Proceedings of NCKP 2021: The Piano Conference

Copyright © 2022 The Frances Clark Center for Keyboard Pedagogy

Printed in the United States of America

Published in the United States of America by

The Frances Clark Center for Keyboard Pedagogy, Inc

PO Box 651
Kingston, NJ 08528
Email: info@francesclarkcenter.org
Web: www.pianoinspires.com

All rights reserved. No part of this book may be reproduced, stored in a retrieval system, or transmitted in any form, or by any means, electronic, mechanical, photocopying, recording, or by any other storage and retrieval system, without permission in writing from the Publisher.

PROCEEDINGS
of NCKP 2021:
The Piano Conference

July 13-31, 2021
VIRTUAL

TABLE OF CONTENTS

6	**FROM THE FRANCES CLARK CENTER**
7	**KEYNOTE ADDRESSES**
49	**PRECONFERENCE SEMINARS**
50	INDEPENDENT MUSIC TEACHERS
51	TEACHING ADULTS
55	INCLUSIVE TEACHING
56	YOUNG MUSICIANS: BIRTH TO AGE 9
69	CREATIVE MUSIC MAKING
73	TEACHER EDUCATION IN HIGHER ED
77	WELLNESS
79	RESEARCH
83	DIVERSITY
86	COLLABORATIVE
89	LATIN AMERICA AND THE IBERIAN PENINSULA
91	CAREER DEVELOPMENT AND INNOVATION
95	TECHNOLOGY
107	**MAIN CONFERENCE PRESENTATIONS**
321	**SPANISH PRESENTATIONS**
335	**PORTUGUESE PRESENTATIONS**

FROM THE FRANCES CLARK CENTER

The 2021 National Conference on Keyboard Pedagogy was an extraordinary achievement at an unprecedented time of great challenges. The staff, extensive volunteer network, and our full community embraced technological innovation when we were not able to gather in one place because of the COVID-19 pandemic restrictions. This publication represents the first fully online conference and the great creativity and dedication that made it possible. Collectively, we transcended geography and gathered to support each other to advance our profession during disruptive uncertainty. As the largest conference in our history with over 200 sessions, attendees contributed from across the world, including representation from almost every state, North and South America, Australia, Europe, Asia, and Africa. This international expansion demonstrated the resilience and dedication of our mission-driven community.

These *Proceedings* document the 2021 National Conference on Keyboard Pedagogy where over one thousand attendees gathered online for seventeen days of programming experiencing powerful preconference tracks, dynamic presentations, thrilling concerts, inspiring keynotes, innovative PEDx, informative workshops, and exemplary teaching demonstrations. The online archive of presentations facilitated extended access to all who attended with new insights for their teaching and performing. The wide range of topics, themes, and research included here attest to the vibrancy and enduring vitality of our profession. Any articles not included in this document were either not submitted for inclusion by the authors or were presented in a format unable to be reproduced here. We hope the wealth of resources, practical teaching suggestions, and innovative ideas contained in these *Proceedings* are informative, relevant, and thought provoking.

The *Proceedings* are a result of the significant contributions of session presenters, committee chairs, and session recorders, all of whom served in a volunteer capacity. In addition, the publication could not have been completed without the dedicated work of Frances Clark Center staff and the editorial team including Sara Ernst, Andrea McAlister, Pamela Pike, Ricardo Pozenatto, and Luis Sanchez. A special thank you to the *Proceedings* Editor-in Chief Craig Sale and to Esther Hayter for her contributions and management of the project. The collaborative spirit of the full organization and community is evident in all aspects of these *Proceedings*.

We appreciate the commitment of every attendee as we engaged in new ways to reflect the ethos of NCKP 2021— "the transformative power of music." We extend our gratitude for your support of NCKP 2021 and your interest in these *Proceedings*. We invite you to join us for the 2023 National Conference on Keyboard Pedagogy from July 26-29, 2023 in Lombard, Illinois, when we will enthusiastically gather together again to celebrate our noble profession on the twenty-fifth anniversary of the National Conference on Keyboard Pedagogy.

Dr. Jennifer Snow | CEO and Executive Director, The Frances Clark Center

KEYNOTE ADDRESSES

Teaching the Musicians Who Will Change the World
Wednesday, July 28, 2021
Keynote Address

Presented by Karen Zorn

I want to thank Jennifer Snow for inviting me to speak at this amazing conference, which has been a really important conference to me for so many years. I am really honored and humbled to be here with you today.

So I have to say even after fourteen years, it's always strange to hear myself introduced as the president of a music conservatory. Because had you told me, let's say thirty years ago, when I was starting out as a private piano teacher, that someday I would be leading a music conservatory, I probably would have protested rather strongly, perhaps with a few choice words thrown in there for good measure. It wasn't that I disliked my own conservatory education, I actually had a really positive experience. But I was happy thirty years ago. As a private studio teacher, I love the idea of bringing music into the lives of a diverse group of people from five-year-olds to adult retirees and everybody in between. It's just that I had too many friends for whom conservatory education was kind of a brutal experience. This is a story you know well, I suspect, one where the focus on perfection has doused the fires of their passion for music, as well as their hopes for a career. Their education left them alienated from their instrument and discipline that they loved so much. I knew that the traditional model for conservatory education that focused heavily on performing skills and culling the best from the rest was absolutely vital for some select students. But it wasn't right for many students. And it wasn't something I wanted to be a part of as a professional.

So what happened to change my mind? Well, in 2006, I was invited to interview for the job of President of the Longy School of Music. And I was intrigued, because unlike the mission of most other conservatories, which typically fall along the lines of training the best students to become the best of the best performers to fill the elite positions on the great stages of the world, Longy had just changed its mission. It wanted to become a totally different kind of music conservatory. Longy's mission was and is to prepare musicians to make a difference in the world, which may not sound that groundbreaking today, but back in 2006, it was. And that idea sparked my imagination and kind of set my brain on fire. I started to think of music as social change, musicians as the change makers, and this was really something I could get behind. So exploring this mission these past fourteen years has changed my life. It has changed my perspective on what it means to be a musician and the types of careers musicians can have, on the types of students who can major in music and go on to find meaningful work in our field, and what we value in music education.

So today, I want to share with you some of the things that I've learned. And especially some of the things that I've seen music students and musicians go on to accomplish, in the hope that you might draw some inspiration from their work as I have. And then it might allow all of us who are teachers to nurture the passions of every student who's potentially interested in making a life and a career in music, as all of us have. But especially those students for whom traditional conservatory education may not be in the cards.

So what are some of those things that I've learned? Number one, students want more meaningful experiences, and students are really driving this change. They don't all want to be performers. In the end, they want their education to prepare them to address big ideas and big issues in our world. Secondly, too many music students lose the connection with what inspires them with what inspired them to become musicians in the first place. Thirdly, when students are inspired and passionate about their work, musical excellence follows. And fourthly, there are so many more ways to be a musician in the world, even more than we can imagine today.

We all know that music is a powerful force in the lives of so many. Music is almost universally beloved as a source of celebration, joy, and so many other things. It's an integral part of the human experience, which makes teaching music such a meaningful endeavor. But what I've learned over these years is that, in addition to teaching and performing, there are so many more ways musicians can make a difference in the world. So, if I could look into my crystal ball, let's say, I don't know, twenty years from now, I see a world where musicians are seen as essential to society; dare I say, essential workers. What if we imagined a world where every neighborhood strives to build its team of artists who bring music to their community to address specific needs, or every Mayor's Commission has a plan for deploying musicians into communities, creating the kinds of neighborhoods that draw tourism dollars and attract new business, or every retirement community sees musicians as essential. In fact, the residents mentioned music as one of the most important factors that improves their quality of life. Retirement communities compete to hire the most exciting and effective musicians on to their staff. I see a future where musicians are seen as essential and in a big way. And it's not just because their performances are so transcendent. Yes, that's always amazing when it happens. But it's because they have the skills to harness the power of music, to help solve issues and needs in society. We are in a moment where we can rethink music education, I actually think it's the next generation that will make the big shift for us, the students of today, some of them are already out there doing this work. Others are taking piano lessons and are wondering whether music might be their thing. And we can all join in and play our part. So let's take a look at some of the people who are already well underway. Early adopters who lead the way for the next generation doing the work I'm talking about using music to make a difference in the world. First up, meet Vijay Gupta, a musician who's making just the kind of change I'm talking about. Let's take a look at what Vijay has to say:

> I auditioned for the LA Philharmonic when I was eighteen. And this orchestra accepted me into their family as a nineteen-year-old boy. Within a couple of months of joining the orchestra, I started to learn about the story of a homeless man named Nathaniel Ayers, who was the subject of a book and a movie called *The Soloist*. And I found myself becoming Nathaniel's violin teacher. And Nathaniel and I would have these amazing conversations through music in this courtyard in Skid Row. And so a couple of questions started to come at that moment: what did it mean to bring music to Skid Row, and how many more Nathaniels were out there? Street Symphony is a community of musicians, my colleagues from the LA Philharmonic, from the LA Master Chorale, professional musicians, and students from all over Los Angeles, of varying different genres of music, who present regular monthly engagements in shelters and clinics in Skid Row, as well as all five Los Angeles county jails. And the goal of Street Symphony is to engage a historically marginalized community of people through artistic performance, dialog, and teaching artistry. We took the *Messiah* to the midnight mission in Skid Row, which is one of our partner organizations. And the *Messiah* project is a chance for the professional musicians of Street Symphony to share our stage with the Skid Row community. Now we work with artists and musicians and singers and composers and instrumentalists, who live in Skid Row. And they are our soloists, and they are our curators, and they are the ones who teach us about the power of their artistic voice in their community. And so when we show up to make music in Skid Row, it's not about being the perfect artistic product. It's about being the most present human being.

I love what Vijay said—"It's not about a perfect artistic product. It's about being a present human being." It's been such a privilege to work with Vijay and a thrill to have him work with our students at Longy. He's such a powerful role model for our future. Now back to the crystal ball. I see a world filled with potential Vijay Guptas and a future with Street Symphony-like organizations all across our country, doing the work their communities need. One of the things I noticed in Vijay's video is his energy when he talks about Street Symphony. It reminds me of this quote from Howard Thurman. "Don't ask what the world needs. Ask what makes you come alive, because what the world needs is more people who have come alive." Now, I love that quote, but I think about it slightly differently. Sometimes the way you find what makes you come alive is actually looking for where there is a need. And in a lot of ways, Vijay said "yes" to a need that he stumbled upon. And then he had the vision to see that need could be solved, in part, with music.

Let's take a look at another musician. I want you to meet Angelica Cortez. Angelica did a master's degree with us at Longy, a Master of Arts in Teaching. And I can see that she applied her teaching skills, working with young people at the largest El Sistema program in the country. While working with these students in grappling with their needs and their aspirations, she really grew and learned how to work with all different parts of a community using music. She gained so many skills and experiences that she was plucked from warm Los Angeles to New York City to help Juilliard rethink its own sense of community and belonging. And now she's the executive director of El Sistema USA. Like so many other musicians in the world, she wanted to be involved where she could make big changes. Musicians who have Angelica's experience and expertise are needed by so many institutions today more than ever.

Next, I'd like you to meet Gabrielle Molina, also an alumna of Longy's teaching programs. Here's a little bit of her story:

> In my undergrad, I was studying clarinet performance. And for years, I had thought that my ultimate goal was to be an orchestral musician, sitting principle and playing solos. This was really my idea of success. And I had a few transformative experiences in my undergrad that profoundly shifted the way that I was thinking about my artistry. And in particular, I came across the TED talk from Jose Antonio Abreu about El Sistema. And after doing more research, and actually leaving the practice room, I found the MET program. And I felt like, at that time, I was finally finding my tribe. Finally, finding a community of like-minded individuals who were also questioning their role in society as musicians. I had spent so many years in the practice room trying to perfect excerpts and my *legato*, and I was trying to figure out how these things actually intersect in making the world a better place. And I have been so fortunate that after leaving MET, I've traveled the world, working with different El Sistema-inspired programs, ultimately going on to do a second master's at Harvard, and founding an international nonprofit, Teaching Artists International. And we do work all around the world.

So one of the things I've learned is that music students want to find this kind of work. They want to be involved in big ideas that can make real change in the world. One of the ways I know this is from reading the essays that students write as part of their Longy application. Here's what one of our recent applicants had to say:

> I have worked on community-based initiatives to create affordable housing and improve food security. This work helped me realize that I could not divorce my calling as a musician from my responsibility to address people's material needs as well. I want opportunities that deeply integrate the arts with social connection and transformation. In our contemporary times, I can't imagine music looking any other way.

And she's not alone. Here's what another applicant had to say:

> During my sophomore year in college, I grew extremely interested in community engagement and prison reform. In an attempt to combine the two things that I felt so passionately about, I directed a concert series at a medium security prison. I was struck

by how deeply the inmates listened, and how profound it is to be able to share music with people from a variety of backgrounds. Music is incomparably humanizing, and in seeing how prisons hardly treat people like human beings, it became increasingly important to me to continue to bring it to the prison.

The prison warden told her "your program has created a safer prison and has given the inmates something vital, a purpose." And here's what she wants:

I want my life as a musician to revolve around supporting my community and helping to create new ones. Finding new and creative ways to teach music is the first step to achieving my goals. I want to continue to bring music into prison systems and create comprehensive plans that make it easier for others to start similar programs.

Wow. Okay, one last excerpt:

The spate of killings from terrorism and religious and tribal clashes in my country have skyrocketed over the years. This has evoked various emotional responses such as anger, depression, violence, sadness, and pain in the populace, and has led to the employment of medical and non-medical approaches to try and curb these emotions. While some of these interventions have been therapeutic and effective, others have failed because they are deemed unaffordable, or are inaccessible. In the future, I want to research the use of music as a means of regulating emotional responses in a troubling social environment.

Now, what I see in those comments is that music can help with affordable housing and food insecurity, prison reform, and can support and comfort communities in crisis. I can imagine that you might be thinking these students and these musicians are not typical, that they're somehow anomalies. But actually, I don't think so. Students like this are more and more typical. And yes, more students who apply to Longy do have these kinds of aspirations because of our social-action mission. But young people like this are all around us. And they come from a variety of walks of life, a variety of disciplines, including music. These students are your students.

What has caused this change? I'm not exactly sure. Clearly, some of it comes from the students' own lived experience. Another is the need to show that you've done some community volunteer work on your college application. Now, at first, they may do this work because it's required. But doing the work actually changes them and what they value. And for some, it shifts how they see themselves and what they are capable of doing. So many students now want a future where they're useful and can effect change. They want to find something that helps them come alive, and they want their work to be needed. Now, there are so many paths we could explore today. It just takes a little bit of research to become overwhelmed by all the ways that musicians are making big change in the world already. Some of the paths have been illustrated in the stories that I've shared. But there's another path that I haven't really touched on yet. One that I think has a huge amount of potential for musicians, and for our music world, and for our world at large. Today, I want to take a deeper look with you into therapeutic music, using music for healing and comfort, and so much more. Just to get us started, I want to show you a short clip from a film that I think illustrates so well what I probably cannot say in words myself. The film is called *Alive Inside*, a documentary that follows a social worker, Dan Cohen, as he explores using music with patients suffering from dementia. Some of you've undoubtedly already seen this film. Let's take a look at Henry's story again from the film *Alive Inside*.

"And look at more or less religious music for him. Because he enjoys his music and he always quotes the Bible. So I would rather have that for him."

We see Henry in it, maybe depressed, unresponsive and almost unalive.

"Henry."

"Yeah."

"I found your music. You want your music now? Let's try your music okay. And then you tell me if it's too loud or not."

And then he is given an iPod containing his favorite music. Immediately he lights up, his face assumes expression, his eyes open wide. He starts to sing, to rock, and to move his arms, and he's being animated by the music.

"And he used to always sit on the unit with his head like this. He didn't really talk to many people. And then when I introduced the music to him, this has been his reaction ever since."

The philosopher Kant once called music a quickening art, and Henry has been quickened: he has been brought to life.

"Yeah, I'm gonna take the music for one second. Okay, just to ask a few questions. Okay. I'm gonna give it back to you."

The effect of this doesn't stop when the headphones are taken off. Henry, normally mute and virtually unable to answer the simplest yes or no questions, is quite vocal.

"Henry."

"Yeah."

"Do you like the iPod? Do you like the music you're hearing? Tell me about your music."

"Do you like music?"

"Yeah, I'm crazy about music, I get to play beautiful music, beautiful sound."

"Did you play music when you were young?"

"Yes, yes I did big dances and things."

"What was your favorite music when you were young?"

"Cab Callaway was my number one band guy."

"What's your favorite Cab Calloway song?"

"Oh, 'I'll Be Home for Christmas.' With plenty of snow. Mistletoe."

So in some sense Henry is restored to himself. He has remembered who he is. And he's reacquired his identity for a while through the power of music.

"What does music do to you?"

"It gives me a feeling of love. Romance! Right now the world needs to come into music. Singing. You've got beautiful music here. Beautiful. Oh lovely. I feel the band of love, of dreams."

I think this is such an amazing example of the power of music. I'm kind of a puddle every time I see it. Such a raw example of how music can reach something that's truly human. I highly recommend watching the entire film, especially if you ever feel like you need a pep talk about the importance of music. Let's go back to something Oliver Sacks said; "Music helps them find their place in the world again." I mean, can you imagine anything more important than that? So then, let's consider the fact that there are over six million people with dementia in the United States alone today. So imagine what that number will be in ten years. And imagine how music could be used to make a difference in all those lives. That's a world that needs more musicians, not less. Okay, so at Longy, we thought, what if we deployed music students who understood how to use music for healing and comfort in hospitals, assisted living programs, and other health care facilities? Now to do that, we added a class as part of our core curriculum. It's called "Music as a Healing Art." Students in this class learn and practice techniques for how to be a healing presence and how to use music to bring comfort. And then they go out into the community and they practice what they've learned. Now on a regular basis, students in this class say that these are some of their favorite and most meaningful experiences as musicians, and that learning these techniques has changed how they think about their own performances, not just those in healthcare facilities. I think this is connected to what Vijay Gupta said. It's not about the perfect artistic product. It's about being present as a human being. Really being present with your audience creates more meaning for our students. Let's take a look at what our music as a healing arts students have to say:

> It makes you feel good. It makes you feel if, just closing your eyes and listening to it, if you had a problem, you can kind of go away a little bit.

> I love music. You both have to come back. Yeah. No, it's great. We enjoy it very much.

> This class changed my perspective on what venues are possible. That's not really just like the concert hall and the traditional stage. There are people who can't get to the concert hall who need the music.

> I think my perspective has changed on what a performance is, and so many times we think of it as being this stiff, I'm-on-the-stage-and-you're-in-the-audience kind of experience. But we were reminded of ways that we could interact with audiences and make it meaningful, not just for us, but for them.

> I think of the one nursing place, in Santa Maria. There was a far corner and there was an old lady in her wheelchair, sitting like this during the whole concert. One moment, I started improvising some jazz, and then I looked in the corner and she was smiling. This class made me think that we need more musicians in this world, because this world is going crazy. And, you know, we have all this bad news. And I think musicians, we have a superpower. We can bring you, with one note, to a present moment.

> I feel like this course has definitely helped me make a difference in the world already. Because I feel like I've been given an opportunity to serve people through my music and having this experience and seeing how it changed our lives, even for those few minutes, really has motivated me to continue to do that.

So students who really get the bug for this kind of work can go on to become certified music practitioners. Now, I've known about the work of music therapists for decades. But I had never heard of music practitioners until about, I don't know, seven or eight years ago. And what really piqued my interest was that music-practitioner training is a skill and a job that you can add to what you are already doing as a musician. Music practitioners are musicians who focus on meeting a patient's present needs in the moment with music. They use music to bring comfort and create a healing presence. Here are just some of the things that they are trained to do: relieve anxiety, reduce stress and stabilize blood pressure, augment pain management, aid mental-focus and Alzheimer's patients, and stabilize vital signs and acute patients. Okay, now let's face it, not all music is therapeutic. In fact, some music can probably cause anxiety. But let's think about how much anxiety there is in this world right now. How can music and how can a music practitioner help with that? Well, you may think the best way to meet the needs of a patient with anxiety is with relaxing music. Now, that can actually cause more anxiety. It's kind of like when someone tells you to relax or calm down, it just doesn't help. A certified music practitioner will sit with a patient with anxiety and notice the pace of their breathing. Then play music that matches that pace. If there's agitation, then they'll play music that has agitation in it. And over time gradually and eventually they bring down the energy and the tempo of the music that they're playing. And the outcome is generally slower breathing, a more controlled heart rate, and an easing of anxiety. So let's hear from two students who are studying to become certified music practitioners. In this video, I just want to explain one thing: the student will mention an acronym, MHTP. It stands for Music for Healing & Transition Program™. This is the credentialing organization for certified music practitioners.

My son was my first patient. He was born prematurely around thirty-two weeks, so he had to spend a month in the hospital. The main thing that he was having trouble with was breathing and eating. So most of his food would be through a feeding tube. My mentor, Alene Benoit, encouraged me to bring my violin and start putting what I was learning in my MHTP program into the hospital. The first time I brought my violin to the NICU, I started playing for my son. And after a little while, I started to notice that the nurse was bringing other cribs into the NICU room where my son was, and all of a sudden I had ten cribs in front of me, and all the babies stopped crying after a little while. And then I started playing a movement of Bach that I used to play for my wife when she was pregnant. As soon as I started playing that song, he just simply smiled. I was amazed how music changed the room and changed the atmosphere of the hospital to where the hospital became a sanctuary of feeling loved and feeling hope. And this particular nurse, who was a little bit skeptical about me coming to play, tapped my shoulder and said "I think you should come at least once a week." Once I started doing therapeutic live music for my son, I started to notice how much it was helping him to breathe on his own and eat on his own. But when he started eating, he started eating on his own one time I think around five to ten milliliters of milk. And as I continued to play, he started to eat twenty, thirty, forty, eighty. Eventually, he was eating on his own without the feeding tube. That was really a miracle for us because we were expecting him to stay there until forty weeks full term. He was able to come home around thirty-seven weeks. The MHTP program really taught me that music is not just an art form. That it is really a powerful force that can help provide an environment of healing.

I hope you can see how meaningful this work can be. Our students are super excited about the future they see because of this training. Right now, there are over nine hundred certified music practitioners employed in healthcare facilities in the United States. And as the healthcare field continues to embrace alternative therapies, more and more, we think this work is just going to grow and grow and grow. Now the training is extremely doable and affordable. It's a matter of days of training, not weeks, months, or years, plus a practicum that you can complete where you live. You can take the training at a variety of locations and online throughout the year. It's really that easy.

Now back to my crystal ball. Imagine all the ways that therapeutic music is needed in the world right now. Nevermind in the decades to come as our population ages. Imagine a world where every retirement community employs musicians full time to play concerts, teach lessons and classes for the residents, and work as music practitioners to bring comfort and care through all the phases of aging. Think of how much this work could help with the opioid crisis and the pain management required during recovery. Imagine a future where every hospice and palliative care unit employs a music practitioner to aid and improve the experience of end of life.

You may be wondering how this paradigm shift affects the way we teach at Longy. What's it like to study at a school where students are preparing to make a difference in the world, rather than preparing to take their role on the concert stage? Without going into too much detail, let me share some of the ways we think and work. Number one, everyone is good enough, full stop. It's not about culling those who can from those who can't. It's another way of saying that we look for potential and passion, that fire in the belly to learn and make things happen. Number two, more musicians, not fewer. Okay, so unlike some conservatories, we're not in the business of saying, "No, you can't be a musician." And obviously, we have our aperture wide open to all the things musicians can do that are needed in this world. Which means we think we need more musicians, not fewer. So we say "yes," more often. Number three, no auditions, no juries. Okay, this isn't quite true, but it's almost true. We do have auditions, but instead of the typical requirements, you know so well, the Baroque piece, followed by the Classical sonata, then something written after 1950; we say, "Give us fifteen minutes that shows us who you are as a musician." That's it. And it's amazing how much we learn about each student, just based on the choices they make alone. Number four, emphasizing passion over perfection, which not unexpectedly, seems to bring out the best in our students musically. Number five, focus on those who otherwise would not have access. A lot of the discussions at Longy are about where music isn't happening, how to get rid of barriers and create access to music and music education for those who otherwise would not have access. Perhaps the biggest shift is focusing on a student's intrinsic motivation. We work hard to find out what each student is really passionate about and what makes them come alive.

Based on that, we help them figure out the courses they should take, the experiences they should have to prepare them for what they want to do after they are no longer a student. Consequently, we have very few requirements. It's much more about meeting each student's needs and desires. And as it turns out, giving students a lot of choice is one of the best ways to tap into their own intrinsic motivation. Self motivation is the best indicator of success, not how well you perform, but how motivated you are. Those are the students who turn into the change makers of the future.

So it all started with a simple idea, that mission, preparing musicians to make a difference in the world. Now, as music teachers, you play such a pivotal role in the lives of your students, and especially those students who have a passion for music and are considering how they might make music part of their life. I hope that some of what we've talked about today may inspire you to encourage your students to see more potential paths for becoming a musician and staying a musician for a lifetime.

Breaking the Sound Barrier: Prioritizing Representation in Classical Music
Thursday, July 29, 2021
Keynote Address

Presented by Afa Dworkin

Greetings, everyone. I'm Afa Dworkin, President and Artistic director of the Sphinx Organization. I'm joining you today from Ann Arbor, Michigan, the ancestral land of the Anishinabe people, including Odawa, Ojibwe, Potawatomi, as well as Wyandot peoples. I am an average height woman with olive skin. I'm wearing a funky brooch and eclectic clothing. I have my mother's wavy dark hair and my father's large dark features. Being a combination of Persian, Jewish, and Azeri heritage, I am a mixed race. It is my pleasure to be with you all, albeit virtually. Today I hope to speak with you about my life's work, how I came to align my creative aspirations with issues surrounding Diversity, Equity and Inclusion, as well as the future that I hope to see for our field.

I was born in Moscow, Russia, in the mid-70s, when it was the capital of the Union of Soviet Socialist Republics. I was raised in Baku, Azerbaijan, a small country just south of Russia and north of Iran. My father was a chemical engineer and my mother was a Romance languages linguist and a professor of French. The arts and music were not part of our realm, and were not seen by my parents as a viable career path. Diversity was also not part of our lexicon, nor mentality, as the ethos was always so centered around unity, solidarity, and a one-minded approach, almost in a utopian fashion, devoid of race and ethnicity.

So my introduction to the violin, my primary instrument, and piano, my secondary one, was reluctant at best. After a couple of years of me attempting to make the case to study them, my folks agreed to take me to my community music school and test my sense of pitch and rhythm, which were the prerequisites for studying music. And I say this with intention, the *only* prerequisites, because for the many faults of my country of origin, the view of musical studies was such that it was not a privilege of the few, but the right of every child to have this incredible hands-on experience with classical music without regard to one's zip code, heritage, or skin tone.

Thus began my incredible journey into music. After playing both violin and piano for several years, I took an exam into the pre-conservatory division of our music academy and entered into this incredible domain, where music literature was studied alongside math and chemistry, followed by mixed chamber music, eurythmics, and world history. I am deeply grateful to my parents for finding the right balance between guiding and allowing for this incredible trajectory which in so many ways, formulated my future, building a pathway to this very moment of speaking before you today. But all fairytale-like beginnings can sometimes offer twists and turns, and mine was a formidable occurrence in my late teens.

It was one cold January afternoon, I found myself watching the center square of my city. And it felt like a scene from a movie. My beloved country, my city, was literally dissolving in front of my eyes, both literally and figuratively. A row of military tanks was appointed right in the center of violent and spirited protests and demonstrations. For so many reasons, I could not comprehend much more than the fact that this meant the news reports were not just alarmist, the country was in fact falling apart, and to my teenage self, it meant that my orchestra was not likely to resume rehearsals this week, go on tour next month, and that my family was likely going to find a way to take us west. So after a number of very careful conversations, my parents explained that in light of concerns related to the fragile state of affairs with everything, as well as our mixed heritage being a likely target, they would simply take us to America to try to build a better and a safer future.

While devastated at the thought of losing our friends and everything that we knew to be comfortable, familiar, and dear, my sister and I accepted our fate and prepared as best as we could. So fast forward to many partly humorous and partly tearful ways in which I could describe my early experiences in this country as a seventeen-year-old. With no fluency with the English language, I met a violin professor from the University of Michigan's School of Music, Theatre and Dance, and had an unexpected opportunity to perform for him. This resulted in auditioning, formally getting accepted by the school, despite repeatedly failing the English test, and staying back in the state of Michigan as my family eventually made the decision to move back home. So my real journey was beginning, just without my full recognition of its significance.

During the early days, I met an incoming studio mate who was a transfer student. Now, this was an African American violinist who had an idea to diversify the field of classical music through the study and performance of works by black and brown composers and presentation of young artists of color on stage. The idea at the time seemed unrealistic, but also unusual to me. Is not classical music the one bastion of meritocracy, I challenged him. How can achievement be significant to race? And how could diversity be an issue when we're all the same? As we were taught back home clearly, until I began to see my own argument fall apart for me, I saw virtually no black or Latino artists on stage, I had never studied a work by a composer of color. We were never taught any examples of literature outside of what was known to be our canon. And for centuries, it seemed whole cultures appear to have been excluded both purposely and implicitly from our entire field. So maybe merit was not as much of a thing as I once thought. So after many conversations with my then classmate, I decided to volunteer and enlist myself as the first self-appointed student intern for what was to become the Sphinx Organization.

Twenty-five years later, I'm still here, albeit in a bit of a different role. The founder of what was to be the Sphinx Organization, Aaron Dworkin, is now my life partner. And together we have dedicated our lives to the vision of having our beloved field reflect the vibrancy and diversity of our communities.

Sphinx began as a small competition for young black and Latino musicians back in 1998. Today, it is more of a movement with eight hundred-plus alumni, reaching ten thousand people through its direct annual programming, two million in audiences, and having awarded more than four million in scholarships and artists grants. We have launched five performing ensembles and are getting ready to celebrate our 25th anniversary next year.

Through the years, the motivating factor for me was a realization that excellence was only possible through diversity. A misfortunate myth has plagued classical music until now, where anytime we speak of diversity, many will assume it means dumbing down our standards of excellence, merit, and rigor. But nothing can be farther from the truth. The fact is, there's not a scarcity of talent or achievement in classical music among black and brown communities, as evidenced by Sphinx's efforts over the past twenty-plus years. When we started, black and Latinx artists comprised about one-and-a-half percent in American orchestras combined. Today, this number is slightly more than four percent, which tells us we have a ways to go. But sometimes folks argue that the talent or the interest is simply not there early on. However, I think it is always so important to quantify and fact check what feels to us to be anecdotally the case.

When we look at the issue more closely, the numbers in our community music schools, which focus on early introduction and afterschool education, are encouraging because they reflect almost precisely the population representation, which indicates to me that the problem is not with a pipeline or early interest, nor the lack of talent. It lies in the lack of intentionality, and directed resources toward retaining, nurturing, and cultivating this talent.

Sphinx's efforts form a pipeline, which begins with early introduction education then continuing to intermediate boot camps, and on to college preparedness, professional performance opportunities, touring, commissioning, and most recently, talent development and placement at the professional level, through performance, administration, and now entrepreneurship. Our work spans all of the various phases of participation, but we do this not alone. We are in partnership with more than two hundred partners across the country, ranging from one hundred and five orchestras, major conservatories, and music schools, presenting houses, and community educational institutions.

I will share from personal experience of running our youth educational programs each year that we select ninety young artists to participate in our summer programs alone. These young people range from ages eleven through seventeen. But if given resources, we could easily welcome three times that many young artists. And, those young people are good enough to enroll in any music school with the right effort on behalf of the school. Sphinx has become a service to the field organization by not just administering and running our programs directly but by creating, amassing, and disseminating the necessary resources to encourage our field to work more decisively in the sphere of presentation and diversity.

Since the twin pandemics of 2020 and until now, we have focused our work on programs which range from beginning private and group lessons online to digital performances featuring hundreds of our artists to funding new commission's assembling online for more than twenty-two hundred people around the globe and beyond. Our work has been to find ways to continue artist-centric support, from offering relief funds, to helping to catalyze and reshape the projects and initiatives by our artists, to working with partners and issuing a concrete call to action to the field.

You see, the organizers of this wonderful event kindly invited me to spend time with you long before our world was brought to its knees back in 2020.

It happened before our artists were to become silenced across the world. Before our family members were to fall ill, before canceled opera premieres and newly commissioned symphonic works were replaced by the Brady Bunch-like squares on our screens. It was also before we lost one of our greatest civil rights icons, John Lewis, and before the murders of Breonna Taylor and George Floyd shook our numb world in profound ways. It was also before the solidarity statements, earlier than implicit bias consultants becoming the hottest commodity on our market, before philanthropic institutions called for racial equity, and before DEI became the code for the scorecard of our conscience. Before we knew that our country and the very foundation of our democracy would be shaken once more, to remind us that division and injustice are still so profoundly at the core of our shared realities.

I knew then, but I certainly recognize now, that the only way we are to survive this costly dual pandemic is through reliance and trust in one another's strength and integrity. We need to stand tall for those who are tired of fighting, by doing and not just saying the right thing when it matters, by taking risks when they're not popularly blessed by consensus, by hearing from those who do not think nor look like us and whose pain and challenge have been greater than ours. Today, this is everybody's fight. Everybody's time to lead, every single one of us who pledge their allegiance to artists and leaders of color, all of those who hold the privilege to act for more than just ourselves. And that's all of us. Last summer, Sphinx called upon our partners to make a fifteen percent commitment to diverse programming, a fifteen percent commitment to diversify their staff and board, as well as a fifteen percent budget allocation to racial equity work. I still stand by that call and stand ready to work together with any partner, any individual educator or artist who is ready to tackle those concrete steps. The talent and the readiness of our artists and leaders will inspire anyone with a resolve to make different choices this year.

Sphinx saw record high participation through our cumulative applicant pool growth by more than sixty percent, quadrupled the number of artists that we reached through our national alliance for audition support, and awarded more than $900,000 in grants and scholarships since last summer alone, while pivoting every single one of our programs to the digital space and ensuring that every student in every household, every one of our artists was accounted for. And before I come to the closing phase of my talk today, I'm hoping that you will ask yourself this one question. "What will I do? What will I do differently this time? How will I go beyond that one work that I program, that one artist that I engaged, that one commission, that one DEI speaker who gave us this zoom talk?" The time has come to join our hands and commit wholeheartedly to the discomfort of real change. And once this talk and this wonderful conference come to an end, once the tears are dried and the urgency of this work yields to the dangerous comforts of *status quo*, may we all pause in remembrance of those we lost in gratitude to those who lead this work today, and in awe of all that we can accomplish together in the name of our collective good.

A gifted African American pianist, one of Sphinx's premier artists and ambassadors, and a recipient of our Medal of Excellence, Jade Simmons, once said that we must not look to impress our audiences but instead to *impact* our audiences. In guiding our artists as educators, we encourage them to uncover the repertoire by black composers, which dates back to the contemporaries of Mozart, such as Joseph Bologne St. George. The very knowledge and realization that excellence and creative expression was present during the times of Mozart within communities of color, creates a sense of connection and belonging. And the latter, I think, is so critical when it comes to creating equitable opportunities for our young people. That realization and pursuit and study of this music then brings about impact by encouraging and inspiring young people to pursue their sense of connection to this music.

One of my own children, our youngest son Amani, is studying piano. While I do not necessarily, and unfortunately, see his pursuits taking him to the professional route, the knowledge and then the opportunity to study classical works by Florence Price, an African American woman and composer, changes his perception of what classical music is, who belongs in it, and why it is that we seek to define something as canon. Furthermore, the opportunity has an effect and impact on his teacher and the rest of her studio. Now, all of a sudden, dozens of young kids of all backgrounds get to hear, study, and know of music that was written by black composers, black women composers at that, which impacts their approach, their mentality, and sense of enormous normalcy which will distinguish them from their parents and the earlier generations for whom something like this was likely unheard of. A terrific and brilliant pianist, Stewart Goodyear, wrote an amazing piano concerto called *Callaloo*. I encourage you all to look it up and listen, paying tribute to his Caribbean heritage and culture. Think about the privilege and the opportunity to live during a time when something like this is not only possible, but it is known and accessible. Now, think about our individual and collective power to go search up the piece, find a score, study it, teach it, and advocate for it. Think about the impact upon your students, our students, audiences, colleagues, critics, and our communities. What an awesome power we all have to do better. To do it differently this time and ultimately to generate some impact.

One of the most dear things I have heard during my entire career from one of our young artists years ago, was that she had never known a world without Sphinx. She was born after we were founded. To her teachers, to her parents and peers, Sphinx has always ensured that the norm was not defined by ignorance, lack of knowledge with a mix of assumptions, but instead, the norm was to see talent and poise and accomplished students of color perform alongside their white peers held to the very same standards of excellence. What is more important is that she knew so many artists of color who came before her and succeeded. The very idea of feeling alone was unfamiliar and odd. Think about that impact that each of us can have. My own kids used to say that growing up in our household, they thought most string musicians are in fact of color, because that's what they saw. So if you are an educator, take the time to reimagine what you teach and how you recruit, find ways to afford a voice to deserving composers of color, and to evolve our canon. Define your own methods to recruit from communities that have not been participating in your program or your studio by forming partnerships with community centers, leaders, schools, and faith-based institutions. If you are a leader, find a way to advocate for and establish that fifteen percent commitment of annual budgets to go toward efforts in the DEI sphere, not just now, but for the next ten years. Our budgets are our moral documents. We all spend precious resources no matter how small or big. Imagine if each one of us decided to do so with an authentic emphasis on diversity.

If you're an administrative recruiter, then commit to at least twenty-five percent of your final administrative staff pool of candidates to be BIPOC candidates and fail the search if you do not immediately succeed. If you're not sure where to start, that's okay, reach out to Sphinx, check out our resource page, and we will do our very best to connect you and work with you. If you are a student, a performer, or collaborator, make the choice when deciding on a program, select the non-white composers who deserve to be heard, studied, and appreciated. But not just this year or the next program, but for the next ten years. To each one of your programs, not just one. I invite you to think of yourself as an investor.

In many ways, however abundant or scarce our means might be, we all have some amount of power and I would argue great power to invest our daily energy actions and resources into our future by simply making intentional decisions, which can have radically different and powerful consequences. And finally, a quote; I mentioned we lost an iconic civil rights leader some months ago, John Lewis, who said, "We may not have chosen this time, but this time has indeed chosen us." We have an obligation and the privilege to lead from every single seat. As educators, as artists, as organizers, as community leaders, as allies, we have the power to make decisions that benefit our beloved art form, and our communities. So let's seize it. So that a year from now, when we reflect and look back and feel pride, when reflecting on ways in which we have helped to empower real, measurable change in our industry, we may all rejoice together. Thank you for this wonderful opportunity to speak before you today.

Music—A Tool for Good
Friday, July 30, 2021
Keynote Address

Presented by Joseph Conyers

Greetings to the National Conference on Keyboard Pedagogy. I'm so excited and honored to be able to speak to you all today. Thank you so much for the invitation. Even as I make this presentation, there is so much light at the end of what has been a very, very long tunnel. It is my sincerest hope that each of you and your loved ones are well and safe. I'm very optimistic about what the fall might bring.

So many of you might be thinking, what on earth is the string player doing giving a presentation at my piano conference? Well, you might be surprised to learn that I started my studies on the piano at the age of five, with my piano teacher Rosemary Smith, down in Savannah, Georgia. And I was pretty good. Starting in eighth grade, I played the piano score to a new musical each year in its entirety, including *The Sound of Music*, *Once Upon a Mattress*, and *South Pacific*. And my claim to fame was the summer of my eighth-grade year. While I was a double bass major at the Brevard Music Center, in a competition open to the whole of the center that included college students, yours truly made it to the finals of the concerto competition on piano playing the first movement of Ravel's *Piano Concerto in G Major*. I'm still very proud of that moment.

Now, I realize that I'm speaking to some of the best educators and performers in the field. And I also realize how difficult this time has been for all musicians as we pivoted to find new ways to use our art to connect, express, and represent all of us as individuals. And despite the difficulties of this devastating pandemic. I've only heard stories of resilience, creativity, and determination continuing to provide precious resources to our students and performances for our audiences. *Bravi tutti* on your excellent work. I also think the pandemic has allowed for a new perspective. It has enabled us to re-examine who we are as artists; for example, for me, it is through our art, our love of music and its power, that I believe we can collectively find our purpose, that purpose beyond performance. Let me explain further. Some might ascertain that as a performing musician, I am pretty good musically. I'll admit, I've had some success in life. But winning my job with the Philadelphia Orchestra was not the end of the journey. For me, it was the beginning. It's because I recognized that my purpose as a human being on this planet wasn't to be found in the score of a symphony, and definitely not in the corner of some dark practice room. Instead, being a member of the Philadelphia Orchestra has given my purpose a platform, the further ability to do the work I was called to do, a calling only complemented by the fact that I'm a musician. This belief system embedded in me, is based on my own life experience, an experience I look forward to sharing with you all in this forum today, hopefully as encouragement in your own enriching musical journeys.

So let's start from the very beginning. I hear that's a very good place to start. Today, you'll learn how, based on my life experiences, I built a career on using my gift to serve others. Now, it's been told to you that the title of my lecture today is "Music—A Tool for Good." But that's not the real title. It's just the one I use to get folks to invite me to do these speeches. The real title of my presentation is surprise… wait for it. That's right. "Be Somebody's Butterfly." Now, I know that might sound super cheesy, but don't worry, I believe this presentation will have plenty of substance. In the meantime, I do want you to marinate on that thought for a second. And while you do that, let me tell you a bit about myself. I, Joseph Conyers, was an odd child. Now, there are two things that have been part of my life for as long as I can remember. Here's the first.

I fell in love with music at an early age. I grew up with gospel music as a child of the African American Baptist tradition. But I was introduced to classical music early on as well. This piece, "Meditation" from *Thais* was played by the cello teacher of my sister, at my sister's cello recital. And even though I was a pianist, I was invited to play piano in the same recital, because we are twins, and they didn't want me to feel left out. I was six years old, and here I was on that very day. Now, when Adele Dwyer, my sister's teacher performed "Meditation" at the end of the recital, I was mesmerized. I was mesmerized by her sound. So beautiful. Now the recital was recorded on VHS and I listened to her lyrical playing no less than one million times, just rewinding and rewinding. Music called me, music found me and boy, was I happy to be found. So that was one love. The other love of my life for as long as I can remember—weather. I am a weather nerd, and particularly when it comes to hurricanes. So get this. I was an official storm tracker when I was in high school for the National Weather Service in southeast Georgia. I had those hurricane tracking charts. Back before the internet, we tracked the storms with pencil and paper. I know—huge nerd alert, and I totally remember Hurricane Hugo, because Hurricane Hugo was supposed to hit Savannah. I remember all the evacuating, and at the last minute, the storm veered to the north, and hit Charleston, South Carolina, instead. Now what I love about weather is hurricanes in particular. Its unpredictability, its ability to bring humankind to its knees. Not so unlike this pandemic. Now, the most amazing thing about hurricanes to me, despite the massive and overwhelming destruction, the chaos of the storms, in the very middle of them, the eye of the storm, the wind is calm. There are no clouds in the sky. There is peace. I've always found that humbling. Now, this is not an endorsement for more storms. But like most in the south, my love of hurricanes is out of sheer respect for Mother Nature, and a humbling reminder that we should never ever mess with her.

So there are two things you've learned about me so far. I was a music geek, and my head was literally in the clouds. But I digress. Butterflies; we're supposed to be talking about butterflies, right? So when I was in sixth grade, I'll never forget it. One of my classmates, Mary Ellen, gave a book report on this science fiction novel by a guy named Michael Creighton. Any guesses on what that novel may have been? Well, if you guessed *Jurassic Park*, you are correct. Many of you might remember the plot to *Jurassic Park*, where humans bring an extinct species from millions of years ago back to life. And they think it's a good idea. I mean, what could go wrong? There's a character, Ian Malcolm, and he's a scientist and he's a constant pessimist. And early on in the story, he introduces the concept of chaos theory as to foreshadow what has yet to come in the plot. Now, chaos theory is a real thing. It's a branch of mathematics focusing on the behavior of dynamical systems that are highly sensitive to initial conditions. Now, here's a famous scene from *Jurassic Park*, where Malcolm, played by actor Jeff Goldbloom, explains this theory to a colleague:

> MALCOLM: You see? The tyrannosaur doesn't obey set patterns or park schedules. The essence of Chaos.
> ELLIE: I'm still not clear on Chaos.
> MALCOLM: It simply deals with unpredictability in complex systems. The shorthand is the Butterfly Effect. A butterfly can flap its wings in Peking and in Central Park you get rain instead of sunshine.
> (Ellie gestures with her hand to show that this has gone right over her head.)
> MALCOLM: Are you saying I'm going too fast? I went too fast, I did a fly-by. Give me that glass of water. We are going to conduct an experiment. It should be still, the car is bouncing up and down, but that's ok, it's just an example.
> (He dips his hand into the glass of water and takes Ellie's hand in his own.)
> MALCOLM (cont'd): Now, put your hand flat like a hieroglyphic. Now, let's say a drop of water falls on your hand. Which way is the drop going to roll off?
> (He flicks his fingers and a drop falls on the back of Ellie's hand.)
> MALCOLM (cont'd): Off which finger or the thumb, what would you say?
> ELLIE: Thumb, I'd say.
> MALCOLM: Aha, ok. Now freeze your hand, freeze your hand, don't move. I'm going to do the same thing, start with the same place again. Which way is it going to roll off?
> ELLIE: Let's say, back the same way.
> MALCOLM: It changed. Why? Because tiny variations, the orientation of hairs on your hand…
> ELLIE: Alan, listen to this.
> MALCOLM: …the amount of blood distending your vessels, imperfections in the skin
> ELLIE: Imperfections in the skin?
> MALCOLM: Microscopic microscopic…and never repeat, and vastly affect the outcome. That's what?
> ELLIE: Unpredictability….
> (Grant throws the door open and bolts out of the moving car.)
> MALCOLM (cont'd): Look at this, see, see?! I'm right again! No one could predict that Dr. Grant would suddenly jump out of a moving vehicle.
> ELLIE: Alan?

(She jumps out too and follows him into the field.)
MALCOLM: There's another example! See, here I am now, by myself, talking to myself. That's Chaos Theory!

I'm sure you found that interesting. And if you could get past Ian Malcolm's flirtatious behavior, did you happen to hear something called the "butterfly effect"? The pioneer of chaos theory was a scientist named Edward Lorenz. And he was at MIT in the early 1970s. And he's the one who coined the term "butterfly effect." The "butterfly effect" is this idea that a butterfly flaps its wings, and that causes a series of events that lead to something like a hurricane on the east coast of the United States. Now, this is a concept of meteorology. Even still today, I'm sure now, regardless of where you live in the country, you've dealt with weather people giving a report saying, "Oh, the model is saying this" and "the model is doing that" and "we've got our spaghetti models." Well, that's the "butterfly effect" in practice, because they're all different solutions based on initial conditions.

This speech is about to get a touch technical, but don't worry, my last math class was in 1999. So it's not going to be too technical. Simply put, Lorenz ran a test, he put that into his computer. And then he ran a bunch of algorithms of math problems on his computer, and the computer would then spit out a solution—test done. Now to check his results, Lorenz ran the test again. And this time he revised the initial numbers; rounded up just a little bit, I mean, we're talking multiple decimal points over. But when the results came back, there was shock. Now, this is the actual computer output from the Lorenz model. So as you see on your screen, there's continuity in the lines, they actually look completely the same. And then the lines diverge. To see the discrepancy in Lorenz's model, hopefully this next slide helps. Now the yellow might be hard to make out, but you can see there's one distinct line. And at first, they are exactly the same. And then they are very similar. And there's kind of a variation, and then they become two completely different and varying solutions over time.

So, let's really dive in here. Why do I like the "butterfly effect"? And what's its connection to our discussion today? I think it's awesome how small, seemingly inconsequential changes in initial conditions can produce such shockingly different outcomes over a period of time. I'll say that again. I think it's awesome how small, seemingly inconsequential changes in initial conditions can produce such shockingly different outcomes over a period of time. Now the actual flap of the butterfly's wing in Bangladesh, if you will, causes a series of events like a domino effect that causes the invisible storm. So through this lens, how does this look when thinking of the role of music, or the arts in people's lives? Let's think about those hurricanes again. Hurricanes are destructive forces of nature. But why do they exist at all? As menacing as this picture may look, we should be reminded that hurricanes are actually good for the Earth. Hurricanes cool the planet; keeping the temperature of the planet regulated is paramount to our survival. That is a good thing. And from this wanna-be meteorologist, while they are destructive, they are still very beautiful. Is it possible then that with all the craziness that seems to swirl about us in our modern world (global pandemic, economic turmoil, social unrest) that we might find beauty in the chaos and the hustle and bustle of our own daily lives? Let's start with a microcosm, the story of my own family.

Everyone, say "hello" to Emma Conyers, my mother. My mom was a child of the segregated South growing up in the Democratic village in Savannah. The world may have viewed my mother as inconsequential, a statistic, which was the common assessment for people of color during that time. But it was a chance encounter, trivial as say the flap of a butterfly's wing that changed her life forever. She heard classical music on the radio, and she thought it was beautiful. And thus began a series of events that affected her future. She went on to become an amateur singer, she decided that all of her children would play, and all three of her children did. And now she has a son in a leadership position in one of the world's great orchestras. Now remember, this is all via a chance encounter that affected my mother's initial conditions as a child. That's one example of beauty in the chaos of the world.

Where my folks find beauty or meaning in the chaos of the larger world, for the Conyers family, that refuge was the church. So I grew up Baptist. And it's important to note now that this is not a presentation on religion. There are many who have similar beliefs, who may not even be religious at all. That said, my church family was a very strong, faithful, and steadfast community of beautiful souls to whom I owe a lot of my success. I had the good fortune of having very loving and supportive parents; both sacrificed for me to find success in life. My parents' protection of children was no different from protection and community found in the church. It is a traditional African American Baptist Church deeply embedded in the heart of that community in Savannah, the very same church my mother attended as a girl. It was there that I learned the true meaning of community and the value of service. I remember constantly seeing our parents helping folks out, going out of the way to visit with elder members of the Church, many of whom could no longer make it to Sunday services. Now, as a child, I didn't understand why we had to visit so many people I didn't know. But as I got older, I realized that it was the elders in the church who had helped my parents, acted as butterflies for them, steering them in the right direction, in a segregated world that was not necessarily on their side. People looked out for each other. And it was at the core of our DNA as a community. There was a pay-it-forward mindset of flapping of wings for others and hopes for a better future for them, even if they never saw that future.

You'll notice with the Lorenz model, there is no timeline on when these changes might occur. The only thing we can be certain of is that change will eventually happen. That's something we can hold onto. Now, listen closely, paying it forward can be difficult. It can be hard, and it can be inconvenient. However, contentment from those elders doing all of that work came in knowing that they were simply paving the way for others. My family, my ancestors, against all odds fought in the world, a world that was fighting just as hard against them, to make things better. And it's upon their shoulders that I stand and I'm able to speak with you here today. Sacrifices were made. Wings were flapped. And in many cases, even lives were lost. I am a proud product of their sacrifice. What else can I do, but also be a servant?

Now, some of you may be asking, "Well, how does this relate to me?" Well, here's my "aha" moment. We were driving down the road and we saw some kids sitting on the porch, and my mom just made the comment that amongst them, one of them could be a genius, this great person no one ever knew. And that was my "aha" moment. As I grew older, what I wanted to do was use my talents and my opportunities to give back, to come back to my hometown in Savannah, and try to inspire some children. I still remember that very vividly. And I remember thinking, looking at those young people in this impoverished situation and thinking, why did they not have opportunity? I've been given an opportunity, and the fact that they couldn't have that same opportunity made me sad. And honestly, it's haunted me. Why don't they have the same chance? The only thing separating those kids from me was opportunity. All human beings have potential. The question is, how do we realize that potential? How do we get opportunity to as many young folks as possible, particularly in our under-resourced communities? How do we help them? Look, I'm just the bass player. And as any orchestra musician will tell you, that's not much. But even as a bass player, I can commit to doing what I can to help whoever I can. Not unlike the family I had at home and at church to help me, I cannot singularly change the world. But collectively, we can change the initial conditions, so that the future is a better place, we could all be somebody's butterfly. People in the world need butterflies. That's the fact. Hard work is important. But life becomes exponentially more difficult if all are not beginning from the same starting line. I'd like to show a powerful film depicting just that. You may have seen it on social media in the last few years. And it's since resurfaced in numerous variations, highlighting privilege and society, a reminder of the inequalities that exist in our communities. This film was produced by Adam Donini.

> The winner of this race will take this $100 bill. Before I say go, I'm going to make a couple of statements. If those statements apply to you, I want you to take two steps forward. If those statements don't apply to you, I want you to stay right where you're at. Take two steps forward if both of your parents are still married. Take two steps forward if you grew up with a father figure in the home. Take two steps forward if you had access to a private education. Take two steps forward if you had access to a free tutor growing up. Take two steps forward if you've never had to worry about your cell phone being shut off. Take two steps forward if you've never had to help mom or dad with the bills. Take two steps forward if it wasn't because of your athletic ability that you don't have to pay for college. Take two steps forward if you never wondered where your next meal is going to come from. I want you guys up here in the front just to turn around and look. Every statement I've made has nothing to do with anything any of you have done, has nothing to

do with decisions you've made. Everything I've said has nothing to do with what you've done. We all know these people out here have a better opportunity to win this $100. Does that mean these people back here can't race? No, we will be forced to not realize we've been given more opportunity. We don't want to recognize that we've been given a head start. But the reality is we have. Now there's no excuse. They still got to run their race, you still gotta run your race. But whoever wins this $100, I think it'd be extremely foolish of you not to utilize that and learn more about somebody else's story. Because the reality is, if this was a fair race, and everybody was back on that line, I guarantee you some of these black dudes would smoke all of you. And it's only because you have this big of a head start that you're possibly going to win this race called "life." That is a picture of life, ladies and gentlemen.

It's a powerful film. And it's controversial for a number of reasons. But we're going to focus on the big picture. The black guys he refers to could be anyone; underserved, disadvantaged, disenfranchised folks who exist in all of our communities. In the video, you'll see that some kids have advantages while others don't. Is that fair? Well, the world is most certainly not a perfect place. My question then is how do we level the playing field as an arts community? Is the answer in the art itself? Could music, yes, even the piano, somehow be an equalizer.

Now this next slide I'm about to show you is also controversial. This picture has sparked many different iterations, corrections. And reimaginings is the mother of the now famous equity-versus-equality illustration. And I want to focus on one aspect of this drawing that resides on a website produced by the Interaction Institute for Social Change. Now, the persons you see before you, like in that race, have different advantages. And in this case, it's specifically height. Now in the first picture, you can see what equality is; each has been given equal assistance to be able to see over the fence, in which case, the individual in the blue shirt, no problem, the individual in the orange shirt, no problem, the individual in the purple shirt, having a few issues. In equity, you can see that their heads are all in alignment, and each is given exactly what they need to be able to see over the fence. Now I was in an argument with one of my colleagues who told me that well, you can see the individual in the blue shirt had to give their box away to the individual in the purple shirt. But if you look at the picture, the individual in the blue shirt didn't need the box at all. In life, what can act as boxes to level the playing field. And I think this is where you come in. It's music y'all. The arts can act as those boxes, and thus lays the groundwork for my work in Philadelphia. Do I believe music can be used as a tool for change, a tool for good? Let's celebrate music not simply for art's sake alone, but as a tool for people's sake, as a tool with which we can engage our underserved, our disadvantaged, and our disenfranchised. And that's our focus at my organization Project 440. We use music as a tool to help young people achieve their dreams.

Now, some might find this a bit strange, as we are a music organization that doesn't teach music. Well, how does that work? On the outside, it might look to be a music program, but on the inside, we are a creative youth development program that uses music as a tool to teach entrepreneurship, leadership, and service. And we don't need to teach music in Philadelphia. There are many organizations doing this work in Philadelphia. Let me tell you about an organization called PMA, the Philadelphia Music Alliance. PMA is a pipeline program, a unique collective, where everyone is not doing the same thing. We all stay in our lane. It is built specifically to create a pathway for students from underrepresented communities to find their ways from working on their music in their communities, to ultimately being on the stages of American orchestras and concert halls. What PMA has done is create and continue to grow an ecosystem of opportunity in the city of Philadelphia. Our mission, at Project 440, is to help young people use their interest in music to forge new pathways for themselves and ignite change in their communities. Our vision is that through music, every young person is provided with the opportunity and tools for individual growth and impact.

We have four flagship programs; the first, Doing Good. It is an afterschool social entrepreneurship training program where students explore the ways that making music, advocacy, and creative community engagement can all interface with local challenges in the community. Basically, students are charged with finding a problem and then are charged with searching for a solution. This is a semester-long course meeting twice weekly.

Next up, we have Instruments for Success. It is an afterschool, college and career readiness course that exposes young musicians in high school to a varied collection of musical-based opportunities and pipelines to the collegiate and professional level across a number of genres and sectors. This is a ten-week course that is two hours a week. Next up we have our college fair, our fourth annual fair was held virtually, of course, due to the pandemic. The fair is usually in partnership with the Kimmel Center for the Performing Arts, which is located in downtown Philadelphia on the Avenue of the Arts. Our in-person featured over fifty colleges and over three hundred participants. Our virtual featured over sixty colleges and over four hundred participants. Project 440 seminars and workshops are held throughout the fair on various topics, all free of charge to students participating. We decided to do our college fair online after a very successful partnership with the Los Angeles Philharmonic. We reached 100 students in sixteen states across the country. We're really excited about our work. We have taken that model and have revised it for various cohorts, a Project 440 all around the country, in cities across America. In this way, the pandemic gave us an opportunity to reach more kids than ever before. The Youth Advocacy Program is an advocacy group for our youth to be able to advocate for music in Philadelphia, but also to advocate for Project 440 and letting others know about the programming that is in Philadelphia. They also develop leadership skills, they learn board governance and hands on board training.

So, what type of musicians do we serve? Well, Project 440 serves all musicians and here's why. I told you at the beginning of our discussion that the church was one of my first interactions with music, and gospel music is still one of my favorite forms of expression today. I chuckled to myself sometimes because when I was a little boy, I was one mean alto. If anyone has seen me perform as a bassist today, they would know that I perform just as passionately when I'm on stage with the Philadelphia Orchestra. It's in my blood. Music is a language and gospel and classical, while two different languages, deliver the same message. Different genres of music don't threaten our form but the celebration, the interconnectivity, and appreciation of all genres of music, diversity, only helped make the art better. We should not only embrace this fact, but we should celebrate it. And as for those reasons, we welcome all musicians into our program.

Where does Project 440 fit in the music and education conversation? In classical music, there is great concern, great concern about our future, particularly now. The industry is evolving and negatively or positively, changes do not come easily. We've heard a myopic, eighteenth-century view of music's role in society. There's too much emphasis on the music itself, versus what the music can do, what it can be for people, particularly in a modern age. We spend too much time focusing on Bach, Beethoven, and Brahms, and I get it. I think Bach, Beethoven, and Brahms are pretty awesome. Brahms is my favorite composer. But here comes a little bit of a reality check. And I say this with the comfort that this is a virtual presentation and that no one can actually throw anything at me. Truth is, most people don't care about Bach, Beethoven, or Brahms. And why should people care? Because we say so, all while willfully neglecting the existing culture of communities we are supposedly trying to serve. So what is the solution? Stop focusing on Bach, Beethoven, and Brahms, particularly since most young people are not going to become professional musicians. I know, I know. And that's okay. Just like most kids in sports programs will not become professional athletes. Instead, think "what if we focus on the music and the arts being used as tools to help young people become the best version of themselves possible." Now what we've done is created a narrative that all communities can stand behind in the advocacy for music education. Music, a tool for equity. That's Project 440's approach. We are adapting to the changes in our industry, ensuring that young people will enjoy and celebrate our art form for years to come. Beethoven is not going to make the world a better place. He's no longer with us. But just as we, as artists, take the notes from those pages to make harmony, we as citizen musicians must use music as a tool to create harmony amongst each other. Music as a tool is how we address the injustice and inequality faced by many of our young people. Through music, we can help youth develop the agency and competencies needed to thrive and the fringe benefits. Folks might just learn a little bit about Bach, Beethoven, and Brahms and given our openness to different genres, we might be mixing in a little Beatles, Brandy, and Beyoncé in there along the way.

More kids of color can both proudly and comfortably enter into new musical spaces, particularly from marginalized communities, if given access to the art form. They can be guided to the pipeline of continued study if that is what they wish, or simply use music as an instrument for success. I'm optimistic about the future of the classical music industry through this lens, the very best days of our industry are not behind us. As I conclude, you might surmise that I'm not very shy on matters relating to music or youth. And I'm not shy because the kids in Philadelphia, the nation's poorest major city, mind you, so desperately need our help. My goal as an artist is to provide young people boxes of opportunity upon which they can proudly stand in concert with other youth, not only in our suburbs, but across our country. Yes, it's true. I do a lot. And it's possible some of my colleagues might think I'm a bit crazy. But I'm made crazy by the deafening silence that permeates our industry when it comes to our many storied institutions, meeting the needs of our communities. We must remember to whom much is given, much is required. "Well, Joseph, I've been told we're doing the best that we can." That statement bugs me even more, the best we can is a qualifier, and allows for the proverbial can to be kicked down the road. Folks, let's stop doing the best we can and just do.

To the members of the National Conference of keyboard Pedagogy, you get my message. Unabashedly be somebody's butterfly for positive growth and change–your neighbor's butterfly, your community's. Remember it is the actions of the butterfly that set into place the domino effect, setting off a hurricane of hope that can change the future for the better. Let that flap of the wing come from you. In a time where folks might be feeling uneasy about the future, given the chaos that seems to spin so uncontrollably around us, I remind you that even in the middle of a hurricane, one of the worst catastrophes of Mother Nature, there are no clouds in the sky. The sun shines brightly, and the wind is calm. There is peace. Art is the beauty within the chaos. It challenges us, it stretches our imagination and can be used as a tool to level the playing field so that everyone has a chance to live the life they want to live. I want to leave you with an excerpt from a poem whose text was used as inspiration for a commission from my inaugural year as music director of Philadelphia's All City Orchestra. It was written by Frances Ellen Watkins Harper, an abolitionist poet, who helped runaway slaves escape via the Underground Railroad. She was a civil rights activist, a women's rights activist who believed in education for all and lived right here in Philadelphia, Pennsylvania, at the turn of the twentieth century. These are the last two stanzas of her poem, *Songs for the People*.

Our world, so worn and weary,
Needs music, pure and strong,
To hush the jangle and discords
Of sorrow, pain, and wrong.

Music to soothe all its sorrow,
Till war and crime shall cease;
And the hearts of men grown tender
Girdle the world with peace.

Don't tell it, just do it. Music gives us all we need to take on the world. Don't delay—be somebody's butterfly today.

Recalibrating Our Teaching to Accommodate Young Musicians' Psychological Needs
Saturday, July 31, 2021
Keynote Address

Presented by Gary McPherson

My training is in music education, education, psychology, and also music psychology. And I've spent my life just studying how children learn musical instruments, how they practice, how they develop skills, how they develop. But a particular love of mine is studying those motivational forces that allow children to thrive and continue and sustain their learning, and particularly sustain their learning when they're having difficulties or they hit the other brick walls or the obstacles that occur with a sophisticated area of learning such as music.

Today I'll talk about two main theories: self-determination theory. And when I talk about that type, pay particular attention to the three psychological needs that need to be satisfied for any child to thrive with their learning, particularly autonomy and autonomy-supportive environments that are just absolutely fundamental to success and developing the right sort of attitude and motivation to sustain yourself as a learner. The second theory is visible learning theory. And one of my colleagues here at the university is John Hattie, a very, very prominent education psychologist, one of the best in the world. And he developed this visible learning theory. And visible learning is about seeing progression as a journey. And especially about making learning visible not only to yourself, but especially to the child so the child understands what they're doing, why they're doing it, and they're a partner in the educational process. So, with those brief comments to start off with, let's watch the video. And afterwards, we can talk about some of the issues that I bring up. Or you could write to me if you're interested in any of this material.

In this presentation, I'd like to talk about what students need in order to thrive and succeed with their music learning. To do this, I'll draw heavily on my own research across the past thirty years studying children who learn instruments, but also related research in other disciplines, and in particular, some of the main motivation theories within education and psychology. And by the end of this presentation, I'd like you to have some sense of the types of basic psychological needs that research now shows are fundamental to effective learning. But I'd also like you to have a sense of the techniques that are being used in other areas of education, and now in music education, to help sustain children's involvement in their own music learning.

Let's begin with self-determination theory. Now, this is a motivation theory that's been around since the 1980s. And it was originally devised by Edward Deci and Richard Ryan, and they have many, many publications on this particular theory. It's a very powerful theory, in terms of explaining the motivational forces that act on any learner when they're trying to acquire new knowledge, or gain extra skill. And the two basic components of self-determination theory are really intrinsic motivation and extrinsic motivation, and contrasting and comparing both of these forms of motivation. Intrinsic motivation is fairly self evident, it's doing something for the inherent satisfaction; you do it because you choose to do it. And you're not doing it because of any external reason for doing it. That's your choice. Extrinsic motivation, on the other hand, is engaging in an activity because you feel others want you to do it. So feeling reinforcement or pressured and even pushed, or in the worst case scenario, even coercion.

Humans are inherently oriented towards growth and well being. That's part of who we are, we want to grow, we want to feel good. And we thrive when we feel in control, and we make choices. Our motivation decreases, however, when others make choices for us, and we feel we don't have control.

Here's the full slide with the complete theory, self-determination theory. And you can see in the middle of the slide, we've got extrinsic motivation, that's when you're completely disinterested in a particular activity. On the right hand side of the slide, you've got intrinsic motivation. And again, that's doing something for sheer pleasure and enjoyment. So there's no discernible reinforcement or reward, externally. And then those four levels of extrinsic motivation in the middle, moving toward intrinsic motivation.

At the top of the slide, we have the three basic psychological needs. Now, a lot of research shows that these three psychological needs are absolutely fundamental to all of us, we won't thrive. We won't grow and won't feel a sense of well being unless each of these three psychological needs are satisfied.

Now, the three basic psychological needs: the first one is *competence*. Feeling able to do an activity, and feeling you can master the activity, a sense of mastery, and competence in what you're learning and what you're doing. *Relatedness* is feeling that you can talk and relate to your teacher, your parents or even your peers, and sharing a sense of valuing of the activity. *Autonomy* is perhaps the most important; it's about feeling that you're learning because you want to learn rather than your teacher or parents want you to learn. Autonomy is about giving students choices. So they feel they're part of the learning process, and that their opinion matters. That's important because whenever a student feels in any way controlled by external factors, they are much more likely to experience frustration, and in the worst case scenario, feel helpless, or even give up. Here's those three psychological needs feeding into intrinsic motivation—competence, relatedness, and autonomy.

So based on the information I've just shared, let's now survey some results from work with musicians who are learning music. And the first group of studies comes from researchers who are looking at different profiles of individuals who demonstrate a passion for an activity, which they're learning. And these are studies about passionate involvement with an activity or basically motivation studies. The second group of studies come from work I've conducted with students in the first couple of years of learning a musical instrument. And in my work, we typically get to the students before they actually have their first music lesson, and do extensive interviews with the students and their parents and even the teachers. And then we follow their progress for the next three to five years, and in fact, in one of the studies I conducted we've followed their progress for fourteen years. And after these results, I'd like to discuss some work with recent studies I've undertaken with university-level pianists who were preparing for their end-of-semester performance examination. So this work is about higher levels of expertise, and typically students who are undertaking a bachelor of music or even a master's degree, and would hope to become professional musicians.

Now the first group of studies about passion show that musical identity—a sense of being a musician—and some sense of musical identity is absolutely fundamental to holding a great love of music or a passion for music, and for music learning. And in this slide, you can see that these other forces come into place. So we've got harmonious passion at the top of the figure. And harmonious passion occurs or is more likely to occur when individuals have been exposed to an autonomy-supportive environment. And I'll talk a little bit more about that in a moment. So they've been supported to make choices and have some ability to shape their own learning. And you can see that autonomy support is positively related to harmonious passion, and also positively related to persistence. They're the type of learner that when they face setbacks, or things go wrong, or hardship in any way, that they're more likely to persist to overcome those obstacles in their learning. At the bottom of the diagram, you can see psychological control. And that's when the student feels that they're doing the activity because mum or dad want them to learn, a teacher's on their back, they've got a recital coming up, they've got all sorts of external influences that are tempering their sense of identity, and also their passion for music. Now, the label we use for this category is obsessive passion. And you can see that psychological control is positively related to obsessive passion. And then obsessive passion is positively related to stress. So they're the type of individuals and musicians who when they feel stress, it can be exaggerated because they feel others are controlling them, or the music's controlling them, instead of them controlling music or them controlling the learning process and stress as negatively correlated with persistence. So again, the types of individuals, when they have those stressful moments, they hit those obstacles, they're less likely to persist. So I think this basic difference between harmonious passion and obsessive passion is a really interesting way of conceptualizing how important it is to provide an autonomy-supportive environment, an autonomy-supportive learning environment for every child that is exposed to music learning.

Here's another diagram by John Marshall Reeve, a wonderful educational psychologist, and he's done a number of studies, where he he looks at learning environments and the type of comments that are being made by a teacher to students, and whether they're encouraging autonomy and personal choice in the students, particularly when asking them to reflect and make their own mind up or their own decisions. As compared to more controlling environments, where the students are, the learning situation is more whether the teacher controls the learning outcome, the students have less choice, for example. And you can see all sorts of positive benefits from an autonomy-supportive environment as compared to a teacher-controlled environment.

Eliza Cooper has done some wonderful work in The Netherlands, and this is from her PhD. She was looking at children learning cello, and the dynamics that are going on in a lesson between the teacher and the child. Now, these were young children, who were seven or eight years of age learning cello. She was looking at the amount of engagement within the lesson, how concentrated the work was, and how engaged the children were in the learning process during the lesson, as compared to the amount of autonomy that were given within the lesson, the amount of opportunities to decide for themselves. And essentially, she has these four quadrants. Now, I won't go into all the details here. But essentially, the top two are mimicry. And this because in a lot of lessons where there's high engagement, the student isn't doing what you're asking the student to do. But essentially, you're just telling the student what to do. So they're following your lead. And therefore it's more of a mimicry result from the students, low autonomy and high engagement. The sweet spot is where we have high autonomy from the student, and lots of engagement. So they're really involved. And we call that autonomous engagement. They're the four prototypes of student engagement during lessons.

And Eliza did really detailed analyses of every comment by the teacher and the student, and what happened before and immediately after that comment was made. And you can see the mapping out there, of the level of engagement of the students from four of these children who are learning cello.

Overall, the results provide quite conclusive evidence that high autonomy support triggers engagement and low autonomy support triggers the resistance. So an authoritarian style of teaching triggers copying the teacher and less meaningful interactions between teacher and student and an authoritative style of teaching triggers engagement, curiosity, persistence, and more positive values about learning music.

And here's the results of a number of studies all collated together by John Hattie and some other education psychologists. You can see autonomy-supportive environments as compared to controlling environments within learning settings. Autonomy-supportive environments create less frustration in the student, less feelings of helplessness by the student, less negative feelings by the students, less self criticism and negative thoughts. That creates more positive feedback, more planning and strategy used by the students. And overall, the students are more motivated, and the teacher is more encouraging.

Now it's well established in virtually every learning and work environment that external rewards erode achievement and motivation. External rewards such as giving stickers, awards, or even pocket money to complete practice, can seem innocent enough. But in all forms of learning and also in music, these types of external reinforcements have consistently been found to reduce motivation over time. And I've done a number of studies on this and, in one of them, we looked at whether our beginning instrumentalists were receiving any pocket money or any tangible incentives to learn or practice from their parents. And we found that not one of the children who were given any rewards or incentives to learn such as pocket money to practice their instrument, continued learning beyond the first year of the progress or the learning. So it was really clear to us that rewards that were given by parents in particular, but also sometimes by teachers, tended to decrease and seriously erode the student's motivation to learn.

So another part of the study was where we asked the children a week before they got their instruments and had their first music lesson, how long they expected to play their instrument. Now remember, this was before they actually had their first music lesson. And some of the children said that they're expecting to play just for a couple of years, we'll give it a go there, they're not sure whether they would continue into high school. And the medium-term commitment children were those children who said, "Yes, I'll play till the end of high school. But after that, I'm just not sure whether I'll continue playing because I want to go to university or get a job." And "I'm not sure that I'll have the time to continue playing my instrument." There were other children, however, who expressed a long-term commitment. And these children typically spoke about learning the instrument, playing the instrument, all of their lives. Now, we looked at how much practice the children were doing in the first year of learning. And we got the parents to map out their practice habits across the first year. So we'd phone them up every few weeks and ask how much practice the child was doing and get the mom or the dad to tell us what they could remember for those immediate couple of weeks. And so we separated it into low, medium, and high amounts of practice. At the end of the first year, we gave them a standardized performance measure, in this case, a sight-reading measure to see how good they were on the instrument, what they have accomplished after one year of learning. And you can see the children who expressed a short-term commitment to music learning—it didn't matter whether they did low, medium, or high amounts of practice, their achievement at the end of the first year was about the same. The children who expressed a long-term commitment with high amounts of practice, are the ones who flourished. And they were the ones who really stood out at the end of the first year, in terms of their ability, and also the desire to continue on into the next year as well. So this gives you a sense of how important motivation is. It's not just about practice, but it's also about the right beliefs, and the right attitude toward learning.

Now, in some of my publications, I talk about children's current musical identity, how they view their musical lives right now in the role of learning their piano, or whatever instrument it is right now. And we'll ask them questions like, "What do you expect to be doing with piano or your music lessons in ten years time?" And so often, we'll see a contradiction between their current musical identity and their future musical identity as shown in that diagram there—what they expect from it, what they value from music into the future as compared to now. And I say in a number of publications that I really do believe that students will give up if they are unable to imagine themselves as musical into the future, if they do not have some sense of what the future might hold for them musically.

This figure shows some of the main features of self-regulated learning, one of the most prominent motivation theories in education. And there are two main features of this theory. First, the forethought performance and self-reflection phases of any learning process which is before, during, and after. And second, each of those terms within the three phases refer to what a learner may be doing, their behavior, what they may be thinking at any particular moment, their cognition, and what they may be feeling at any particular moment before, during, and after, which is their ethics. So it's about behavior, cognition, and ethics, and itemizing all of the things that are important for us as researchers to understand in order to really understand how self-regulated learning operates, and can evolve in children as they develop a sense of mastery on their instrument.

When we study the dynamics of one-to-one studio teaching, we often find teachers who focus on just the behavior of the student, and quite often the language they use is more like a monologue, rather than a dialogue with the students. For example, we often hear comments such as "that was wrong, try it again." "Can you do that again and try to make it more *legato*?" So the emphasis is on what the student is doing, rather than what they are thinking or feeling.

In the next section of this presentation, I'll talk about some techniques that you might consider, that are based on a huge amount of research in other areas of education. And they show that effective teachers focus their students on what they are thinking, their cognition, and feeling their effect, as a means of more effectively being able to change what the student is doing with their behavior.

So with self-regulated learning, it's about behavior, cognition, and ethics. And there are three phases of the self-regulated learning process, there's the sorts of activities and thinking and behaviors and feelings that occur in any learner, before they do something. And these processes can enhance or impede performance.

You can see that one component is task analysis—goal setting and strategic planning. And these are cognitive processes, thinking processes. And it is ways that musicians organize a practice session, for example, and it would be questions that they ask themselves like "What am I intending to achieve today?"

At the bottom of that figure, we've got self-motivational beliefs. And these are personal beliefs and feelings, *etc*. And they relate to feelings of confidence, outcome expectations, interest and passion, such as "Why am I doing this?" And self efficacy is a particularly important one in that list there. In the performance phase, we've got self-control mechanisms, and also self observation, and these impact on performance. And they're about "How can I optimize my efforts?" "By controlling my performance?" "How do I monitor and control what I'm doing when I'm actually doing it?" And then the bottom one is metacognitive monitoring and self recording which has a real impact on concentration. How can I mentally track what I'm doing? So if I make a mistake, I can correct it, if the section is repeated. And then the self-reflection phase is what occurs after practice, or after the performance of a work.

These are the musicians' responses to the performance, self judgments and self reactions. We can see that self judgments are about how and why we choose to engage in activities that are satisfying, and avoid experiences that are frustrating or stressful. Self reactions are the processes that give direction to our actions and create self incentives to persist with our efforts. Motivation to achieve doesn't stem from the goals we set ourselves, but rather our reactions to experiences trying to fulfill our goals. So our motivation is not necessarily so linked to what we want to do. But our feelings and thoughts about ourselves once we've done it, and we've started to evaluate the success, or otherwise, of our efforts.

Now, I could probably talk for hours about my research into all of the dimensions on this self-regulated learning three-phase model. But to give you a sense of how powerful the theory is for explaining effective learning, let me quickly show you two results. The first result deals with self efficacy. And we define self efficacy as your confidence that you can do something immediately before you do it. A good example would be your confidence immediately before you walk on stage that you can accurately perform a difficult section of a piece that you're about to perform. So self efficacy is about how you feel and what you're thinking immediately before you do it.

And in the studies I've undertaken we see that self efficacy is a much better predictor of success on the music performance examination, then is the amount of practice the student completed in the month before the performance. So in effect, self efficacy tells us more about what the student will do in the performance examination then does the amount of practice they've done in the month before that examination.

In recent years, in using the self-regulated learning three-phase model, we've been examining how pianists practice as they prepare for an end of semester performance examination, and we've also been trying to devise techniques to help make their practice more efficient. Now, as expected, we observed wide variations in the practice habits of more successful as compared to less successful pianists. And these, again, were university students. The most successful pianists are what we refer to as proactive learners. They tended to report just a few goals for the practice session. But these goals are typically very clear and very targeted. And they also report higher self-motivational beliefs. And they are called proactive learners, because they display high forethought and performance phase behaviors, cognition, and effect. So more is happening before and during their practice.

In contrast, the less successful learners are very different. We call them reactive learners, because they spend less time on thought processes, and jump right into the performance of a piece or exercise without planning out first what they want to achieve. And then after they're finished, and they weren't quite successful, they tend to report less self-regulated goal setting, and reactive habitual strategy use. And because of this, they are more likely to feel bad about their practice efforts. So what do all of these results tell us? For me, they reinforce the power of motivational beliefs, those thoughts and those feelings that are fundamental for anyone to succeed at a high level.

So in the next section of my presentation, I'd like to frame what I've covered so far, with comments and suggestions about what you can do in your everyday teaching, to help bring about the best in your students, and also be known to them as someone who inspires them.

Let's now turn to this perspective from Simon Sinek, an author whose work is being widely cited in education. And he suggests that there's only two ways you can influence human behavior. You can manipulate human behavior or you can inspire human behavior. Simon Sinek's ideas help us differentiate between the everyday teacher and those teachers who seem to make a profound impact on their students' lives and music learning. Teachers who inspire their students produce musicians who want to go home and practice after the lesson, or achieve at a level they never thought might be possible for themselves.

Now, as teachers, we know what we do, and we know how to do it. But in every lesson, few of us ask why we do it. And great teachers reverse this by starting with why. They go from why, to what, to how. And here you can see on the slide the Golden Circle, Simon Sinek's depiction of the why, what, and how.

We understand the why in terms of the purpose, cause or belief; or why we are teaching something at that particular moment, or why we want the learner to learn something at that particular moment in the learning cycle. And the main point here is that it needs to be understood by both the teacher and the learner. So the teacher needs to understand why they are giving the student that particular task at that particular moment, in terms of the purpose, or the reason why that's needed. And then also the cause, what change will occur as a result of the student being able to accomplish or master this task. Now we know that the purpose and the cause have a huge impact on not only the teacher's beliefs about the student, but the student's beliefs about their own potential and their own ability to master something. So again, the why concerns the purpose, cause, or belief of why we are teaching something or attempting to learn something at that particular moment.

Another view on education now that I particularly like is John Hattie's visible learning, these are used extensively in school education in many countries around the world. And it's based on three concepts, seeing learning through the eyes of students. And this means focusing on your students perspective about their learning, rather than our perspective on the learning, helping students to become their own teachers to become self regulated with their own learning.

And really importantly, learning is seen as a journey. Development is seen as having reached a particular point along that journey. So the emphasis is on focusing students on where to next, rather than what they may have just done, that was right or wrong. That's looking to the future rather than the past. Within visible learning, I really like John Hattie's concept of feedback, feed up, and feed forward. So let's tease out the details of each of these. Now, most of the feedback that we give to students, most of the comments that we give to students in our everyday teaching, is what he would label feedback. The focus is on the past and what you've just done. So it's very person based. Feedback aimed at the individual often involves praise or criticism, such as "That was great," "You're really good at this," or "No, that's not quite right."

This type of feedback has virtually no impact on learning, because it doesn't include information about the learning process. And I'll tease that out in a little bit more detail in a moment. It also reinforces ability rather than effort, perceptions of oneself. So it gives the sense to the student, if they're exposed to lots of this over time, and this is the main vehicle of communicating with the student about their progress, it gives them a sense that they can do it or they can't do it, or they're good at that, or they're not good at that, rather than if they put more work in, they can be better.

So it reinforces ability rather than effort, perceptions of oneself. And in fact, excessive ongoing praise can sometimes lead to a reduction in one's willingness to try in some learners. So there are learners, who if you praise them all the time, they'll start to feel actually less motivated to learn, often because they actually can see through what you're saying, and they know themselves that they're not progressing as fast as you might be inferring in the lesson.

There's also a difference, a major difference, between constant praise versus intense praise. Now, when we study lessons of teachers teaching their instrumentalists, quite often, what we'll see is this constant praise, constant positive reinforcement. But if you look at really great teachers, often they will give a lot less constant praise. And there will be these moments within the lesson where they stop, and they really celebrate what the student has been able to achieve at that particular moment, after they can actually do something that they couldn't do before. So we know that intense praise is much, much more effective, and much, much more motivating for a student. But I should say that praise and criticism are problematic because they reduce students' focus on the task. They stop them from thinking about what to do next, and we have to be careful of that.

Now feed forward is the next type of way of communicating with students. And that's about where to next, it's about the future. So the focus is on the future, let's focus on the journey ahead. And students prefer where-to-next-type comments to virtually any other form of communication from a teacher or feedback from a teacher. They really want to know what they should do next, in order to master a new challenge. So feed forward isn't simply about what a teacher says to a student, though, but what a student can also say to the teacher. So with all of these forms of feedback, it's really important that it's not just a one-way communication between the teacher and the student. But there are moments in the lesson where you stop and you ask the student for an opinion, or to give thoughts on whether they feel that they're learning or not learning at all, whether what they're doing is succeeding or not succeeding or whether the comments that you're providing as a teacher are useful to them. That's extremely important. And that's part of this concept of feed forward.

Feed up probably occurs less often in a lesson. But it's these unexpected moments when you focus on challenging the student to get them to do something, to really push them to think outside the box, or challenge them to do something that they feel that they may not be able to do. The best way of doing this is to compare the learner's current state with his desired target state. So for example, you might say to the student that that performance is about sixty-percent accurate. See if you can get to seventy-percent accuracy with this next attempt, or next lesson, do you think you could get to eighty-percent accuracy on that particular piece. So give them a sense of the journey. And you give them a sense that quite often, even within an individual practice, session, or lesson, we can't accomplish everything, that this journey may take a month or two to complete.

To summarize, the best forms of feedback feed forward and feed up, they focus on quality, not quantity. They're given during the instructional cycle, not too far, either beforehand, or after the event. It's most powerful when learning becomes visible, not only to the student, so that the student knows what you're thinking and what you want from them. But they're also powerful when learning becomes visible to the teacher. And some of the most powerful instances of great learning occur when the student explains what they're doing, thinking, and feeling with their teacher. And together, they both negotiate a way forward.

Feedback, feed forward, and feed up work best when you provide clear information on how to correct errors, and how these errors can be avoided in the future. And yes, we should identify errors in the students playing. But our real focus should be on the process whereby errors can be corrected. So if I was to summarize the main elements of visible learning, and what I've said so far, I'd say I'd encourage you to think about engaging more in dialogue, and try to avoid monologue. And that means the short utterances that we often make to students. "Now that wasn't right, do it again," that sort of comment, and engage the student in a conversation. It's slower, but it's more meaningful for the student.

Learning should be based on why, as well as what and how. We should stress progress over achievement. And we should see learning as a journey, we should also stress achieving your personal best over comparisons with others, the worst thing you can get a student to do or you can do yourself is to compare the student's progress or abilities at any particular point with another student that may be in the same studio or that they're competing against.

So in conclusion, let me stress that it's okay to be demanding as a teacher. Like you, I have very high personal standards that I don't want to compromise in any way whatsoever. I want my students to achieve at a very high level. But we have to be careful. So that we're not seen as authoritarian in that we don't give our students opportunities for those basic psychological needs I spoke about earlier to be satisfied. They need to feel they can do it themselves, that they can talk to us and share how they're feeling with us. And most importantly, they need to feel that they are in charge of their own learning. So providing an autonomy supportive environment is extremely important if we want them to thrive, and be able to overcome difficulties and obstacles.

And finally, I'd like to end with two quotes that for me summarize everything I try to achieve as a music teacher. The first one is from John Hattie's visible learning. It's about teaching. And he makes the really important comment that "my role as a teacher is to evaluate the effect I have on my students." The second one comes from Wayne Booth, who wrote a wonderful book called *For The Love of It*, about being an amateur musician. And he actually taught himself to play cello after he retired from the University of Chicago. He was one of the English professors and it is a beautifully written book. It's about practice and he says that, if practice feels like the thing you want to do, you found a good teacher. So at this point, I'd like to thank you all for listening. And I hope that what I've covered is of some use in your daily lives as musicians and music teachers.

PRECONFERENCE SEMINARS

INDEPENDENT MUSIC TEACHERS PRECONFERENCE
Tuesday, July 13, 2021

Chair: Jason Sifford
Committee Members: Rebekah Healan Boles, Elaina Burns, Wenjing Liu, Jodi Stewart-Moore, Rebecca Pennington, Stephen Pierce, Veena Kulkarni-Rankin, Kenneth Thompson

NCKP 2021: The Piano Conference kicked off with the Independent Music Teachers preconference day. Packed with a variety of sessions, this day explored topics such as helping students successfully navigate music study, rote teaching, healthy attitudes towards performance, technology, studio design, and diverse repertoire.

Jihea Hong-Park began the day with "A Year of Experimentation: Piano Studio as a Place of Belonging, Engagement, and Ownership," in which she explored how to create a studio where students experience belonging, engagement, and ownership throughout their musical studies. Next, Julie Hague, Paula Dryer, and Anne Davis explored strategies and tips for rote teaching, while Mary Brostrom Bloom and Adam Matlock discussed how to encourage students to have healthy attitudes towards performing.

Ying Zhao then presented "Roll the Ball! The Use of Positional and Directional Words in Learning Wrist Motions," in which she explored how to teach effective technique with a tennis ball, as well as effective language to use while teaching technique. Rachel Hahn presented "Green Screen, Eggs, and Ham: MacGyvered Music Classes for K-8 Remote Learning," and explored the pedagogical lessons and applications stemming from the wide variety of technology used during the COVID-19 pandemic. Christie Sowby then presented "Stunning Studio Spaces," and listeners were taught how to design studio spaces that promote effective learning.

The next portion of the day was devoted to diverse repertoire, and included "Let it Shine! Celebrating Piano Music by Black Composers," presented by Aaron Mathews, "More Diverse Children's Albums: Finding Variety in Teaching Literature," presented by Angela Miller-Niles, and "Raag-time: Incorporating Non-Western Musical Traditions" by Omar Roy. These sessions explored music by underrepresented composers that teachers can include in their repertoire lists.

The day concluded with a lecture recital by the faculty of the New School for Music Study who presented "Teaching the Gillock *Lyric Preludes*: An In-depth Analysis and Practical Guidelines." The session included teaching suggestions and performances of the complete *Lyric Preludes*.

TEACHING ADULTS PRECONFERENCE
Wednesday, July 14, 2021

Chair: Jackie Edwards-Henry
Committee Members: Yeeseon Kwon, Sarah Moore, Debra Perez,
Pamela Pike, Mary Sallee, Thomas Swenson

Adult Students—The *Now* Frontier

Learning to play the piano, resuming piano study or continuing to refine skills is becoming increasingly popular with adult students of all ages. As such, adding adult students can help piano teachers increase student numbers and add diversity and new opportunities to teaching schedules. During this track, the Committee presented new pandemic-era discoveries as well as tried-and-true ways to attract, retain, and meet the needs of this growing student population. Following a brief welcome of attendees and committee introductions, individual sessions were presented simultaneously in two time blocks with a break between to emulate the topic-focused experience of a face-to-face preconference track.

PART ONE
"The Question/Answer Cycle of Teaching Adults"
Presented by Pamela D. Pike and Thomas Swenson

Dr. Swenson highlighted how each adult piano student has unique goals by presenting brief case studies of three of his adult students who study private piano: Student No. 1 (stay-at-home mom and wife who is taking lessons along with her two sons; intermediate level; wants instructor to take control of the learning environment); Student No. 2 (retiree; living alone who is preparing for ABRSM level 8; involved in two local performance groups); and, Student No. 3 (widowed; early-advanced level who participates in two performance groups and an out-of-state adult piano camp). Then, Dr. Pike described a third-age piano group that she has been studying for nineteen years, highlighting how they learn music together, support each other, have become friends, stretch themselves to learn new musical styles, participate in low-stakes ensemble performances, and have diversified in the past decade.

When working with adult piano students, it is important to remember the six assumptions of andragogy, consider the curriculum, teaching/learning climate, lifespan stages that cause changes in learning and outside-of-lesson responsibilities, and assessment of progress at the piano. Teachers are *facilitators* of learning and, as such, they should consider whether the adult is a serious amateur, an amicable amateur, or a late bloomer (who comes to piano lessons late in life). Each adult's past musical experiences, expectations, and motivations for piano study will impact the type of teacher the learner is seeking. The presenters ended by reminding attendees to consider feedback, assessment, learning climate, curricular design, and teaching style when working with the adult student in both the private and the group setting.

Why Teach Them?
Presented by Sarah Moore

Adult students and teachers of adult students submitted videos of their responses to select questions from a list created by the committee. Videos were selected and shown during the session to feature piano study from the perspectives of adult students and their facilitators. Students elaborated on why they are engaging in adult piano study at this point in life and provided diverse reasons for why piano study is important to them. Adult students emphasized the importance of instructor flexibility and the use of a variety of instructional approaches. Instructor videos spotlighted the rewards of teaching adult students and the importance of flexibility in mindset.

How We Teach Adults, Part 1
Presented by Mary Sallee

The first of this two-part instructional video series highlighted effective techniques one might use for adult-aged students.

Short video examples of the committee members teaching their own students were used to illustrate how teachers can develop more of a "facilitator" or "partner" rapport as opposed to a "teacher-student" relationship. Through the various examples, attendees were exposed to adult students varying in ages from thirty to eighty with various musical backgrounds, playing experience, and interests in musical styles. The presenter made a point of showing some of her older students facing health issues such as Parkinson's, declining memory, and hearing loss to demonstrate their ability to persevere and accomplish unique musical and performance goals.

Real-Time Lesson Demonstration
Presented by Jackie Edwards-Henry and Sarah Moore
Repertoire: *Prelude in A Major,* Op. 28, Nr. 7 by Frédéric Chopin

Student bio: Stanly Godbold is Professor Emeritus of History at Mississippi State University. His retirement activities have included piano study, hiking, gardening/landscaping, yoga classes, and completing the second volume of his two-volume biography of Jimmy and Rosalynn Carter for Oxford University Press. Stanly began piano study prior to retirement by enrolling in one of Jackie Edwards-Henry's adult beginning piano classes. Following the class, he has continued piano study, on and off, primarily independently. He has resumed piano study with Jackie, as their schedules allow, since 2019.

This session was managed with Zoom. Stanly and Jackie worked together, face-to-face, in her studio and Sarah Moore commented and provided additional coaching via Zoom. Stanly selected a segment of the *Prelude in A* by Chopin that was problematic. Jackie assisted him with dotted-rhythm accuracy and the technical challenge of chord moves. Smaller steps included clapping and counting aloud and hands separate approach. Sarah also suggested approaching the rhythmic feel by saying words that matched the rhythm, then playing and saying the words rhythmically. She also suggested starting at the end of the phrase and working backwards to connect the rhythm pattern.

PART TWO
Adult Students Making Music
Facilitated by Yeeseon Kwon

The second series of sessions for the preconference track on teaching adults began with ten-minute videos of various adult students playing excerpts of repertoire from their study. Levels ranged from the elementary to advanced and from Classical to Popular styles.

How Do We Teach Adults in Groups?
Presented by Mary Sallee, Debra Perez, and Yeeseon Kwon

One option suggested for teachers wanting to explore teaching in a group format included Partner Lessons. Presenter Mary Sallee shared how she paired and scheduled students that were either friends or were similar in level, which added the ability to "change-up" the routine and make lessons more fun! She covered the importance of selecting user-friendly duet repertoire that would develop ensemble skills and, at the same time, build confidence in their rehearsal abilities to practice together outside of the lesson.

Debra Perez discussed the philosophy of the teaching environment and the "dos and don'ts" of recreational/leisure music making. She recommended the incorporation of music wellness and the importance of giving students varieties of ways to participate in classes to manage different student abilities and allow all to enjoy and benefit from the activities. In addition, she encouraged teachers/facilitators to participate in class activities and music-making with their students to model the team aspect of learning and making music together.

Yeeseon Kwon presented the virtual aspects of group teaching, including the ways to enhance student engagement through technology, the comparisons of teaching live versus virtually when in group settings. She also addressed other group teaching aspects such as the size of groups ranging from partner lessons and beyond, types of instruments, and setups of groups.

How We Teach Adults, Part 2
Presented by Mary Sallee

The second part of this series featured more video clips of committee members Yeeseon Kwon, Thomas Swenson, Jackie Edwards-Henry, and Mary Sallee teaching their students. Similarities were observed between several of the teachers in the way they demonstrated concepts and musical elements by demonstrating from a second piano, singing or tapping/playing on the fallboard. A variety of custom practice strategies were used to secure note reading, fingering of note sequences, memorization, and focus on listening. Other lesson elements covered included asking questions to assess what students knew or understood, making time for improvisation or music-making with the teacher, troubleshooting insecurities when memorizing, and drawing upon adults' experiences and intuitive abilities when learning a new concept.

Real-time Lesson Demonstration
Presented by Sarah Moore and Jackie Edwards-Henry
Repertoire: *Sonatina in G Major,* Op. 36, No. 5 (III. Allegro di molto) by Muzio Clementi

Student bio: Sarah Baxter is a Professor of Mechanical Engineering at the University of St. Thomas in Minnesota. She has been taking piano lessons off and on since she was in elementary school; mostly off. After a long break, she began taking lessons at the Community Music Program at the University of South Carolina and studied with Sarah Evans Moore from 2009–2013. After she moved to St. Paul, Minnesota in 2014, they resumed via online lessons in 2017.

Once again, this live demonstration was managed by Zoom, and all three participants were participating via distance. Sarah Moore's adult student, Sarah Baxter, has been studying virtually with her for several years. Sarah Baxter played an excerpt of the sonatina and Sarah Moore shared how to practice the right-hand articulation of the melodic phrase and then softly balance the left-hand chords. Jackie Edwards-Henry shared the articulation differences found in different editions/scores and then shared how to "ghost" the accompaniment on the music rack or fallboard or lap while the right hand plays the melody. Experiencing two ways to approach and teach melody/accompaniment balance was valuable for the student and attendees alike.

Cata-tonic, Virtual Happy Hour

Zoom Breakout Rooms provided a highly successful close to the preconference day. Participants brought their own questions, and some shared their feedback on the day. It was wonderful to see that some participants felt comfortable enough to share their own teaching experiences and reflections on teaching adult students.

INCLUSIVE TEACHING PRECONFERENCE
Thursday, July 15, 2021

Chairs: Beth Bauer and Melissa Martiros
Committee Members: Derek Kealli Polischuk, Scott Price

The Inclusive Teaching preconference at NCKP 2021: The Piano Conference began with a session by Cherisse Miller entitled "Undefined by Hearing Loss: My Career in Music," in which she shared her personal journey of studying music while having hearing loss. Miller shared what it is like to have hearing loss and shared the struggles of navigating social environments. Miller's story of pursuing music study, including receiving a doctoral degree in piano pedagogy, was inspiring and informative for teachers who have students with physical disabilities.

The day continued with Jasmine Harry, who presented a session entitled "Music, Autism, and ADHD: Successful Strategies and Resources for Music Educators." She began her session by defining autism and ADHD, as well as explaining stigmas surrounding autism and ADHD. She gave principles for teaching students with autism and ADHD, including creating rules of positivity, the Care Method (care, authenticity, respect, and empathy), positive reinforcement, mindful language, using person-first language. Finally, Harry summarized different teaching methods and strategies for students who are special learners.

The next session, entitled "Inclusive Parents: What Every Teacher Needs to Know," was moderated by Scott Price, who spoke with a panel of parents of music students with special needs. During this inspiring and informative session, the parents gave many helpful suggestions and strategies for working with students who are special needs.

Next, Michael Thaut gave a session entitled "The Brain that Engages in Music is Changed by Engaging in Music." In this session, he showed how the brain and neuroplasticity is positively affected by music study. Musical training results in a higher density of neurons and connectivity in neural pathways as well as higher motor coordination.

Azusa Higatoni gave a touching session entitled "Perspectives on Music and Human Wellness: Stories from Hospice," in which she shared stories from her work as a music therapist with patients in hospice and music had a positive effect on their well being.

The final session, "Key to Autism: Out of the Box Techniques for Out of the Box Students," was presented by Connie Wible, an independent studio teacher who shared numerous creative techniques for teaching students with special needs. The day concluded with a question and answer session featuring committee members.

YOUNG MUSICIANS: BIRTH TO AGE 9 PRECONFERENCE
Friday, July 16, 2021

Chair: Janet Tschida
Committee Members: Gregory Chase, Linda Fields, Janna Olson, Amy Rucker

Setting the Stage—Strategies for Developing Young Musicians
(Why - When - How - HELP!!)

The Young Musicians Committee's incredible lineup of presenters revitalized even the most experienced early childhood music specialists and teachers of young musicians. The sessions "All I Need to Know I Learned from Early Childhood Music" and "Music is Child's Play" demonstrated how understanding early childhood music transforms our teaching and performing. Valuable strategies for successfully transitioning students from early childhood music to study on an instrument were experienced during the interactive sessions "The Aural Underground" and "Movement for Musicianship." Similarly, seeing innovative aural-based activities for developing rhythm, tunefulness, and artistry during the "Activity Share" gave ideas for rejuvenating one's teaching. To encourage connection and collaboration, the committee included time for a "Snack and Chat, Discuss and Dine," and Q&A panel "From Floundering to Flourishing."

All I Need to Know (About Teaching and Performing) I Learned in Early Childhood Music
Presented by Linda M. Fields, NCTM
Friday, July 16, 2021
Recorded by Linda Fields

Fields began by referencing Robert Fulghum's essay, "All I Really Need to Know I Learned in Kindergarten." Twenty lessons from early childhood music that apply to all levels of teaching and performing were explored during this session. They will be numbered in this report.

Successfully playing a musical instrument requires six capabilities: be *emotionally* connected, love the *contrasts*, have control of our *body*, have control of our *instrument*, know the *language*, and *decode* the notation. Many traditional piano methods begin at the bottom of this list with decoding notation. However early childhood music specialists believe that:

1. Every child is musical, and so they start at the top with emotions, developing musicality on the way to reading music. The six capabilities divide into three areas, Story, Sound, and Symbol, which served as the outline for Fields' talk. A popular teaching song, "Clap, Clap, Clap," from *Music Keys*, the Musikgarten curricula for school classroom was used in illustrations throughout.

Beginning with Story (the artistic ideas we want to convey), Fields led attendees through lessons from early childhood music focusing first on *emotions*. At any age, it's important to:

2. Use emotional attachment to motivate learning. Additionally,

3. The learning environment is important. It should be comfortable and evoke good feelings, ideally including something beautiful from nature.

When choosing pieces, it's important to remember that:

4. Excellent repertoire touches the soul. And certainly,

5. Parents are our partners. In a good story, being emotionally connected is related to drama, highlighted by *contrasts*. In early childhood, contrast is often the basis for identifying patterns, and, Fields said, is a basis for art itself. Musicians…

6. Communicate form by highlighting contrast, exaggerating differences in dynamics, tonalities and more.

Next, the presenter pointed out a basic principle of learning:

7. We know what something is by what it's not.
Since paying attention is required for learning, good teachers know to:

8. Minimize talking; model instead, letting the student observe and discover for themselves. An excellent teacher also will:

9. Be an observer, especially of their students, noting what makes each student unique. Additionally, a good teacher knows their curriculum, like a piece of music. With an internalized lesson plan, sections can be presented with flexibility, according to the student's need. Observe and follow the child, so you can:

10. Teach the class, not the plan.
After telling a powerful story about creating a strong emotional transition for children and parents, by settling down rowdy toddlers with the use of a contrasting lullaby, Fields stressed that feelings, in the framework of contrast, are the foundation for musical artistry.

Sound (the aural expression of our ideas) requires control of our *body* and of our *instrument*. At every performance level, control of the body helps us express musical ideas effectively. With young children, especially…

11. Learning begins with the whole body. It's helpful at any stage to experience a musical idea with the body before expressing it on an instrument. And, as we engage the body, it's good to remember that:

12. Large motor comes first. Brain development starts from the center of the body, and even advanced players minimize tension by starting with large motor gestures, before extending to wrists, hands, and fingers.

A musician must also control the external instrument. Players must know what their instrument can and can't do. And the more a student knows about different instruments, the more imaginative their playing can be. Therefore,

13. Experience with a variety of sounds teaches about timbre.
Being knowledgeable and in control is also a good starting place for creativity, demonstrated by an excerpt of a clarinet improvisation on "Clap, Clap, Clap." But students require time to explore and gain knowledge before being creative. When they are ready, a student can use what is known to create something new. Fields made the point that creating the desired sound with an instrument requires both physical control and aural imagination.

Next, the presenter talked about the ear and its dual processing. Using an illustration of the brain, she explained the ear's auditory and vestibular functions, demonstrating that:

14. Hearing and movement are powerful partners. Moving to the beat while singing creates a strong connection between pitch and rhythm.

In addition, research shows that:

15. The ear plays a central role in learning. It is the first sensory organ to fully develop, four months *in utero*, and many believe it is the last to die.

Continuing to Symbol (the musical languages that represent our desired sounds), Fields showed that *languages* of pitch and rhythm are best secured through the dual function of the ear, after which students can *decode* notation. Many teachers agree that it's best to:

16. Teach pitch and tonal sense by singing.
Vocalizing proves knowledge, demonstrated in a video of a college class from Maranatha Baptist University singing "Hot Cross Buns," switching between major and relative minor. Echo activities…

17. Make use of the Learning Loop in which a student listens, thinks, vocalizes, hears their own voice, adjusts, and repeats to improve accuracy.
Just as we teach pitch by singing, we:

18. Teach rhythm by moving. Marching and galloping help students feel the difference between duple and triple meters. Many music teachers:

19. Apply language learning strategies to music learning.
Fields showed another video, demonstrating steps taking a student from echoing neutral syllables to use of tonal or rhythm language, to reading notation.

20. There are non-musical benefits.
Fields listed several, including confidence, memory, social dynamics, anticipation, and math concepts such as one-to-one correspondence, patterns, graphing, and fractions.

There were three follow up questions she addressed, all of which involved observation of the student:

- *How does one compensate for cramped space with toddler locomotor movements?*

The children will compensate on their own; follow their lead.

- *How can you tell that a student is ready to be creative instead of just exploring?*

After plenty of random play, they may become more intentional about using the instrument or concept.

- *Will the student become creative one concept at a time, or all at once?*

Typically, one at a time, but sometimes things will come together in clumps.

Music is Child's Play
Presented by Joy Morin
Friday, July 16, 2021
Recorded by Janna Olson

This presentation offered a unique learning opportunity for observing some of the earliest music experiences of a child. Morin presented her observational research with her daughter, Aria based on her exploration of Music Learning Theory and as an application of her early childhood professional development certification with the Gordon Institute for Music Learning.

Morin began by giving us a synopsis of her education background and interest in Music Learning Theory and her exploration of early childhood music education. Morin's Early Childhood

Certification with the Gordon Institute for Music Learning prepared a foundation for her practical exploration of Music Learning Theory with her daughter which she began even before Aria was born.

Next, Morin offered a summary of Music Learning Theory and outlined the principles of preparatory audiation showing the audience the types and stages that occur during a child's musical development. Morin briefly explored the history of observational research starting with Milicent Washburn Shinn and went on to include Maria Montessori, Jean Piaget, and John Holt.

Morin chose her musical material from the *Music Play* curriculum with the rationale that children learn from difference rather than sameness. This collection offers songs and chants in various tonalities and meters. She stressed the importance of maintaining the same key for songs and also shared her choice of technical equipment for recording, storing, and documenting her video footage.

The practical aspects of her music sessions with Aria included using the practice of whole-part-whole repertoire engagement, attempting to interact intentionally on a daily basis, and using the time with Aria to bond, focusing on a playful, joyful approach to musical interactions. Morin ended up recording 490 video clips! She chose ten video clips where Aria was the most responsive and engaged. She was quick to remind the audience that in the natural course of a day there are ups and downs and variations of mood and interest.

Each video offered an excellent example of Aria's various responses to songs and chants. Morin took time to highlight the importance of various responses and discuss the significance of Aria's movement and vocal responses. It was fascinating to hear Aria begin to vocalize the tonic and Morin explained Edwin Gordon's theory that children audiate first in a range of a 5th (from D to A above Middle C). Morin also performed stepwise *legato* patterns to encourage responses. It was also fascinating to see Aria's familiarity with songs or chants previously heard and her anticipation of what was coming next. In video clip #8 Joy showed the audience how she experimented with imitation patterns (skips from dominant to tonic).

In closing, Morin shared practical suggestions for creating a music environment at home. She shared her insights as a piano teacher into why early childhood musical experiences are so important with the potential to change the world! She stressed the importance of teaching music in a similar way to teaching language, observing student responses and approaching music education with joy.

Movement for Musicianship: PreK & Beyond
Presented by Dr. Wendy Valerio
Friday, July 16, 2021
Recorded by Hannah Creviston

Dr. Wendy Valerio is Professor of Music Education, Director of Student Teaching, and Director of the Children's Music Development Center at the University of South Carolina. Her session was a wonderful demonstration of how movement can bring meaning to one's instrument. Dr. Valerio's background in Orff-Schulwerk, Kodaly, Music Learning Theory, and Laban movement merge together in her study of how humans coordinate with themselves and others. In music, movement is used to do this.

Dr. Valerio believes that she "cannot teach anybody anything," she is "not supposed to teach anybody anything," and that her job is "to facilitate situations (by modeling breath and movement) that help humans enjoy their musicianship birthrights" or the idea that everyone is born with the potential to learn music.

The session began with some breathing exercises—feeling the difference between one's body and breath when slumped versus long—and some stretches based on Qigong. Participants remarked that they felt "open," "relaxed," and "free."

When working in a group setting, Dr. Valerio has three rules:
1. Be kind.
2. Be in your place.
3. Be doing your music jobs.

Music jobs are listening, watching, moving, singing/chanting or playing. These three rules guarantee a respectful and productive music learning environment. Music class time always begins with a Hello Song, such as **I Said "Hello"!** (Hello Song Example #1). While the students engage in their music job, the teacher models breath, singing, and continuous fluid movement, thereby encouraging students to join in. The teacher should also notice who is moving eagerly and who is hesitating to inform their later interactions.

Let's Sing Hello Together (Hello Song Example #2) is another wonderful greeting song which encourages continuous fluid movement. Continuous fluid movement is the movement that occurs in, through, and between beats. In this teaching example, "sing" can be replaced with words such as "swim," "swing," or "sway"—all actions which encourage continuous fluid movement.

For **Hello, Hello, Hello** (Hello Song Example #3)[1], Dr. Valerio focused on body part awareness, an important skill for young children. Each child can (silently) input the names of different body parts by modeling continuous fluid movement with that part while everyone else imitates. For a challenge, each student could use two body parts.

Dr. Valerio then moved on to activities featuring the four Laban efforts of Space, Weight, Time and Flow. Using Dr. Edwin Gordon's *Stretch & Bounce* and *Go and Stop*[2], we practiced getting stuck vs. getting loose, self space vs. shared space, stationary vs. locomotor pathways, curvy vs. straight pathways, and quick vs. slow movements. In all of these movement activities, teachers and students are encouraged to move differently each time and to add purposeful silences to encourage audiation. Valerio noted that if there is continuous sound, young musicians will tend to only listen and watch, but, in silence, students will begin to respond through movements and sound.

At the end of the session, participants remarked that they felt rejuvenated and excited to incorporate these movement activities into their teaching.

NOTES
[1] Wendy Valerio, *Hello, Hello, Hello*, 2007.
[2] W. H. Valerio, A. M. Reynolds, C. C. Taggart, B. B. Bolton, E. E. Gordon (1998). *Jump Right In! The early childhood music curriculum, Music Play*, (GIA), 1998.

RESOURCES and REFERENCES
Gordon Institute for Music Learning - https://giml.org/
Feierabend, J, & Kahan, J. (2003). *The Book of Movement Exploration*. GIA.
Reynolds, A. M., Valerio, W. H., Taggart, C. C., & Gordon, E. E. (2020). *Jump Right In! The early childhood music curriculum: Music Play 2, Part A*. GIA.
Reynolds, A. M., Valerio, W. H., Taggart, C. C., & Gordon, E. E. (2020). *Jump Right In! The early childhood music curriculum: Music Play 2, Part B*. GIA.
Valerio, W. H., Reynolds, A. M., Taggart, C. C., Bolton, B. B., Gordon, E. E. (1998). *Jump Right In! The early childhood music curriculum, Music Play*. GIA.

"See it In Action" Activity Share
Host: Gregory Chase
Session Presenters: Linda Fields, Janna Olson, Amy Rucker
Friday, July 16, 2021
Recorded by Gregory Chase

The goal for this session was to "show" aural-based activities that can be done with young musicians to develop their artistry and musicianship. The session included videos along with pre- and post-commentaries. Each video was introduced drawing attention to things to observe, and then after "Seeing it in action" the reasoning and importance of such activities were shared.

Video #1: *Wiggle Song*
Video Description: In this video we catch them singing the last part of the "Wiggle Song" by Beth Bolton in Dorian tonality. Between verses the teacher sings tonal patterns to both children. These patterns are different, depending on the musical age of the child.

Post-viewing Commentary: Two things occurred in this video, the first is acculturation to Dorian tonality. The second item is the beginnings of building a tonal vocabulary in Dorian. With the older toddler (age 3), the tonal patterns were based on an arpeggiated tonic triad in Dorian. With the younger child (around 15 months), the tonal patterns were diatonic (stepwise) based on the tonic function of Dorian. During acculturation stages, tonal patterns move in stepwise motion and are *legato*—the way young children first learn to make sound and vocalise—so with informal instruction, we meet the child where they are and then move on from there. In the imitation, assimilation, and formal instruction level of learning, we sing tonal patterns based on the essential chord functions of the tonality, and we sing the pitches of the tonal pattern slightly separated. This allows students to hear the individual pitches clearly, but yet they hear the tonal pattern as a whole. With the older child echoing the patterns back, although at an imitation level, this is a necessary preparation and readiness for audiation—he's starting to create those neural pathways in his brain.

Video #2: *Singing Resting Tone*
Video Description: Students singing the Resting Tone (tonic) through various activities and at various times were observed throughout the video.

Post-viewing Commentary: We always want to establish a sense of tonality through an aural affinity for a tonal center or final resting tone. In this case, we saw how the teacher had students retain that resting tone (tonic or tonal center) throughout the playing of the folk song. The instructor stopped playing and then the students sang the resting tone. She did not always stop when the next pitch was *do*, which then makes this more of a challenge. The teacher first had them sing the tonic–dominant melodic cadence establishing a sense of tonality. Since our resting tone is *do,* we know we are in major tonality.

Video #3: *Mouse Mousie* - Musikgarten MM2 neutral syllables moving to notation
Video Description: This was parent time in a Musikgarten class. The object of this activity was to demonstrate the children's ability to connect playing, hearing, and singing tonal labels and reading a familiar melodic pattern.

Post-viewing Commentary: Here we saw them learning through "playing" a game of Mouse Mousie. Both Piaget and Vygotsky emphasize the importance of play with learning. However, what happened afterwards was wonderful. The child was asked to play a tonal pattern on the barred instruments—he played a descending tonic triad. Without any cues, the students knew the tonal syllables (they started singing *before* their instructor sang). This demonstrates that, when developing tonal audiation and building a tonal vocabulary, students know and understand what they have heard. And then the crux of all this, is that the students were able to bring meaning *to* the symbols, rather than *from* the symbols. Attendees saw this notational audiation occurring when the student was then able to pick the symbols on the card to match the sound.

Video #4: *Lightly Row* - Musikgarten
Video Description: Another Musikgarten class parent time. This activity was about linking a tonal notation pattern with its sound, then associating the scrambled patterns with a familiar song, and lastly hearing and singing the Resting Tone (*do*).

Post-viewing Commentary: Here we saw the teacher and students sing tonal patterns with the tonal syllables. This is so important when learning music as the tonal syllables become the "words" for sound-pattern relationships that appear again and again in melodies. Tonal patterns become the building blocks for a sense of tonality and facility with pitch relationships. After students sang the "words" or tonal patterns, students had the comprehension of *what* they were singing when they sang "Lightly Row."

Video #5: *Listen for Bells* - Musikgarten Keyboard
Video Description: Jill Hannagan teaching a Musikgarten Keyboard class. This is a look at the Sing-Play Process and applying *solfège* to the Keyboard.

Post-viewing Commentary: Here attendees saw the application of tonal patterns and tonal syllables to the keyboard. After we sing, then we play. Participants also saw how students did it together as a class/group, and then were given the opportunity to do it individually, helping them to "own" that pattern.

Video #6: *Dr. Wendy Valerio with Dr. Sara Ernst, FCC PTL, The Beginner Course Tonal 1* - early experience with harmony
Video Description: Dr. Wendy Valerio and Dr. Sara Ernst work with early-elementary piano students, inviting them to hear, sing, play, and identify harmonic patterns. This segment, and two others today with Valerio and Ernst, are part of *The Beginner Course*, an online course offering from The Frances Clark Center.

Post-viewing Commentary: Here we saw the students making connections to the sound, and giving them meaning, based on the tonic and dominant harmony. This is an example of how meaning is brought *from* the sound. By hearing the tonal patterns with the use of tonal syllables they were able to identify if the patterns were tonic or dominant. They did this through singing first, then they applied it to the piano. Again, it is important to recognize the purpose for using tonal syllables—to verbally associate with sounds of melodic patterns of two to five tones and to develop a vocabulary of tonal-pattern sounds that may be recognized and retrieved through their functional syllable labels.

Video #7: *Dr. Wendy Valerio with Dr. Sara Ernst, FCC PTL, The Beginner Course Tonal 2* - early experience with improv
Video Description: A student tries her wings at improvisation, flowing from her budding knowledge of tonic and dominant harmonic patterns. The next step will be notating the patterns, not shown here.

Post-viewing Commentary: As soon as students can play a few patterns, they should be encouraged to make up their own patterns or tunes using the patterns. In this case, we saw the student create her own patterns based upon the pattern of her teacher. By doing so, she is now "owning" the patterns, they are becoming part of her own vocabulary. A future step is to sing and then play a chained-together series of familiar patterns with simple articulations and rhythms—what we call improvisation.

Video #8: *Music Makers Keyboard Class* - Improvisation
Video Description: Students respond to a CD for improvising with a specific key, meter, and to use tonic and dominant chords.

Post-viewing Commentary: Here we saw students adding a harmonic accompaniment to their improvisation. The development of a sense of tonality and a tonal pattern vocabulary is enhanced by the use of harmonic accompaniments. The tonal function of any given pitch in a melody is immediately more obvious if harmonic reinforcement is available.

Video #9: *Dr. Lorna Heyge, Musikgarten for Infants* - Introduction to microbeat & timbre; Introduction to Drums
Video Description: Musikgarten author, Dr. Lorna Heyge with an infant class. She gives these infants an experience of exploring drums, playing with timbre, leading into microbeat. Parent modeling and a clear stop mid-stream plants the seeds of impulse control.

Post-viewing Commentary: Two things to mention are the importance of "modeling" and microbeats. Social Learning Theory, devised by Albert Bandura emphasizes modeling, in which a behaviour is learned from the environment through the process of imitation or observational learning. We saw evidence of that here with the little boy in blue beating the drum to the microbeat.

Which brings us to the second point, the purpose of moving with continuous flow and pulsations is to be able to model those pulsations in coordination with microbeats in songs, rhythm chants, and rhythm patterns that are being performed. Very young children typically attend to microbeats before macrobeats when responding with rhythmic movements or chanting. As they grow, musically, they will respond to macrobeat and microbeat movement—this is something to watch for in their movement to signal when *they* are ready for macrobeat and microbeat movement activities.

The Aural Underground: Laying the Ear-Brain-Body Foundation for a Lifetime of Piano Success
Presented by Amy Rucker
Friday, July 16, 2021
Recorded by Linda M. Fields

Rucker started with a question for attendees: "If I had more time in the piano lesson, I'd include…" Answers included: rote teaching, sight reading, singing, movement, listening to orchestral works, etc. These things are all important, but often students need help with more basic things like note or rhythm accuracy. Using examples of teaching pieces in triple meter often distorted to duple meter, Rucker admitted that short-term solutions such as using words that reflect the proper rhythm can help, but what the student really needs is movement. However, many are not comfortable using their voice, much less leaving the bench. In addition, finding time for these kinds of activities is an ongoing challenge.

So, Rucker had participants take a step back to consider the student's "aural pathway," and what may be missing there. Displaying a matrix, Rucker showed two progressions that start from birth. In the Child Development list, Listening is the beginning. Motor Response follows, leading to Language, then Social and Emotional milestones, culminating in Cognitive skills. Next, she traced Musical Development, again starting with Listening—"the cornerstone of all learning." Movement in response to music comes next, followed by Vocalizing (language), then Ensemble (social music making) and Creativity (expressing feelings). Reading and Writing music are a natural final step.

Yet, she pointed out, we typically start lessons with Reading and Writing—having missed many, if not all, of the earlier steps. Using the example of struggling to open a tightly shrink-wrapped bottle, ignoring the perforations, Rucker made the point that we don't have to open the child's musical mind the hard way. Instead, we can seize upon "open windows" (sometimes called "critical periods") along the developing aural pathway.

Neural science shows that the window for developing an internalized and controlled steady beat is three to six years of age, when the frontal lobes are developing toward their future role as executor of the brain. Experience with steady beat enables neural connections, priming the frontal lobes' awakening, possibly avoiding symptoms of weak executor function (similar to ADHD) that may surface later.

Referencing Dr. Dee Joy Coulter, a neuro-science educator, Rucker shared that, in infancy, a steady beat is basically a subconscious reflex. Around age three to four, as the child is realizing they can control their own beat, they may play around, often with syncopation and other "messy" rhythmic expressions. Around the fourth year, many will regain control, evident in the ability to stop and start, to move at different speeds, to fit their steady beat with an external rhythm, etc. This can be an ideal time to introduce short rhythmic echoes, with the goal of helping them move from beat awareness to owning an independent steady beat. At any age, a steady beat is best heard and absorbed into the body, using the aural pathway from ear to brain to body to instrument. Rather than making pianists into musicians, she stressed, we want to help musicians become pianists.

Rucker agrees with many that age six to eight is a good time to start lessons, but *music* learning can occur earlier. The challenge for us today is to find ways to bridge the cultural gap in social musical experience that would normally build the aural pathway. Rucker listed some options for helping to fill that gap right now. She suggested experiences beyond the method such as:
- Sing, especially the resting tone.
- Chant rhythm patterns.
- Start early with movement and even drumming.
- Look at the music, focusing on what should be heard. Express an element with the body before playing it on the piano.

Sample activities followed. Attendees were invited to use a scarf to move with Beethoven's "Ode to Joy," keeping a half-note beat until the phrase ending, when the gesture became a loop.

Rucker then modeled, and had participants try, a variety of physical movements to help a student feel triple beat in the body, using a dance called "Cathrineta" from Musikgarten's *Music Makers Around the World*. She recommended clapping, drumming, or dancing, using both macro and micro beats, noting that it's important to keep moving through the large, slow beats, so students feel the space in their body. Additionally, when students change their movement with sections, it leads to awareness of form.

The presenter wrapped things up with some suggestions for additional steps to take as educators, to foster an "underground" aural pathway in our students. These included:
- Add an early childhood department to your studio.
- Take early childhood music training.
- Grow your own musicians and educate parents at the same time.
- Teach in groups.

Finally, Rucker made the point that it all starts with the ear. If we don't help them focus their listening, how many will be able to develop it on their own? From steady beat on, she admonished, give your students the gift of deeply ingrained musical awareness and they will thank you!

A Questions and Answer period concluded the session: :
- *Is it possible to compensate for lack of these experiences from 3-6 years?*
  Yes! The learning will take longer, but it's worth it.
- *What size is best for a group?*
  6-8 is ideal; 4-10 at the outside.
- *Please talk about the ear-body activities that encourage parent involvement.*
  A curriculum-provided CD with suggested home activities for parents is ideal.
  Include parents for the last 10-15 minutes of class.
- *How to encourage families to buy CD players?*
  Many publishers are moving to links to be downloaded to various devices.
  Rucker still likes a child-dedicated listening area with a CD player, scarves, sticks, etc.
- *Do you use any childhood education methods, such as Orff?*
  Rucker has found success with a curriculum that pulls the best from Orff, Dalcroze, Kodaly, Montessori, Tomatis, etc., in development-appropriate pacing.

RECOMMENDED REFERENCES:
Dr. Dee Coulter - *Mind and Music: Insights from Brain Science* (4 CDs, c/o Worldcat libraries)
Dr. Edwin Gordon - *Music Learning Theory for Newborns and Infants*
Eric Bluestein – *The Way Children Learn Music, an Introduction and Practical Guide to Music Learning Theory (*an easier-to-read, partner book to Gordon's)
Paul Maudale – *When Listening Comes Alive* (about children and their possible aural needs)

CREATIVE MUSIC MAKING PRECONFERENCE
Saturday, July 17, 2021

Chair: Jeremy Siskind
Committee Members: Yoshiko Arahata, Chris Goldston, Kristina Lee,
John Mortensen, Bradley Sowash

What's Pop Got to Do with It? Building Piano Skills with Today's Music
Presented by Todd Van Kekerix

Introduction
- Personal experience was shared about growing up with popular music.
- Folk music was in early lesson books. Its value was in being known. Are folk tunes known today?
- Todd van Kekerix described informal learning practices and made the case that pop music encourages experimentation.
- Listening, imitating, enculturating, experimenting, and group interaction are elements from "informal learning practices" from Lucy Green's *How Popular Musicians Learn*.
- This encourages an absence of formal teaching. These methods are something the students did on their own.
- Listening is also pointed out by Lucy Green. Different listening strategies: purposive, attentive, distracted. Popular musicians are focused on listening more than elements of formal training.

Where to Start
- Start by asking students what music they're interested in.
- Listen to intervals, rhythmic repetition, form, melodic repetition, etc.
- "Roar" (Katy Perry) arrangement; meter is altered to avoid syncopation, notation just used to "jog memory," teacher duet added.
- Arrangements take "creativity and breaking the rules by the teacher."
- It's important to "strike while the iron's hot" with pop pieces.
- It's also possible for students to just play the bass note while the teacher plays the more complex material, allowing students to listen purposefully. It can be done in the lesson and shouldn't necessarily be practiced at home.
- You can show students different lead sheets to demonstrate that there's more than just one way to play a piece. They can play block chords in their left hand or a fully composed piano arrangement.
- Holiday lead sheets, like "Feliz Navidad," are universally known pieces. Give students lead-sheet-reading practice to practice their chords and to practice finding the closest positions.
- Pop music supports technique and ear training. Ear training with pop is a much less "sterile setting" than traditional testing.

- Musicnotes.com is a great resource that gives top songs, new songs, and recommended songs. Van Kekerix recommends focusing on new songs to "strike while the iron's hot."
- You could record each track on the clavinova with the student to help the student's ensemble playing and encourage purposive listening.
- Basic accompaniment patterns—broken and blocked fifths, boogie woogie, rock and pop fifths, arpeggiations
- Van Kekerix demonstrated how to teach ear training through the song "Piano Man"

Teaching Strategies for Making Creative Music using K-pop Melody in Piano Lessons
Presented by Sumi Kwon

- Is music learning for creativity development? Or is creativity developing essential musical growth?
- Most teachers don't have experience with improvisation so it's difficult for them to develop teaching materials for improvisation.
- Improvisation is the art of thinking and playing music at the same time; improvisations are meaningful activities, not random, that express ideas on the spot.
- The educational benefits allow musicians to express themselves actively with interest and immersion, improve their creative keyboard playing skills, make music by aural learning.
- Planned training is important for improvisation—involve indicated musical elements and question and answer; rhythm, pitch, chord, scale, and form.
- Use simple rhythm patterns before melody patterns.
- Utilize teacher accompaniment and don't worry about dissonance.
- Start by making music with a single note, then move to two notes and three notes; BTS, Exo Dancing King, Zico and Mino examples given ("Not Today").
- Why K-Pop? It's familiar and fun, simple tunes in modes, repetitive rhythms, melodies are between speaking and singing.
- How to use K-Pop? Choose a simple, repetitive rap passage. Arrange the melody for teacher accompaniment, designate limited tones and rhythm patterns for students' counterparts, and transpose if necessary.

Bringing the Pop Back to Popular Music
Presented by Nicholas Lira and Bridget O'Leary

- Pulse, beat, and meter are similar but not the same and important.
- Groove needs to be maintained with "machine-like consistency" whether in straight eighth notes or swung.
- There are different idioms in pop piano music—heavy, separated chords in quarter notes; students should subdivide.
- Syncopation is often accented and rests are used in pattern #2. Rests need to be viewed as active part of style and be played with intentionality.
- Dotted-quarter-note pattern requires subdividing.
- Flowing sixteenth-note patterns can be a good place to introduce the sustaining pedal.

- Considerations for pop idiom—meter, subdivisions, swung vs. straight; when does piano drop out? Is piano part melodic/rhythmic/both? What's the texture? Is it doubling the melody? What is the articulation?

Sara Bareillies – Love Song
- Percussive sound, relying on articulation and register.
- Listen to the original performer to guide interpretation.
- Both right hand and left hand have specific articulation that need to be interpreted correctly for a convincing performance.
- Consider if a rock band were playing the piece, which instruments would be playing which parts?

Alicia Keys – If I Ain't Got You
- Listen for the two-measure hyper meter created by the harmonic rhythm.
- Even the performer performs the pieces differently depending on the performance; compare different recordings—studio vs. live can be a good activity for lessons.
- Melody is a typical pop melody, using the pentatonic scale, syncopation, and blue notes; articulation has a lot of details.
- How are dynamic swells heard or felt? How does the meter and rhythm change between the verse and chorus?

Elton John – Your Song
- Hyper meter is a metrical grouping longer than a measure.
- Right hand and left hand have different accent patterns.
- Notice the texture changes as the song moves from one section to another.
- Why is the piece in 2/2 rather than 4/4? How would the piece be different?

Adele – Hello
- Great piece for discussing harmony, since the piece comes from the Aeolian mode, which gives the piece a feeling of suspension and unsettled emotion.
- How to differentiate the bridge, verse, and chorus?
- Syncopation makes subdivision crucial.
- Adding octaves or making use of a wider section of the keyboard can help get a more expansive sound as pieces build to a chorus.
- Adele swings the subdivisions in the verses; listening and singing along can help to nail the subdivisions.
- Student questions—experiment with different voicings and inversions. How does this change the sound of the pieces? Which chord receives the most emphasis?
- Important questions: Are we playing on the beat, aligned, or ahead of the beat? Where are the strong beats? Is there a hyper meter? What is the piano part doing?

Songwriting Custom Shop: Interactive Songwriting Masterclass with Grammy-Nominated Music Educator
Presented by Shane Adams

Prosody – a constructional element is used to augment or magnify a lyrical element (constructional elements include melody, harmony, space, articulation, instrumentation, bassline, meter)
- Examples were given of "Somewhere Over the Rainbow" where the melody reflected the meaning of lyrics.
- Example was given with the lyric "I love you" in each of the different modes.
- Quote from Yip Harburg—"words make you think a thought. Songs make you feel a feeling. Songs make you feel a thought."
- Shane Adams gave an example of a song he wrote that has rhymes that get more and more precise as song continues.

Two-dimensional vs. three-dimensional songwriting—does the meaning of the chorus change or does it remain stagnant?

A verse is to move the story forward and a chorus is intended to sum up the verse using your title/hook.
- Shane Adams gave the example of a song about colors and suggested that each verse should be a different color instead of just talking generally about colors in each verse to create a song with progression.
- He gave an example by Melissa Etheridge to show progressions of the verse.
- Adams showed that each part of the song can be dependent on what happens in other parts of the song.
- He suggested introducing words like "but" and "therefore" to make connections between sections.
- Adams gave titles and an emotion map and instructed students to construct three parts of the song with an emotion, a "but" statement, and a "therefore" statement.

TEACHER EDUCATION IN HIGHER ED PRECONFERENCE
Monday, July 19, 2021

Chairs: Courtney Crappell and David Cartledge
Committee Members: Bradley Beckman, Michelle Conda, Diana Dumlavwalla, John Ellis, Barbara Fast, Ivan Hurd, Midori Koga, Franklin Larey, Andrea McAlister, Artina McCain, Pamela Pike, Carolyn True, Yu-Jane Yang, Lisa Zdechlik
Jennifer Snow, ex officio

The Teacher Education in Higher Education committee's preconference day was divided into two substantial sections. The first dealt with professional microaggressions, and the second with concerns with repertoire choices in the collegiate curriculum.

Professional Microaggressions

This section of the day was led by Michelle Conda, of the Cincinnati College-Conservatory of Music. Entitled "Why Do I Feel Like a Second-Class Citizen?", Conda explored subtle experiences of discrimination against practitioners of pedagogy experienced in the Higher Education workplace.

Conda began with a survey of the virtual "room," where she asked participants whether they had experienced professional situations where their ability to do their job had been doubted. She asked participants whether their feelings had ever been hurt in a professional context, whether it was intentional, and whether it resulted in self-blame, or blaming the other person. After encouraging this introspection, Conda gave specific examples of professional microaggressions, including statements to pedagogy practitioners such as: "The recital adjudicators should be from the applied faculty or theory faculty"; "No need to sit on auditions"; "You play well for a pedagogy person"; "We would love you to do a masterclass of the precollege students"; "Could you sit on committee X, Y, Z? We are just too busy to participate and know you would do a wonderful job since you don't have to spend all that time practicing."

Noting that it was important to understand that microaggressions are directed at groups, not individuals, and that no one is immune from the possibility of committing microaggressions, she encouraged exploration of participant reactions to things like bad drivers, tattooed people, a group of motorcyclists, people playing loud music in their cars, and people wearing skin-tight clothing. She noted that being judged solely based on group membership is "like a slap in the face" with powerful feelings of being hurt, unwanted, unwelcome, and devalued. Even if the microaggression is aimed at groups, it is still deeply destructive at a personal level.

Conda suggested constructive paths forward to move beyond microaggressions, to move towards productivity, self-esteem, and cooperation. She suggested that some paths forward to avoid a climate of microaggressions include: to learn about the cultures and identities of other groups of people; to surround yourself with diverse people; to quiet your own voice; and to pledge to be a champion against injustices. She suggested that if we experience professional microaggressions, we can ask colleagues to rephrase their questions, to be supportive of colleagues who observe microaggressions, and to step up when someone is ignored. She encouraged participants to suppress their fight-or-flight reactions to microaggression, and instead to maintain a professional tone and explain to the microaggressor your experience of their remark. You should document your experience so there is a record of the interaction. If your colleague responds positively and changes their behavior, be appreciative; but if it continues, present an account of the behavior and your documentation to the administration of your institution.

If you discover that you have inadvertently committed a microaggression, apologize, and thank the person for alerting you of your mistake. Ask them how it made them feel, and observe that the more you know, the less likely you are to do it again. Conda observed that no one is perfect, and we all have room to grow.

This portion of the day then moved to group discussion, where Conda presented a series of case studies of possible interactions and encouraged the groups to explore how they would deal with these particular incidents. Later in the day, participants were given the opportunity, in small-group discussion, to present situations where they encountered professional microaggressions, and to receive support and ideas from other participants.

Repertoire Concerns

Discussion on repertoire concerns began with a panel discussion featuring Jeriel Jorguenson and Natalia Vanegas Escobar, both of the University of Memphis, together with John Patrick Murphy, of the University of Oklahoma. The panel explored the use of folk songs in teaching repertory: traditional or folk songs typically characterized by stanza form and simplicity of melody. Such songs are typically transmitted orally and exist in multiple versions. Discussion was coordinated and moderated by Jorguenson.

Exploring the use of folk songs in group piano, Murphy described new trends in the public schools for teachers to educate themselves about the origins of music used in their curriculum. In his experience, folksongs are incorporated as skills-based devices. Vanegas Escobar described the experience of interacting with folk songs as an international student in the United States. She was surprised that she knew very few of these folk songs—they were new to her. She noted that she developed an understanding of these folk songs and their social role through her students.

Murphy noted that we have well-developed curricula that have been assembled by master pedagogues. He sees folk songs used to develop harmonization skills, and reading fluency, noting that there's a flexibility and potential for rearrangement that gives these songs utility in a wide spectrum of the curriculum, curating representation of cultures from around the world.

Murphy also identified that folksongs are often in the public domain and can be reproduced without royalties.

Jorguenson added that folksongs offer a benefit of familiarity, which can provide a pathway of access for students—using a familiar tune to teach more complex ideas. Vanegas Escobar agreed that the simplicity of the folksong offers a vector for students to concentrate on other parameters. She offered that folk songs can provide a path of access to music for the non-music major. Folk songs can be a path to musical content, even without higher reading skills.

There are, however, concerns associated with the use of folk songs. Vanegas Escobar offered that these folksongs may not be accessible to all. International students, for example, may not know the songs. Jorguenson affirmed, as an international student himself, that it can be isolating to be "the person" in the room who doesn't know the cultural touchstone being referenced via a folk song. The use of folk songs identified with particular cultural groups can also be problematic in particularizing or isolating given groups.

Murphy mentioned again the public domain nature of these works, identified as "American Folk Songs." He noted that public domain is pre-1920s, and that very often folk songs have questionable origins, and often offensive content. Particular care is needed with folk songs of the late-nineteenth and early-twentieth century. Additional curation is needed when choosing folk song repertoire to make sure that it explores a balanced variety of cultures, in order not to be exclusive.

Murphy presented the concept of "repertoire swaps" in the group piano curriculum—swapping out folk songs used in harmonizations with folk songs from under-represented regions. He suggested the possibility of a multi-week assignment where students could be given the opportunity to select their own folk song, and transcribe, harmonize, and perform at the keyboard. The Smithsonian "Folkways" was used as the resource site for this project. Murphy has used this approach, and found that students reacted positively—as did the graduate instructors.

Jorguenson asked Vanegas Escobar about the use and validity of contextualizing folk songs. Vanegas Escobar described this as a need for a "call for awareness," to expand students' curiosity. She noted the presence, often in children's textbooks, of callout text such as "Who is Beethoven?", and suggested that similar callouts could be used to highlight and contextualize folk music.

Jorguenson observed that, in the current climate some care is called for. Those who constructed these tunes did not imagine that they would be used for learning *Alberti* basses. We also need to understand what the context was for these tunes originally, and how they were used. He suggested that callout text might amplify student curiosity. Murphy highlighted the importance of presenting the origins and contexts of folk songs. Vanegas Escobar noted that the first challenge, as an international student, was actually to figure out the origins of the music she was using—to make sure that there was nothing problematic in those origins. She explained the importance of embracing the culture in which she is teaching, even if it comes to her as a new culture. She stressed the importance of inclusion and a sense of justice. She described being alarmed at learning the backgrounds of songs that superficially seemed pleasant, but have racially problematic origins.

The presentation closed by sharing resources to support appropriate use of folk songs. Those resources were:

1. Resources "Songs With a Questionable Past" by Lauren McDougle, docs.google.com/document/d/1q1jVGqOgKxfiUZ8N3oz0warXefGIJill2Xha-3X5nUY/mobilebasic?fbclid=IwAR3s8_zEtc97xSL7P0AdOPjxRhJg8D4BIz9Ky6HtmHJbEiAPnmwvEEFTZb4
2. "Crowdsourced Anti Racist Songs" by Martin Urbach, docs.google.com/spreadsheets/d/113kfyv68Pv_Afk9GefvPfdc9eXNhqRrdck7IfJEJGa4/edit#gid=1214992227
3. Decolonizing The Music Room, decolonizingthemusicroom.com/resources
4. Smithsonian Institute's Folkways Recordings, folkways.si.edu
5. Beth's Notes Plus, bethsnotesplus.com/countryregion

This panel discussion was followed by individual group discussion which encouraged exploration of broader problems in the mainstream "canonic" piano repertoire.

The preconference day closed by encouraging participants to identify changes that they could make in their professional lives which would address the concerns related to professional microaggressions, and to repertoire featured in the day's discussions.

WELLNESS PRECONFERENCE
Tuesday, July 20, 2021

Chair: Lesley McAllister

Committee Members: Linda Cockey, Vanessa Cornett, Jessica Johnson, James Litzelman, Artina McCain, Paola Savvidou, Brenda Wristen

About YOU: How Superheroes Care for Themselves during Turbulent Times

The 2021 Wellness Preconference Seminar of the National Conference on Keyboard Pedagogy was designed to give participants an opportunity to consider their own wellbeing as they have weathered the storm of the pandemic, supported their students, adapted to teaching virtually, and coped with their own financial and personal stressors. For many teachers, supporting their family and their students has been their highest priority, and their own physical and mental wellbeing has taken a backseat to the needs of those around them. The Wellness Committee members decided that "superhero teachers" needed a day dedicated to facilitating awareness of their own needs as they processed the events of the previous academic year and prepared for any unexpected challenges in the future.

For many teachers, the sacrifice of their own mental and physical health had been just one component of the many adaptations they had to make since early 2020. Through those adaptations, many had confronted their own perfectionism and anxiety. As the pandemic raged around the world, resulting in quarantines, mask mandates, and the loss of physical touch through social distancing, music teachers were faced with unexpected demands on their time, energy, and mental and physical wellbeing. They were forced to adapt to the new world of virtual teaching with all its technological and pedagogical challenges while still trying to connect with students whose lives had also been uprooted. And they succeeded in making some incredible adaptations—learning new technological skills, reaching students in unexpected ways, and staying on the frontlines as they worked with students who felt isolated and alone. Yet, many suffered despite their own best efforts to stay positive for students and family. They faced unexpected financial challenges or reduced their teaching hours to stay home with their own children in virtual school. Physical health, for many, was compromised by long hours of screen time, resulting in vocal stress and vision fatigue as well as back, neck, and shoulder pain caused by awkward positions and hunched posture. Anxiety over the unknown and concerns about the health of loved ones and students resulted in mental health concerns.

Aiming to provide tools and discussion around the wellness needs of teachers, our Wellness Preconference Seminar was packed with a combination of interactive workshops, panel presentations, and informative sessions. In the opening keynote session, "Luxuriant Piano Playing," William Westney shared how the physical enjoyment of playing the piano can serve as a way of promoting personal "wellness." Next, a panel presentation by Laura Amoriello, Vanessa Cornett, and Jessica Johnson explored self-care for teachers during turbulent times. Then Kay Hooper, author of *Piano Moves* and licensed Body Mapping Educator, led an interactive session on the easiest ways to correct and avoid limitations in technique and musicianship for students of all levels. Hooper's session was followed by another panel presentation by Lesley McAllister, Laura Amoriello, Paola Savvidou, Andrea McAlister, and Sara Ernst on "Parenting and the Pandemic: A Guide to Promote Wellbeing." Next, vocal health specialist Dr. Rachael Gates guided participants through exercises as well as diet and lifestyle choices to help optimize the speaking voices for teachers who have often overused their voices while teaching virtually. Later, Adam Mayon and Stephen Pierce illustrated how physical fitness fosters healthier, more optimal piano technique. The final session by Lesley McAllister explored the use of yoga movements and breath work in the piano studio with three different populations of students—preschoolers, adolescents, and senior musicians—as well as how professional musicians can use yoga to decrease anxiety and optimize performance. Sprinkled between each session, committee members led five-minute "Mindful Moment" sessions to allow participants to move around, breathe deeply, center, and experience the profound benefits of mind/body relaxation techniques. At the end of the day, participants were armed with a variety of strategies to enhance their own wellbeing and promote wellness in their music studios.

RESEARCH PRECONFERENCE
Wednesday, July 21, 2021

Chairs: Grace Choi and Joann Kirchner
Committee Members: Carla Davis Cash, Minju Cho, Cynthia Stephens-Himonides,
Margaret Young

Scientific Research: What Has That to Do with Piano Pedagogy?
Presented by Gilles Comeau
Wednesday, July 21, 2021
Recorded by Joann Marie Kirchner

Dr. Gilles Comeau, the founder and Director of the Piano Pedagogy Research Laboratory at the University of Ottawa, began his session by discussing how piano pedagogy has relied a great deal on past experiences and how research has the ability to question what we have been taught. Research brings elements to help further our musical learning. Dr. Comeau introduced attendees briefly to the Piano Pedagogy Research Laboratory, which brings researchers from various disciplines to closely examine piano learning and piano teaching.

He then proceeded to outline some of the major research works taking place at the Research Laboratory that he is involved with. The following are some of the areas outlined:

Motivation and the factors affecting motivation
- Age of starting piano lessons: The earlier a student begins, the more motivation will grow and the later one begins, the greater the risk of a downward curve
- Gender
- Methods used
- Private versus group lessons
- Exams and competitions
- Parental involvement: This was the most influential factor affecting motivation. Parental involvement resulted in strong intrinsic motivation.

Cross-Cultural Analysis
- Strong level of motivation among Chinese students

Music Reading
- Eye-tracking system—the presenter shared a chart of eye tracking. The children actually spent a lot of time looking at the pictures as opposed to looking at the notes.
- Illustrations in piano method books—notes versus pictures. When the student looks at the pictures, they are moving away from reading the notes. Pictures have a great deal of

impact. Dr. Comeau suggested the possibility of having music on one side of the page and the pictures on the other side of the page.

Music Dyslexia
- Few of us know what to do with students who have dyslexia or how to detect it.
- Dr. Comeau is currently doing research in this area.

Sight Reading
- Reading ahead and not looking back.
- Experts look mainly at the treble clef and can figure out the left hand.

Cognitive Enhancement
- There is not strong support that music will enhance cognitive skills. The studies that show there is an impact are methodically weak.
- While making music changes the brain, there is actually little transfer to other skills.

Pain/Injuries
- 47% to 80% of professional musicians report pain and/or injuries, while only 20% of music students report the same.

Warming Up
- We know very little about this area.
- Dr. Comeau and his researchers have done some work with thermal imaging and have discovered that the body works hard to prevent warming up. There is no such thing as "no tension."

Dr. Comeau concluded his session by stating that research promotes greater effectiveness in terms of musical learning and teaching.

Current Trends of Research in Piano Pedagogy Panel
Panel by Grace Choi, Pete Jutras, Cynthia Stephens-Himonides, and Margaret Young
Wednesday, July 21, 2021
Recorded by Grace Choi

Panel members introduced themselves with descriptions of current job and teaching situations. The panel also introduced an initial path to and involvement in research.

Panel members described how they got started in research. All described journeys starting in the graduate school years and beyond. Conversations occurred regarding the importance of the academic community to support and sustain oneself throughout a research career. Audience questions involved graduate degrees and dissertation-writing process, and panel members answered questions as they came up and as time allowed.

A changing approach to research over the years emerged as panel members transitioned from graduate students to working life. The paths and steps to introducing research to students continued and panel members each shared their advice and steps in how they have taught and are currently teaching research.

Panel members discussed how to help students shape and focus their research as it is easy to get lost in the sea of information. Helpful advice and website resources were distributed to the audience as live questions kept coming in. Interdisciplinary research and collaboration between disciplines were emphasized throughout the panel as all members have formal education and experiences in multiple disciplines related to music teaching and learning.

Panel members talked about surprises encountered in the research process and what they hope to see in the years to come regarding research. Advice and tips on how to disseminate information were shared with the audience. The panel ended by directing attention to the next session, a Student Spotlight.

Student Spotlight Featuring Research in Progress
Presented by Alysse Cagle, Viktoria Juganzon, and Jeyeon Kim
Wednesday, July 21, 2021
Recorded by Joann Marie Kirchner

Three students were featured and shared their current research projects with the audience.

Alyssa Cagle, a senior at the University of Georgia, is a double major in piano and biology with an emphasis in neuroscience. Her research focuses on pedagogical methods to optimize the benefits of piano instruction for students with cochlear implants. Alyssa shared that while she has not had the opportunity to work with a piano student with cochlear implants, her interest in this area arose as a result of her grandfather, who has cochlear implants. Students with cochlear implants suffer from a decreased capacity for pitch and timbre perception, but as a result of musical training develop an enhanced pitch capacity, as well as the ability to recognize and discern melodic contour, rhythm, and timbre. Alyssa suggested two approaches when working with a student with cochlear implants. The first thing is to ask for an audiogram, and secondly inquire as to whether or not the student has previously worked with a music therapist.

When working with students, Alyssa recommends the following best practices:
1. Avoid speaking while the student is playing;
2. Remain visible to the student at all times;
3. Avoid background noise; and
4. Choose exercises wisely.

In the actual lesson, Alyssa suggests the following:
1. Focus on Dalcroze-inspired listening and movement activities;
2. Begin with familiar tunes;

3. Singing can be helpful especially when paired with visual representation;
4. Hanon exercises may be beneficial due to their pattern orientation; and
5. Make use of music mapping and highlighting.

In a qualitative approach through individual, semi-structured interviews with secondary music teachers across England, Viktoria Juganzon hoped to identify the potential of a musical genre crossover learning approach. Viktoria sought to examine whether learning classical music via popular music and music technology instead of acoustic instruments would be engaging to children from different backgrounds. One result that surfaced from this study was that music teachers adhered to the notion of classical music as popular music to involve students in classical music. In addition, classically trained musicians saw greater value in the musical genre crossover learning approach contrasted with musicians with popular music training. Viktoria recommended that the music classroom should offer a mixture of music technology and acoustic instruments. Some of the benefits as reported by the participants include direct involvement with a music history topic without studying an instrument; development of arranging, composing, and producing skills; and developing deep learning. In the fall, Viktoria will begin a PhD program at Kingston University in the United Kingdom.

A recent graduate with a DMA in Piano Pedagogy from Texas Tech University, Jeyeon Kim presented a survey of which specific software programs and computer applications (apps) were being used in group piano class during the COVID-19 pandemic and whether or not there was an intensification of new and improved technology to assist in virtual education.

Her survey consisted of three parts:
1. Demographic information;
2. Questions regarding the use of technology; and
3. How technology was being used during the pandemic.

Jeyeon found the following results from her survey:
1. There was an increase in video communication programs for both students and teachers;
2. There was an increase in the use of *Classroom Maestro*, but a decrease in the use of other apps for teachers; and
3. Teachers were focused on Zoom.

Jeyeon concluded that such a reduction in the use of technology may be due to the teacher deciding to simplify their use of technology for dictation or composition assignments following the start of the COVID-19 pandemic. On a personal note, Jeyeon discovered that designing a survey was more complicated than she originally thought.

DIVERSITY PRECONFERENCE
Thursday, July 22, 2021

Chairs: Leah Claiborne and Desireé González-Miller
Committee Members: Minju Cho, Diana Dumlavwalla, Leonard Hayes, Veena K. Kulkarni-Rankin, Franklin Larey, Artina McCain, Astrid Morales, William Chapman Nyaho

NCKP: The Piano Conference continues to offer robust, dynamic, and innovative practices in keyboard pedagogy. This year, NCKP welcomed a new Diversity and Inclusion committee which fostered engagement with leading scholars in the field who champion equitable practices in teaching, scholarship and performance.

Since the conception of the new committee, chairs Dr. Leah Claiborne and Dr. Desireé González-Miller have spearheaded various town hall discussions, webinars, articles, a new course release, and a diversity summit which all examine how teachers, students, and performers can begin to take steps to create a more inclusive field in piano pedagogy. The 2021 preconference continued to highlight these efforts by providing various levels of engagement and scholarship centered around these practices.

The Diversity Committee created a dynamic preconference for its participants to explore, engage, and reflect upon. The diversity committee centered the preconference on two large areas in the pedagogy field: Diversifying Piano Repertoire and Building Anti-Racist Practices. The diversity track also highlighted other proposals centering around cultural appropriation, Latin American music, female composers, and contemporary piano music. Below is a description of the various presentations that created the diversity track for NCKP 2021.

Building Anti-Racist Practices
The year of 2020 brought forth many social, political, and personal challenges. Among those challenges was the spotlight on racism in our country. This spotlight has created an opportunity for professionals to examine how they can begin to ensure that their work not only shuts down racist practices that they may or may not be aware of, but also equips members in our field with the tools to ensure they create safe spaces for learning to occur.

The Diversity Committee held a 90-minute panel discussion (and breakout rooms) with leading scholars in our field who shared their work with developing anti-racist practices in piano pedagogy for the independent teacher and piano guilds. BIPOC panelists began the session by first sharing intimate stories of unfortunate times they have experienced racism in the piano field and then moved toward sharing how teachers can take action steps to prevent continued racist practices in piano pedagogy. This session was geared toward the private piano teacher as they have great influence on opening the landscapes of equity and fostering a positive change for the next generation of pianists.

Break Out Sessions
Olivia Adams: "Do I Belong Here?"
In this presentation Olivia Adams discussed methods of decolonization, anti-racism, and feminist theories as they relate to piano literature. The workshop highlighted how indigenous musicians must be the authority on their own music and how music teachers must be mindful when method books practice "cultural theft."

Holly Kessis: "How To Tackle Cultural Appropriation In Piano Music"
Classical music is the basis of our formal training. Everything is originating from western cultural framework. Kessis explained how she grew up studying the 3B's: Bach, Beethoven, Brahms. These composers also incorporated music by other cultures, but the lack of context always left her wanting more. Where is the information about where this music originated from? Kessis shares pictures from method books and discusses examples where cultural context should be provided. A very powerful and informative conversation regarding appreciation vs. appropriation was also examined in this presentation. Kessis gives practical and thought provoking questions that teachers should be mindful of when engaging in music from other cultures.

Piano Repertoire Around the World
The presentation highlighted various piano pieces that have largely been left out of the canon and worthy of bringing to the concert stages as well as being used for pedagogical purposes. Attendees listened to prerecorded performances of the engaging repertoire as well as information on where they can locate the music. Piano music from the Americas, Asia, and Eastern Europe were performed and discussed, showcasing the beautiful variety of available piano music for our students.

Creating Piano Recitals for a More Diverse Tomorrow
Penny Lazarus, Lynn Jones, Sue Ruby, and Sally Richie discussed how challenging it is to find diverse repertoire. They also discussed how the pursuit could be intimidating. The presenters shared resources for where you can find music from around the world and created a useful self reflection tool for teachers to begin the process of diversifying their studio.

University of Memphis: Innovative Intermediate Music from Latin America
The University of Memphis MTNA chapter highlighted three Latin American composers: Jesus Alberto Rey Marino, Violeta Hemsy de Gainz, and Eduardo Caceres. The presenters discussed the didactic and pedagogical compositional techniques of these composers

Lift Every Voice: Diverse Contemporary Piano Compositions

In this 25-minute lecture recital, Andrea Johnson highlighted diverse piano repertoire by composers: Connor Chee, Rachel Grimes, Meredith Monk, Brittany Green, Evan Williams, and Errollyn Wallen.

Town Hall Reflection and Social Hour

The committee ended the day with a thirty-minute town hall reflection, which allowed participants to ask questions and give comments on what they experienced. Many teachers shared they enjoyed the presentations and also shared ways that they have begun creating more diverse and inclusive practices in their own teaching.

COLLABORATIVE PRECONFERENCE
Friday, July 23, 2021

Chair: Alexandra Nguyen
Committee Members: Dana Brown, Jocelyn Dueck, Steven Harlos,
Andrea Merrill, Spencer Myer, Joy Schreier

The last several years have been tumultuous, with the COVID-19 pandemic and social justice crises significantly impacting our lives. The pandemic upended the performing arts field, decimating musicians' work and professional lives. Organizations historically considered pillars in the profession, such as the Metropolitan Opera, Broadway venues, and the Kennedy Center, shut down. Teaching entailed massive investments in technology, energy, and time, not to mention major shifts in pedagogical approaches. Collaborative playing came to an abrupt halt with physical distancing and safety protocols, wreaking havoc in virtually every aspect of music performance and education. To add to that, social justice movements have forced us to question biases inherent in ourselves and our field, exposing vulnerabilities that we may not have wanted to acknowledge. As we tentatively emerge from the pandemic, these issues remain at the forefront of our consciousness. We all long for the ease, comfort, and routine of our pre-COVID lives. Yet, as Sonya Renee Taylor so eloquently posits, is that a life that we should wish to return to?

> We will not go back to normal. Normal never was. Our pre-corona existence was not normal other than we normalized greed, inequity, exhaustion, depletion, extraction, disconnection, confusion, rage, hoarding, hate, and lack. We should not long to return, my friends. We are being given the opportunity to stitch a new garment. One that fits all of humanity and nature. - Sonya Renee Taylor

This is the spirit in which the collaborative preconference day for the National Conference on Keyboard Pedagogy 2021 was conceived. The collaborative committee felt strongly that the virtual gathering was an ideal occasion for active reflection and discussion of these issues. With these challenges came growth: the lessons learned and knowledge gained in this difficult process will transform how we do things when life returns to "normal." To this end, the preconference sessions highlighted topics that been thrust into the spotlight, through a collaborative lens: teaching and performing in times of physical distancing, professional development and evolution, recording, and exploration of repertoire by underrepresented composers.

The day opened with an honest conversation among the collaborative committee members about the pandemic's effects on how collaborative work was delivered—the good, the bad, and the questionable: low-latency platforms, adjustments to pedagogical approaches, and an examination of what practices might continue to be constructive post-pandemic. Themes that emerged from the discussion included:

1. Long-term implications for how we teach collaboration. Clearly Zoom was not ideal (or feasible, in most circumstances) for collaborative teaching. However, it allowed for a more in-depth approach to score study and concepts that may have been glossed over in usual in-person teaching circumstances. Finding ways to balance these would certainly be beneficial. Teaching using low-latency platforms, while more promising than Zoom, was dependent on all participants' access to, and comfort with, technology and raised challenges as discussed under point #2 and equity issues, as presented under point #4.

2. Long-term implications for how we perform collaboratively. Though initial low latency platforms proved to be laborious and required complex technology in order to work effectively, development has continued in earnest, with several new and much improved options that can and should be implemented in the future, removing the limitation of geographic proximity, and allowing for distanced ensemble performances across countries and continents.

3. Identity crises. As any other performing musician, collaborative pianists' identities are closely intertwined with our work. The cessation of performances caused many to question their purpose and intention—so many of us are so wrapped up in our work yet forget to ask ourselves whether the path we are on aligns with our goals. While the financial implications of lost performance income were significant, it became clear that gains were made in terms of realigning priorities and interests.

4. Equity and access. The quality of a student's learning experiences during the pandemic was directly related to their access to technology, instruments, and space. As was observed in many other sectors, the pandemic highlighted the systemic failings that disproportionately work against those with lesser financial means. This must be addressed if we truly believe in diversity, equity, and inclusion.

Our second session, "Independent Entrepreneurship" featured panelists Christopher Foley, Andrea Merrill, and Valerie Dueck, who each presented strategies for re-defining one's professional goals and activities. Related to point #3 above, forging one's own path in the musical profession has always been a rite of passage for emerging pianists given the broad scope of possibilities. As a new work landscape emerges post-pandemic, reinventing oneself professionally is critical to ensuring success in an unknown market. The discussion was followed by a town hall forum intended to address individual case studies solicited from participants, but ended up being a space where people shared their transformative experiences. One of the rather onerous tasks for pianists that transpired thanks to the pandemic is the production of recorded tracks for singers and instrumentalists. Digital applications have also been used to supplement these, causing concern that pianists might be replaceable by electronic media—a sobering thought.

In our third presentation of the day, "Artistic Digital Self-Representation," presenters Joy Schreier and Spencer Myer provided strategies for best practices in this realm, and ways to retain a sense of artistry and the truly interactive nature of personal collaboration despite the rather artificial nature of producing recorded tracks.

The day ended with a session presented by Dana Brown dedicated to the music of voices not normally represented in our everyday teaching. The music of the Western canon that we encounter is predominantly by white men, yet the demographic of composers is far more diverse. An overview of vocal and instrumental repertoire by underrepresented composers was shared, as were resources to research these works. There is a wealth of undiscovered repertoire to which we must bring voice, and this will enrich our programming in immeasurable ways. The day's discussions were thought-provoking, energizing, and provided a clearer path to move forth from the pandemic, with renewed and clearer purpose and intention in our teaching and performing.

LATIN AMERICA AND THE IBERIAN PENINSULA PRECONFERENCE
Saturday, July 24, 2021

Chair: Luis Sanchez
Committee Members: João Paolo Casarotti, Alejandro Cremaschi, Sebastian Colombo, Elena Dabul, Claudia Deltregia, Desireé Gonzalez-Miller, Fanarelia Guerrero, Ana Orduz, Luis Pipa, Ricardo Pozenatto, Carla Reis, Ricardo de la Torre, Alberto Urroz, Miriam Vasquez, Paulina Zamora

The Latin American and Iberian Peninsula committee made its debut in NCKP 2021 with a curated preconference program that featured eighteen sessions in Spanish and Portuguese that focused on wellness, piano pedagogy, and repertoire. Attendance was not limited to speakers of these languages, as all presentations included English subtitles.

After the round table discussion sessions in Portuguese and Spanish, that focused on teaching in the times of COVID, the morning continued with two tracks, one in each language. The sessions in the Portuguese track featured three presentations that focused on piano pedagogy. Bibiana Bragagnolo's presentation, "Decolonized Piano: Emancipating Teaching Practices" explored the outcomes of her research which proposed a piano teaching methodology from an independent perspective. Practical strategies to increase interactive activities in private and group online lessons were explored in Daiane Raatz and Mirka da Pieva's session "Distant but Connected: Practical Steps to Stay Engaged and Humanize Online Classes." A close look at the pedagogical works of Brazilian composer Clarisse Leite was the topic of Iracele Vera Livero de Souza's presentation. The morning Spanish track featured two presentations that offered different perspectives on wellness. Mónica Zubzuk's presentation "Corporal, Auditory, and Emotional Aspects in Musical Interpretation," described how the knowledge of the body's capabilities influences the ability to achieve the demands of the score and its sonority. "Mindfulness: A Significant Practice to Pianists," by Yasmin Fainstein discussed the importance of mindfulness and surveyed ways in which it may help to meaningfully prepare the mind for everyday practice and performances.

The afternoon Portuguese track included two sessions on wellness. "Anxiety in Musical Performance: Reflections of Music Students from Experiences with Alexander Technique" and "Mindfulness Meditation" by Fernanda Zanon took a close look at coping strategies for anxiety. Carina Joly, in her session "Preventive Pedagogy: a Project That Starts with Teachers," aimed at providing the tools so that current and future teachers can find more confidence to reduce physical problems related to musical performance. In "Every Student is an Artist! Developing Artistry in the Earlier Years of Study," Vicente Della Tonia and Claudia Fernanda Deltregia discussed various learning stages of a musical work, with the focus on developing students' artistry. In the Spanish track, Luis Sánchez presentation, "Mozart and Performance Practice: What the Fortepiano can Teach Us," used a replica of Mozart's 1782 Walter fortepiano and provided examples from elementary through upper intermediate works by Mozart addressing stylistic elements of his music and suggesting teaching strategies. Jacqueline Gutierrez's "Exploring Audiation in Professional Piano Students: an Approach to Gordon's Pedagogies" focused on the findings of research carried out with college piano students and their development of ear training skills.

Lesser-known repertoire by composers on both sides of the Atlantic were also part of this preconference day. Jacqueline Petitto's "Sisterhood: The Piano Works of Nadia and Lili Boulanger," highlighted the important contributions that both composers made to the piano repertoire. Elena Dabul explored the works of Argentine composer Roberto García Morillo, providing insight into his compositional styles. She addressed the artistic value of these works and their place both in teaching and performance. Lúcia Barrenechea introduced attendees to the music of four contemporary Brazilian composers: Caio Senna, Dawid Korenchendler, Lea Freire, and Marcos Lucas.

Before the closing social gathering, four more sessions in Spanish brought the preconference day to an end. The works of Nicaraguan composer Luis Abraham Delgadillo and their pedagogical value were explored by Fanarelia Guerrero López. In "The Toolbox: Encouraging Independent Learning in Beginner and Intermediate Piano Students," Lorena González Brougher explored different learning strategies that students can apply independently. Additionally, Jorge Briceño González discussed the importance of listening to recordings in the preparation of a new piece, and how to develop listening skills in students. Finally, those that always wanted to perform Latin music without having a score or a piano arrangement enjoyed Julio Barreto's presentation. This session focused on how to acquire the tools to create an arrangement from a chart with melody and chords and use different Latin rhythms.

The closing social gathering brought the day to a conclusion giving attendees the opportunity to network, exchange teaching tips, and develop new friendships.

CAREER DEVELOPMENT AND INNOVATION PRECONFERENCE
Monday, July 26, 2021

Chairs: Kellie Cunningham and Jani Parsons
Committee Members: Myron Brown, Sarah Buckley, Fabiana Claure, Leonard Hayes, Annie Jeng, Jonathan Kuuskoski, Astrid Morales, Clinton Pratt, Allison Shinnick, Trevor Thornton, Andy Villemez, Meggie Young

Part 1: New and Emerging Professionals

The first session of the day began with Jennifer Snow giving a brief introduction. Jani Parsons gave an overview of the day and invited people to engage in the chat. Each of the members of the sub-committee (New Emerging Professionals) took a moment to introduce themselves. Clinton Pratt summarized the polls where participants answered a series of questions that helped us gauge our audience. "What best describes the stage of your career?" Half of those responding answered mid-career (six to thirty years of teaching). Responses to the question "Which career is most desirable to you?" were varied.

Allison Shinnick, Trevor Thornton, and Astrid Morales presented a short session on transitioning from college to career and shared their own stories. Shinnick shared stories about transitioning from professional teacher to doctoral student and how she adapted to these changes. She spoke about balance, juggling her life, and the challenges of each degree and how she approached them. Morales, an international student, spoke about income as a student in the United States. Thornton spoke about balancing many different jobs after he graduated and finding joy.

Jani Parsons, Clinton Pratt, and Sarah Buckley gave a short presentation on building a career in the post-graduate years and discussed the advice they would give their former selves. Parsons shared tips about scheduling, balancing performance, teaching, and projects, and the patience necessary to develop a career of your dreams. Pratt spoke about the freedom and flexibility to do and try lots of things in the early stage of careers. Buckley discussed her roles as a faculty member and independent teacher and how she redefined success for herself.

Buckley gave a presentation on establishing a studio in a new location and finding community. She gave tips on how to gain attention in one's community, build trust, amplify word of mouth, provide clear communication, and establish easy-to-use processes for clients. In addition, Buckley hired a business coach and marketing professional to help her to fill her studio.

Parsons spoke about diversifying income strands as a pianist, finding joy in the combination of skills, and finding balance. She spoke about finding a place where your own passions overlap with the needs of a community. She then directed the participants to the break-out rooms where everyone spent approximately ten minutes to talk more intimately about the topics addressed.

After the break-out session, Pratt gave a short presentation on "Launching a Successful Studio Business." He shared his own story of combining all of his various teaching locations into one studio space before transitioning to a larger studio space where he hired an additional teacher. Pratt also described the differences between a gradual and all-at-once studio launch. After listing the benefits of launching gradually (less risky, learned experience from working at other places, build a reputation), Pratt outlined the pros and cons of working from a home studio, a travel studio, teacher at another studio, or online. He gave some tips on marketing and branding, with specific tips on building your website with regards to values, mission, purpose, and branding. Pratt concluded his presentation with information on building a website and the benefits of free trial lessons.

Thornton shared a short presentation about the "growth mindset" and how to organize oneself as a multitasking musician. He emphasized the need for detailed lesson planning, event planning, and communication. Shinnick and Morales then spoke about establishing policies and contracts with our clients, with specific items that should be included in a teaching contract and policy. Parsons finished the panel by sharing examples of performance contracts.

The group assembled as a six-member group to answer any final questions and wrap up the session, sharing contact information.

Part II: Career Development Segment

Hours three and four of the preconference for the Committee for Career Development and Innovation were divided into three parts and were opened by our host Kellie Cunningham. She explained the intent of the upcoming three sessions, with a focus on sharing our stories. Within the Zoom platform, committee members first shared their individual sessions, and then groups entered breakout sessions led by the various committee members to discuss and delve into deeper questions regarding career building, mentorship, and the development of soft skills. The hours culminated in Leonard Hayes sharing his story, bringing together these various sessions as exemplified in his own career journey.

Committee members first introduced themselves, starting with Kellie Cunningham (who also introduced Meggie Young, who led her session via pre-recorded video). Then, Leonard Hayes, Andy Villemez, and Sarah Buckley each introduced themselves before moving into the session.

Part 1: Behind the Scenes: Stories from Different Career Paths began with Sarah Buckley, Andy Villemez, and Kellie Cunningham each describing their career journeys. Each gave inspirational tidbits from their own personal experiences as a means of encouraging upcoming professionals as they build their careers. This was followed by a ten-minute breakout session in which participants introduced themselves to one another within their various Zoom breakout rooms, sharing their name, location, current teaching position, and a fun fact.

Part 2: Setting Yourself up for Success: Talks of Intentional and Accidental Mentoring in Music, a twenty-minute session, was a pre-recorded Zoom interview by Meggie Young with Dr. Martha Hilley and Dr. Cynthia Stephens-Himonides. Young was a student of both Drs. Hilley and Stephens-Himonides while Stephens-Himonides also studied with Hilley—so this interview represented a "mentorship triad," as they called it. Young asked each of these mentors about their perspectives on the process by which they built mentorship relationships within their lives (and the lives of their students) as a means of both personal and professional development. Stories about how they were influenced by one another were shared. This session was also followed by a discussion in the Zoom breakout room setting, with questions such as:

> 1. "Mentoring is a brain to pick, an ear to listen, and a push in the right direction." - John Crosby. What kinds of support do you feel you need to be successful? (Encouraging words, constructive feedback, regular meetings, sporadic check-ins, etc.).
> 2. "I've learned that people will forget what you said, people will forget what you did, but people will never forget how you made them feel." - Maya Angelou. When you think back on the teachers or mentors you had, what made those relationships particularly effective or ineffective?

Part 3: Preparing New Skills for New Stages of Your Career. Andy Villemez challenged participants to think outside the box when it comes to developing the skills needed for a career. Moving beyond the typical performance and pedagogical preparation, he encouraged thinking regarding the "soft skills" of creativity, leadership, ability to work with a team, conflict resolution, ability to persuade, organization, strategic thinking, conflict resolution, communication, emotional intelligence, punctuality, ability to "read a room," flexibility, patience, attention to detail, time management, risk tolerance, social skills, and cultural awareness and sensitivity. He framed our understanding of communication in terms of storytelling, making an accessible connection for participants in how to build this soft skill.

Villemez encouraged viewers to see leadership in terms of "leveling up," with Level 1 starting with leading yourself, Level 2 including realizing and refining your influence, and Level 3 broadening to exercising and increasing influence. He reminded us that our hard skills within our field are useless without these soft skills. When turning to the breakout rooms, he encouraged participants to discuss questions on the topics of leadership and communication. Some questions for the breakout session included:

- Describe how you have influence in the current stage of your career.
- What people or groups of people do you know you have personal power over?
- Describe one change or step you can take in the next few months to LEAD UP!

- What specific situation(s) in your life would most benefit from improved storytelling skills?
- Describe one situation or event coming up where you can practice these strategies.
- Take an event from your life, run it through the story questions, and share with us a "rough draft" of a story you could use in your personal/professional life.

In the final segment, Leonard Hayes shared his musical journey.

TECHNOLOGY PRECONFERENCE
Tuesday, July 27, 2021

Chairs: George F. Litterst, Stella Branzburg Sick
Committee Members: Mario Ajero, João Paulo Casarotti, Linda Christensen, Alejandro Cremaschi, Shana Lynne Kirk, Christopher Madden, Michelle Sisler, Jennifer Stadler, Kathleen Ann Theisen

Inspired Teaching with Technology in the Post-Pandemic World
Welcome to the 2021 NCKP Preconference Track

Jennifer Snow welcomed conference attendees to the Technology Preconference track and invited everybody to join the conference starting the next day.

Stella Sick and George Litterst introduced the Technology Committee members and provided an overview of the day's activities.

George Litterst concluded this segment by providing a perspective on the work that the Technology Committee has undertaken since the inception of NCKP in 2001. He pointed out that the committee has frequently produced leading-edge, creative sessions that were both timely and well ahead of their time including:

- multimedia performance (2005)
- the power of virtual reality when studying a piano concerto (2007)
- NCKP's first long-distance presentation (2007)
- workshops on building studio websites (2007)
- long-distance teaching (2007)
- NCKP's first long-distance concert performance (2009)

Building Community/Overcoming Distance: 2021 NCKP Virtual Piano Ensemble
Presented by Laura Silva

This session reflected on the process of making a Virtual Piano Ensemble for the 2021 NCKP Conference with performance contributions from presenters and attendees.

The presentation described eight steps for creating a virtual ensemble:
1. set up goals,
2. evaluate resources,

3. get the music ready,
4. engage participants,
5. prepare the music and necessary technologies,
6. record,
7. edit, and
8. share.

During the presentation attendees and the participants of the ensemble had the opportunity to talk about the music. The ensemble performed *Mi Teresita (Little Waltz)* written by Teresa Carreño, a Venezuelan virtuoso pianist and composer of the late-nineteenth century, in a piano-ensemble arrangement written by the presenter for this project. The ensemble consisted of fourteen pianists who sent their recordings from fourteen different locations of the United States and Venezuela.

A "pre-premiere" of the resulting collaborative video was shared and the session finished with a brief reflection on the practical application of creating such projects in piano studios. The presentation concluded with an invitation to join the Geeks in Concert and the official premier of the video at a Lightning Talk during the conference.

Distantly Social:
Creating Meaningful Virtual Recital Experiences for Students, Families, and Communities
Presented by Mario Ajero

In 2020, most piano teachers had to adapt to restrictions not just in teaching, but also providing meaningful music-making experiences for their students due to COVID-19. Teachers became creative with technology and using the internet to create virtual recitals to keep students, teachers, and their families connected with musical experiences during a time when it was needed the most.

It is important for teachers to have the technological proficiency to provide alternatives to traditional face-to-face recitals. This presentation highlighted virtual recital solutions for both teachers with limited technological experience and also for teachers who want to make their online recitals more engaging and interactive for online audiences.

Among the technologies demonstrated in the presentation was how to set up a playlist of individual student performances on YouTube and how that can be shared with audiences in an asynchronous manner. The presenter also showed how to set up a "premiere" of a pre-recorded video through YouTube (but can also be achieved through Facebook) that allows teachers to release a pre-recorded recital video but make an event that allows students and their families to experience it together at a scheduled time and interact with one another in a live chat.

Finally, the presenter showed how to broadcast recital performances live using limited resources including a computer, external video camera, and a microphone. The free open-source software application, OBS (Open Broadcaster Software), enables teachers to broadcast a performance live to multiple platforms including YouTube, Facebook, and Zoom in order to create a live musical event that anyone with a high-speed internet connection can access.

Creative Solutions for Using Orchestrated Accompaniments
Presented by Lori Frazer

With the introduction of MIDI in the 1980s, the door was opened to develop orchestrations for piano study and music education. Almost forty years later, technology has greatly improved and so have the options.

MIDI files are available for almost every piano method on the market, as well as many supplemental books. Once USB drives were used in place of floppy disks, many publishers were not sure how to distribute MIDI files. Some hired companies to provide downloads, and some publishers included the files embedded with their audio CDs. The presenter recommended Keys to Imagination (www.keystoimagination.com) as a location from which a large number of these files can be purchased as a download.

Frazer also recommended the iPad app, *SuperScore*, by TimeWarp Technologies.

Now, with the use of tablets and cell phones, using audio files are more popular than ever. In the past, using audio files had been challenging due to tempo issues. Hal Leonard has many books that include a code to enter on their website to download free audio accompaniments. These accompaniments can be used with their free app, *My Music Library*.

Using Yamaha's free app *Chord Tracker*, tempos can be adjusted, songs can be transposed, as well as markers can be used for practice. Some Yamaha instruments interface with this app allowing you to record your performance along with your favorite song to create your own audio recording. All of your favorite teaching audio accompaniments can be used with this app. To do it, import your CDs into iTunes on your computer and copy them to your device. The *Chord Tracker* app will automatically load your audio songs into the app, and you're ready to teach.

Remote Instruction and Young Beginners: A Little Bit of Technology, A Lot of Creativity!
Presented by Nicha Stapanukul, Timothy Stephenson

This presentation was designed to reframe online teaching in a positive light and highlight simple, effective strategies that make starting young beginners over a screen less stressful. Nicha Stapanukul and Timothy Stephenson explored multiple practices for online instruction to help build modern piano teachers' toolboxes as they continue to navigate their remote piano studio through real-time demonstration.

The presentation was split into two sections: the first outlined pros and cons, common expectations, best practices, and key characteristics of the successful online teacher, while the second featured demonstrations of specific usage of programs, applications, and hardware that has been found to be most effective. The demonstration showed and emphasized specific strategies for effectively adapting in-person teaching habits for remote instruction.

Throughout this presentation, piano teachers learned how to effectively use their existing devices to enhance their teaching in order to confidently start young beginners through a screen. They demonstrated specific methods for content delivery of basic pianistic concepts, utilizing easily accessible and user-friendly technology in real time.

Bringing Your Online Teaching to the Next Level: Using OBS Studio and Creative/Fun Activities
Presented by Daiane Raatz and João Paulo Casarotti

Dr. Casarotti focused his portion of the presentation on the visual communication aspect of piano lessons and the use of multiple cameras with Virtual Cameras (OBS Studio). He showed the best scenes used in his online studio and explained why and how he uses each one for his instructions. Dr. Casarotti also showed examples of tutorials made with the OBS Studio and demonstrated how this can be beneficial for online instruction. In particular, he demonstrated:

Scene 1: Welcome (face cam + logo): usually used at the beginning of the lesson or during a close-up conversation or explanation/demonstration of the fingers, hand, wrist, or forearm.

Scene 2: Score + top + face: great for score annotations and side views; in-and-out and forearm rotation movement demonstrations.

Scene 3: Right side + top: recommended for showing right hand close up and movements such as up and down, circular, and forearm rotation and in-and-out movement demonstrations.

Scene 4: Left side + top: recommended for showing left hand close up and movements such as up and down, circular, forearm rotation, and in-and-out movements.

Scene 5: Top + pedal: important angle to demonstrate the alignment of the elbows, arms, and sideways; in-and-out and forearm rotation movements.

Scene 6: Studio + top: great scene to demonstrate whole-body movements.

Scene 7: Multiple cam: recommended for more-advanced students; allows them to have a bigger screen or watch the replay, concentrating on different angles.

Scene 8: *Classroom Maestro* + top: recommended for engaging with the visualization of the keys being played as well as analysis (intervals, scales, or chords).

Scene 9: Score + top + *Classroom Maestro*'s keyboard: offers a great visual combination.

Scene 10: iPhone: visualization of music apps or even display social media links (YouTube, Facebook, Instagram)

Daiane Raatz noted that the unprecedented COVID-19 pandemic has caused piano teachers around the world to face a new reality and forced them to rapidly switch their usually in-person lessons to an online environment. A major challenge was keeping lessons fun and engaging especially for kids.

Many teachers use a variety of creative activities such as board games, sight-reading and rhythm cards, as well as music apps in their private and group lessons. The online challenge was to adjust the fun in-person creative activities to a new virtual learning environment. Zoom tools made it possible to adapt a variety of fun activities to online lessons in order to teach and reinforce subjects on music theory, ear training, sight reading, among others, in a creative and unexpectedly interactive way.

The presenters demonstrated Zoom tools to engage students during online piano lessons, such as screensharing, the whiteboard, and annotation tools. These tools enable creative music theory activities in addition to music games and music theory including:

- Virtual background with music theory activities and games
- Mirroring the iPhone/iPad screen to show music apps for note reading and interval recognition that use the microphone to listen as the student plays from his/her home
- Remote control tool to enable students to control their teacher's mouse and keyboard remotely while playing music games in a more interactive way

During the session, the following apps and games were demonstrated:

- *Teach Piano Today:* teachpianotoday.com/2019/11/18/holiday-themed-note-reading-printables-for-your-level-1-piano-students/
- *Note Quest:* apps.apple.com/us/app/note-quest-piano-flash-cards/id1176943393

- *Teachers Pay Teachers:* teacherspayteachers.com/Product/Elementary-Music-Distance-Learning-Interactive-Rhythm-Games-Splat-5584932st=718a639486091398a6c95941d5de7854
- *Boom Cards:* melodypayne.com/product/boom-cards-major-minor-root-position-chords-2/

Dining with the Best
George Litterst, Stella Sick, Mario Ajero, João Paulo Casarotti, Linda Christiansen, Alejandro Cremaschi, Christopher Madden, Michelle Sisler, Jennifer Stadler, Kathleen Theisen

During lunchtime the attendees had a choice of five different rooms hosted by the members of the Technology Committee. The topics areas were:
- *Video and Audio Hardware* with João Paulo Casarotti and Alejandro Cremaschi
- *Multimedia and Long-Distance Recital Ideas* with Mario Ajero and Jennifer Stadler
- *Long-Distance Teaching Success Stories* with Kathleen Theisen and Christopher Madden
- *Interactive Software* with Michelle Sisler and MIDI Keyboards
- *Computers and Tablets* with George Litterst and Stella Sick

Creating a "Snowball" Collaborative Recorded Ensemble
Presented by Lori Frazer

A "snowball" recording is an ensemble recording that is assembled by adding students one at a time. Some of the first decisions to be made for a "snowball" performance is the piece to be used include:
- Will it be something the students create?
- Will it be a commercially prepared ensemble?
- Where will you find these ensembles?

A few great resources include:
- *Susan Ogilvy Ensembles* (Ogilvymusic.com & SoSpace.com)
- *Way Cool Keyboarding/Piano Band* (Musicalmomentsrmm.com)
- Dennis Alexander *5 Star Ensembles* (Alfred Publishing)
- *Hal Leonard Student Piano Library* (Hal Leonard Publishing)
- *Alfred Piano Method* (Alfred Publishing)
- *Mayron Cole Piano Method* (Freepianomethod.com)

Once you have decided on repertoire and the students are rehearsed, it's time to film. For recording purposes, all students will film playing along to a pre-recorded track. These pre-recorded tracks can be ones you have created, or commercially prepared tracks.

Having students play along with pre-recorded tracks will allow you to be able to sync the parts in the video after you have collected each video from the students. Parent cooperation is a must. Provide a list of requirements prior to beginning the project to make sure everyone is on board. This is a process, so allow yourself plenty of time. Research and reach out to others who have done these projects for recommendations. Visit vibrantvalleymusicstudio.com for some great videos, and great ideas! Melody Payne at melodypayne.com has a helpful article on her website titled "How to Create a Virtual Piano Ensemble Recital Video."

Green Screen, Eggs, and Ham: MacGyvered Music Classes for K-8 Remote Learning
Presented by Rachel D. Hahn

Looking back on 2020, we can marvel at how the world's teachers adapted to the remote education necessitated by COVID-19. Using a variety of resources and technologies, music educators and studio teachers ensured that their students would continue to make music, learn, and grow. This session explored the pedagogical lessons learned from teaching K-8 music and studio piano in this unprecedented situation and provided recommendations for applying these lessons in remote and in-person teaching.

The Urban Dictionary defines "macgyvered" as "the use of seemingly useless objects in your close vicinity to accomplish otherwise impossible tasks." It's what many other teachers did to set up remote learning music classes, including general music, group piano, band, private lessons, and a musical at a K-8 school with 48-hours' notice.

Using a "green screen, eggs, and ham," the presenter's community developed new skills, explored content, and remained connected and engaged. Session attendees viewed sample remote learning videos and materials, and analyzed how various approaches could be used to assess student needs and facilitate individualized exploration, practice, and feedback in isolation. In addition to viewing sample teaching videos, participants also shared their own experiences in the platform chat.

The practicality of "macgyvering" is an invaluable opportunity for pianists, general music educators, and all other teachers. This presentation concluded with the story of "Inspire Piano" – a cross-generational group-piano outreach program that connected elementary-age piano students with senior-citizen residential communities in the era of COVID-19 and was the recipient of an MTNA Community Engagement Grant. Attendees were encouraged to "macgyver" their own teaching and look for creative innovations for pedagogical excellence during and beyond the pandemic.

Better Video Performances from Your Students
Presented by Aaron Garner

Recognizing that video is quickly rising as a crucial aspect of piano studies, yet many studios are falling behind with respect to video and audio editing capabilities, Aaron Garner addressed these issues:

- Do your student video performances adequately reflect your quality of program?
- How do you help your students create better video performances?
- How do you capture better audio?
- How do you inspire creativity?
- How do you inspire the viewer through cinematography?

Constructing Semiotic Bridges through Multimedia Performances
Presented by Jonathan Scofield

One of the many advantages of living in the 21st century is the opportunity to enjoy music anytime and anywhere we please through technology. The global COVID-19 pandemic has caused us to rely almost exclusively on technology to experience music, but while some artists thrive in the digital medium, others suffer from a lack of in-person interactions with their audiences.

Classically-trained musicians are especially vulnerable at this time as our art is usually experienced in person. Instead of simply incorporating technology into traditional concert hall conventions, we can reinvent our performances to exploit the power that technology gives us. Unless your audience is composed of trained musicians, they probably do not assign nearly as much meaning to the music as the performer.

Teachers face a similar challenge when teaching interpretation to young students. The reason for this challenge is simple: classically-trained musicians have acquired a set of learned associations with their repertoire that allows them to enjoy the music and interpret it in a holistic manner.

The study of the way we derive meaning from art is called semiotics. Our audiences often do not have the same associations to help them understand and enjoy the music as completely as we do, but we can use technology to help narrow that gap. By combining elements such as film, art, literature, and even food in a multimedia format, we can build semiotic bridges to help our audiences enjoy and understand the music we perform in a much more impactful way than we could in a traditional concert setting.

Many professional performing organizations such as symphonies, operas, and chamber ensembles have been employing multimedia elements long before the pandemic, but modern technology has made it possible for anyone with a phone, projector, or a network of artists to create a production that audiences will remember for the rest of their lives.

Google Drive Can Do All of That?
Presented by Linda Christensen and Michelle Sisler

When you think of innovative uses of technology, Google Drive may not be the first thing that leaps to mind. However, Sheets, Slides, and Forms are powerful tools that can be used to create interactive PDFs, drag-and-drop worksheets, clickable choice boards, escape rooms, auto-corrected worksheets, registration forms and more!

In this session, the presenters demonstrated how to go beyond the basics of Google Drive to add excitement to lessons and save time on administrative tasks. Demonstrations and printed instructions included the following:

- Google Slides: Interactive PDFs and Drag-and-Drop Worksheets
- Google Slides: Clickable Choice Boards and Escape Rooms
- Google Slides: Flipped Classroom Assignments
- Google Forms: Registration for events, recitals, or registration
- Google Forms: Auto-corrected and graded worksheets, including pre-and post-activity assessments, and how to provide feedback, including video feedback, for incorrect answers so students learn from their mistakes.
- Google Forms: Check-in forms (*i.e.* How are you feeling? How is practice going? Do you have questions? How can I help you?)
- Google Sheets: View and manage forms data all in one place or create a new sheet for assignments or tracking music

Fast, Clear, and Musical: How to Solve Issues of Sound and Synchronicity
Presented by Kathleen Theisen, João Paulo Casarotti, Stella Sick, George Litterst

The first part of the presentation covered the intricacies and challenges that are present in any internet connection. George Litterst and Stella Sick talked about the terms and concepts of bandwidth, ping, latency, jitter, Wi-Fi vs. ethernet and such, and how each of these elements affects an internet connection and especially the quality of picture and sound in the online teaching environment.

The second part of the presentation focused on the specialized tools available for distant learning, and especially on the possibility of synchronous connections for teaching, rehearsals, and performances. Kathleen Theisen and João Paulo Casarotti described a number of scenarios where high-quality audio sound and synchronous connection are essential for the learning process, both during the pandemic and looking forward, as a viable method of long-distance instruction in the future, supplementing and expanding musicians' horizons.

Throughout the session Theisen and Casarotti focused on technical components to create successful low-latency connections (equipment, internet connection, *etc.*) and shared several examples of recordings that they made using several of these platforms. Some software programs that provide lag-less or low-latency solutions for connections:
- *JamKazam*
- *Musicology*
- *Rock Out Loud*
- *Musical Overture*
- *JackTrip*
- *SonoBus*
- *SoundJack*
- *Jamulus*
- *CleanFeed*
- *Aloha(Elk)*
- MIDI alternative: Internet MIDI

Geeks on Stage
Members of the Committee

Kathleen Theisen presented herself as pianist and vocal quartet, performing as a "virtual choir." The work was *Open the Eyes of My Heart, Lord*, which she had recorded for a remote service at First Congregational Church, Ridgefield, Connecticut. The performance featured Theisen in five roles simultaneously. Remarkably, the entire video was produced on an iPhone.

Jennifer Stadler gave a fifteen-minute presentation "Geeks on Stage: Virtual Reality." In this presentation, Jennifer explored the educational potential of VR technology using the Oculus Quest 2. She shared her *BeatSaber* gameplay to show the benefits for rhythm coordination. She also played the trailer for *Virtuoso*, a fully immersive music production app. Stadler presented the opportunities provided by two apps that can be calibrated to a MIDI keyboard: *VRTuos*, a *Synthesia*-style app with notes that fall directly onto the keys of the instrument, and *Grand Reality*, a lighted keyboard. Both apps offer a learn (wait) mode and a score mode, which she demonstrated through a screen recording of a student inside the VR headset. She concluded with a clip from a live VR Concert held in February 2021. She closed with a statement on the positive implications of this technology for the future.

João Paulo Casarotti, piano, and duet partner Ekaterina Skliar, mandolin, presented a beautiful performance of *Odeon (Tango Brasileiro)* by Ernesto Nazareth, transcribed for this instrumentation by Amaral Vieira. Casarotti recorded his part from his studio in Baton Rouge, and Skliar added her part from her studio in Philadelphia.

George Litterst gave a mini lecture-performance, presenting *Waltz in C for Piano with Accompaniment for Triangle and Tambourine*, Op. 38, No. 9 by Muzio Clementi. Putting the piece in historical perspective, Litterst discussed the period of the early 1800s during which time there was an emerging class of consumers that could afford musical instruments, sheet music, and lessons. During this time, the range and features of the new *fortepiano* expanded considerably. There was a popular interest in exotic instruments, such as the tambourine and triangle, and the waltz became a highly popular—although controversial—dance form.

Taking the presentation in a humorous direction, Litterst proceeded to clear space on the right side of his music desk and invited his son, Patrick, and his virtual twin, Pietro, to join him in this performance. At this point, miniature percussionists appeared from behind the music desk carrying triangle and tambourine, and they joined George in a highly unusual performance of the work.

For the next performance, Alejandro Cremaschi offered a video collage of his own duet performance of *Otoño Porteño (Autumn in Buenos Aires)* by Astor Piazzolla, in its arrangement for piano four-hands by Giannantonio Mutto. Cremaschi recorded himself performing both parts of the arrangement in alternate fashion. He used a Yamaha Disklavier to record the "leading" part for each section (sometimes the *primo* part, other times the *secondo*), and then recorded the other part in a second pass while the Disklavier performed the leading part that had been previously recorded.

The MIDI information produced by the Disklavier was recorded in real time by a Mac computer with the software Reaper. Reaper was used to play the MIDI back, to record the second part, and then to edit together all the sections and parts to create a seamless performance (Note: Cremaschi only edited MIDI information, not audio). Lastly, he rendered the MIDI recording as an audio file using a virtual Steinway piano provided by the software *GarageBand*. This audio file served as the backbone for the final video product. The audio was combined with video recordings of his playing as well as with preexisting video footage of Buenos Aires.

The final video was assembled using *Screenflow*, sparkled with some color filters in some of the sections to add variety. Geeks on Stage concluded with a reprise of the Virtual Piano Ensemble performance of *Mi Teresita (Little Waltz)* created for the 2021 NCKP by Laura Silva. At the beginning of the day, Silva had provided a step-by-step explanation for how this performance had been put together. The work provided a fitting ending to Geeks on Stage.

MAIN CONFERENCE PRESENTATIONS

Innovative Intermediate Piano Music from Latin America
Presented by University of Memphis MTNA
Wednesday, July 28, 2021
Recorded by Melissa Coppola

This session explored the importance of diversity of repertoire and representation in the piano studio through the lens of pieces by Latin American pedagogues Violeta Hemsy de Gainza from Argentina, Eduardo Cáceres from Chile, and Jesus Alberto Rey Mariño from Colombia. The University of Memphis MTNA aimed to stimulate instructors to diversify their students' repertoire by introducing works by these composers that address a variety of musical styles for elementary through late-intermediate piano levels.

It is important that young musicians are exposed to music outside of the traditional canon in order to diversify their musical ear. Latin music has specific characteristics that are beneficial to the young pianist; this style of music is characterized by rhythm and challenges a student's concept of typical musical expectation. Exposure to new rhythmic patterns, especially syncopation, can improve sight-reading skills. Additionally, teachers can expand their knowledge of music and diversify the types of music they teach in their studios by including Latin American music.

Jesus Alberto Rey Mariño (1956-2009) graduated from the National Pedagogical University of Bogota. He was the director and founder of regional bands in Medellin, served as Advisor for the Ministry of Culture, and was a Colcultura Scholar in 1996. Mariño was deeply involved with his community and was a prolific pedagogue. He was also a composer and was First Prize winner of the 6th Vieco Ortiz National Competition. *De Negros y blancos en Blancas y Negras* was composed in 1996 in conjunction with Colcultura. This book contains fifty pieces and emphasizes articulation, texture, syncopation, rhythm, voicing, Latin rhythms, folk songs, and ensemble work. Most pieces in this collection are appropriate for intermediate to advanced students. A short piece from the collection, "Timba," was demonstrated. The piece showcases rhythmic variation and is appropriate for elementary to intermediate levels. The dance-inspired piece, "Estudio de Joropo," which challenges the student to use different articulations in both hands, was also demonstrated. "Pasillo," the longest piece in the book, was also showcased, as well as "Caña" and "Mambito," a four-hand work. These pieces include mixed meter, cluster chords, seventh chords, and dissonance.

Eduardo Cáceres (b. 1955) was trained in Chile and Germany. He organized over 600 concerts of contemporary Latin American composers and was awarded a UNESCO Medal of Music. As an arts leader, he serves as Associate Chair at Chile State University, is Artistic Director of the Contemporary Music Festival in Santiago, Chile, and is Music Director of Bartók and Trok-Kyo Contemporary Ensembles. *Fantasies Ritmicas* was written in 2009 and is pedagogical in nature.

It includes nineteen programmatic gradual pieces and addresses difficulties found in contemporary music.

The final composer explored during this presentation was Violeta Hemsy de Gainza (b.1929) from Argentina. She is the author of over forty musical publications and served as the President of the Latin American Forum for Music Education. Her publication, *Nuestro Amigo el Piano,* was published in 1970 and is a collection of piano pieces written by children during their first two years of lessons. It includes major, minor, modal, and chordal harmonies.

The presentation concluded with a question and answer session with the presenters.

The Music of Marianna Martinez and Maria Hester Park
Presented by Olga Kleiankina and Kristen Turner
Wednesday, July 28, 2021
Recorded by Allison Fog

This presentation features a lecture recital of the music of eighteenth-century composers Marianna Martinez and Maria Hester Park. Most people associate the Classic era with the composers Haydn, Mozart, and Beethoven. However, eighteenth century audiences as well as critics felt their music was often too complex and harmonically confusing. Composer Ignaz Pleyel was more popular during this time, and many critics preferred him to Haydn. The music of Marianna Martinez and Maria Hester Park represented the standard of musical taste at the time, which favored simplicity over complexity. Musicians craved a "natural" melody, supported by simple harmonies and phrases that were clear and uncomplicated.

Marianna Martinez was born in 1744 into a wealthy family, with connections to Pietro Metastasio, who was the Imperial court poet and who later took up residence with the Martinez family. He could see the talent in Marianna and directed and encouraged her academic and musical education. She was also a student of Haydn for three years when she was a child. Metastasio gave his fortune to the family after his death, and because of this wealth Martinez had the freedom to remain single, thereby becoming the most important salon hostess at the time. Many of her compositions were lost, and many possibly went unpublished during her lifetime, because it wasn't considered respectable for a woman of her status to publish music. She wrote over sixty-five pieces, including over thirty piano sonatas, however only three remain today.

Martinez' *Sonata in E Major* is an example of one of Martinez' early works, which may be one reason certain passages are somewhat problematic. The first movement is monothematic in form, with the theme presented in different keys. The melody is beautiful, with much ornamentation, and would most likely have appealed to audiences at the time. Dr. Kleiankina performed *Sonata in E Major*, by Marianna Martinez.

Maria Hester Park was born in 1760 in London. She was a popular and well-respected teacher, whose students came from the upper class and nobility, as young women were encouraged to acquire a "genteel" education. Park had a full performing career that stopped when she got married, which was quite common at the time, since it wasn't considered respectable for a married woman to have a professional life. Park's career didn't end after marriage like many of her contemporaries. She had five children, and maintained a career as a composer, teacher, and performer. She remained in London for her lifetime and met Haydn at a salon; he even dedicated a sonata to her! Unlike Martinez, Park's music was published while she was alive; this was more acceptable because she was a middle-class woman. In addition, all of her compositions are written for piano, and she frequently performed her own music. Her pieces were also used for students who sought sheet music to play for in-home concerts and other amateur events. Park's compositions were accessible with natural, balanced phrasing. Like most popular pieces of the day, her music centered around a beautiful melody and simple harmonies. Dr. Kleiankina performed Maria Hester Park's *Sonata, Op. 2, No. 2*. It features a brilliant melody and lots of "showy" passage work.

Piano Sonatas by Twentieth-Century Soviet Female Composers
Presented by Helena Hyesoo Kim
Wednesday, July 28, 2021
Recorded by Allison Fog

In this lecture recital, Helena Hyesoo Kim introduced Soviet composers Galina Ustvolskaya (1919-2006) and Sofia Gubaidulina (b. 1931). Both women had access to education and were able to pursue their musical and compositional careers, however life in the Soviet Union throughout much of the twentieth century was repressive and presented many challenges for artists and musicians living there. For example, a powerful union was formed that had full control over publishing, banning many types of music and only allowing tonal, traditional, neoclassical music, and folk tunes with a Russian theme. Gubaidulina was blacklisted by the Sixth Congress of Composers of the Union of the Soviet Socialist Republics. Ustvolskaya had many works concealed because they were incongruent with Soviet ideology.

Both women had strong personalities and favored music that was atonal and experimental. Composition teacher Dimitri Shostakovich once encouraged Gubaidulina to take her "mistaken path" and continue composing avant-garde music. Ustvolskaya was nicknamed "A Lady with Hammers," for her unconventional sounds that explored the whole range of expression at the piano.

Galina Ustvolskaya's music is difficult to categorize and features unusual tempo markings, frequent dissonance, cluster chords, repeated use of accents, and extreme dynamic ranges, from *pppp* to *ffff*. There are no clear forms, and the number of movements within a sonata is not consistent. Her compositional output includes six piano sonatas, one concerto, *Twelve Preludes,* and many works for orchestra, chamber ensembles, and solo instruments.

Kim performed excerpts from *Sonata No. 1*, and while the music on the page looks to be without structure, a contour graph showed the arc of the melody and the general shape of the piece. Ustvolskaya did not use barlines in *Sonata No. 2*, nor did she use them in subsequent compositions. The composer was inspired by spirituality and Russian chant, and favored creating a linear line without interruptions. Kim performed this very slow movement from *Sonata No. 2*, as well as excerpts from *Sonata No. 6*. She explained and showed how the thumb is used to play cluster chords in the middle of the texture, while the rest is heavily accented and percussive. The cluster chords were written to express pain and trauma, both emotionally and physically. The performer may feel physical discomfort while playing these chords, and often the entire hand and arm is used.

Next, Sofia Gubaidulina's compositions were examined from the standpoint of two categories: extended technique and dichotomy. The composer used extended techniques like *glissandi* with bamboo sticks on tuning pins, muted strings using *con sordino* (mute with one hand, play with the other), plucked strings, and non-pitched cadenzas. Gubaidulina liked to experiment with the piano to create different sound "worlds." Her compositional output includes large works for orchestra, concerti, film scores, and chamber works. Her works for the piano include *Chaconne*, *Piano Sonata, Musical Toys, Toccata-Troncata,* and *Invention.*

The dichotomy in Gubaidulina's pieces is shown by contrasting characters in her music. The composer believed that divine and human natures exist within us and all around the world. Within the same piece, one may hear a theme that is consonant, followed by one that is dissonant. Five expressive qualities are used to analyze and compare her music: articulation and sound production, melody, rhythm, texture, and compositional writing.

Kim played excerpts from Gubaidulina's *Piano Sonata* and showed how dissonance and consonance are used as a compositional tool throughout the piece. The presentation ended with a performance of the third movement.

In the Company of Ladies: Rediscovering Piano Duets by Women
Presented by Bonnie Choi
Wednesday, July 28, 2021
Recorded by Jessie Welsh

While piano duet music is immensely popular, works for piano ensemble by women composers remain largely unknown. In her introduction, Dr. Choi discussed some of the long-held beliefs, stemming from the eighteenth century, which have led to an all-male duet repertoire even today. She acknowledged that while some women were encouraged to perform (*e.g.* Clara Schumann), there was a widely held belief that women could not (or should not) compose. Because of this, audiences and publishers at that time were unreceptive to works by female composers. However, a modern survey of four-hand repertoire by female composers reveals a wealth of pieces from the late-intermediate to advanced levels.

This session examined brief, biographical information about a variety of composers, pedagogical information about the ensemble repertoire, and performance clips demonstrating the style and character of the works discussed.

Galant composer Jane Savage (1752-1824) published a variety of pieces, including the recently discovered, earliest-known anthem for the Church of England. Her piece, *A Favorite Duet for Two Performers on One Pianoforte or Harpsichord* (1789), contains four movements. Dr. Choi and her colleague performed an excerpt of the first movement "Maestoso," which featured short phases, clear cadences, and clear textures between *primo* and *secondo*.

Maria Szymanowska (1789-1831) was a Polish composer and perhaps the first piano virtuoso. She was employed as a pianist at a Russian court, was praised by Robert Schuman for her compositions, and is considered a forerunner of John Field and Chopin. Her *Grand Valse* duet is an example of an ensemble work at the early-advanced level. It features a lively character, a highly ornamented melody, and a waltz bass. Dr. Choi and her colleague demonstrated these elements in a brief performance.

Fanny Hensel (1805-1847), eldest of the Mendelssohn siblings, was a prodigy. She was encouraged to perform, but she was not permitted to travel and pursue a concert career. She was instead expected to pursue a domestic life. Still, she composed over 460 works, including four pieces for piano duet. Three of these are often performed as a set of *Three Character Pieces* and are published by Furore. The second work, in C minor, demonstrates the composer's maturity and is an advanced work requiring technical facility. The performance demonstrated the dark, bold character of the work and the continuous virtuosic passages of sixteenth notes.

Clara Schumann (1819-1896) remains one of the most highly celebrated pianists of all time, but she is often still considered the "other Schumann," fading to the background in light of her husband's fame. She performed more than 1000 concerts but published only twenty-three works in her lifetime. These included solo piano pieces, *lieder*, and her famous piano concerto. Her *March in E-Flat Major* is an ensemble piece at an intermediate level. A performance of the opening "fanfare" and the following contrasting trios demonstrated the wide variety of characters within Clara Schumann's work.

Marie Jaël (1846-1925) was a Parisian child prodigy, student of Liszt and Saint-Saëns, and the First Prize Winner of the prestigious piano award at the Piano Conservatoire. Her husband was a student of Chopin, and they often performed together. Jaël was also the first known individual to perform Beethoven's sonatas in their entirety. Due to a struggle with tendonitis, she also studied neuroscience and created her own method of piano playing. Her *Waltzes and Finale*, an advanced set for four hands, was admired by Liszt and features a variety of characters. The performance excerpts by Dr. Choi and her colleague demonstrated these contrasting characters and moods.

Cecile Chaminade (1857-1944) began composition at the age of 10, but her father refused her the privilege of studying at the Paris Conservatoire. She was the first female European composer to have a work published in the United States, and she even met President Roosevelt when one of her works was premiered. Her music is a late-Romantic French style. Her *Pieces Romantiques*, Op. 55 are tuneful, feature chromaticism, and are highly accessible for late-intermediate students. In the first piece of this set, the *primo* melody appears mostly in unison or sixths, and the *secondo* features broken chords. The other works evoke their particular titles and feature musical imagery throughout. The chosen selections for performance showcased these various characters and the charming nature of the melodies.

Amy Beach (1867-1944) was the first successful American female composer to create large-scale works. After marriage, Beach greatly limited her performances but resumed performing widely and to much acclaim after her husband's death. Amy Beach became a figurehead of the American women's suffrage movement, co-founded the Society for American Women Composers, and aided many other women in their compositional careers. She wrote roughly 300 total works across genres, including pedagogical materials. Her *Summer Dreams* for one piano, four hands is a set of six character pieces based on poetry. They are impressionistic miniatures that feature the depth of Beach's creativity in small-scale works.

Mel Bonis (1858-1937) was a classmate of Debussy at the Paris Conservatoire, and she studied harmony and organ with Cesar Franck. The majority of her works were composed for solo piano, and her solo work *Valse Espagnole* was also arranged by the composer for piano, four hands. Dr. Choi suggests that the title does not accurately denote the expected musical elements of Spanish style but is more broadly evocative of early-twentieth-century exoticism. The duet score is highly specific, has clearly marked phrases, and evokes a dance feeling.

Germaine Tailleferre (1982-1983) was the only female member of *Les Six*. She studied harmony, accompanying, and counterpoint at the Paris Conservatoire, eventually winning First Prize in each of those categories. After graduation, she also studied orchestration with Ravel. She produced a series of concerts with Satie, who was very enthusiastic about her compositions. Her *Suite Burlesque* is for late-elementary/early-intermediate students. The pieces are tuneful, simple, representative of French style, and feature different moods in both title and musical expression. The Neoclassic textures, forms, and length (seven minutes total) also make this work approachable for younger students.

Dr. Choi summarized her presentation with three words: accessibility, attractiveness, and advocacy. She ventured that these works are approachable for intermediate to advanced pre-college students and are rewarding to perform, even for professionals. The attractiveness of the music extends to the audience and makes it easily understood by both performers and the audience. Finally, Dr. Choi argues for programming these works to advocate for lesser-known composers, top females in the field of composition, and bringing pedagogical music to life. In the discussion following the presentation, Dr. Choi recommended the following sources for locating scores: imslp.org, Ferrari Publishing; Hildegard Publishing; and utilizing interlibrary loan.

Finding Opportunity in Times of Change
Presented by David Cartledge
Wednesday, July 28, 2021
Recorded by Charl Louw

David Cartledge's presentation highlighted the most persistent issues faced by every individual of society since the COVID pandemic started. The pandemic wreaked havoc in the personal and professional lives of people and was unprecedented in the sense that few measures were in place to counter the disastrous effects. Dr. Cartledge gave an account of the major crises and issues dealt with by every individual and explored the entrepreneurial spirit that arose under these conditions.

One of the major challenges was the economic recession and loss of jobs faced by people all over the globe. Companies had to lay off employees, leaving major chunks of the public jobless. Dr. Cartledge suggested that there is an entrepreneurial spirit in every individual, and that the time has arrived to put one's own creativity to practice. Entrepreneurs in recent times have come up with innovative techniques and business ideas to cater to the needs of the public despite the pandemic.

Studio teaching in particular was highlighted. Despite rough beginnings, teachers came up with ample opportunities using technology. Addressing student queries and using the digital media for education led teachers to find new and better ways to deliver their lessons to students. Even the students have become active participants in the education sector using a hybrid approach. Although traditional education is preferred, the digital approach allows students to distantly learn from teachers from other states or countries. It also expands the reach of education by reaching out to students living in remote areas.

Higher education can also address the major challenges that it faces. Dr. Cartledge's presentation addressed issues like curriculum, recruitment, lack of funding, and shortage of experienced personnel. There will be challenges when things return "to normal," but with the hybrid approach including technology and digital teaching, these issues can be resolved to some extent.
The presenter explored the term "intrapreneurship" which is acting like an entrepreneur *within* an established company, and its potential role in the development of "business within the business." He described an example where he saw a decline in the number of students who were recruited for the music major and other electives. Advertising, flyers, and other options were suggested to enhance recruitment. They also played a key role in the curriculum awareness among the students. Development of facilities that cater to the needs of a high number of students is needed but requires greater revenue.

Dr. Cartledge emphasized going online in the education sector to a greater degree. It is important to change the system at this stage with the COVID-19-based impacts. He highlighted the need for change for better community engagement on campuses. Music education, also, has been undergoing major changes, changing just as the rest of the world is changing. He emphasized that the education sector needs to adapt more readily to these changes. They should not lag behind as it is time to plant the seeds for the future and be "ahead of the game." The future is bright and full of possibilities for everyone.

Echoes in Time: Understanding, Teaching, and Creatively Programming Contemporary Works as Parallels to Standard Classics
Presented by Monica Kang-Sasaki
Wednesday, July 28, 2021
Recorded by Charl Louw

Kang-Sasaki's presentation centered around contemporary piano music spanning a myriad of styles, (post-) tonal languages, and mediums. This presentation viewed various new works as parallels to standard repertoire from past eras in order to stimulate understanding through connection. Practical ways to introduce standard and non-standard contemporary works to students of various levels were discussed. Different programming possibilities integrating new music into student's recitals as a twenty-first-century pianist were also explored.

Her presentation featured forty composers whose music can expand the teaching and performing repertoire. She highlighted and compared the levels and features of contemporary works with parallels from standard classics including:

Late Elementary
- Schumann *Album for the Young,* Op. 68: No. 1 "Melody," No. 2 "Soldier's March"

Early Intermediate
- *Notebook for Anna Magdalena Bach*: Minuet in G Major, BWV Anh. 114; Kabalevsky *24 Pieces for Children,* Op. 39: No. 20 "Clowns"

Intermediate
- Clementi *Sonatinas*, Op. 36; Burgmüller *25 Progressive Pieces*, Op. 100: No. 10 "Tender Flower," No. 13 "Consolation"

Late Intermediate
- Kuhlau & Diabelli *Sonatinas*; Haydn *Sonatas*; Bach *Inventions*

Early Advanced
- Bach *Sinfonias*; Beethoven *Sonatas,* Op. 49, and Op. 79; easier Chopin *Nocturnes* Op. 9, No. 2; Op. 55, No. 1

Advanced
- Repertoire beyond those previously described

The first work discussed was Bartók's *10 Easy Pieces* (1908), *Mikrokosmos* Vol. 1 which includes pianistic concepts like parallel motion, imitation, inversion, counterpoint, and

Mikrokosmos Vol. 4 with silently depressed chords, and bitonal sounds resulting from symmetrical constructions.

She discussed the works of Bolcom including *Monsterpieces (and others)* (1980), mentioning that the beginning pieces were rather traditional while later pieces were more contemporary. The works of Chen Yi, such as *Ba Ban* and *Northern Scenes,* are virtuosic pieces based on folk melodies and rhythms and feature dense textures, long sweeping lines, and rhythmic chordal sections.

Kang-Sasaki performed works of Henry Cowell, including *The Snows of Fujiyama* and *Piano Music,* Volume 1: "Aeolian Harp" highlighting the quiet, beautiful sonorities. Works by George Crumb included *A Little Suite for Christmas,* based on seven pieces requiring extended techniques (strumming/plucking, muting, finding harmonics, etc.). His musical language includes use of whole-tone, pentatonic, and octatonic scales. Another work, *Makrokosmos,* Vol. 1 was also explored.

Richard Danielpour's *The Enchanted Garden* consists of five pieces inspired by dream and reality. Norman Dello Joio's *Suite for the Young*, and Henri Dutilleux's *Piano Sonata: III. Choral et Variations* highlight melodic interest in different textures. Emma Lou Diemer's *Sound Pictures* includes ten pedagogical pieces introducing contemporary sounds, whereas Ross Lee Finney's *24 Inventions* use twelve-tone technique with each piece containing a musical puzzle. An interesting novelty, Annie Gosfield's *Brooklyn* is played with fingers, baseballs, and baseball mitt on and inside the piano. Darius Milhaud's *Accueil Amical,* containing seventeen one-page pedagogical pieces for children, was also included.

Other featured composers included Mazzoli, Nakada, Yoshiano, Ornstein, Papp, Pentland, Persichetti, Pinto, Poulenc, and Rochberg whose music is full of free and mixed meters, key changes, and quick shifts in character. In the final portion of the presentation, she covered Satie's *Gymnopédies* containing three simple dances that describe ceremonial dances at ancient Greek festivals, *Gnossiennes* which has three slow pieces, and *Embryons Desséchés* with three movements, each prefaced by a description of a crustacean dried-up embryo. Other works included Shostakovich's *24 Preludes* (each with defined character), Sifford's *Incognito (Jazz Nocturne)*, Starer's *Sketches in Color*, Stravinsky's *Les Cinq Doigts* (where the right-hand five fingers remain in the same position), and Takács's *Sounds and Colors* with fifteen pieces ranging from tonal to avant-garde. Tanaka's *Techno Etudes,* Villa-Lobos' *Francette et Piá and Petizada,* Vine's *Five Bagatelles* and Webern's *Kinderstück* (featuring twelve-tone technique) concluded the presentation.

Create to Motivate! Giving the Gift of Musical Ownership
Presented by Chee-Hwa Tan
Wednesday, July 28, 2021
Recorded by Luís Pipa

In this interactive workshop, the presenter shared the ways in which she has taught creative skills in a sustainable way over the years—by using repertoire. The main points of the presentation were the importance of having a whole teaching philosophy, selecting the right kind of music, knowing what to do with that music in the lessons, and providing examples of applications for music at different levels.

Creating, or recreating, gives the gift of ownership, and that is empowering. When we discover we can create, explained Tan, we become curious about learning more, and thus, curiosity is motivating. Using repertoire as a basis for composition or improvisation provides a concrete model for ideas and inspiration. Students need structure, and there is structure in creativity, as music is all about structure. The selection of repertoire needs to provide students with pieces that they may enjoy, possess clear patterns and forms, and include inspiring sounds. Principal elements to look for in the music should incorporate patterned or left-hand *ostinato* accompaniments, use of specific modes, consistent rhythmic motives, strong melodic motives, clear use of question-and-answer phrases and tonic-dominant relationships, and repetition of a single technical, musical, or theoretical concept. In the matter of how to approach repertoire, Tan advises to identify first the following features of any piece:
- Teaching/Learning Value
- Compositional Elements
- Assignment Parameters

More important than teaching the "what" and the "how" of music, is teaching the "why." The presenter reported that, as teachers, one imprints a "feeling," a feeling about the student's identity in relation to music study. Even if they will not remember much of the lesson, students will remember how they felt.

Tan presented examples of repertoire suited for different learning levels:
- For the beginning level she chose the piece "The Schumanns" from Unit 3 of *The Music Tree*: *Time to Begin* by Frances Clark;
- For the elementary and late-elementary levels the presenter chose two of her own compositions, "Black Bear Boogie" and "The Land of Nod," respectively;
- For the intermediate and late-intermediate levels the choice went to Bach's "Musette in D Major" and "Fountain of Diana" and "Seascape" from Gillock's *Lyric Preludes*. There was, at this point, a video presentation of a performance by an advanced student

improvising on "Seascape." Another video of several intermediate-level students improvising in different ways on "Mazurka" by Maria Szymanowska was also shown.
- Finally, Bach's "Prelude in E Minor" (BWV 941) served as the basis for a composition made and performed by a college student in the same style and using the same harmonic structure. The title was "Fan Mail for Sebastian," and the performance was seen on video.

All these pieces contained the elements that Tan specified in the introductory part of the session, with the creation component always present. The audience participated interactively throughout the presentation answering questions posed by the presenter. The presenter ended the session with a group of helpful tips:
- Patterned or *ostinato* accompaniments are great for improvisation
- Experiment with rhythm motives
- Experiment with modality – major to minor, or minor to major
- Use repetition
- Use question-and-answer phrases and tonic-dominant relationships
- Copy the form
- Melodic dictation/mapping with first four measures of theme
- Rhythmic dictation of two-four measures of theme
- Transpose a section or theme to different keys
- When in doubt, block it out!

Applying Video Modeling and Motor Imagery to Remote Piano Lessons: Creative and Practical Approaches to Enhance Piano Technique

Presented by Huiyun Liang
Wednesday, July 28, 2021
Recorded by Omar Roy

Dr. Liang began the presentation by highlighting the challenge of teaching piano technique in a virtual learning environment where the nature of instruction creates barriers for close monitoring and physical contact. This is especially important for young students who are learning and developing new skills. Dr. Liang emphasized that teachers may find it difficult to adequately describe elements of movement, weight transfer, and touch that are involved in piano technique compared to the natural physical demonstrations common to in-person instruction. Dr. Liang's presentation covered several different ways to incorporate video modeling and motor imagery to aid in the virtual instruction of piano technique.

First, Dr. Liang defined "Video Modeling" as:
Learners watch and analyze recorded performances of others or themselves, and utilize the information acquired from the videos to imitate, modify, and improve target skills.

Dr. Liang emphasized its application in training for various sports and included examples from her dissertation which explored and adapted elements of video modeling to private piano lessons. In her research, she used video cameras to record students and teachers playing from various angles to provide modeling feedback for motion analysis and comparison. All participants in her study were classified as late-elementary students, and her results indicated that video modeling resulted in immediate improvement in the technique of students. Dr. Liang noted that video modeling allowed participants to more immediately detect and correct problems due to the visual nature of the exercise.

In the next segment of the presentation, Dr. Liang explained her setup for online studio teaching, including software like *ManyCam* and the use of multiple camera angles. She also elaborated on the following strategies to enhance video modeling in online lessons:

- Design camera views and layouts based on the needs of the demonstration.
- Direct student attention to specific aspects of the demonstration through an ordered sequence of viewing the demonstration from different angles.
- Provide prompt visual cues by using drawing tools.

Dr. Liang also provided strategies for helping students utilize self-modeling and self-observation. These included:

- Observe self-performance in real-time and adjust movements accordingly by using their camera as a "mirror."
- Screen record a student's performance for self-evaluation.

Dr. Liang also elaborated on "Motor Imagery" and defined it as "a cognitive process in which a subject imagines he or she performs movements without physical actions." For implementation, she provided two principle strategies: Visual and Kinetic Motor Imagery.

Visual motor imagery is an external form of imagery that requires students to imagine their movements as they would see it from a third-person perspective. Dr. Liang demonstrated visual motor imagery through basic technical elements and using drawn visual cues to indicate the positioning of the hand. This exercise in visual motor imagery also included singing to reinforce the aural skills.

To build upon this example, Dr. Liang also included an excerpt from Tchaikovsky's *Italian Song*, highlighting the importance of smooth wrist motions in the left hand's waltz-like accompaniment pattern. She achieved this with overhead and side-view camera angles to provide students with multiple angles of the different planes of motion, as well as visually drawn cues to highlight the motion of the wrist and the overall range of motion.

Kinetic motor imagery is an internal or first-person sense of imagery where the subject performs the skill to feel the kinesthetic sense of the movement(s). To illustrate this, Dr. Liang demonstrated a warm-up exercise she uses with her students involving the fingertips of each hand being placed against the other, and pressing the corresponding fingers against those of the opposite hand. This sensory experience was reinforced using examples from Faber's *Piano Adventures*.

The presentation concluded with video footage of Dr. Liang working with a student in a lesson, employing strategies of video modeling, as well as visual and kinesthetic motor imagery.

Teaching Little Hands: Building Three-Dimensional Piano Technique from the Beginning
Presented by Fred Karpoff
Wednesday, July 28, 2021
Recorded by Omar Roy

Dr. Karpoff began the presentation by highlighting that one of the great challenges in teaching piano is instilling a great technical foundation with child beginners due to inadequate muscle definition and coordination. In this session, he systematically presented essential three-dimensional movements that are important in developing technique from the very first lesson.

The presentation included videos with his five-year-old student, Allison, where Dr. Karpoff introduced these techniques in a lesson, and concluded with the student demonstrating their assimilation of the movements in repertoire and improvisational settings. Throughout, the presenter advocated for the use of *kinesthetic transference* to allow the student to feel movements more organically. Before addressing movement, however, Dr. Karpoff highlighted that a key entry point to building technique is to first address seating position, ensuring that students are sitting at the proper height and distance, with proper balance and support.

The three-dimensional movements covered in this presentation included:

- *Quiet Hand:* The lack of excess muscle tension achieved in conjunction with adequate preparatory motion(s). Dr. Karpoff's demonstration highlighted that tension can manifest in excess finger movement.

- *Arm-Weight Drops*: This movement emphasizes the use of arm weight to drop into the key, rather than relying solely on the action of the fingers. Dr. Karpoff emphasized the importance of establishing this movement early on in a student's development as it becomes the foundation upon which other movements are built.

- *Portato*: The *portato* articulation involves the application of both arm-weight drops and the quiet hand as a precursor to *legato* technique. Dr. Karpoff noted that *legato* is often challenging for child beginners to execute without introducing excess tension.

- *Basic Vibrato Motion*: This refers to the cycling motion initiated by the larger arm muscles and distributed into smaller bursts of energy through the fingers. Dr. Karpoff demonstrated by loosely bouncing his fist on the closed fallboard while moving his arm towards the piano. This motion eventually evolves into the advanced technique necessary to play elements such as repeated notes, chords, and octaves.

- *Two-Note Slur*: This movement is characterized by a continuous lift and drop, followed by the arm continuing to move forward before the note is played. Dr. Karpoff introduced this technique with a C-major scale, using only fingers two and three to illustrate the two-note slur.

- *In and Out*: This movement involves moving the arm horizontally towards and away from the piano. Dr. Karpoff illustrated this movement using a pentascale, moving away from the piano when ascending and towards the piano while descending.

- *Under and Over*: This movement illustrates the larger fluid and continuous three-dimensional movement necessary to *legato* playing. Dr. Karpoff introduced this with a pentascale, building upon the "in and out" movement.

After introducing these movements, the presentation featured repertoire performances by the student, including Alexander Reinagle's *English Minuet* and *Hopak* (anonymous). In the *English Minuet*, the student demonstrated successful incorporation of three-dimensional movements including in and out, under and over, and the two-note slur. In *Hopak*, the student demonstrated incorporation of the two-note slur, quiet hand, and consistent alignment and connection to arm weight drops.

Dr. Karpoff emphasized the value of improvisation as a pedagogical tool, allowing students to experiment without fear of making mistakes. The presentation concluded with his student demonstrating, in addition to a sense of musical sensitivity and creativity, many of the same three-dimensional movements employed in repertoire to illustrate the assimilation of these movements into their technical foundation. In this improvisation, Dr. Karpoff drew inspiration from Forrest Kinney's "World Piece," published in *Pattern Play* Vol. 1.

Keys to Inclusion: Reimagining the Piano Canon
Presented by Brian Hsu, Daniel Pesca, Sun Min Kim, Susan Tang, Sonya Schumann
Wednesday, July 28, 2021
Recorded by Charl Louw

This presentation on the subject of Keys to Inclusion (KTI) was a panel discussion. Dr. Daniel Pesca started the presentation by discussing the advent of Keys to Inclusion, started in summer 2020 with the murder of George Floyd which led to a call for action against racism. It has led its way to the piano community as well. He talked about the programs and lectures started in four of the universities he has worked at where students and teachers learned a lot about racism and explored the music by Black American composers. With music of all styles and lengths, these works can greatly expand the teaching repertoire. He further highlighted that students are keen to study the music of African American piano composers.

Dr. Brian Hsu discussed the lectures held last year in which four speakers were involved:

Dr. Ramsay, one of the speakers at the presentation, elaborated on the issues related to music education and performance. He asked participants to judge music fairly within their own studios and institutions and discussed the example of the Grammys where the initial intention to celebrate and acknowledge the best music/performers has been replaced by a tendency to celebrate popularity and record sales. He articulated that KTI is a project which is aimed at the celebration of the work of the marginalized composers, empowering piano students of diverse backgrounds, and enriching the pianist's repertoire. He further elaborated that KTI aims to bridge the gap between the renowned composers, the audience, and the marginalized composers.

The presentation continued with Dr. Sonya Schumann who is a founding member of Keys to Inclusion. She discussed master classes held in five institutions where selected pieces of musical diversity were presented. The aim was to increase the interaction of the students with the KTI faculty and advocate that students study these pieces at the highest level. She shared a few demonstration videos.

Dr. Sun Min Kim, Assistant Professor of Music and a founding member of Keys to Inclusion, highlighted that the students not only received instruction but also performed in public to increase their learning outcomes and confidence. The recitals were done with hybrid methods using digital technology for distant students while students close by had in-person recitals with a live audience where students also shared their reflections on African American musicians and composers.

Dr. Susan Tang, an Associate Professor of piano at Northeastern Illinois University and another founding member of Keys to Inclusion, highlighted the way forward. She said that the organization is still evolving and aims to help diversity in the music industry. She expressed the desire to create a more inclusive environment for teachers in other institutions. The KTIs current season in this presentation sheds light on the works of African American composers through lectures, master classes, recitals, and recordings, fostering community among the presenters' five piano studios which span the country.

Creating Multi-Level Duets and Ensembles from Standard Piano Repertoire
Presented by Paul Myatt
Wednesday, July 28, 2021
Recorded by Olivia Ellis

In this interactive session, the presenter began by saying that ensemble playing is important to a student's growth and is enjoyed by many. However, Myatt posed the problem that there is a lack of published keyboard ensembles to meet a variety of student abilities in one setting. He claimed that creating original duets and ensembles allows teachers to gain independence from finding published ensemble works.

First, Myatt discussed a few of the many benefits of collaborative playing. He also discussed the importance of the beat in ensemble work. Activities that work on keeping a steady pulse can build a foundation for other collaborative playing skills. At this point in the session, the presenter asked audience members to try some clapping exercises. Myatt used ocean-themed rhythm words to assist in counting. For example, to count a whole note, the audience used the phrase "great – big – blue – whale," while the pattern "quarter – quarter – quarter – rest" was counted by using the phrase "shark – shark – shark – sh!" After the audience clapped and said each of the phrases with him, he then had attendees try it again with a fun accompaniment playing in the background.

Continuing with the importance of beat, the presenter outlined several benefits of creating a percussion ensemble for students. These included:
- Every student can participate in a percussion ensemble.
- Percussion ensembles allow easy integration of movement.
- Students are able to use their voice, eventually leading to saying rhythmic names such as "ta ti-ti ta."
- Students are able to clap or play the rhythms.
- Score reading can be easily extended to rhythmic note reading.

Myatt said the music itself helps to engage the students.

Moving on to piano ensembles, the presenter suggested that teachers arrange standard repertoire works as a duet or other ensemble. For example, he suggested Cornelius Gurlitt's "A Deserted Garden," (also known as "Andante"), Op. 82, No. 35. In his arrangement of this piece, he added full chords as well as chord symbols. He also added an introduction so one student sets the pulse from the beginning. In the B section, he included a rhythmic motive to keep the students together. He suggested other pieces, including Ray Moore's "Waltz Mystique." As shared by Myatt, the benefits of doing collaborative playing before learning the original solo work include understanding the voices or parts in the work, understanding harmonies, engaging in collaborative learning, creating a memory-enhancing learning environment, and exploring orchestral and other instrument sounds. Myatt claimed that this kind of ensemble provides great opportunities for vacation programs where you may have a variety of student abilities or levels.

Myatt gave several points for teachers to remember when arranging ensembles:
- Consider the style (*i.e.* band or orchestral).
- Brush up on four-part harmony rules.
- Double the hands for an octave part.
- Double up on the same part, making sure to balance the overall sound.
- Start with the end in mind; know which students will play the piece.
- Create a piece at a lower level than the actual playing ability of the student.
- Make sure instrumental sounds blend together.
- Consider sound registrations (*i.e.* trumpet and violin for solo, French horn and cello for countermelody, electric piano and organ for accompaniment, tuba and bassoon for bass, and guitar and harp for moving accompaniment).
- Ensure the notes used are correct for the instrumental range.
- Look at the articulation and choose the instrument appropriately.
- Think about the balance in the duet; there should be a strong melody that stands out, a solid bass for foundation, and a rhythmic pattern or *ostinato* to keep things in time.

At this point in the session, the presenter put attendees into five-minute breakout rooms. He asked each group to use a Miro board to create a four-bar piano and percussion ensemble based on "Hot Cross Buns."

To close out the session, Myatt shared an arrangement of *Bourrée* by Gottfried Heinrich Stölzel. The original piece had three main parts, so he arranged it for three instruments: B-flat clarinet, oboe, and bassoon. He also added a harpsichord continuo part to outline the harmony. He explained that arrangements like this allow students to better understand multiple parts in the piece. The presenter also shared several video examples of his projects, including an example with a group of young children playing piano and percussion and an advanced teacher group performing Dennis Alexander's *Toccata Ritmico*.

Teaching Composition to Young Beginners
Presented by Christopher Oill
Wednesday, July 28, 2021
Recorded by Olivia Ellis

Taking creativity to new heights, Oill presented an interactive session highlighting the process of putting together a student composition. Before beginning, he said it is important to be in the right mindset. Oill suggested the following:

- Introduce one concept.
- Collaborate with the young beginner.
- Move on quickly rather than getting stuck.
- Give them choices sometimes.
- Make only a few changes throughout the composition.
- If the composition is not working out, throw it away.

He claimed that music compositions could be successfully completed using his five-step process, which allows students a great deal of creative freedom.

Asking the audience to work through the creative process as an example of how to work with a student, Oill began with "*Step 1: Think*." For this step, he asks students what the composition is about. Oill recommended encouraging students' imaginations by asking what happened at school, what they had for breakfast, *etc*. He suggests basing the piece on students' experiences. One audience member suggested it could be about a pet, so the collaborative piece of the day started with the image of a dog. Then, Oill asks students to elaborate. He asked the audience about any special features of the dog, so the next audience member suggested that the pet could grow wings when no one is looking and fly.

Oill then moved on to "*Step 2: Outline*." Comparing it to other examples such as painters needing a canvas and actors needing a stage, Oill said that music needs form. He also claimed that stories make more sense to students. Therefore, his next step focused on writing the story and outlining the form of the composition. To help create a story, the presenter recommended drawing the action with pictures in three to five parts. As part of the presentation, Oill took the time to draw the audience's suggestions, which included:
- A section, in which the dog's owner wished on a star that the pet could fly.
- B section, where the dog snuck past the owner and sprouted wings before flying to the lake.
- A1 section, in which the dog's owner is standing in confusion that nothing happened.
- Coda, where the dog is having a grand time splashing in the lake.

Oill suggests that students "reuse, recycle, repeat." Teachers can guide students through elements of form, such as returning to an A section but altering it slightly to make it a modified A1 section and adding a Coda. He mentioned that through-composed form was also fine, reiterating that it is more important that the student simply has a beginning, middle, and end.

Moving on to "*Step 3: Experiment*," Oill suggested using various sources as inspiration when students begin playing their piece. These sources could include the teacher, the lesson book, YouTube, TV, video games, radio, and live music. Students should take note of the different aspects of the piece, like rhythm, dynamics, texture, melody, harmony, timbre, and form. Then in lessons, student and teacher can talk about what it sounds like on the piano and try out each section. Oill suggested tweaking the ideas as you go to improve them.

In "*Step 4: Sketch*," Oill advised doing a whole piece improv at first, followed by the teacher modeling the piece for the student. Teachers should guide students, and it was recommended to record for this stage.

Finally, for "*Step 5: Shape*," the presenter said students should practice their composition. As they work with their pieces, they can trim, add, and adjust, changing it as they go. However, he does recommend that they treat it comparably to a repertoire piece they might be practicing for lessons, giving it equal attention and importance.

Once the piece is ready, Oill said there are many places for students to share the composition, such as competitions, performances, MuseScore, SMP Press, Soundcloud, CD Baby, YouTube, and social media. He promoted sharing as a way to encourage students.

Online Piano Lessons for Young Beginners
Presented by Rebecca Pennington
Wednesday, July 28, 2021
Recorded by Olivia Ellis

In this session, the presenter posed the question: How do we create online lessons for young children that are as effective and engaging as in-person lessons? Pennington explained that she taught more than twenty beginning students while online during the past year, and she created a formula that worked well for both her and her students. The session was a compilation of ideas gleaned through her teaching.

After engaging with the audience on their own experiences with online beginners this year, Pennington proceeded to share her ideas. First, she recommended that teachers consider the lesson format. For her students, a typical time frame was too long for young online students, so she decided to implement half-hour lessons twice weekly and offer online group classes as a possible substitute for one of the lessons. Students chose if they wanted all group instruction, all one-on-one instruction, or some combination of the two.

Next, she advised teachers to have a routine in place. In her lessons, she makes sure to move quickly through material and keep a fast pace, returning to concepts later in the lesson if students do not understand the first time. For online lessons, she suggests having a balance of activities that are known to be successful along with more difficult tasks that are presented in "bite size pieces" to limit frustration. She never spends more than five minutes on a given lesson element. Pennington's template includes a short hello. She claims that a longer hello may result in a younger student becoming bored or perhaps telling a lengthy story. Instead, Pennington jumps right into the content of the lesson. She typically reviews concepts from previous lessons, such as "wiggle your 1s," so students are engaged and learning right from the start. Another review activity might include putting the musical notes in order. For a technique warmup, she runs several quick drills and often asks parents to attend this portion of the lesson. This allows the parent to help reinforce concepts throughout the week. They can also send a video to Pennington if she is not able to see something through the online platform. Pennington typically includes review pieces before moving to new repertoire. To introduce a new piece, she sets the stage with several preparatory activities, such as tap and count, finding the starting position before playing, and other efficient steps to help the student succeed.

In between review and new pieces, Pennington staggers miscellaneous concept work. She shared that Google Slides can be used to teach line and space notes, intervals, and landmark notes. She also uses an online whiteboard for rhythm activities like labeling counts, clapping back rhythms, and other activities with large movements to internalize the pulse. At the end of lessons, Pennington has an improvisation prompt, which often reinforces concepts from that day's lesson.

She keeps goodbyes short but has a song she likes to sing at the end. She reminded the audience to end each lesson with a smile!

The presenter also suggested using friendly language because having a positive attitude sets students up for success. Some of her favorite phrases include "I heard X and Y, that is two thumbs up for your performance today!" and "Follow with me, do what I am doing, make your hands look the same as mine." Rather than reacting to what they have done, she suggests using reminders ahead of time to make the performance more successful. In general, she also suggests ignoring any negative behaviors. If there is negative behavior in her class, she disregards it and focuses on the positive behavior.

At the end of this session, Pennington addressed a few questions from the audience which gleaned more information. When asked about ideal student age, she re-emphasized the need for a tailored lesson plan. She shared that she uses *The Music Tree* method as part of her curriculum. When asked about the number of students in her group classes, she said she would take as many as seven beginners in a class, but four is best. The following statement by the presenter summarizes the session well: "Efficient lesson plan plus efficient language = no down time."

Creating Piano Recitals for a More Diverse Tomorrow
Presented by Sally Ritchie, Sue Ruby, Lynn Worcester Jones, and Penny Lazarus
Wednesday, July 28, 2021
Recorded by Charl Louw

The presentation highlighted the quick change to virtual learning and performing formats in 2020. As a result, students everywhere connected, shared, and performed for one another more easily. With rising expectations for cultural awareness, piano recital programs are evolving to reflect the diversity in our piano studios. An exploration of repertoire resources and recital repertoire "swaps" by women and composers of color formed the main body of the discussion.

The repertoire "swap" idea is a selection device used to replace a popular teaching piece by a white male composer with a lesser-known piece by a minority composer. The main considerations are:
- Time period
- Character or style
- Difficulty
- Musical principles
- Endorsing and promoting diversity, equity, and inclusion in the piano studio

Ms. Lazarus, along with the other presenters, developed a self-reflection tool to help people explore the diversity in their studios in three broad areas: the teacher, the studio, and the curriculum.

Three themes were explored:

Night Music: In this category, it was established that no matter where we are on earth, we all share in the wonder of the night sky and its significance in marking the end of one day and the beginning of another. Even though the alignment of the stars are different from place to place, the theme of Night creates a beautiful umbrella for pieces from different periods, cultures, and experiences. In addition to the first movement of Beethoven's "Moonlight" Sonata, Brahms' "Lullaby," Mozart's "Twinkle Variations," Chopin *Nocturnes* and Schumann's "Träumerei," consider expanding the repertoire to include works like *Rock-a-bye* by Florence Price, *Notturno* by Fanny Mendelssohn, Bangambula Vindu's *Twilight Hour, Pray (Prière)*, "Rock-A-Bye Song" from *Miniatures*, and "Lullaby" from *Suite for Piano*. Other options include *Day's End* by Hale Smith, "End of Day" from *Soundshots* by Louise Talma, *Berceuse* by Wanda Landowska and "In the Cold Moonlight" ("In De Col' Moonlight") from *From the Southland* by Harry T. Burleigh.

I've Known Rivers: Lazarus and the fellow presenters highlighted this evocative title, including a recitation of the poem *The Negro Speaks of Rivers* by Langston Hughes that has been set to vocal music by several black composers including Margaret Bonds and Howard Swanson. Songs about rivers were used as a secret code to call black people to the Underground Railroad to escape slavery. Themes of water abound in both classical, folk, and popular literature. In addition to Handel's *Water Music Suites*, Burgmüller's "The Storm," Felix Mendelssohn's "Gondola Song," and popular favorites *O Shenandoah, Bridge Over Troubled Water, Moon River*, and *River Flows In You* by Yiruma, consider other pieces for a broader repertoire. Some recital recommendations in this case are "River Flows" in *Piano Discoveries*, *Thunderstorms* by Dianne Goolskasian Rahbee, *Dream Boat* by Florence Price and *Troubled Water*, based on the Spiritual "Wade in the Water" by Margaret Bonds.

Songs without Words: In the category inspired by Felix Mendelssohn's *Songs without Words* (Lieder ohne Worte) by and Edvard Grieg's *Lyric Pieces*, it was recommended that the piano pieces by Fanny Mendelssohn Hensel (1805-1847) could be included. Her Opus 2, 4, 5, 6 and 8 for piano were composed while her brother Felix was composing his piano sets. Fanny is only recently given equal credit to Felix in inventing the idea of Songs without Words; piano pieces, written in ABA form, with a singing, lyrical melody that soars over arpeggiated chords.

**All I Need to Know (about Teaching and Performing)
I Learned from Early Childhood Music**
Presented by Linda M. Fields, NCTM
Wednesday, July 28, 2021
Recorded by Angela Leising-Catalan

The presenter began by stating that early childhood music has become synonymous with music and movement. She reminded the audience that training the ear and the body can begin in infancy, but its benefits extend far beyond young childhood. The principles of early childhood music can inform how we teach older students, and even enrich our own performances.

The presenter explained that to successfully play a musical instrument, one needs to:
- Be emotionally connected.
    - Fields referenced Marvin Blickenstaff's quote: "Music is sound that expresses feelings."
- Love the contrasts.
    - Contrasts are the basics of form.
- Have control of our instrument
- Know the language
- Decode the notation

Using the chat function, the presenter took a poll of attendees about which of the above are most important. The results were as follows:
- Be emotionally connected – 50%
- Find the contrasts – 12.5%
- Have control of the body – 25%
- Have control of the instrument – 0%
- Know the language – 12.5%
- Decode the notation – 0%

The presenter moved on to discussing twenty lessons from early childhood music, and further grouped them into the broader categories of Story, Sound, and Symbol. Fields played an audio recording of the children's song *Clap Your Hands* to highlight these lessons.

STORY: As storytellers, musicians communicate feelings. Feelings, in the framework of contrast, are the foundation for music artistry.
- Every child is musical.
- Use emotional attachment to motivate learning.
- The learning environment is important.
- Excellent repertoire touches the soul.

- Parents are our partners.
- Communicate form by highlighting contrast.
- We know what something is by what it is not.
- Minimize talking; model instead.
- Be an observer, especially of your students.
- Teach the class, not the plan.

Fields stated that when the musician is ready to express a story, we use an instrument. This first requires being able to control the body, as the body is the first instrument. Singing and dancing started it all!

SOUND:
- Learning begins with the whole body.
- Large motor comes first.
- Experience with a variety of sounds teaches about timbre.
- Hearing and movement are powerful partners.
- The ear plays a central role in learning.

SYMBOL: Stimulating the ear by singing and moving gives meaning to what the eye will eventually read.
- Teach pitch and tonal sense by singing.
- Make use of the Learning Loop – Listen, Think, Vocalize.
- Teach rhythm by moving.
- Apply language learning strategies to music learning, such as using neutral syllables.
- There are non-musical benefits, such as confidence, leadership, story telling, understanding order, and awareness of patterns.

The presenter stated that these lessons from early-childhood music can shape pedagogy at any level. The concepts of story (the artistic ideas we want to convey), sound (the aural expression of our ideas), and symbol (the musical languages that represent those sounds) apply to all stages of learning. She encouraged attendees to observe their students in the near future with any of the twenty lessons in mind, as these lessons are directly related to all levels of musicianship.

Who's That?: Creating a New Standard Repertoire
Presented by Artina McCain
Wednesday, July 28, 2021
Recorded by Elizabeth Smith

The presentation began with an explanation of the disconnect between conversations about diversity and what is being played in most piano studios. The goal of this presentation was to help remedy that disconnect, and the presenter explained that she will leave the audience with ten different programs meant for their own piano studios. Dr. McCain then explained her approach. After examining 135 competition/festival pieces, she created a programming formula, which was put into use during her presentation. Dr. McCain then added a note that she is very excited about the plethora of diverse repertoire presentations at NCKP 2021 and began the presentation by highlighting a few other sessions that focus on similar topics as her own.

Dr. McCain listed the various projects she herself is involved in (DEI Editor of *Piano Magazine*, Program Advisor for the Frances Clark Center, the McCain Duo, and the LA Phil YOLA National Symposium), but admits she still feels like sometimes she fails when she looks at the repertoire of her own studio. In her research, there was only one female composer, one black composer, three American composers, two Latin American composers, and two living composers in the 135 competition pieces she examined. The most programmed works were Bach, Beethoven, Chopin, and Liszt, and less than 9% of composers were from marginalized groups.

The presenter then asked the audience to jot down on a sheet of paper the various composers that they are programming in their own studios. She shared her own findings first: the presenter found she programmed Scarlatti, Beethoven, Chopin, Debussy, Kabalevsky, Mozart, Fauré, Copland, Bach, and Clara Schumann. She admitted that her own list is disappointing for herself and emphasized that this list is exclusive to her precollege students; her collegiate students play a lot of underrepresented composers. The presenter then explained her formula for the inclusion of diverse repertoire in her students' program. The six different aspects for students to think about are:
- Gender
- Ethnicity
- Race/colorism
- Country of origin
- Living composers
- Underperformed

Dr. McCain helped the audience imagine a revitalized world of competitions, where there is a diverse range of music chosen by the teachers. The group then went into breakout rooms and were instructed to create two intermediate programs of three pieces, and to brainstorm two other resources for intermediate students. The breakout rooms had five minutes to create their programs. The breakout groups came back, and Dr. McCain asked each spokesperson from the group to explain their program. The pieces and composers shared by groups were:

- "Star Light, Star Bright" (Alexina Louie)
- Nathaniel Dett (no intermediate piece was found)
- Florence Price
- *Circus Sonatina* (Chee-Hwa Tan)
- *Portraits in Jazz* (Valerie Capers)
- Johann Jacob Froberger
- "When Rivers Flow on Mars" (Nancy Telfer)
- Brazilian composers
- "Just for Now" (Diane Hidy)
- "Mean Little Monsters" (Diane Hidy)
- "The Months Song" (Diane Hidy)

Dr. McCain then shared the program she designed using her template:
- Fantasia in G Minor TWV 33:8 (Telemann)
- "Dance from a Deserted Plantation" from *Piano Works for Children* (William Grant Still)
- "Recess" from *Naughtycal Glimpses* (Maria Corley)

Dr. McCain shared information concerning the Hal Leonard free showcase later at the conference. The presenter explained that the group will go into breakout rooms again, this time to create advanced programs using the formula. They are also asked to categorize composers into five categories (Baroque, Classical, Romantic, Impressionistic, and Contemporary). Dr. McCain's four programs are as follows:
- Prelude and Fugue No. 6 in D Minor BWV 851 (Bach)
- *Six Variations on an Original Theme in G Major* (Beethoven)
- Scherzo No. 2 (Clara Schumann)

- Les Sauvages (Rameau)
- Fantasy in C Minor (Mozart)
- "Forest Scenes" Op. 66 No. 4 (Samuel Coleridge Taylor)

- Piano Sonata in G Major HOB XVI: 40 (Haydn)
- Piano Sonata in C Minor, Movement 1 (Chaminade)
- *Cowherd's Flute* (He Luting)

- Sonata in F-sharp Minor (Clementi)
- "The White Peacock" (Charles Griffes)
- Etude No. 11 in G-sharp Minor (H. Leslie Adams)

A participant asked Dr. McCain about accessibility of music, specifically regarding unpublished and copyright issues when performing this music. Dr. McCain explained that the music can be difficult to find, but all of the music on her programs are easy to find and accessible for teachers.

Loud & Clear:
Looking at Piano Pedagogy and Female Composers Through an Intersectional Lens
Presented by Olivia Adams
Wednesday, July 28, 2021
Recorded by Todd Van Kekerix

This presentation explored the history of gender and racial inequity through the lens of the piano syllabi of various Canadian schools of music and presented strong data suggesting that women composers of color have been underrepresented. Adams shared her findings of unconscious gender- and racially-biased syllabi by sharing over fifty years of data points that indicate why these syllabi have an intersectionality problem.

Polling data from a recent survey by Adams indicated that 57.3 percent of the respondents agree that racism is a problem in music education. However, only 16 percent of teachers were actively addressing this problem by teaching music by BIPOC composers.

Adams then shared data analysis of her examination of the syllabi of Conservatory Canada and the Royal Conservatory of Music over the last fifty years. The data specifically explored what percentage of music by female composers and BIWOC composers is featured in each syllabi. Both syllabi have expanded their inclusion of women composers over the fifty years, but the inclusion of BIPOC women composers has been statistically insignificant.

To argue the point of how the problem is perpetuated, Adams presented the Conservatory Cycle of Exclusion and used it to explain what has kept students from learning music by BIPOC women composers. Since they are only marginally included in the piano syllabi, their music is not heard at festivals or exams.

Adams used intersectionality, an intellectual framework by Kimberlé Crenshaw, to argue that there is not only a gender problem to consider, but also a racial one. The problem is not addressed by simply adding more BIPOC women composers. The process for choosing music for the syllabi must be reframed and reshaped. Adams argues that it is crucial to consider an intersectionality approach to inclusion practices of Conservatory Canada and the Royal Conservatory of Music.

Adams concluded the presentation with suggestions of pedagogical piano repertoire by BIPOC women composers to consider when addressing the aforementioned problem in music education. The presenter suggested the following teaching collections and individual pieces:

- *Piano Teaching Music, Vol. 1 & 2* by Florence Price
- *Flake upon Flake upon…* by Hope Lee

- *Children of Light* by Karen Tanaka
- *Star Light, Star Bright* and *Small Beautiful Things* by Alexina Louie
- *New Music for New Musicians* and *Clavierstuck* by Melika M. Fitzhugh
- *Portraits in Jazz* by Valerie Capers
- "Dança das fadas" by Chiquinha Gonzaga
- "Falling in the Water" by Karen Sunabacka
- *Canadian Floral Emblems* by Beverly McKiver

Adams closed her session by suggesting the following action steps for moving forward: educate, incorporate, advocate, elevate, and celebrate the music of BIPOC women composers.

Absolutely! Pathways to Expression and Artistry for Special Learners
Presented by Scott Price
Wednesday, July 28, 2021
Recorded by Stephanie Mercer

In this presentation Dr. Price discussed how his special-learner students with autism have actually taught him what the best practices are for teaching them expression in piano playing. Even though these special learners may not communicate or understand social behaviors, they can still play expressively. He emphasized that just because a special learner has less ability to express thoughts and emotions doesn't mean they have fewer thoughts or emotions. In his presentation, Dr. Price discussed specialized vocabulary and concise, detailed teaching strategies that address balance, voicing, dynamics, phrasing, articulations, tone quality, and pedal usage that help students express themselves at the piano.

Breaking down the teaching process, Dr. Price came up with five factors that guide his teaching. The first is correct body position and proper bench height. The student may have to gain strength to sit correctly. The special learner's teacher will have to teach the student to adjust the bench themselves if needed. The ideal position at the piano is the same as for neural-typical students. The upper arm and forearm should be relaxed and suspended above the keyboard creating a plane of motion so the fingers can move freely. Once these are correct, the fingers usually follow along correctly.

The second factor Dr. Price brings attention to is to teach special learners the meanings of the words we as teachers are using. Musicians have specialized vocabulary that may not make sense to every learner. Musicians also have different uses for words that may confuse students. Teachers need to make sure the student hears the word, has time to comprehend the word, and teachers need to explain what the word means in the context of the music.

The third factor for teaching special learners is use of the correct vocabulary. Analogies and metaphors will not always work with these students. Teachers need to use very specific and literal vocabulary. Teachers need to say what we mean and mean what we say with the correct tone of voice.

The fourth factor for teaching special learners is to give the student time to hear, understand, process, and put into action the instructions. Some students may need two minutes to process whereas some may need twenty minutes. Teachers should let students take as long as needed to fully comprehend what is being asked of them.

The fifth factor is that the special learner student needs constant assurance, reassurance, celebration, and validation. It is hard for younger students to conceptualize and to be consistent. The teacher should celebrate every attempt and reassure the student's attempts with validation. Possibilities for teachers who work with special learners include using concise, literal, and specific language. The first possibility Dr. Price discussed was dynamics. Instead of using *forte* or *piano,* Dr. Price suggests using the words strong or gentle. Balance is hard for special learners as it is for neural-typical students. He suggests using specific instructions in the score so the student can see the two different instructions for the different hands. In the place of the *crescendo* and *diminuendo,* Dr. Price suggests using very literal and specific terms to explain the desired effect. Instead of using abstract words, the teacher should use words that tell the body what to do.

Articulation markings should be translated into literal directions. For example, when explaining *staccato*, the teacher should tell the student that the dot under or over the notes means to have a space between the notes. For *legato,* a very detailed instruction can help a student play the desired effect. Instead of explaining that, in a two-note slur, there is not a "hiccup" on the last note, one can explain that the first note is strong and the second note is weaker.

For the term *ritardando,* Dr. Price says to never use the shortened word *ritard* because of its possible negative misinterpretation; instead, teachers should use *r-i-t-*. when requesting the student to slow down. For a *fermata,* Dr. Price recommends writing in counts for the students to hold the note. Pedaling may require the building up of strength in the student, but is possible to do so expressively with lots of repetition and guidance using very specific terms. For tempo, Dr. Price suggests using familiar descriptive words rather than the given musical term.

These are some ways of approaching the teaching of expressive playing with special learners. The goal is for the students to be able to follow all the markings in the score. To make this happen, teachers should always use specific literal vocabulary and use a step-by-step breakdown of the music. Dr. Price reminded teachers that it is also important that the teacher has a lot of patience and faith that the student will master expressive playing in their own time.

Does One Size Fit All? Interpreting Ragtime Piano
Presented by Glenn Utsch
Wednesday, July 28, 2021
Recorded by Sarah Leonard

Eubie Blake's *Charleston Rag* was played at the start of the presentation. Dr. Utsch, who previously presented on lesser-known ragtime piano composers at the 2019 NCKP, put together this lecture recital to explore interpretation of the style. In a literature review, the presenter found that there are many writings about historical and theoretical approaches to ragtime, but very little information on its interpretation.

In reference to the title, "one size fits all" refers to use of the same interpretive style when playing all ragtime pieces, typically loud and fast. Dr. Utsch hypothesized that all ragtime pieces should have their own unique sound and emotional feel. The presenter used the following quotes to illustrate this point:

"Indications for tempo, dynamics and phrasing on rag scores show that loud and fast interpretations are not adequate," says Ronald Nadeau in John Edward Hasse's *Ragtime: Its History, Composers, and Music*. "We wish to say here that the Joplin ragtime is destroyed by careless or imperfect rendering. And very often, good players lose the effect entirely by playing too fast," states Scott Joplin in his *School of Ragtime*.

Rags are notated with a variety of tempos. Classic rags, specifically those by Scott Joplin, James Scott, Joseph Lamb, and May Aufderheide, are notated with slower tempos such as "not fast," "slow march," and *moderato*. More lively tempos, *allegretto* and *allegro vivace* for example, can be found in the works of Eubie Blake and Charles L. Johnson.

Max Morath, a long-time performer of ragtime, shared the following advice with the presenter, "Ragtime is music, so it should be played musically and expressively." Dr. Utsch noted the importance of a well-tuned instrument when playing musically. However, the condition of pianos traditionally used to perform ragtime were often poorly kept and out of tune. This resulted in the "honkytonk" sound associated with old ragtime styles, though this is not necessary in today's performances.

The presenter's first interpretive point of interest was to include *rubato* periodically to feature "special" chords and phrases. This helps the music breathe. Dr. Utsch performed Joseph Lamb's *American Beauty* to illustrate the effect of *rubato*. In this performance, he illuminated the German-augmented-sixth chord on beat two of the second measure by use of *rubato*, which draws attention to what he calls "its special beauty." The presenter noted that, because of the repeat, this is not necessary to do both times.

The next element was to observe the marked dynamics and add more when needed. Muriel Pollock's *Rooster Rag* and Charles L. Johnson's rendition of Doc Brown's *Cakewalk* were used to illustrate additional dynamic markings in the B sections.

Additionally, performers should play with balance between hands and voicing similar to classical music performance, favoring the top of each chord. Using the opening of Scott Joplin's *Easy Winners*, Dr. Utsch demonstrated how these two aspects combine for musical interpretation. Another tactic that can be used for interpretation is varying the pedal on the repeat. An option includes *legato* vs sparse pedaling to bring out the ragtime rhythm. The presenter used this combination of pedal techniques in his rendition of *Dusty* by May Aufderheide.

There are additional options for varying repeats. The presenter offered ideas about variations of previously mentioned elements, bringing out an inner voice rather than the top voice, leaving out *rubato*, and changing the dynamics for some examples. Aside from this, the performer may alter the bass and melodic lines. To illustrate this point, he used the B section of *Dusty* by May Aufderheide. As written, the bass line is made up of eighth notes. In order to alter the bassline, the presenter improvised with passing notes and repeated tones with sixteenth notes. Using the same piece, he utilized continuous sixteenth notes along with patterns and sequence to vary the melodic line on the repeat. His intention was to use these elements to give more rhythmic motion and overall change the repeated section.

The aforementioned points can be summarized:
- Include *rubato* periodically to feature "special" chords and phrases.
- Pay attention to dynamics and add more when necessary.
- Play with balance between the hands, and voicing towards the top.
- Vary pedaling on the repeat.
- Vary the repeated sections with differences in previous elements, and/or modifying the melody and bass lines.

The presenter believes ragtime should be performed evenly, both eighths and sixteenths, as the style came before jazz. Dr. Utsch does not believe ragtime should be played like classical music at all, though many of the interpretive concepts are similar. Ragtime was traditionally performed in bars, clubs, and brothels. There should be a rhythmic edge to the performance. Because ragtime was played for entertainment, it should be performed musically with joy and vitality. To close the lecture, Dr. Utsch performed *Maple Leaf Rag* by Scott Joplin.

The Blues: A Colorful Framework for Igniting Creativity
Presented by Leila Viss
Wednesday, July 28, 2021
Recorded by Curtis Pavey

In this session, Leila Viss shared her passion for teaching the twelve-bar blues and making this relevant and engaging for young piano students. Already a pathway to creativity and improvisation, the presenter's approach to teaching the twelve-bar blues included numerous creative activities for students from the beginning to advanced level of study.

In introducing her topic, Viss explained the importance of understanding the origin of the blues and her personal connection with the genre. Developed during the enslavement of African Americans, the presenter shared that a full history of the blues deserves its own session and she reflected upon the tragedy that such a beautiful and creative musical style was born in such tragic circumstances. Viss first heard and developed her teaching methods while teaching group piano and studying as a master's degree student at the University of Denver. During this period of exploration, she fell in love with Eric Clapton's song *Walkin' Blues* and became more interested when she began working alongside pedagogue Bradley Sowash. Together, they developed a partnership called "88 Creative Keys," which offers workshops for teacher development.

The presentation began with a discussion of her personal reasons to teach the blues, which included the numerous creative elements within a strong formal structure. Reminding session participants of the basic form, she asked them to find a nearby keyboard and play along in C major. Throughout the interactive presentation, Viss called on participants to try out her suggestions in real time. She broke down her approach to teaching the blues in many different steps, beginning with hands separately. In her work with students, she first helps them to develop a left-hand pattern to maintain a steady beat. This can include a single bass note, an open fifth, or the "back-and-forth" pattern alternating between a fifth and a sixth. Once this harmonic foundation is established, she has students explore a right-hand melodic pattern. The melodic pattern is based on words from the titles, which she helps students to choose creatively. For students who struggle to come up with an imaginative title, Viss suggests using paint strips, Crayola crayon colors, favorite books, and even the *Decide Now* app to get a student started.

Once the student has a title, Viss works with the student to develop a melodic pattern that matches the rhythm of the words. By chanting the words together, they can explore a melodic pattern that best reflects the title. She specifically asks students to develop their melody based on scale degrees: 1, flat 3, natural 3, and 5. These scale degrees function as members of the blues scale and match the harmonic foundation being performed in the left hand. After establishing some melodic material, she asks students to develop bookends–an intro and an outro based on the same musical material.

Viss demonstrated her success with students through several videos of their compositions. She showed how she used the twelve-bar blues in a beginning music group class, having students on a variety of different instruments besides keyboard including drums. She also helped students to record their compositions, placing the recordings in a book-creating app that allowed the student to create a finished product that they could show to family and friends. She also suggested apps such as *Music Clock* and other programs that could develop backing tracks for the blues.

Encouraging others to explore this in their own teaching, Viss told participants that mistakes will happen and are part of the important musical and creative process. She asked participants to break down their own perfectionism, give students opportunities to improvise in low-stakes scenarios, and to make it fun for all.

Parents, Pianists, and Pedagogues: Prioritizing Self-Care During a Pandemic
Presented by Lesley McAllister, Laura Amoriello, Sara Ernst,
Andrea McAlister, and Paola Savvidou
Wednesday, July 28, 2021
Recorded by Curtis Pavey

In this presentation, five leading pedagogues and mothers discussed their experiences of balancing their work as faculty members with their busy lives as parents during the COVID-19 pandemic. Throughout the session, the panelists discussed important lessons they learned as they struggled to not only take care of themselves, but also serve as an effective teacher and parent during a challenging time.

Dr. Lesley McAllister opened the presentation with her personal experience working at Baylor University while also being a parent to two young children. In her experience, Dr. McAllister struggled initially with the anxiety of trying to balance taking care of her children and meeting their educational needs while still working full time. Dr. McAllister, whose research focuses on yoga and movement activities at the piano, described the importance of developing self-care routines that included regular exercise such as daily walking or jogging as well as a daily yoga routine. Besides this, Dr. McAllister shared how she dealt with prioritizing tasks; a person with a very high work ethic, she discussed personal acceptance that she could not always complete each task to the best of her abilities. In other words, she stated that she could sometimes earn a "B" instead of an "A" in particular tasks as she worked vigorously to maintain control over the many competing interests in her life. Additionally, Dr. McAllister suggested concern for future employment culture and expectations. Given the flexibility of virtual teaching, she expressed fears that employers may expect more from employees and overstep healthy boundaries between work and life.

Dr. Laura Amoriello shared her experiences next, and began by providing context into her unique situation. While her husband worked from home before the pandemic, she struggled with work-life boundaries due to her living room becoming her new office. Dr. Amoriello's young daughter suffered from some sleep difficulties during this time and this caused her to also suffer from extensive sleep loss and migraines. Dr. Amoriello's experiences led her to discover five lessons that she shared with participants. Impermanence was an important realization—that everything is only temporary and that this challenging time would eventually pass. She described feeling a constant duality of emotions between frustration and languish while at the same time feeling joyous. Dr. Amoriello, similar to Dr. McAllister, described the importance of accepting her own imperfection and knowing that parenting was a continual learning experience for all. This led her to develop a deeper sense of personal compassion along with mindfulness, meditation, and self-care practice. Dr. Amoriello similarly closed her portion with comments about the need for continued conversations about how to improve life as a parent in academia.

Dr. Sara Ernst offered similar lessons learned from her experiences during the pandemic, focusing on the positive changes she made to cope with the anxiety she faced. Dr. Ernst developed a number of self-care routines to help her focus on being the best parent she could be to her two young children while maintaining a busy teaching schedule at the University of South Carolina. Time that would have otherwise been spent commuting could now be focused on restful walks in her neighborhood, baking for relief from anxiety, and practicing daily gratitude. In her daily work, she noticed herself becoming more open with her students about personal struggles and acknowledging that some days were more hopeful and positive than others. Despite her increased concern for her children's safety, Dr. Ernst was able to develop traditions and routines that kept her focused on the many positive elements of her life.

Dr. Andrea McAlister's discussion followed and she similarly focused on sharing some of the positive lessons she had learned as she developed coping mechanisms during the pandemic. A mother of two with a husband who worked from home, Dr. McAlister described how the initial onset of the pandemic led her to balance her busy teaching schedule at Oberlin with the need to take care of her children and their concerns. During this time, Dr. McAlister insisted that one of the most important lessons for her was continuing daily routines to keep her and her family focused on completing their work. For instance, Dr. McAlister took daily walks with her son in the morning to get him into the mindset of going to virtual school each day. She added that she had to embrace imperfection during this time and regularly reevaluate daily priorities using her family's unique numbering system. Besides this, Dr. McAlister shared her family's "Happy Jar," in which they would collect memories of happy occasions throughout the pandemic. These memories helped the whole family develop a deeper sense of gratitude during this dark time.

Dr. Paola Savvidou concluded the panelists' remarks and shared the challenges of balancing her life as an academic and a mother of a toddler and a newborn during the pandemic. Dr. Savvidou's experience during the pandemic was challenging due to anxiety, sleep deprivation, and the high expectations she set for herself as a scholar and as a mother. A wellness expert, Dr. Savvidou's role at the University of Michigan gained increased importance as she led wellness initiatives throughout the pandemic and was working to finish a manuscript for a new book. The stress of these experiences required her to reflect about her own sense of perfectionism and how she could give herself permission to make mistakes. She accepted that she needed to give kindness to herself on a daily basis through yoga, baking, and time devoted to her children. She cited Bruno Bettelheim's book *The Good Enough Parent* and the encouraging research that helped her to accept her own limits as a parent, especially during this challenging time.

The session ended with a few questions about the role of performance in each of these pianists' lives and concluded on a hopeful tone about the ways in which all had found ways to positively adapt to the stresses of being pedagogues, pianists, and parents during the pandemic.

Music & Empathy: Ambassadors for Tomorrow
Presented by Susan Bruckner
Wednesday, July 28, 2021
Reported by Todd Van Kekerix

Bruckner's presentation contained three parts and began with a poll inquiring how often attendees have their students get together to share or make music. Possible answers were: 1) weekly, 2) monthly, 3) four to six times a year, or 4) three times a year or less. The results were not discussed.

Part 1 – What's the Connection?

Bruckner states that researchers are looking at two types of empathy: cognitive and affective. Cognitive is described as a rational understanding or the ability to take one's perspective. Affective empathy is an emotional connection or the ability to feel what they feel and take their perspective. Empathy is not a fixed trait.

In 1999, a mirror neuron system (MNS) was discovered which has shown an intimate relationship between imitation and empathy. Oxytocin, the "feel good" hormone and dopamine, which is connected to the reward system, most closely relate to music and are seen in the bloodstream when making music together. Thus, the more you make music with someone, the more you relate to that person.

The functional near-infrared spectroscopy (FNIRS) device has allowed researchers to gather data with the MNS.

Part 2 – Research Around the World

In the second section of her presentation, Bruckner shared research and projects that are taking place around the world. She introduced the lead researchers and project masterminds.

Laurel Trainor, Director of McMaster University Neuroscience and Music Lab.
- Interpersonal synchrony increases presocial behavior. In other words, this study found that babies who were bounced in synchrony (rhythmic entrainment) with a researcher were more likely to help retrieve a dropped item.
- McMaster University also has a "Livelab" which is outfitted with devices to study the differences between actively making music and actively listening to music.

Assai Habibi, University of Southern California Brain and Creativity Institute
- Studied the effects of music lessons, soccer, or no extracurricular activity. All the music students show a much higher rate of prosocial behavior.

Eiluned Pearce, Oxford University
- Studied choir group vs journaling group vs crafting group of middle-aged people. The study showed that after just a two-hour session there was a higher level of prosocial behavior in the music group as well as a higher pain threshold.

Music for Life project in Capetown, Africa
- Music therapists supplanted gangs with music therapy. After school, subjects could choose various styles of music making. The results from the project are that there are now fewer gangs.

Part 3 – Music: A Social Superpower

The last section was how music has an ability to be a superpower. Bruckner illustrated this point by sharing the work of Daniel Barenboim and Edward Said and their Western-Eastern Divan Orchestra, which is comprised of young people from Israel, the Palestinian territories, Lebanon, Jordan, Syria, Egypt, Turkey, and Iran with the intention of developing empathy in the musicians.

She shared a powerful quote from Edward Said to illustrate the power of music: "Presiding over our efforts, students and teachers alike, has been the spirit of music, which I would want to insist is neither a sentimental panacea, nor a facile solution for every problem, but rather a practical utopia, whose presence and practice in our driven world is sorely needed and, in all sorts of ways, intensely instructive."

She concluded the presentation by emphasizing that music teachers have the power to cast a long impact through our work with the young and socially connected, as they learn affective and cognitive empathic skills which come naturally to musicians, and ultimately, leading to stewards of commitment, motivation, the ability to listen and to work together in difficult situations.

How Our Brains Learn Best: Surprising Practice Tips We Tend to Avoid
Presented by Barbara Fast
Wednesday, July 28, 2021
Recorded by Cicilia Yudha

When our brain encounters a new task, it works the hardest. It is also when learning takes place. Naturally, we tend to avoid this hard work. In this session Dr. Barbara Fast shared four main thoughts on practice habits:
- Interleaved vs. Blocked Practice
- Variable vs. Constant Practice
- Hardest First vs. Easiest First Practice
- Developing an Aural Model vs. Just Playing the Notes

Interleaved vs. Blocked Practice

What is Interleaved or Interspersed Practice? It is a technique to organize and divide study materials in smaller divisions that then could be re-arranged to promote enduring and flexible learning. It is the opposite of the Blocked Practice method where there is only one concept that is learned repetitively at a given time. Interleaved Practice could feel unnatural at the beginning. It requires planning, greater focus, more effort, and time discipline. Furthermore, it delays instant gratification. However, studies suggest that when we learn music by interleaving our practice, the brain functions more effectively. As the brain restarts the learning process, it facilitates long-term retention. Fast notes that in the class piano setting, when Interleaved Teaching is applied, whereby various activities are rotated, the pacing of the class and students' engagement increase. In learning repertoire or a technical drill, such as establishing fingering for a difficult passage or securing tricky transitions, a cell phone timer can be a great tool in interleaving practice.

Variable vs. Constant Practice

In discussing Variable Practice vs Constant Practice, Fast highlights performance psychologist Noa Kageyama's research.[1] Constant practice is a common approach to practicing; "practice the same skill over and over again, exactly the same way." Constant practice creates the illusion of rapid learning because one tends to see improved performance during that practice session. However, this technique is not effective and reliable in the long run because it trains a skill under one specific condition. Inspired by his research on the world of sports, Kageyama suggests variable practice. Practice under various comfortable and (un)comfortable conditions. For example, practice when one's hands are cold or stiff. Practice slower or faster. Wear restrictive clothes. The variable conditions allow the learner to extract the essence of the transferable skills that need to be mastered, regardless of varying performance conditions. Fast also mentioned her engaging interview with pianist Spencer Myer about practicing.[2] In addition to muscle memory work, Myer believes in the importance of strengthening the "other memory" work which engages the brain to help enforce security in a performance. One can achieve this by practicing slowly and deliberately, by doing rhythmic variations (and maybe altering the variation midway), by transposing a passage to a different key, by committing to a non-stop run-through, *etc*. As any performance on stage will always feel different, we need to create "extreme change in physicality" during our practice to ensure the brain stays engaged.

Hardest First vs. Easiest First Practice
In the last two points of Fast's presentation, she introduces two concepts from *iPractice*, a book that Jennifer Mishra and she co-authored.[3] The idea of Hardest First Practice vs Easiest First was also inspired by research on sports.[4] Studies of Olympic figure skaters' training sessions suggest that the successful skaters practice more difficult moves first. In practicing a piece of music, addressing the hardest passages immediately makes way for a more secure final performance. For example, difficult transitions in and out of passages or the ending of Leopold Mozart's *Burleske*, where the left hand must secure the octave jump from G to D and back to G.

Developing an Aural Model vs. Just Playing the Notes
Lastly, instead of "Just Playing the Notes," Fast suggests "Developing an Aural Mode" to make practice more efficient. She shared many excellent teaching and practice tips teachers can do with technology already at hand: the cellular phone. Engage students to record and immediately evaluate their performance during their practice. In her experience, assigning students to submit "Slow Perfect Recording" proves a successful long-term result. Another idea is to assign students to record their performance three times throughout the week. Assign review of a specific musical detail for each recording, *e.g.*, dynamic, steady tempo, *etc*. Teachers can also model this practice during a lesson. Record the student's performance and review it together. Asking the students "Did you reach your goal?" helps them to listen more critically and prepares them to be more engaged during their practice at home. Practicing with a metronome can also help identify hesitations and correct the problems. In learning new music, where no recording is available, Fast suggests slow-downer applications, such as "ASD." Additionally, one could create an Aural Model (by recording at 50% the speed) or enter the notes to NoteFlight or similar online notation software.[5]

In summary, as studies suggest, when the brain encounters a new task, it requires more effort. Most learning takes place when the brain works hardest. By understanding this concept, musicians can capitalize this learning opportunity and practice more efficiently. Fast offers valuable takeaway phrases: "Change things up," "Teach Hardest First," and "Practice Makes Perfect *If You Change It Up*."

Notes

[1] Noa Kageyama, The Bulletproof Musician – bulletproofmusician.com

[2] Barbara Fast, "Engaging the Brain: Practice Tips from an Interview with Spencer Myer," *Piano Magazine,* Summer 2020.

[3] Jennifer Mishra and Barbara Fast, *iPractice: Technology in the 21st Century Music Practice Room* New York: Oxford University Press, 2019.

[4] J.M. Deakon and Stephen Cobley. "An Examination of the Practice Environment in Figure Skating and Volleyball: A Search for Deliberate Practice," *Expert Performance in Sports: Advances in Research on Sport Expertise,* Janet Starkes & K.A. Ericsson, 2003. 116-135.

[5] Jennifer Mishra and Barbara Fast, "Practicing in the New World: A Case Study of Practicing Strategies Related to the Premiere of Contemporary Music." *Music Performance Research.* 7.

Go Forward and Make Beautiful Music
Presented by Spencer Myer
Wednesday, July 28, 2021
Recorded by Jessie Welsh

This session explored tried-and-true techniques for achieving a full, warm, and beautiful tone at the piano. The presenter included three main ways to produce a free and resonant tone and provided numerous exceptional demonstrations of these techniques with musical excerpts from standard piano literature. The three main points included a diagonal-motion approach to the keyboard, a circular (or "oval") motion of the hand/wrist/arm as a complete mechanism, and natural follow-through movement from the arm aiding the hand.

Dr. Myer began this session by describing how one creates sound at the instrument. He advocates for sound created with the freest bodily motion, as this creates the most resonant and colorful sound. Vertical, downward motions, on the other hand, lock the arm and increase the velocity of the hammer striking the string. This creates a "knocking" or percussive sound and often breaks the harmony of the hand/wrist/arm unit. While a certain amount of "pushing" and even tension is, in fact, required to create sound, it is the efficient release of this sound that must be considered.

Next, Dr. Myer turned his attention to the three main ways of "going forward" into the key to create this beautiful tone. The first, a use of a diagonal-motion approach to the keyboard, is a combination of a down *and* forward motion. This adjustment slows the velocity of the hammer, takes advantage of the natural use of arm weight, and applies to both loud and soft passages by freeing the arm and allowing it to have the most natural movement. The presenter provided the caveat that these motions must be efficient and judicious, as tempo often requires quick combinations of movement patterns. The inclusion of musical examples was highly effective, as Dr. Myer beautifully demonstrated the effects of this natural, diagonal movement pattern.

The next "forward" movement pattern Dr. Myer identified was a circular gesture. (He provided the caveat that he now refers to this as an "oval" gesture, as this visual image allows the arm to remain aligned and prohibits additional elbow movement.) This movement pattern is best utilized for successions of notes in two different directions. Without this gesture, the fingers are often forced to overwork, which may lead to tension or overuse. In order to achieve a full sound with this choreography, the presenter noted, the movement pattern must begin with the full arm and the elbow must remain free and aligned. The presenter again included beautiful demonstrations, showing the efficacy of his movement approach at the keyboard.

The final "forward" motion discussed in the presentation was the follow-through, which the presenter described as the natural outworking of the release or end of a movement pattern.

Dr. Myer compared this to the natural movement of a baseball bat after it is swung. He carefully pointed out, however, that this movement must not be artificially *added*, but it should instead be a natural movement pattern that allows the whole arm/wrist/hand to breathe and prepare for the next movement pattern. It is a subtle upward motion that is a natural result of thinking forward. Once again, the presenter showcased the value of this movement pattern by demonstrating elegant, resonant, and carefully crafted phrases.

Dr. Myers's ideas were succinct, effective, and validated by his beautiful performances. The musical excerpts were well-selected and included some of the best-known passages in all of the piano repertoire. The effect was such that—even over distance—the session participants could hear the changes in his sound when he utilized these forward movement patterns: it was rich, resonant, and free. The session concluded with a brief question-and-answer time during which the presenter fielded questions about scale crossings, rotation, repetitive passagework, and other technical challenges. The presenter warmly engaged participants and demonstrated his technical solutions to their questions.

Chopin's *Polonaise Fantasy*: A Love Story Expressed through Song and Dance
Presented by Carol Leone
Wednesday, July 28, 2021
Recorded by Allison Fog

Chopin juxtaposes a love story using song and dance together with a dignified Polish dance in his *Polonaise Fantasy, Op. 61*. Some musicians view this piece as a complicated jumble of ideas, however Dr. Carol Leone presented a cohesive and passionate story. She highlighted five special features, walked the audience through the story and structure of the piece while playing excerpts, and concluded with a performance.

The first special feature is Character, which includes "Polish heroic gestures." These are indicated by the *Maestoso* marking, which meant dignity and pride to Chopin. A short video excerpt from Tchaikovsky's *Eugene Onegin* illustrated this dignified character. The second special feature is that Chopin's title reveals the structure of the piece; introduction, polonaise, fantasy, conclusion. The third special feature is the key that Chopin also chose for many of his works, A-flat major. This key is full of feeling and expression and is considered to be delicate and tender. The fourth special feature is Chopin's use of two main rhythmic motives, one of which appears in the introduction, and one that is a more typical polonaise rhythm. The fifth special feature is the use of two main melodic themes, which Dr. Leone identifies as "Let Us Dance," (which appears five times in the piece) and "How I Love You." In addition, she has created lyrics for the melodic themes to help us imagine the song-like character in the piece.

The structure of the *Polonaise Fantasy* is in four parts, beginning with the Introduction, which is twenty-one measures long. The introduction features the first rhythmic motive, punctuated by arpeggios, which give the *Maestoso* designation a dreamy quality. (Interestingly, Chopin's first version of the piece did not include the arpeggios). The first song-like theme occurs at the end of the introduction and is a duet between soprano and bass.

> *I hear the Music stirring my soul tonight, dear.*
> *It casts away all sorrow and grief and pain.*
> *All sorrow and Grief.*

The Polonaise is the second part in the overall structure of the piece and is presented in three sections. First, the polonaise rhythm signals the start of the dance, followed by the "Let Us Dance" theme. After that, Chopin writes a special theme A, which is only presented once in the entire piece. The dancing theme is played in two keys before Chopin returns to a transformed, dreamy version of "Let Us Dance" that uses a triplet figure in the bass. The third section of the polonaise opens with a new "thoughtful" theme, which leads to special theme B. The conclusion of the third section transitions to the dream-fantasy world.

The Fantasy is the third overall part in the structure of the piece, and in this section, Chopin changes the key to B major, and the tempo to *Piu Lento*. The left hand plays a nocturne-like accompaniment while the "I Love You" theme is played in the right hand.
Dr. Leone expressed this theme lyrically:

> *How I love you*
> *How I love you*
> *How I want you*
> *How I need you*

The "thoughtful" theme makes a second appearance, followed by special theme C. (Each of Chopin's special themes appear just one time, and always follow the thoughtful theme). After an extended trill, the fantasy concludes with a reminiscence of the "I Love You" theme.

The Conclusion of the entire piece features a return to the *Maestoso* introductory theme, delaying the dramatic end somewhat. Now in the key of C major, there is a return to the thoughtful theme, followed by a suspenseful build-up to the climax of the piece. This climax is virtuosic in nature, and is paired with the following lyrics:

> *Oh! What a Glorious Life!*
> *Oh how our spirits light with the music in view, as we're*
> *Turning, spinning, loving, yearning,*
> *When I am dancing with YOU!*

"How I Love You" is heard again, transformed by dotted rhythms in the left hand, ushering in a spirit of triumph and hope:

> *When we sing and dance together,*
> *Hearts entwined forever,*
> *We can dream of sharing our lives...evermore!*

The music of the dance dies away after an impressive Coda based on "How I Love You," followed by one final, "dignified" chord.

Next, the attendees heard a performance of the lyrical excerpts, sung by Camille King (soprano).

Before concluding the presentation with a performance of *Polonaise Fantasy*, Dr. Leone explained how she uses a DS keyboard, which features an octave range that is five and a half inches wide, instead of the standard six and a half inches. Playing this piece on a narrower keyboard allows her to avoid injury and reach all the keys.

Promoting Students' Creativity: A Linear Approach to Piano Harmony and Texture
Presented by Christos Tsitsaros
Wednesday, July 28, 2021
Recorded by Michael Clark

Dr. Tsitsaros' session sought to generate ideas to awaken students' musical creativity. Emphasizing that creativity is not limited to composition, he recommended harmonization and improvisation as valuable creative activities and prerequisites to composition. To begin, Dr. Tsitsaros' performed an arrangement of "Silent Night" harmonized with blocked, root position primary chords. Though this harmonization is technically correct, it represents only the beginning of many possibilities. Dr. Tsitsaros suggests that students whose harmonic creativity stops at this level may have no other tools to work with and therefore no other options. They may understand certain theoretical concepts cognitively but do not know how to apply them functionally. Perhaps they have not made the connection between theoretical knowledge and sound. As a result of this lack of preparation, they may not take pleasure in creative activities.

Dr. Tsitsaros proposed that a systematic approach to creative activities can help students unleash their expressive potential. Rather than a dry, theoretical approach, he favors relating multiple musical elements to facilitate learning in a "cognitive, creative, and functional way." Dr. Tsitsaros' approach involved four main elements:

- Short improvisational assignments and games. These allow students to be inventive and spontaneous as they creatively use patterns like artists play with clay.
- Harmonization and chording assignments on simple melodies. These experiences allow students to experiment with harmonic, melodic, and textural (voice-leading) elements within a more structured frame.
- Free improvisation and composition in various genres, forms, and themes.
- Study of excerpts from the standard musical literature so that students can recognize compositional elements in music. He illustrated this type of analysis through the opening of Mozart's *Sonata in G Major*, K. 283, observing the contrary motion of the outer voices.

Dr. Tsitaros used two familiar tunes to illustrate the many possibilities for creating piano textures. He outlined three main ways in which the voices may be distributed between the hands:

- The right hand may have the melody while the left hand plays the bass line and other harmonic layers;
- the right hand may play both the melody and harmonic layers while the left hand plays the bass line;

- or the right hand may play the melody and some harmonic layers while the left hand plays the bass line and other harmonic layers.

When crafting textures, he encourages students to avoid thinking of chords, but to instead think of layers of lines. Dr. Tsitsaros presented many tools for giving interest to the linear motion of the supporting layers, including combinations of primary and secondary chords in root and inverted positions, diatonic and chromatic passing notes, imitation, counter-melodies, chromatic chords (secondary dominants, diminished, and augmented chords), and pedal points (tonic, dominant, subdominant). He advised students to let the linear motion generate the choice of harmony and chord position, rather than merely moving in blocks.

The final portion of the presentation focused on specific harmonies. He explored Chopin's "sixth chord," better known as a 13th chord which features a quartal arrangement in the upper voices. Dr. Tsitsaros traced how Debussy and Ravel built on this chord in their music. He also examined how chromatic linear embellishments of dominant sevenths lead to French and German augmented-sixth chords and tritone substitution. Dr. Tsitsaros advised using modal melodies as starting points for improvisation and harmonization because they free students from the constraints of functionality. He closed with a rich arrangement of "Silent Night" that featured many of the linear harmonic embellishments discussed in the presentation.

The Social Impact of a Socio-Cultural Piano Group Project in Brazil
Presented by Chiesa Goulart and Maria Luisa Avello
Wednesday, July 28, 2021
Recorded by Ricardo Pozenatto

In this session, the presenters discussed the social impacts of a Brazilian socio-cultural group piano project called *PianoForte*, which was an initiative of the private business school for the art *Piano Studio Chiesa Goulart*. The first part of the presentation highlighted how the project came to fruition while the second focused on the business strategies utilized to further expand the music program.

The *PianoForte* project was born in the city of Bagé, south of Brazil, where Goulart voluntarily taught group piano classes for a small group of under-privileged children at the request of Avello, who donated a piano as a start-up to a studio business. The classes became popular through community engagement, increasing the number of children who enrolled in the program. Goulart's motivation and interest in the group piano teaching methodology made her seek professional training in São Paulo. The presenter highlighted that the group piano teaching setting at the pre-college teaching level was not yet utilized on a large scale in the country. Therefore, Goulart sought to implement this teaching methodology in the south of Brazil through the socio-cultural project while attending to children in need.

The presentation continued with Goulart talking about the organizational aspects of the program. The group piano classes were offered to children and teenagers and were organized by compatible age groups, apart from students with cognitive disabilities. There were six students per class, accommodating two students per piano. Students' selections for enrollment happened through nominations from public school management teams and drawings from email applications. Additionally, selections occurred through a list of students who resided in orphanages.

The presenter shared the need of developing a curriculum that included varied abilities. The permanence period of the first project cycle—which was four semesters—and a logical and systematic sequence of musical concepts were established with the concern of promoting creative and student-centered music education. Extensive research occurred seeking what types of individuals the project would serve, accounting for students' particularities and musical tastes which would inform the best musical abilities to be fostered amongst students.

Goulart mentioned that to provide accessibility during at-home study and practice, students utilized paper keyboards. Additionally, the technology supported the study routine where assignments were addressed via the *WhatsApp* app, and classes were held online during the COVID-19 pandemic. The presenter shared how pleased she was for overcoming the instrument (piano) expenses while still being able to offer musical education to children and teenagers in need. Moreover, Goulart spoke about complementary activities that students were exposed to besides the piano classes. The project offered drama and visual arts workshops, musical concerts by students and guest artists, and constant participation in events held locally and in other locations.

As the program grew, music teachers from other parts of the country implemented the curriculum of the *PianoForte* project in their school, expanding the project to the north and central regions of Brazil. At no cost, these teachers received training on how to develop affiliations of the project at different locations. Goulart highlighted that one of the concerns of the program was the continued professional development of the teachers. Teacher training was also offered at no cost to instructors involved in the program.

Avello carried on the session talking about the business path taken by the project. The presenter highlighted the decision of opening a small/individual business that could be subsidized by the government through low costs and low taxes. Avello also mentioned that the *Piano Studio Chiesa Goulart* offered scholarships at a 50% cost of private instruction while the remaining 50% was covered by a sponsor who could be an individual from the community.

After discussing the growth of the project—which was 28.1% between 2020 and 2021—the presenters shared additional actions taken to expand the program. These actions included visiting potential patrons, seeking recommendations of new patrons from current ones, and seeking sponsorship from the bank they worked with. The presenters further mentioned that the Rotary Club of Bagé offered a donation in 2020, which made it possible to purchase instruments and winter uniforms and provided scholarships to two students. Finally, the presenters commented about additional activities that supported the project's growth, such as individual donations of instruments (*e.g.*, digital pianos, acoustic pianos, flutes, guitars, percussion instruments, *etc.*), individual donations of cash, fundraising campaigns, sales of *PianoForte* project t-shirts, massive online publicity targeting patrons partnership with private companies, and other types of publicity through diverse means (*e.g.*, radio, newspaper, television). The presenters then shared the project's achievements. Currently, the project has over 100 enrolled students throughout Brazil in their five affiliated locations in the north, central, and southeast regions of the country, in addition to its founded location in Bagé, south of Brazil. The session ended with the presenters listing the project's social contributions. They included the development and improvement of the student's self-esteem and feeling of belonging, the involvement of the students' families with the project, the shaping of audiences in a part of the population without access to art forms, and the positive effects the project had (and has) in students' future, inserting them in the world of music and arts.

Baroque Basics:
Improvising Ornamentation with Intermediate and Advanced Piano Students

Presented by Curtis Pavey
Thursday, July 29, 2021
Recorded by Amy Glennon

Curtis Pavey's interest in adding ornaments in Baroque keyboard music began with his own harpsichord lessons. This session focused on how to add ornaments upon repeats and how to teach this skill to our students. The outlined "Agenda" is shown below, with notes on each topic.

Purpose of Ornamentation
Ornaments are about beauty and creativity. They take a beautiful music structure and make it even more beautiful. Ornaments are about expression, moving the listener. In addition, there is a practical element to ornaments: to help lengthen the sustain of the instrument. Ornaments are part of the regular vocabulary of Baroque music; an understanding of ornamentation will help us to understand the musical language of the time.

Ornament Tables
The most well-known ornament table appears in the *Clavier-Buchlein* for Wilhelm Friedemann Bach. The Ornament Table from *Pieces de clavecin* (Jean-Henri d'Anglebert, 1689) shows some of these same ornaments, along with additional ornaments, such as the *Cheute ou port deVoix en montant,* the filling in of thirds, and rolling chords.

How are Ornaments Used?
The richly ornamented "Courante" by Elisabeth Jacquet De La Guerre was performed. The second example, the "Sarabande" from the *English Suite in G Minor* is a good example of the way Bach added ornaments upon a repeat. These ornaments make the music more beautiful and expressive.

Where Should I Add Ornaments?
Start small: It is important to find the appropriate repertoire. Starting with less-ornamented music is a good place to start. Begin with one ornament per phrase. Practice repeating numerous times, each time with additional ornaments. Where to add: repeats, melodic lines, long sustained notes, strong beats, filling in leaps, and cadences. An example: "Sarabande" (Louis Couperin). This was performed to show one possibility for ornamentation upon repeat.

Practice!
The participants were invited to add ornaments to this same example and performed after a few moments of practice time.

Lightning Talks

Moderated by Sara Ernst; Presented by Laura Silva, Eneida Larti,
Natali Burton, Ivan Hurd, Shitong Sigler, and Brianna Matzke
Thursday, July 29, 2021
Recorded by Jessie Welsh

This lightning talk session featured the research and best ideas of six different presenters. Each presenter summarized their project, idea, and/or research in this compressed, five-minute setting, leaving the attendees with the big picture and a thirst for more. Presenters shared their various projects in pre-recorded videos and attended live for a question-and-answer session with attendees at the end.

The first lightning talk, **Building Community/Overcoming Distance: 2021 NCKP Virtual Piano Ensemble** by Laura Silva, featured a work for fourteen pianos that was arranged by Silva. The arrangement was based on a melody by Venezuelan pianist Teresa Carreño and is published on SuperScore. Using video editing and TimeWarp technologies, Silva created a "real time" experience for the performers and an edited, completed project with NCKP attendees. The performers featured in the performance video were all NCKP attendees (previously selected) from the United States.

Next, a lightning talk by Eneda Larti, **Bridging the Divide Through Non-Traditional Collaboration**, featured two innovative collaborative piano projects that arose during the COVID-19 pandemic. Compelled to curate creative collaborative experiences for her university students, Dr. Larti joined forces with student composers and paired them with her collaborative piano students. Together, these composer-pianist teams created and showcased contemporary compositions, which featured interesting effect chains, layered sounds and loops, multimedia elements, and experimental effects. Ultimately, this project showed that creativity continues amid uncertainty and opened the possibility for future collaborations between departments and with technology and performance.

How Private Music Teachers Can Contribute to Equity in Music Education by Natalie Burton discussed the positive effects of private music study for all children and examined three specific and practical ways teachers can provide music instruction to a wider economic group. This lightning talk discussed utilizing local music schools in one's community, connecting with the MusicLink® Foundation, and setting up studio scholarships as concrete steps for music teachers to contribute to equitable opportunities for music education. Burton also gave useful tips for studio teachers to participate in this work while also running a business, including group lessons, bi-weekly lessons, shorter lessons, bartering systems, donation pools, fundraisers, and using a portion of registration fees to build a scholarship fund.

Pandemic or Not—Online Lessons for All! by Ivan Hurd, took a persuasive approach by featuring the benefits and positive outcomes of online teaching. Dr. Hurd identified positive outcomes he's seen in his own studio, including increased independence, familiarity with the score, musical growth, patience and respect for the teacher, and increased parental involvement. Dr. Hurd also noted other benefits of the online platform, including fewer make-up lessons, sharing musical annotations through useful technology, and the necessity of succinct teacher communication/delivery. The results of a live survey during this NCKP lightning talk revealed that 61.5% of session attendees plan to continue teaching online in some capacity post-pandemic.

The fifth lightning talk, **An Entrepreneurial Blueprint for the Twenty-First-Century Musician**, by Shitong Sigler, provided an overview of the leading literature in the field of music entrepreneurship. Dr. Sigler described music entrepreneurship as composite skills that equip students to be creative and meet the needs of audiences. Specifically, she discussed and recommended the following resources to attendees: *Beyond Talent* (third edition), *The Entrepreneurial Muse, The Entrepreneurial Artist, Creating the Revolutionary Artist*, and *Engaging the Concert Audience*, citing *Beyond Talent* (with its third-edition updates) as her personal top resource.

The final lightning talk featured Brianna Matzke with **Arts Entrepreneurship 101: Six Steps to Make Your Creative Ideas Come to Life**. Dr. Matzke referred to these steps as her "tried and true method" to take an idea from conception to execution. These six steps included generating an idea with a solid, artistic vision and measurable short-term goals; choosing your team from individuals you respect, local artists, businesses, and non-profit collaborators; finding funding sources by examining the financial support for similar projects; implementing the plan and making the idea come to life; creating publicity from press releases, local news and radio, and social media; finally, documenting everything for future projects, funding, and reflection. Dr. Matzke's experience corroborated each of these steps, as she shared brief anecdotes and tips from her own journey.

Following the presentations, Dr. Ernst moderated the question-and-answer time, and presenters attended live to engage with NCKP session participants.

Voices Silenced: Piano Music of Composers Killed in the Holocaust
Presented by Hannah Creviston
Thursday, July 29, 2021
Recorded by Charl Louw

Hannah Creviston's presentation focused on the music and legacy of composers who lost their lives during the Holocaust. The presentation featured piano music of several of these composers, including Erwin Schulhoff, Rudolf Karel, Pavel Haas, Karel Berman, and Gideon Klein. She started her presentation by discussing the fact that society needs to mitigate a great injustice by reviving and performing the music of those whose "crime" was to be Jewish. She emphasized that this revival could serve as a reminder to resist any contemporary or future impulse to define artistic stands on the basis of racist, political, sectarian, or exclusionary ideologies.

The first composer featured was Gideon Klein (1919-1945), a Czech pianist, composer, writer and educator. He arranged Hebrew folk melodies, wrote quarter-tone compositions, and served as repetiteur for the production of the Verdi *Requiem* in the infamous Terezín ghetto. Taking the discussion further, Creviston discussed Pavel Haas, another Czech musician murdered during the Holocaust and an exponent of Leoš Janáček's school of composition. He was notable for his song cycles and string quartets. The performance of his *Praeludium* provided an excellent demonstration of his skills.

Creviston also included Rudolf Karel in her discussion. A Czech composer involved with resistance to the Nazi occupation, composed *Nonett* in short score before his death in 1945 (while imprisoned in the ghetto in Theresienstadt). His composition *Notturno* was included in the presentation as well. Czech composer and pianist, Erwin Schulhoff, whose composition *études de jazz* (1926) has recently gained more prominence, formed a major part of the presentation. Bass singer Karel Berman (1919-1995), who was deported to Terezín in 1943 sang in operas and recitals during his interment, wrote extensively about his time in Auschwitz and his new life after he was released. His compositions were played during the presentation to highlight his style. The melancholy associated with his work and memories provides much insight into the emotional experiences shared by victims of the Nazi regime.

Creviston put a lot of effort into highlighting the works and the style of the composers/musicians under the Nazi Regime. Their works represent a major discovery for music enthusiasts. The impact of their music is vast and deeply enriching in the sense that a younger audience is being introduced to the forgotten music and experiences of those who lost their lives to a brutal tragedy and major historic event.

Creviston finished her presentation by discussing the reunion of people and families who survived the holocaust, and the impact this event has had on society and the music community.

Her performances throughout the presentation revealed the great musical diversity and expressive range of the piano compositions discussed.

Why Can't We Be Friends?
Informal Music Learning and Pop Pedagogy for Classical Teachers
Presented by Kate Acone
Thursday, July 29, 2021
Recorded by Michael Clark

Kate Acone's session offered an introduction to Informal Music Learning and practical suggestions for applying its principles in piano lessons through the teaching of pop music. Acone defined pop music as anything other than classical or jazz. She began by offering five reasons to teach pop music. First, pop music is important to adolescents because it contributes to their self-identity and their ability to connect with peers. Pop can also function as a mental health tool to provide consolation or soothe anxieties. It provides opportunities for culturally responsive teaching, allowing students to bring their own culture into the classroom through music that is meaningful to them. Studying pop music also encourages intrinsic motivation and skill formation. Finally, there is a wealth of excellent pop music to explore.

Acone then summarized the main components of the Informal Music Learning approach. This system was first explored by Lucy Green in *How Popular Musicians Learn* in 2001 and further developed in *Music, Informal Learning, School* in 2008. It has five main principles:
1. Students choose the music—it can be from any genre, at any level of difficulty, and for any instrument or ensemble.
2. Students learn by copying recordings, doing the work of listening and reproducing themselves rather than the teacher providing a rote or written model.
3. Students learn by playing with their friends in ensembles.
4. The learning process is unleveled: students learn what is actually being performed, even if the result is a haphazard approach. It is understood that students improve as they go.
5. Various musical components such as improvisation, composition, aural skills, and performance are fully integrated rather than addressed separately.

Acone offered practical ideas for applying this approach in private piano lessons. Her typical lesson plan begins with asking students to bring music that they like through curating a playlist, making sure to give them enough time to choose music that is significant to them, not just the first thing they think of or something that they think the teacher would like. Then, the teacher and student listen together, and the teacher takes their own notes. Acone recommends some scaffolded steps to help the student get started. These could include determining the key, working out the melody, finding the chords, and putting together an arrangement. All along the way, student and teacher continue to refer to the recording and play along with it.

The role of the teacher is different in Informal Music Learning than in traditional classical pedagogy, Acone argued. She suggested teachers should view themselves as guides, not instructors. They should observe, allowing extra time for students to struggle. They should ask questions that direct them to notice aspects of the recording, elements of the piano, or other options they have not yet tried. Teachers should encourage their students, reinforcing their natural instincts that will help them progress in their project. Acone suggested that the teacher even leave the student alone for a few minutes to give them more autonomy. In private lessons, teachers must seek ways to simulate the peer learning experiences available in group settings. Possibilities include having students work on duets with siblings, overlapping students' lessons, or playing the role of "co-creator" with the student through accompanying or cuing the recording.

Acone concluded her presentation with two case studies from her own studio. The first student was at a primer level with basic prior music knowledge. She picked a song that was meaningful to her family, and Acone created a reference guide with some of the notes in the song. The student's deep knowledge of the music helped her figure it out on the piano with only minimal assistance. The second student had more experience and an understanding of major and minor scales and basic accompaniment patterns. She selected a Frank Sinatra tune and Acone created a rough lead sheet and provided a brief introduction to seventh chords. She sent her home with the recording to work it out on her own, and the student returned the next week with a fully formed accompaniment.

How to Implement a Video Lesson Library in Your Studio
Presented by Joseph Harkins
Thursday, July 29, 2021
Recorded by Louie Hehman

Goals with elementary repertoire, according to the presenter, include experiencing artistry, as well as proper utilization of technique (coordination and use of arm weight) and recognizing patterns. The lesson plan is based on these goals. A video demonstration was included in which the students "take the teacher home" with them. This demonstration was given using the piece "Graduation March." Three demo videos were included, showcasing the artistry, technique, and patterning (referred to as outlines by presenter). Eye contact was kept consistent through several of the demonstrations.

Harkins then pivoted to goals relating to theory and interval recognition. Singing intervals and recognizing them away from the instrument was particularly emphasized. He reminded teachers that making mistakes in front of students can provide the foundation for a good-humored rapport. Harkins showed a demonstration of take-home assignments for interval recognition, using familiar songs ("Twinkle, Twinkle, Little Star" as an example of a perfect fifth).

The presenter's next topic was improvisation for intermediate learners. The focus was upon the ii-V-I progression in jazz. Harkins discussed the possibility of using a video to be given as preparation before the lesson, as opposed to reinforcement after the fact. These videos occurred in three parts: root notes, addition of the 3rds and 7ths, and voice leading with 3rds and 7ths. This topic has allowed students to create their own demos to share with fellow students. An example was shown from one of the presenter's students, explaining the 3rd and 7th voicing leading in his own terms.

Another intermediate improv concept to be covered was the blues scale. A demonstration video included: coordination on a boogie-woogie pattern, daily improvising (with practice limits), and blues scale technique.

In the question and answer period, Harkins explained that he uploads his videos to YouTube or texts them to the students' parents. One final question concerned printed resources for students, to which Harkins stated that, when it comes to jazz, he emphasizes playing first, reading later.

Music and Nationhood
Presented by Catherine Kautsky
Thursday, July 29, 2021
Recorded by Karen Gerelus

This lecture was based on Dr. Kautsky's reflections on the current global pandemic, where music could have the potential to bring people together in a universal language. Historically, countries have used it for their own individual political reasons. She focused on certain composers that have "been aligned with an image that a nation wanted to project": Beethoven, Chopin, Debussy, and more briefly, Clara Schumann. Her lecture-recital captured the sounds of these composers and their national affiliations.

Beethoven's music had been taken up by conflicting German political movements throughout the twentieth century, from social democrats to Nazis to East-German communists. The audience viewed recordings of Beethoven's ninth symphony played in celebration of Hitler's birthday (1942), and the same recording celebrating the fall of the Berlin Wall (1989). Beethoven's own biography was full of adversities, and overcoming those personal obstacles became "triumphs of bravery" that political leaders wanted to draw upon. Dr. Kautsky performed excerpts from the final movement of Sonata, Op. 110, with analytical comments. In particular, Beethoven's masculinity and bold sound seemed to match the needs of a country that calls itself "the fatherland."

As Dr. Kautsky quoted Paderewski's admiration of Chopin, she said "the whole of Poland lives, feels, and moves in *tempo rubato.*" Chopin's flexible music encapsulated the flexibility that Poland needed in order to survive. Poland aspired to keep its soul intact while it was subjugated by one nation after another. The country may have been physically weak but was spiritually strong. Dr. Kautsky described its history as tragic and suffering—much like Chopin's music and personal life. The audience viewed photos of the Chopin monument in Warsaw that the presenter connected to the *"Military" Polonaise*, the Chopin rose that was connected to his *fairy music*, and pieces which reflected both the talons and the petals. For example, Dr. Kautsky performed *Mazurka*, Op. 53 in C-Sharp Minor as a "crossover piece." Next, the audience listened to *Nocturne*, Op. 27, No. 2 in D-Flat Major and were encouraged to listen for the love song, the melancholy, the gender implications. Chopin's music "sighed," as did Poland.

Dr. Kautsky presented that Clara Schumann overcame many of her own personal adversities, which came primarily from being a female in the nineteenth century, and were well-represented in a performance of her *Nocturne*, Op. 6, No. 2. Why was this music not chosen to represent a nation? Perhaps because it did not have enough "hard edges" for Germans, like their language and military, if they were going to do battle with it. Dr. Kautsky wondered whether if Clara Schumann had lived in France it might have been different.

Debussy found himself in Paris amongst beautifully manicured gardens, people, and pastries. Despite the blurred, impressionistic lines of his music, Debussy became the composer to represent the French nation's spirit. The French wanted to assert their muscle, but also to be as different as possible from Germans who were defined by muscle. Debussy's music may equally have lacked muscle, but he was enthusiastic about being defined by differences. For example, he despised Wagner's bombastic style. Debussy wanted emotion without epilepsy. The audience viewed images of Debussy's soldiers which were not from a bona fide, real-life army but rather came peeking out of a toybox. Dr. Kautsky described Debussy's *Berceuse Heroique* which was written with the Belgian national anthem, the sounds of bugles and drums, and in homage to King Albert's soldiers upon the German occupation of Belgium. In a performance of this piece, the audience heard that this war composition was also equally a lullaby.

This presentation used performances of musical examples, photographic images, audio-visual excerpts, and a compelling lecture to bring the topic of music and nationhood to life.

Using Performance Cues as a Memorization Strategy
Presented by Maria Eduarda Lucena Vieira
Thursday, July 29, 2021
Recorded by Luís Pipa

In this presentation, Vieira introduced the primary results of her on-going PhD research focused on the implementation of Performance Cues (PCs) as a memorization strategy among group piano students, using teacher- and student-directed approaches.

The presenter started by comparing two learning approaches: (1) *teacher-directed* and (2) *student-directed*. In the first, students rely mainly on the teacher's knowledge to guide their learning process. In the *student-directed*, pupils assume a more independent role and teachers work as facilitators, giving students time to find answers and allowing them to learn in their own way. Different students can benefit from both approaches, depending on their learning styles.

Vieira dedicated the second part of the presentation to a specific memorization strategy known as Performance Cues (PCs), which has been extensively investigated by Roger Chaffin and colleagues. PCs are mental markings that help musicians keep track of their progress during learning and performance of a given piece. They work as a mental map guiding the musician during memorized performance. PCs can be based on different features of the score, which have been categorized in previous studies into different types, such as basic (*e.g.*, notes, fingering, hand placement), interpretation (*e.g.*, dynamics) and expression (*e.g.*, feelings brought by the score). Several studies conducted by Chaffin and colleagues with different professional musicians and students have explored the role of PCs as a strategy to secure memorization, finding that such strategy can indeed help reinforce and consolidate the memorization process.

Vieira argued that PCs can be used as a pedagogical strategy to help students memorize more effectively. The instructor can encourage students to find different PCs and mark them on the score while practicing. In such an approach, teachers encourage students to start memorizing at the beginning of the learning process, by developing and practicing the PCs that will later guide their memorized performance.

In her study, Vieira attempted to help a group of piano students to develop different types of PCs while learning three pieces of different composers and styles. The purpose of the research was to compare the effect of teacher-directed and student-directed learning approaches, by using PCs as a memorization strategy with Level III group piano students.

During the data collection, the participants learned three different pieces, which matched their level of studies. Each student had five days to learn the piece, ending with a recording from memory. The students were divided into two groups, the first following a student-directed approach and the second a teacher-directed approach. In the first group students received the piece and had up to eighteen minutes of practice before discussing with the teacher what they thought would work as effective PCs. In the second group, the teacher provided her own markings of different PCs to the students. All students performed three pre-tests and three post-tests. The recordings of the tests were rated by two external judges who had experience with group piano teaching. The judges rated the recordings on a seven-point Likert scale, evaluating three main aspects (note accuracy, rhythm accuracy, and phrasing). Findings showed that all groups improved from the pre-tests to the post-tests. There was no significant difference between student-directed and teacher-directed approaches, as both groups improved.

Vieira closed the presentation with a list of different aspects she plans to investigate further in the future, namely the exploration of different repertoires and the use of a larger number of students. The presenter also plans to improve the evaluation process, by implementing a stricter training for the raters and by developing grading rubrics, which will be given to the raters for consistency.

Piano Music by Female Composers and Composers of Color
Presented by Jenna Klein
Thursday, July 29, 2021
Recorded by Sonya Schumann

This presentation addressed a lack of representation for female and BIPOC students and pianists, and highlighted pedagogical repertoire available to explore through all levels of pre-collegiate study. Jenna Klein expressed that throughout her studies, she wished to see more representation from female composers and composers of color. Now in her PhD program, she researches the music and lives of composers from these groups. She outlined a piece from each level, 1–10, in accordance with Jane Magrath's leveling system. Klein only demonstrated one piece at each level during the presentation.

She began with a Florence Price piece, "On Higher Ground," a level 1 piece that is pattern based. She noted that it could be taught as a rote piece, and could be useful for experimentation of different dynamics and fingering choices at the piano.

The level 2 example was "Waltz" from *Minute Music for Small Hands* by Violet Archer, a quirky piece that works well for small hands and requires expressive playing.

Next, the level 3 piece was *Sonatine No. 1* (II) by Germaine Tailleferre. In binary form, the piece uses interesting dissonance and resolution, and a lilting melody.

The piece for level 4 was *Tender Thought* by Ulysses Kay. This piece requires the sharing of unexpected harmonies between the hands and relies on chromaticism throughout.

The presenter's choice for level 5 was Joseph Bologne's *Adagio in F Minor*. It features a broken chord LH, with octaves, and is in 6/8 time.

For level 6, Klein chose to highlight the Amy Beach piece "Sliding on Ice" from Opus 119. She introduces it as a level 6 for its syncopation, more difficult form, and exciting transitions.

"The Monk" by Valerie Capers was featured for level 7, imitating the style of Thelonious Monk with triplets, syncopations, contrary motion scales, cluster chords, and accents.

Her level 8 example was "Prayer Before Battle" by Amanda Aldridge, a piece from the collection *An Eastern Suite*. The piece features frequent rolled chords, creating a pensive and dramatic air. It is useful for students who appreciate serious sounding, dramatic pieces who are prepared to explore more difficult pedaling.

The level 9 featured work was "The Goblin and the Mosquito," a Florence Price piece found on IMSLP. This work is a quick character piece with exciting rhythms and flare.

Finally, Lili Boulanger's "D'un Jardin Clair" is an impressionistic and atmospheric level 10 piece with beautiful harmonic variety to offset voicing and pedaling challenges.

Florence Price: Underrepresented Repertoire for Pianists of All Levels
Presented by Shannon Wettstein-Sadler
Thursday, July 29, 2021
Recorded by Sonya Schumann

This presentation focused on the life and music of Black American composer Florence Price. Dr. Shannon Wettstein-Sadler began with a brief biography of Florence Price, before diving into Price's elementary, intermediate, and advanced piano literature. She focused on certain works that highlight how to use Price's works to advance students in progressive and cumulative choreographic elements, develop healthy tone production, and cultivate compositional textures to create *cantabile* phrasing.

Florence Price attended the New England Conservatory, graduating with honors in 1906 in piano and organ, receiving an Artist Diploma and Teaching Certificate. As a teacher and pedagogue, she rose to become the head of the music department at Clark University in Atlanta. After marrying in 1912, she returned to Arkansas and later moved to Chicago where she had a thriving private piano studio. She is known well now as the first African American woman to have a symphony performed by a major American orchestra in 1933. However, solo piano music was her largest output of compositional work. She also mentored another Black American female composer, Margaret Bonds.

Dr. Wettstein-Sadler began with some of Price's elementary level repertoire. The first example is found in *Three Sketches for Little Pianists*. The most important elements of each are: 1) key drop choreography, 2) tone from arm weight, and 3) single note and melody with triad textures. Each piece from the set of sketches is easily accessible to students between levels 1–2. Another example of Price's elementary level repertoire is "Etude." This simple melody is found on one staff, with upper eighth notes for the right hand and lower eights for the left hand. The texture requires the student to cross hands, and the texture shows chord blocking—with possible pedal training for early to early-intermediate level students.

The next examples are more appropriate for an intermediate level student: *Meditation, Quiet Lake*, and *Clouds* share several traits, but may differ on individual techniques required. *Meditation* has a beautiful *cantabile* melody, and now adds a jump bass accompaniment with very few octaves. *Quiet Lake* is primarily highlighting the tenor register, with a more complex accompaniment texture bantered between the hands throughout the piece. Finally, *Clouds* features an impressionist air, with greater complexity of texture for the student to learn to balance. Both hands will require shared arpeggiation and a comfortable octave reach.

Finally, Dr. Wettstein-Sadler featured two pieces from Price's advanced repertoire. First is "At the Cotton Gin," from the suite *In the Land o' Cotton*. The accompaniment shared between the hands will imitate the sound and motion of the cotton gin. The melody and accompaniment are both found simultaneously in the right hand, requiring voicing and dexterity. The second piece was *Fantasie Negre No. 4*, another brilliant piece that requires *cantabile* in all registers, as well as large chords and orchestral textures throughout.

Raag-time: Incorporating Non-Western Musical Traditions
Presented by Omar Roy
Thursday, July 29, 2021
Recorded by Hannah Roberts

Indian classical music is largely absent from traditional Western piano pedagogy, and little is known among piano teachers about the Indian genre of the *raag*. This presentation shared valuable information, teaching examples, and pedagogical suggestions for incorporating the Indian tradition of the *raag* within the teaching studio. By doing so, teachers can diversify the repertoire they present to students and expand cultural representation within their curriculum.

To begin, Dr. Roy educated the audience on what a *rāga* is, defining it as a genre that features structured improvisation and uses scales unique to Indian classical music. *Rāgas* can be context-dependent, varying based on the time of day. Traditional performance forces for *rāgas* include one or more melodic instruments, such as a *sitar* or *bansuri*; a "continuo" instrument that plays a drone or ostinato figure, such as a *tampura* or harmonium; and percussion instruments, such as the *pakhawaj*. The mixture of these various timbres lends a unique and compelling soundscape to the *rāga*.

Rāgas follow a sectional form, with distinct attributes assigned to each section. The *alaap* is a slow, exploratory section that begins with a pulseless drone. It explores the scale and gradually unveils the main features of the *rāga*. In a typical *rāga*, two *gat* sections follow the *alaap*. The first *gat* section begins with a pre-composed, moderate-tempo melody accompanied by a strictly metered drone. This is followed by an improvisatory interlude, still accompanied by the drone. After this comes the second *gat* section, which is faster than the first. After the *gat,* an optional *jhala* section, typically fast and flashy, may precede the ending. The ending of the *rāga* includes a descending scale passage, repeated three times, and a conclusion. To help musicians better understand the *rāga*, Dr. Roy suggested considering it as an improvisatory jam session, which can vary significantly in length. Some *rāgas* are brief, while others may extend up to an hour. The *rāga* can also be reduced so that only the *alaap* section is performed. However, the *gat* and ending sections should not be performed alone.

Because of the rote traditions inherent to Indian classical music, few scholars have transcribed this music into Western notation. Accordingly, Western audiences have had little exposure to the *raag,* and advanced music students may only encounter the genre in an ethnomusicology or world-music class. Before the twenty-first century, the only published transcription of Indian music for the keyboard was a collection created by William Hamilton Bird. Titled *The Oriental Miscellany: Airs of Hindustan,* Bird's collection was published in 1789. When creating these transcriptions, Bird made various musical concessions which would not have been authentic to the Indian performance practice. These included harmonizing the melodies with traditional

Western harmonies, avoiding the complex rhythmic figures that would have been used in traditional performances, and foregoing improvisatory elements by notating all musical components.

After Bird, no known adaptations of Indian music for the keyboard were created until 2016, when John Pitts published *How to Play Indian Sitar Rāgas on a Piano* (2016, revised 2020) and *Indian Rāgas for Piano Made Easy* (2018, revised 2020). In his books, Pitts notes that several unique elements of the *rāga*, such as tuning, timbre, the natural reverberance of Indian instruments, and the ensemble nature of the genre, may have prevented earlier efforts to adapt it for Western audiences.

Pitts' first book, *How to Play Indian Sitar Rāgas on a Piano,* suits intermediate to advanced pianists. The book outlines the history of the *rāga,* offers explanations for how to perform solo and ensemble *rāgas*, discusses the musical components of the genre, and provides all necessary ingredients for pianists to create authentic *rāga* performances. His second book, *Indian Rāgas for Piano Made Easy*, includes eight *rāgas* at varying levels of difficulty and is appropriate for the elementary to late-intermediate pianist. This resource offers accessible explanations of the *rāga* and provides notated examples to guide a student's improvisation.

According to Dr. Roy, the pedagogical benefits of incorporating the *rāga* into the studio are numerous. First, exploring Indian classical music in the form of the *rāga* offers opportunities for authentic cultural exposure to students at all levels. Second, Dr. Roy described the *rāga* as an ideal playground for improvisation. In their musical exploration, students have no need to worry about playing incorrect notes as long as they remain within the pitches of a particular scale. Additionally, given the ensemble nature of the *rāga*, it can easily be performed as a duet in which the teacher or another student plays the ostinato or drone. This simplifies the hand coordination and allows the student to focus solely on their improvisation. Other benefits of incorporating the *rāga* into the piano studio include the potential for student collaboration, either with fellow pianists or in mixed ensembles; the development of independent hand coordination, with a metrically-played left hand and a freely-moving right hand; and the development of aural skills, as students learn to translate musical thoughts to the piano.

Throughout the presentation, Dr. Roy shared engaging audio and visual examples of *rāga* performances. The audience was treated to a video of a traditional Indian *rāga*, an audio example of Bird's adaptations for the harpsichord, and a video of a *rāga* adapted for piano and performed as a duet by Dr. Roy and his student.

Advocating Musicians' Health for ALL
Presented by Gail Berenson, Linda Cockey, and Charles Turon
Thursday, July 29, 2021
Recorded by Hannah Roberts

Musicians of all ages face physiological and psychological challenges that can negatively impact their musical activities. Teachers must be aware of these challenges and knowledgeable of their remedies in order to cultivate a lifestyle of healthy music-making in their studios. This panel presentation examined the need for musician's health education and offered examples for promoting healthy practices in the piano studio. Panelists addressed every stage of a student's development, from pre-collegiate and collegiate students to young professionals, mid-life musicians, and retirees.

To begin, the presenters stressed the need for a holistic approach to teaching, citing Frances Clark's familiar maxim: "Teach the student first, the music second, and the piano third." They also emphasized the importance of teaching a student for their whole lifetime; a teacher will rarely accompany a student through their entire journey, but each teacher adds foundational layers that the student will build on as their journey progresses.

In his segment discussing pre-collegiate students, Charles Turon used the analogy of time capsules to illustrate how habits formed during the beginning years of study can lead to undesirable results later. During a student's pre-collegiate years, poor physical habits, unhealthy psychological behaviors, or ineffective learning processes can become ingrained habits. While these poor habits may not be immediately apparent, they can become problematic when the "time capsule" is opened later in their life. To illustrate his analogy, Turon shared his own experience as a beginning piano student, in which he studied from a piano method that utilized the middle-C reading approach. In this approach, students learn to play by anchoring both thumbs in front of the body on middle C. Because this requires non-ergonomic positioning of the hands, Turon unknowingly developed an unhealthy habit of ulnar deviation. Decades later, when he began experiencing physiological issues, he recognized the unfortunate impacts caused by chronic ulnar deviation. Using this example, Turon emphasized that piano teachers undoubtedly impact the health of their students, either positively or negatively. It is critical for teachers to recognize their role in training healthy musicians and actively promote healthy practices in their studios.

In addition to addressing poor physical habits, Turon also discussed how psychological behaviors and learning processes developed in early years of study can impact a student's development later in life. Using relevant examples of his own students, Turon shared how unfortunate psychological effects of students' personal lives can impact the learning that occurs in the studio. He also explained how poor learning processes ingrained at the early levels of study can lead to negative performance experiences. By adopting informed pedagogical approaches, pre-collegiate teachers can avert many of these potential physical and psychological problems.

Next, Linda Cockey addressed teaching collegiate students and young professionals. Her remarks emphasized the importance of tailoring one's teaching to each student's individuality and unique skills. She offered three steps teachers can take to achieve a tailored teaching approach. First, teachers should take steps to learn a student's personal story, as it relates to their musical goals; second, they should select repertoire based on the student's interests and needs; and third, they should cultivate supportive communities within their studios. Additionally, Cockey discussed the importance of teaching physiological and psychological awareness to one's students. Strategies for improving physiological awareness include working with students on posture, gestures, tone, and muscle contraction, while strategies for improving psychological awareness include working on goal-setting strategies and learning skills.

In the closing segment, Gail Berenson addressed healthy teaching practices when working with graduate students, mid-life musicians, and retirees. When teaching graduate students, Berenson stressed the teacher's role as a mentor, helping students make school and career decisions. She also addressed the importance of the teacher as an intermediary for international students, helping these students adapt to their new environment. When working with mid-life musicians and retirees, Berenson's strategies included treating these beginning students as intelligent and successful adults, involving students in repertoire selection and lesson content, and providing meaningful and gratifying performance opportunities. She also stressed the value of focusing more on the learning process than on the product. Doing so allows students to develop independent learning skills and discover more fully the joy of making music.

Teachers working with adult students should also be aware of how the aging process can affect a student's piano studies. Vision problems and arthritis were two problematic areas addressed in this segment. Berenson encouraged piano teachers to be knowledgeable about practical strategies for combating these potential issues.

Throughout the presentation, the panel recommended several resources for further study. Recommendations included *Teaching the Whole Musician* by Paolo Savvidou; *What Every Pianist Needs to Know About the Body* by Thomas Mark; *The Mindful Musician: Mental Skills for Peak Performance* by Vanessa Cornett; and *Making Music at the Piano: Learning Strategies for Adult Students* by Barbara English Maris.

In the Key of Now: 21st-Century Ways to Teach 19th-Century Concepts
Presented by Karen Gerelus
Thursday, July 29, 2021
Recorded by Sonya Schumann

This presentation focused on the research of Karen Gerelus on motivation and the beginner piano lesson. Gerelus discussed her most effective teaching props, best used during lessons. The props can be divided into five categories: hand position and technique, touch and tone, music reading, rhythm and tempo, and practicing. By utilizing props, one can create a stronger bond with students, harness emotional memory, engage the imagination, focus on student-centered learning, and use play to build knowledge.

For the first category, hand position and technique, Gerlus recommends using silly putty to encourage students to check knuckle strength. Alternatively, one might squeeze a clothespin with two fingers, watching each knuckle as you do so. For a quality hand shape, she has found foam lady-bugs that she places under the student's hand. Ping pong balls also work under smaller hands. Students can use washable markers on fingertips (only for plastic keys) to see finger placement. She uses an elastic headband for arm weight, encouraging a gentle motion over the keys.

For touch and tone, Gerelus uses a variety of textured fabric samples to encourage visual and kinesthetic attachments. She also uses paint cards, found at any hardware store, to help bring more vibrancy to a student's sound. When addressing balance, she works with her students to feel the literal weight of objects.

In her play-work on music reading, she uses laser pointers, magnet boards, magnifying glasses, finger stick pointers, and teeny-tiny alphabet cards. She has a variety of other musical percussion instruments to play with for rhythm learning. Additionally, she has created musical legos to help assemble complex rhythms. To encourage healthy metronome work and attention to tempi, she has created custom speeding tickets for her students. She also uses a printed stop sign during lessons to get her students to think ahead.

Finally, her treasure box helps encourage students to practice during her twice-yearly practice challenges. Completing the challenge means students gain access to the treasure box! For repetition in practice, she has a set of dice and sets of cards. This means that the student must have repetition determined randomly. She also uses visual aids like cute small animals to cross the piano with correct repetitions.

The Powerful Pedagogy 3Ps—Prepare, Present, Practice
Presented by Janet Tschida
Thursday, July 29, 2021
Recorded by Linda M. Fields

The activities shared in this session focus mostly on dynamics, but they can easily be adapted for other concepts. Tschida recommends a method book's Table of Contents as a good place to look for which concepts to prepare. Budget only about two–three minutes per lesson for these activities, spending several weeks for preparation in the body, the ear, and the hands, leading up to presenting the symbol and label, and then assigning practice of a new piece with the concept.

Tschida often starts with graphing activities. For ideas, she recommends *Teaching for Musical Understanding* by Jackie Wiggins. Good recordings to graph include: "Keeping the Beat" by Feierabend, "Carnival of the Animals" by Saint-Saëns, and recordings from the method book.

As a first step, Tschida plays a musical excerpt for students to "Listen and Describe." With no wrong or right answers, this is a good way to learn where a student is in their listening skills. In a subsequent week students may "do what the music tells you to do," where they create an emotional connection between their body and the music, ideally using (judgment-free) continuous flow movement. Another week, students are invited to "Listen and Respond" with instructions for contrasting movements that highlight specific changes heard, without using musical labels or visual symbols.

After plenty of experience with their bodies, students are shown several simple line drawings of changing sound levels and then asked, "Which picture *best* represents what you are hearing?" The emphasis is not on one "right" picture, but rather on stimulating thinking and discussion. Then, following the example of the pictures, students are told, "As you listen to the music, draw what you are hearing." Tschida explained that this can be in a lesson, with the teacher graphing along with the student, or in a class with everyone graphing together. As a next step, students may compare their drawing with a friend's as they listen again and discuss together. Again, the value of this is not to draw a perfect graph; rather Tschida's goal is active, repeated listening.

Next Tschida moves to preparing dynamics in the hands. This can start with gesture (apart from notation), with the teacher modeling technique and tone quality and the student observing levers used (*e.g.,* elbows, wrists, fingertips, *etc.*) and then imitating, similar to Suzuki piano. This is followed (typically with students at the five-finger-pattern level) with playbacks (*i.e.,* copycats), using combinations of loud and quiet patterns, for students to imitate with their fingers. Rote pieces can follow, with the goal of focusing attention on listening to tone quality and feeling the proper gestures, undistracted by a score.

Sources of rote pieces Tschida recommends include Katherine Fisher's *Piano Safari* (especially "Crocodile in the Nile" for dynamics), *Solo Flight* by Elvina Pearce, and Paula Dreyer's *Little Gems for Piano*.

At this point students are ready to create, using their skills with loud and quiet sounds, familiar rote pieces, copycat/playback patterns or previous improvisations. Recommended sources for creativity templates include materials by Forrest Kinney, Leila Viss, and/or Bradley Sowash.

Once the student can hear the concept, expressing it in their body and with their hands, score study is a good way to present the concept visually. The student watches the music as Tschida plays, exploring "How do you think I know when to play loud or quiet sounds?" Or "What do you think ___ means, based on how I am playing?" With an understanding of the symbols, they may label the music and take home an assigned piece that includes the markings for *forte* and *piano*. (Tschida took care to note that other elements of a new piece, besides dynamics, would also have been prepared similarly.)

For reinforcement, Tschida has students write dynamic markings in pieces they have already learned. Additionally, she gives sight-reading assignments using *forte* and *piano*, and brings back the graphing activities, assigning the student to ask someone to graph the dynamics heard as they play. To reinforce accuracy, the student may listen and watch the music, deciding "Which way is more accurate?" Or the teacher may play and state, "This way is less accurate." (Play), "This way is more accurate." (Play), and then ask "Why was the first way less accurate?" or "Why was the second way more accurate?"

To prepare form in the body, use similar activities as above with the addition of circle games in the "Listen and Respond" step. Moving to music, with a specific movement for each section, brings the music's organization into the body. Choosing a picture (or putting contrasting pictures in order) according to the form could come next. Recommended resources for activities relating to form are *Drumming & Dancing* published by Musikgarten, and *Beginning Circle Games* by Feierabend.

Tschida listed some key phrases to use with students:
- Listen and describe.
- Do what the music tells you to do.
- Which picture best represents the music?
- Following the example, draw what you are hearing.
- Copy me.
- Create.
- Watch the music—how do you think I know when to play ___?
- Which way is more correct? Or Why was the first way incorrect?

The following questions were addressed afterwards:

What can we do with a student that has inhibited movement?
Tschida suggested starting with small movements, referring to Dr. Wendy Valerio (start with thumbs, move to large motor, like elbows, *etc.*) Uninhibited modeling by the teacher helps!

How can we help older students around ages 11-14 to use their bodies?
Tschida has found success inviting students to imitate various sports—surfing, baseball, etc.

Pianist, Heal Thyself! —Developing and Maintaining Healthy Practice Habits
Presented by James Litzelman
Thursday, July 29, 2021
Recorded by Autumn L. Zander

Establishing habits that optimize one's own playing and teaching are paramount to the longevity of a pianist's career. Ideally, healthy practice habits are established in the early years of study and refined throughout a lifetime. Yet, practice-related injuries do occur and historically they were often accompanied by a certain stigma. Thankfully that stigma is eroding and being replaced by multiple resources and support networks to help pianists who do develop a practice-related injury during their careers.

Litzelman recounted his own experiences with a performance injury, focal dystonia. Unlike a repetitive-practice injury that might be caused due to poor technique, focal dystonia pertains to an issue with the brain rather than with muscles, tendons, or ligaments in the hand. Valuable steps in his retraining have included symmetrical inversion practice that uses the symmetry of the keyboard to do the exact same thing in each hand, therapy with a gifted Rolfer, and a daily stretching program called Classical Stretch ® or Essentrics ® that works the connective tissue.

The recovery process for any performance related injury requires that an individual take responsibility in healing themselves and tending to their own well-being. Litzelman stressed that being a pianist is at the core of who we are as human beings and how we self-identify in many aspects of our life. Because of these factors, a musician's injury can be psychologically difficult, leaving an individual feeling lost and "self-less." However, Litzelman reminded attendees that playing the piano doesn't injure us, it is the *way* we play piano that injures us. He then addressed a unique idea that institutes of higher education may in some way contribute to playing-related tension issues by pushing students to perform repertoire that they may not be ready to play, only to have them learn more challenging repertoire the following semester.

In combating performance injuries, knowing how to use the body efficiently is crucial. Yet Litzelman shared that, "most students think that an injury will never happen to them—despite being in pain! This shows that they are ill-informed of the realities." This statement was further expanded upon by citing a study of piano majors at the University of North Texas in which eighty-six percent of the students reported having pain associated with their playing. Despite this shocking statistic, progress has been made in the awareness and treatment of performance-related injuries including support from teachers, doctors specializing in musician's injuries, musician wellness sessions at conferences, and the creation of the Performing Arts Medical Association.

Preventing injuries in the first place, via solid playing habits, is the most successful way to prevent performance related injuries later in life. Litzelman believes that the root of most, if not all, performance-related injuries stems from unnecessary tension. The first step in developing healthy practice habits that avoid unnecessary tension is establishing good posture. This entails determining the proper height of the bench, the distance of the bench from the piano, and where to sit on the bench. For young students the use of a pedal extender to stabilize the feet in order to avoid key bedding and unnecessary tension is crucial. Interestingly, the mention of pedal extenders for proper posture dates back to Francois Couperin's treatise *L'art de toucher le clavecin* from 1716. Litzelman also discussed Thomas Mark's book *What Every Pianist Needs to Know About the Body.* Body mapping (the representation in the brain of what one's body is like, and how we use our body to do any physical activity) and how faulty body mapping results in faulty movement was also addressed.

It is a fact that some muscular tension is necessary when playing the piano, and Litzelman described finding the proper proportion of muscular tension as the three R's, "the *right* amount, at the *right* place, and at the *right* time." The *right* amount of tension depends upon the sound one wishes to produce. The *right* place almost always is in our fingertips since that is the only part of the body that comes in contact with the keys. The *right* time occurs when playing a given note, not before or after playing the note.

As a parting thought Litzelman provided three main aspects to think about during one's practicing and teaching; posture, the three R's of muscular tension, and a "release" after every note, that is the amount of muscular activity needed to activate a key vs. the amount needed to remain on the key.

Collaborating via Technology
Presented by Dana Brown, John Gunther, Alexandra Nguyen, and Jeremy Reger
Thursday, July 29, 2021
Recorded by Elizabeth Smith

Alexandra Nguyen painted the picture of March 2020: the majority of activities moved online due to the COVID-19 pandemic, music making online posed many problems, the biggest problem being latency between devices. The presentation surveyed the different programs available, and the preferences of the panel regarding the programs. Nguyen presented the disclaimer that these are the opinions of the panel presenters and that none of the presenters represent the companies or software developers.

Platforms are categorized in the following ways:
1. Synchronous (low latency): allows for playing together in real time due to little lagging
   a. Programs include:
      - *SoundJack* – free to use, no additional hardware officially required
      - *JamKazam* – fee structure depending on usage, requires additional equipment
      - *JackTrip* – requires massive bandwidth, audio only (unrealistic for students)
      - *Jamulus* – open source, private room (with fees)
      - New platforms: *Musicians Together Apart* and *Aloha*
2. Asynchronous: recordings and layering tracks
3. One-sided: Applications with pre-recorded tracks (not necessarily considered to be collaboration, but commonly used)

The presenters went into detail about *SoundJack* and *JamKazam*. Dana Brown spoke on *JamKazam*. His school ended up using the program due to its ease of use. The additional equipment he used was wired internet, ethernet cable, and was given a new Macbook Pro by his school. At home, he was able to use the "audio interface" setup. The presenters then walked the audience through *JamKazam*, first by explaining the dashboard, and then showing how to set up an account. There is a troubleshooting element built into the program; if your equipment isn't completely set up, you are unable to continue in the program. In Brown's opinion, the interface is much easier to use than *SoundJack*. He describes the program as low latency, with static sometimes being an issue. The app frequently crashed last fall, and the presenter explained the difficulty of crashing mid-semester. Brown prepared two recitals using the program, and the students prepared the programs online. He also shared an anecdotal opinion that students must be more organized when collaborating together. Nguyen shared that she had initial troubles with the program, due to its detailed sound (you can hear breathing, bow use, etc.), but is a fantastic alternative to Zoom.

Jeremy Reger then took over the presentation to explain the use of *SoundJack*. He first explained that there is a steep learning curve to *SoundJack*. His school, the University of Colorado-Boulder, spent about $10,000 on audio interfaces, open-backed headphones, ethernet cables, and microphones. As a result, the school was able to plan two operas and countless coachings. The most frustrating thing with *SoundJack* is the need for a separate video interface. *SoundJack* isn't necessarily great at transmitting nuances over the computers, and the ability to communicate can be difficult. The equipment to get everything you need to successfully use *SoundJack* was around $1,000, and it was difficult to ask students to pay for that. The presenters then displayed the dashboard of *SoundJack* like they did for *JamKazam*, walking the audience through the technical requirements to start *SoundJack*. *SoundJack* has great customer service and has been updated based on requests from students. Reger shares that he will continue using the program, but he won't necessarily plan a recital using the program. It's difficult for students to not want to compensate for the lag, resulting in pianists tending to run ahead of other instruments.

The presenters then turned to some asynchronous options when collaborating. One student can record their part, and then another student can play with that track. It does require a level of basic editing of the two tracks, and file size can be an issue. There is a website called OperaTracks.com, where singers and pianists can buy either pre-recorded or customized aria tracks and can pay to spend time with a coach. The presenters then gave a detailed demonstration with *SoundTrap*, which the jazz department at the University of Colorado-Boulder used for the past year. John Gunther had a lot of initial issues using *JamKazam* and *SoundJack* and turned to *SoundTrap*. The only equipment needed is a laptop and headphones, and it's an easy-to-use interface. As an administrator, there are a lot of different options with pairing students, and students gain basic editing experience. Reger then shared two examples: one with the big band, and one in his own applied teaching.

The final asynchronous program is *Acapella* but is available for Mac users only and only records short snippets. The presenters usually prefer other programs.

In the last category (pre-recorded tracks), programs include *Music Minus One, Appcompanist*, and *4D Music Pocket Player*. Each includes a recorded track that can be sped up, slowed down, or transposed on your phone. Issues arise when comparing sound quality to a real performer, but it is more financially efficient.

Self-Monitoring of Muscle Tone During Piano Practice
Presented by Maria Hordynskyj Holian
Thursday, July 29, 2021
Recorded by Luís Pipa

This presentation addressed self-monitoring of muscle tone during piano practice, an important component of piano pedagogy. The presenter started by pointing out the extensive amount of research dedicated to the relationship between piano practice and the musician's wellness. Existing studies have pointed out different difficulties and solutions for this problem and emphasized the importance of assessing muscle tone for musicians' wellness.

Holian introduced the audience to her research project, where ten subjects (five teachers and five students) assessed their muscle tone and contentment with the sound produced during the performance of C major five-finger patterns, using two physical approaches: Method A focused on playing the patterns with a firm metacarpal arch throughout the performance. In this case each participant determined his/her level of firmness; Method B focused on maintaining a neutral wrist position throughout the performance. Different strategies were used by the participants to obtain information about their muscle tone:
- Vision, which consists of finding the key and recognizing the alignment of the wrist during the placement of the finger on the key
- Proprioception (self-perception), achieved by the sensory organs of the fingers of the monitoring hand
- Hearing, where musicians assess contentment with the sound that is produced.

Findings from the study indicated that when pianists know where to locate and self-monitor the area of muscle contraction, they are able to distinguish between soft and hard muscle tone during piano practice. Method A was related to a stronger muscle tone than Method B. There was also a difference in contentment with musical tones between both methods, as participants indicated greater contentment with tone in Method B. Regarding strategies of muscle tone assessment, the participants initially indicated hearing as the best strategy, but after the study selected proprioception as the primary approach. The ability to perceive muscle tone and contentment with musical tone was not different for right-handed and left-handed participants. All these results were initially hypothesized by the author and later confirmed by the results of the study. The results of this study also suggested that even though muscle tone may be imperceptible to pianists, there is enough muscle activity to depress the key. While playing a passage, each finger may be operating at a different level of muscle tone, thus producing different musical tones.

The presenter concluded with a list of benefits of self-assessing muscle tone, namely the fact that musicians are then able to understand how their movement is produced and correct their position based on the information obtained. This approach can be used with distance learning. Also, the teacher's touch may alter the student's muscle tone with touch. Self-assessment of muscle tone can be used throughout the process of learning a composition on all aspects of the body. This may guide the pianist to find a balanced position that produces the tone quality needed.

Teaching Expressive Playing Through the Use of Words and Singing
Presented by Margarita Denenburg
Thursday, July 29, 2021
Recorded by Angela Leising-Catalan

The presenter began by describing the value of spoken word followed by musical vocalization as part of piano instruction. According to Dr. Denenburg, these elements can provide a meaningful experience and help create an expressive player. Words can help students focus on the known rather than the unknown, and the power of words can help with ear training, imagery, technique, rhythm, memorization, and more.

Rather than the typical Alexander Nikolaev method of See, Play, Hear, the presenter proposed a different approach: Hear, Sing, followed by See, Hear, Play. Dr. Denenburg stated that expressive singing should transfer to expressive rote playing.

The presenter addressed the common concern that many teachers have: what if a student refuses to sing, or doesn't want to sing? She encouraged teachers to maintain an understanding attitude, and never insist that students sing, especially since students come from a variety of backgrounds. Dr. Denenburg stated that teachers can, and should, sing during these student's lessons. Singing will become an innate part of piano lessons, and soon students will join in. Students will still absorb the expressiveness of singing.

Next, the presenter described a lesson activity that included the goal of students internalizing major and minor triads, through singing these triads with words. A video was shown of Dr. Denenburg with a six-year-old student doing this activity, Another video was shown, demonstrating a question-and-answer activity using I-V7 harmony. Lyrics, in this case, were created based on the student's love of cats. The teacher played and sang a question, and the student sang the answer. Teacher and student then played together at the piano.

Moving on, the presenter discussed the presence of pre-written lyrics in commonly used method books. The presenter said that she is constantly singing during lessons, especially with young beginning students. Discussions with these students might include what the song is about, what the mood of the piece is, and what kind of sound would be appropriate for the piece. Dr. Denenburg emphasized the importance of a diverse musical exposure, beyond the typical major tonalities.

Dr. Denenburg continued on, addressing how to approach music that does not come with lyrics already written. She described three approaches.

1. Writing words that include note names. This method was demonstrated using an arrangement of the theme from Liszt's *Rhapsody No. 2* by Artobolevskaya. The presenter created the words, "I jump to B flat, I jump to B flat, I jump to A, I jump to A, I cross to D, I cross to D, and up to F, and up to F!"

2. Using syllables to help fingers (neutral syllables such as "la" or "ba.") A video clip was shown of a teacher with a young student using this method. Another video clip was shown, demonstrating the usefulness of adding words to help accomplish a particular articulation. This video showed a young student playing a Czerny exercise, singing on the syllable "ti" to help achieve an even tone and articulation.

3. Writing words to tell stories. The presenter showed a lullaby from *The Russian School of Piano Playing 1, Part II.* She demonstrated two different sets of lyrics for the same piece, and discussed why one was more effective than the other, based on matching emphasis of the musical phrase and of natural word stress and syllabic emphasis. Continuing with a discussion of intermediate and advanced works, the presenter acknowledged that while it may not be possible to create lyrics for an entire Beethoven sonata, it is possible to create a story that fosters a deeper understanding and atmosphere, as well as a deeper emotional connection to the piece in question. A video clip was shown of a student describing a piece, stating "This piece is about a boy who really misses his mama, but she is not returning". The student then played Schumann's "First Sorrow." Dr. Denenburg then described the lyrics that she wrote for the student.

In closing, Dr. Denenburg gave a list of points to consider when writing lyrics.
- Identify character of the piece
- Identify rhythmic pulse, meter, and rhythmic figures
- Pay attention to the natural "stress" of the music
- Use simple words and phrases that are easy to remember
- Repeat words for identical or similar motives
- Ask students to help write the lyrics!

The presentation ended with an opportunity for attendees to ask questions. An attendee asked, "Do you encourage the same amount of singing from students of all ages? If so, how do you encourage tentative adult and teenage students to incorporate singing?" Dr. Denenburg stated that the key is not to force anything, and to lead by example. She believes that since her own singing is such a central component of how she teaches, singers who are reluctant to sing will still internalize her singing, even if the students themselves choose not to sing.

No Student is an Island: Integrating Collaborative Piano Pedagogy into Your Studio
Presented by Adam Salas and Lauren Koszyk
Thursday, July 29, 2021
Recorded by Angela Leising-Catalan

Adam Salas began the presentation by invoking the words of poet John Donne: "No man is an island entire of itself." The presenter stated that this is a truth also experienced by our piano students. Young student's piano studies can feel isolating at times. Collaborative studies create the opportunity to excite and inspire students. Lauren Koszyk stated that collaborative studies can be a worthwhile and fulfilling addition to the pre-college student's curriculum. Salas shared the goals of the session—to explore the laying of groundwork for successful and straightforward step-by-step approaches to making music with other instrumentalists and vocalists; to provide an overview of the repertoire available and an explanation of introductory collaborative piano skills, partnership techniques, and realistic rehearsal and performance methods.

The presenters continued by describing the benefits of including collaborative piano education into a pre-college studio: the joy of making music with others, learning a specialized skill, and exposing students to a diverse pool of repertoire and experiences. All this leads to more engaged students, with the added bonus of potential additional revenue streams for the teacher. Additionally, the prospect of working with their peers is highly motivating for young students, especially during periods of isolation such as the current pandemic.

Koszyk stated that there are many ways to develop a community of music-making and collaboration. Salas and Koszyk outlined the following opportunities for collaboration.
- With studio mates
- With family members (siblings, parents, friends)
- Connect with another studio teacher
- Summer camp
- Self-recording, along with the use of a track-merging app

The presenters informed the attendees of a number of pre-college collaborative programs at a variety of schools. Those include:
- Eastman School of Music Community Music School in Rochester, New York
- Young Performer's Workshop in Winston Salem, North Carolina
- Texas Christian University Collaborative Piano Summer Workshop in Fort Worth, Texas

Next, the presenters gave a step-by-step plan for introducing collaborative piano to pre-college students.
- Choose music with familiar melodies and/or texts
- Tackle technically challenging spots

- Learn vocal part, by singing or playing on the piano
- Discuss the student's findings and the interconnectedness of the parts
- Discuss rehearsal strategies. In particular, talk about respectful communication, setting standards and expectations, discussing flow of rehearsals, and allowing time for discovery and troubleshooting.

In conclusion, the presenters stated their wish for teachers to share their love of the collaborative art form with the next generation of pianists, and they encouraged attendees to approach the teaching of collaboration with integrity, intentionality, and concrete steps to success. This, in turn, will encourage a wider diversity of students into the field, especially at a time when collaboration and community are more important than ever before.

Intermediate and Early Advanced Piano Gems by Florence Price
Presented by Cole Burger
Thursday, July 29, 2021
Recorded by Ivan Hurd

The presenter directed the audience to the recently published biography of the composer, *The Heart of a Woman: The Life and Music of Florence B. Price* by Rae Linda Brown. The presenter and Florence Price share a connection in that they are both from the state of Arkansas.

Dr. Burger began the lecture recital by performing Price's *Breezes*, a level 4-5 piece (Magrath), written in E Major. The audience was encouraged to listen to how the melody of the piece sounds like a breeze that changes as it passes over various landscapes. Students would be encouraged to analyze the various key areas of the piece and work to achieve a flowing sound as if there were no barlines. It works as an etude as well, helping students to play with an even tone quality.

The second piece, *Rainbow Waltz*, is one of several waltzes by Price. Dr. Burger believes the title might stem from the left-hand crosses which create the gesture of a rainbow passing over the right-hand. The piece features a left-hand melody in the A section, which then transitions to the right-hand. Rainbows might also be a reference to the sunny quality of the harmony.

Dr. Burger noted that, like Debussy's *Reverie*, Price's piece of the same title is also in the key of F major. Price wrote approximately eleven pieces with similar titles, such as *Dream Boat*. Dr. Burger graded this as the most difficult of the five pieces shared in the recital and is also one of his favorites. Before proceeding to the fourth piece, the audience was provided with information on where to purchase the music.

The fourth piece, "Move Behind a Cloud," is from the collection *Snapshots* written toward the end of Price's life between 1947-1952. The harmonic language of this piece uses pentatonic and whole-tone pitch collections. There are several tempo changes in this piece, as if the moon is out in the sky but is covered by moving clouds. Burger compares the difficulty in musicality of this piece to the technical difficulty of *Reverie*.

To conclude the lecture-recital, Burger performed "The Park," from the cycle *Village Scenes* written in 1942. He asked the audience to envision the various people and actions happening throughout the park.

The pieces shared in the lecture-recital displayed a variety moods, tempi, and length, yet are of a similar level of difficulty. The audience was encouraged to explore Price's music despite any reading challenges of how rhythms may be beamed or lack of pedal markings. Dr. Burger directed the audience to explore other collections, some of which highlight social issues of the time, such as *Thumbnail Sketches in the Life of a Washer Woman*, *Scenes in Tin Can Alley*, and *Three Miniature Portraits of Uncle Ned.*

Rhythm Without the Blues: Have a Blast Teaching Rhythm in 45 Minutes
Presented by Beth Sussman
Thursday, July 29, 2021
Recorded by Ivan Hurd

The presenter works in school systems with classroom teachers and pre-K through fifth-grade children that have little to no musical background. The goal of the presenter's work is to covertly connect music to the academic subjects students are learning.

The presenter began by leading the audience through a chant from Ghana called *Kye Kye Kule* by call and response. The first time the chant is done at a *forte* dynamic, the second time *piano* and *staccato*, and the last time *forte* and *legato* while clapping. The last time is challenging as two things are happening simultaneously: singing the rhythm and clapping the beat. Sussman makes the point that rhythm and the beat are two different things. Rhythm is always changing but beat remains the same. Start by clapping and counting a steady beat.

In the next part of the session, the presenter introduced various symbols used during the class for when to stay silent, when a question is being asked, when to answer questions, and when to clap a rhythm together. This provides a means of organization for the lesson. The activity is first done in complete silence as the presenter places four blue plastic cups on a table and signals that each cup is one beat (quarter notes). Four red cups are introduced with two claps each (eighth notes). After the red cups, clear cups are used to represent a beat of silence (quarter rest). Before moving on to yellow cups, the blue, red, and clear cups are reviewed. Each yellow cup receives four claps (sixteenth notes). There are always four cups on the table indicating 4/4 time. Each cup is one beat, and the various colors represent different rhythms that can be used for each beat.

Sussman led the attendees through various rhythm patterns, noting that, when in person, individual students would join at the front of the class. Sussman used a descriptive counting system. "One" is used for quarter notes (blue cups), "two-ooo" is used for eighth notes (red cups), "four-or-or-or" is used for sixteenth notes (yellow cups), and "rest" is used for quarter rests (clear cups). From here, Sussman transitioned to using the Takadimi system, a syllabic counting approach, and led the audience through several examples.

To help kids learn to read left to right, gain an understanding of the space in which beats exist, and track several lines of rhythm, Sussman uses a grid of sixteen squares each representing a beat. First, students use Cheerios to place on the grid for one beat and leave blank squares for rests. Students point and chant their example on the grid.

In the next activity, "Silly Conducting," Sussman demonstrated how to use hands, elbows, teeth, and body movement in a fun way to help students learn to keep a steady beat to recorded music.

Sussman provided endless ideas for body movement gestures during the recording, such as shooing away flies, nodding yes and no, shrugging shoulders for "I don't know," etc.
After leading a class through several examples of clapping rhythm exercises with the cups, Sussman introduces rhythmic value symbols that are color-coordinated with the cups as a smooth transition to reading traditional rhythm.

Sussman provided helpful resources: joppity.com and her YouTube channel, Miss Beth Piano.

Teaching Chopin From Early-Intermediate Through Advanced: Same Concepts Just a Lot Harder!
Presented by Ingrid Clarfield
Thursday, July 29, 2021
Recorded by Curtis Pavey

In this session, Professor Clarfield helped participants understand the necessary concepts and skills to develop in piano students from the early-intermediate through advanced levels as they study music by Frédéric Chopin. Throughout the presentation, Professor Clarfield was assisted through the playing of Dr. Kairy Koshoeva, an accomplished concert pianist and a faculty member at The New School for Music Study.

To begin the presentation, Dr. Koshoeva performed Chopin's *Ballade No. 3 in A-flat Major,* Op. 47. Before the performance began, Professor Clarfield asked participants of the session to take out a pad of paper and to write down ten different concepts that appeared in this work and other works by Chopin. After Dr. Koshoeva's very musical and impressive performance, Professor Clarfield offered her seven stylistic traits that must be mastered before diving deeply into the advanced piano works of Chopin. The first stylistic trait that is necessary for a student to master is creating a beautiful singing tone at the piano. Professor Clarfield remarked that the human voice was Chopin's favorite instrument, apparent by his regular attendance of operatic performances and also by his beautiful singing lines in both the right and left hand. Voicing of complicated textures in both hands, was the second of the stylistic traits, and was demonstrated with the opening of the Chopin *Ballade No. 3*. A clear understanding of harmonic tension and release was Professor Clarfield's third stylistic trait. She demonstrated how shifts of mode, surprising color changes, and Chopin's use of non-chord tones helped to create a musically rich experience for the listener, but only if played in a sensitive way. Citing several quotes of Berlioz discussing Chopin's free approach to *rubato*, Professor Clarfield remarked that a clear understanding of *rubato* and tempo flexibility was certainly necessary for any performance of Chopin's music. Additionally, students need to have mastered a variety of pedal techniques and the ability to make interpretive decisions based on a number of different options in Chopin's publications. Besides these, Professor Clarfield also emphasized the need to develop a student's sense of color, emotion, and character along with pacing large-scale *crescendos* and *decrescendos*.

With these traits in mind, Professor Clarfield offered a number of pieces that she recommends students to study prior to learning the challenging works of Chopin. Most of these pieces came from publications she has co-authored including: *Keys to Stylistic Mastery* (Book 3), *Keys to Artistic Performance* (Book 3), and *Classics for the Developing Pianist* (Book 3 and Book 4). In discussing each of these pieces, Professor Clarfield and Dr. Koshoeva performed excerpts as a duet team, demonstrated the stylistic traits hidden in each work, and offered practice and interpretive suggestions as needed. Among the highlights were appropriate lyrics given to Chopin's *Prelude in B Minor* (Op. 28, No. 6), suggestions for pedaling in Chopin's *"Minute" Waltz*, and demonstrations of voicing material in the left hand. The presentation concluded with a world premier of a piece from Tom Gerou's new book, *Novellas, Book II,* titled "Evening on the River Nile." The piece demonstrated a number of the stylistic traits needed to perform Chopin's works at a high level, with interesting harmonic and melodic material, complicated rhythms, and more.

In sum, Professor Clarfield's presentation gave participants a more thorough understanding of the concepts needed for their students to play the works of Chopin at the highest level both musically and technically.

Special Needs and Creativity: Improvisation as a Blueprint for Learning
Presented by Scott Price
Thursday July 29, 2021
Recorded by Leonidas Lagrimas

Teaching improvisation in the piano studio yields a wealth of musical, social, and intellectual benefits for both teacher and student. For piano teachers of special needs students, improvisation's greatest benefit of all might be as a template or "blueprint" to engage all learners. Price's presentation showcased the possibilities of utilizing adaptive pedagogy as a tool for exploring improvisation with special needs pianists. Adaptive pedagogy is largely built on the premise that special needs students should be thought of as *part of*—and not *less than.* Teachers who work with special needs students should be willing and able to adapt their teaching strategy to fit the individualized, unique needs of the special learner, as well as the unpredictability that may accompany these needs, from one moment to the next. With a focus on exploration and continual validation of student success, improvisation is a natural fit for adaptive pedagogy to engage special needs students.

As part of his overall definition of adaptive pedagogy process, Price emphasized that the term "special needs" encompasses a wide range of issues—developmental disabilities can be physical, such as fine motor skills or visual impairment, or they can take the form of mental/intellectual and emotional impairment. A useful reminder to all teachers is that much of what we consider common knowledge in music is actually built on abstract and non-intuitive concepts, so we should be mindful to give directions as literally and exactly as possible. Finally, all teachers need to be mindful to avoid the layering of multiple thinking processes for students and focus on step-by-step instructions that are clear and easily demonstrated/modeled for the student. Another key aspect of adaptive pedagogy involves conceiving the piano studio as a "safe space" for students. Among the essential components that comprise a safe space include:

- Allowing both teacher and student the opportunity to decompress and feel comfortable in their own identity.
- The necessary teacher persona for utilizing adaptive pedagogy with special learners, which includes remaining calm at all times, using appropriate body language to model calmness and patience, using a "perpetual" smile and encouraging tone of voice, and the avoidance of any negative self-talk or directions.
- Rather than casting critiques or advice in a negative light, ask students to try again in a different manner. In short, every moment in a lesson is an opportunity for validation, a teachable moment, a chance to celebrate success, no matter how small.
- The importance of establishing a manageable and consistent teaching routine that avoids layering of directions.
- Allowing special needs students to "invite you in" regarding the lesson activity. Asking permission and ensuring that students are truly ready to begin is a good way to ensure the

"safe space" atmosphere throughout the lesson. If the student exhibits negative or avoidant behavior, teachers can utilize what Price calls a "gentle insistence" in getting them to participate and continue to model desired behavior at all times.

One component of improvisation that makes it so potentially worthwhile and rewarding for special needs students is the idea that improvisation is essentially the exploration of sound; a process that can be shaped by a minimum of rules and structure. Price notes that success in allowing improvisation to be part of the lesson means placing the process within the context of adaptive pedagogy. For example, a musical concept such as keeping a steady beat can be taught as a guided coaching, with exact modeling and the use of guide words (*e.g.* chanting in strict rhythm "play-different-play-different-play-different" while moving around to different notes on the keyboard.) Teachers must take extra care and plan activities that avoid the "layering" process of combining multiple thought processes or directives at once. Counting in rhythm, for example, presents multiple potential intellectual/physical pitfalls for a special needs student, as does modeling left- and right-hand activities in a face-to-face set up, which reverses the orientation for the student.

The presentation concluded with valuable opportunities to watch improvisation being taught to special needs learners in lesson footage. Price shared a wonderful experience of a 14-year-old male student on the autism spectrum progressing through multiple lessons of exploring improvisation, from exploring melodic steps on the piano, through adding simple harmonization to his melodies, and finally melodic/rhythmic improvisation over harmonies with a steady sense of meter and pulse. Recital footage of special needs students improvising in a performance setting with Price providing harmonic duet accompaniment was also an enlightening experience. Perhaps the most powerful message to be taken from the recorded footage was Price's assertion that improvisation provides an opportunity for special needs students to express themselves through sound, explore their creative potential, and experience success as music performers—opportunities that they might not normally have in their daily lives. Indeed, this was a valuable reminder of the life-changing impact our work as music teachers can have on our students.

Time to Unmute:
Adapting Cooperative Learning Activities for Hybrid and Virtual Group Piano Labs

Presented by Todd Van Kekerix and John Patrick Murphy
Thursday, July 29, 2021
Recorded by Omar Roy

Dr. Van Kekerix initiated the presentation by highlighting the issues many teachers faced at the onset of the pandemic and the rapid pivot to virtual instruction, and encouraged teachers to use this as an opportue moment to reflect on how teachers can enhance the virtual environment for students. He also highlighted that "top-down" instruction became prevalent due to the circumstances and relative inexperience of teachers with the virtual format. This session explored how to adapt cooperative learning structures to the group piano lab to foster student-centered learning in a virtual format, and was divided into four parts:

I. Psychological, Instructional, and Technological Challenges
II. A Brief Introduction to Cooperative Learning
III. Adapting Cooperative Learning Structures
IV. A Virtual Cooperative Learning Activity (Audience Participation)

Part I: Psychological, Instructional, and Technological Challenges

Psychological Challenges:

Dr. Murphy introduced the first segment of the session by reflecting on four psychological challenges associated with virtual instruction:

- Isolation
- Zoom fatigue
- Eye gaze
- Transmission delay

To address isolation, Dr. Murphy suggested having students actively participate in class by unmuting and encouraging them to turn their cameras on, facilitating pre-class conversations by asking open-ended questions, calling on students by name, and having students add or update their preferred names in Zoom's settings.

In his exploration of "Zoom fatigue," Dr. Murphy referred to the article *Nonverbal Overload: A Theoretical Argument for the Causes of Zoom Fatigue* by cognitive psychologist Dr. Jeremy Bailenson, in which he identifies "eye gaze" as one of the four possible causes of Zoom fatigue. Students and teachers are prone to this as Zoom interactions amplify behaviors typically reserved for close relationships, such as long stretches of direct eye contact. As a solution, Dr. Murphy suggested hiding self-view, preventing users from seeing themselves in the video display, and also employing a variety of camera angles. Additionally, he suggested using audio-only meetings when possible, though it may not necessarily be applicable for a group piano class.

Transmission delay describes how technological delays in audio-video transmission can alter an individual's perception of a speaker. Consequently, Dr. Murphy cautioned that instructors may inadvertently perceive students as inattentive due to delays as short as one millisecond, and suggested that teachers be mindful of this in their interactions with students.

Instructional Challenges:

Dr. Van Kekerix highlighted that the barriers of virtual instruction often led instructors to default to a top-down approach to teaching. Other challenges included adapting non-verbal communication to virtual instruction, such as using chat-features to send messages directly to students. He also emphasized the use of programs like ReClipped or Collabra as more effective ways to give feedback in student-submitted videos. Lastly, Dr. Van Kekerix stated that pacing in online classes and lessons is dramatically different than in-person instruction, and that it is important to allow students time to digest content without feeling the need to fill the entire class time with lectures or activities.

Technological Challenges:

Dr. Murphy noted that, by design, the virtual format reduces interaction in addition to other practical issues. Some technology and interaction tips for Zoom include:

- Using an ethernet connection
- Turning on "High Fidelity Music" Mode
- Utilizing background noise suppression
- Unmuting and encouraging discussion
- Breakout Rooms and Polls

Dr. Murphy emphasized setting reasonable expectations for students like having reliable internet access and having access to a keyboard instrument in addition to standard expectations like having required materials and attending class on time. Additionally, he emphasized that a virtual or hybrid lab shares similar routines with a standard classroom, and encouraged consistency in distribution of materials, communication, and assignment submission. Some communication strategies included pre-made slides, including page numbers, annotating slides during presentations, screenshotting, polling, and saving the chat from a class session.

Part II: Cooperative Learning

Dr. Van Kekerix referred to Alejandro Cremachi's definition of Cooperative Learning and emphasized its focus on student-centered learning:

"Cooperative learning provides opportunities for the students to talk, listen, share, and to teach each in an active mode, to develop higher-order thinking and to apply what they are learning in a safe, peer-to-peer environment."

There are five elements to successful cooperative learning, all of which are possible in a virtual learning environment:

- Positive interdependence
- Face-to-face interaction
- Individual accountability
- Social skills
- Group processing

Dr. Van Kekerix cautioned that successful implementation requires proper planning before class, and instructors must lay a solid groundwork of communication of instructions. He also noted the benefits of cooperative learning such as building leadership skills, learning how to work as part of a team, building communication skills, and learning conflict management.

Part III: Adapting Cooperative Learning Structures

Dr. Van Kekerix noted that cooperative learning structures are common in many group piano classrooms. However, successful implementation in a virtual classroom requires going beyond the traditional classroom strategies. Dr. Murphy and Dr. Van Kekerix suggested implementing the following structures:

- *Think-Pair-Share*: Students are assigned a problem to solve, and they are given a brief amount of time to independently develop a solution before convening with a classmate and generating a unified response to share with the class. This can be facilitated using breakout rooms in Zoom.
- *Pair Check*: Students are held accountable to individually contribute and engage through peer-learning interactions. In this scenario, paired students alternate between developing a solution for a problem and acting as a supportive coach for the other member. The presenters noted that this can be especially effective when addressing harmonization exercises.

- *Jigsaw*: This structure works best with a broad topic where students can work out smaller details. In this structure, students are split into groups where each group is responsible for a specific piece of content within a larger context. The groups are then remade so that each group contains one student from the other groups who each teach their content to the group, before content assignments are made again.
- *Send a Problem*: This structure involves individual groups being assigned a problem and given time to work on a solution. The problems and solutions are then circulated to other groups and these groups assess the feasibility of the solutions and develop alternatives. Dr. Van Kekerix highlighted score-reading exercises such as a Bach cantata and the necessity of making decisions regarding fingering.

Part IV: A Virtual Cooperative Learning Activity (Audience Participation)

The final segment of this presentation was a modified "Think-Pair-Share" activity in which the audience was given one minute to reflect on a question prompt before sharing their responses within small groups in breakout rooms. The discussion prompt was as follows: *What interactive group learning activities do you find to be most successful in virtual or hybrid group piano labs?*

Kaleidoscope Career:
Adaptive Strategies for Teaching Students Interested in the Music Industry
Presented by Andy Villemez
Thursday, July 29, 2021
Recorded by Luís Pipa

The presenter teaches at the University of Cincinnati, where there is a relatively new degree in Commercial Music Production. For the past three to four years, he has been teaching a two-semester keyboard skills class in this curriculum, becoming more intimate and knowledgeable with the needs and activities of these students and how keyboard skills play into their careers. With a little bit of knowledge, teachers can easily adapt materials and pedagogical strategies of traditional private and group piano lessons to meet what the students are going to encounter.

First, it is important to define what "Commercial Music," or "Music Industry," means. In that context, it is crucial to know what the student's expectations are in this career, to define how the keyboard is used, and to be aware of the importance of an efficient workflow. The pedagogical approach includes learning reading, rhythm, and technique, but all these elements must incorporate creativity.

The most common paths students take are:
- Audio Engineering
- Digital Music Production
- Songwriting
- Studio/Touring Musician
- Studio Film Composition

For this, they must be skilled in technology and software, but they are also often trained in multiple instruments and get knowledge in creative composition. Because of the students' expectations, their computer is as valuable as their instruments. So, how they use their software is a hugely important part of their career. Thus, compared to the conventional training of a classical musician, composition and creativity are essential for this type of students.

The keyboard is a performance tool, whether it is an acoustic or an electric piano, or even a synthesizer; but it works also as the primary interface and tool with which the students interact with the software that they will use—a digital audio workstation.

A classical student typically has reading and technique as first priorities, then theory and aural skills, and creativity and technology at the bottom. However, the music industry student has aural skills and creativity at the top, then technology, theory, and technique, with reading coming last.

The reason why these things are different has to do with the workflow. The fact that reading appears on opposite sides in the priorities has to do with the fact that students use this skill in different ways. In order to compose, students in the music industry course do not use programs such as *Sibelius* or *Finale*, but rather use recordings of different lengths in their workstations. Working with small sections will help their workflow. The curriculum encourages them to work creatively on patterns that they learn. The presenter emphasized the following elements:

- Rhythmic accuracy is important, but these students learn simple patterns, where feeling the pulse is most important.
- Technique is given in a simple manner by practicing mostly scales and chords, but always applied creatively. Scales are played with one hand only, and students must introduce different rhythms and articulations.
- Reading is done in "Keyboard Style," which means that students read a melody line in the right hand using the top finger or fingers; the indication of chords through cyphers has to be filled with the other right-hand fingers, and the bass line needs to be created by the left hand. This type of exercise prepares the students to tackle any style. Villemez gave a few examples of how he teaches this skill, particularly concerning voice-leading.
- Incorporating creativity is done by making the student harmonically explore a given pattern such as "Twinkle Twinkle Little Star," or complete the remaining part of a prelude with fourteen bars given.

The presenter has published a textbook with these and other examples, available in autumn of 2021. The session ended with Villemez summarizing the principal ideas of his presentation, after which he answered a few questions posed by the audience.

Learning Through Imagery: A Multi-Sensory Approach for Successful Outcomes
Presented by Eneida Larti
Friday, July 30, 2021
Recorded by Autumn L. Zander

All too often, phrases such as "just visualize it" or "hear the melody in your mind" creep into conversations about performing and teaching. However, what these phrases mean and how to execute them can feel like a mystery. With a clear understanding of what imagery is, tangible scientific evidence that supports the benefits of imagery, and the sage teaching experiences of master pedagogues, pianists and teachers are presented with strategies to help develop a greater sense of ease and confidence in learning and performing repertoire.

When introducing the concept of imagery, Larti provided a common definition as created by researchers Donald J. Wright, Caroline J. Wakefield, and Dave Smith. They state that, "Imagery is the process of using multiple senses to simulate an experience in the mind, typically in the absence of overly physical movement."

Historically speaking, great pedagogues such as Karl Leimer, teacher of Walter Gieseking, and Rosina Lhevinne were champions of "mental practice." In an interview excerpt with John Browning, student of Rosina Lhevinne, he discussed the specificity of mental practice that Lhevinne expected. This included knowing each note, each fingering, each dynamic marking, *etc.* in a piece without having to consult the score. Lhevinne believed that if one could not do this, one does not know the music and will not be confident in public performance.

Outside of the musical world, opinions varied regarding the value of imagery in practice, particularly with the early twentieth-century behaviorist movement and their skepticism around this practice. Yet by the 1960s and the "cognitive revolution," opinions began to change regarding its value. Larti then shared her research on fMRI, "functional Magnetic Resonance Imagining," and how these results support the value of imagery in music study.

A 2013 study tracked brain activity with both auditory and visual imagery. The auditory sessions involved participants recalling/imagining familiar melodies in the "mind's ear" while the visual sessions involved the recall and imagining of a specific object. Scientists discovered that when engaging in one modality (visual or auditory) an individual uses a wider network that includes elements of attention, memory, motor retrieval, and semantic processing. Larti stated that these significant findings reinforce the multi-sensory effect that takes place during imagery.

Another study explored whether musical perception and musical imagery in musicians activated the same areas of the brain. Surprisingly, the study showed that more areas of the brain were activated during the musical imagery moments. Larti stated that scientists believe that musical imagery requires more involvement and engagement from the brain and that, in turn, resulted in more brain activity.

There are several important factors to consider when addressing mental and musical imagery. Mental imagery can be involuntary, it can involve all the senses, and it can be focused on a specific sensory modality. Musical imagery can include imagining the sound without hearing it, imagining notation without seeing it, and feeling movement without musculoskeletal activity.

Imagery utilizes many different senses but Larti addressed the following categories:
1. **Motor imagery** - feeling a movement, such as how one's fingers move on the keyboard.
2. **Visual imagery** - visualizing a movement in either first or third person, such as visualizing oneself making a specific movement or acting as a spectator watching oneself on stage making the specific movement.
3. **Auditory imagery** - organizing sounds without external sources, such as hearing a piece away from the instrument.

The Pettlep model developed by Caroline Wakefield and Dave Smith in 2001 explores seven components to enhance the effectiveness of imagery application. The components include: physical, environment, task, timing, learning, emotion, and perspective. For example, the researchers suggest trying to recreate the specific physical issues regarding performance anxiety, such as racing heartbeat, during the imagery sessions to help build confidence during a performance when the racing heartbeat may occur.

Larti shared several ways in which imagery can be utilized in the teaching studio with younger students. Utilizing the book *Visualizing and Verbalizing* by Nancy Bell, Larti developed a chart with a series of questions to help develop a guide for imagery. The chart explores aspects of phrasing, the mood of the piece, *etc.* Another worksheet addressed the technical aspect of the piece such as meter, rhythm, the highest note in the music, *etc.* The final technique addressed was mapping music, as per Rebecca Shockley's book, *Mapping Music: For Faster Learning and Secure Memory*. With more advanced students Lari suggested that mental practice can be addressed via the exploration of large ideas, such as musical structure, and then exploring smaller details such as harmonic changes, until a complete representation of the piece can be achieved.

As a parting thought, Larti stated that combining mental practice with practice at the instrument will result in stronger memory for the performer, greater ease with technical passages, and potential reduction in performance anxiety due to the solid foundation of knowledge. A reduction in the overall learning time of repertoire is another possibility when imagery is incorporated into practice. To summarize these concepts, a video clip of the movie *Free Solo* was shown. Climber

Alex Honnold discussed his visualization practices in preparation for his climb of the 3,000-ft. mountain El Capitan without the use of ropes, harnesses, or protective equipment.

How to Run a Conservatory–Online!
Presented by Emily Ezola
Friday, July 30, 2021
Recorded by Angela Leising-Catalan

Emily Ezola began the presentation with a brief overview of Utah State University's Youth Conservatory. Since 1978, it has been a training lab for aspiring piano teachers, while inspiring pre-college students to foster a life-long love for music, in an environment filled with enthusiasm and enjoyment. Utah State University piano majors teach in the conservatory as part of their studies. Each week, over 100 young pianists come to the conservatory for private lessons, group classes, and performances opportunities. The presenter expressed her wish that attendees leave this presentation feeling equipped to administer a similar program in scope and size with confidence, online or in-person.

Ezola stated that one of the most helpful and important technological tools is MyMusicStaff, in her experience. She described how it helps her manage lesson scheduling, invoicing, and communication. All student info is stored and shared with teachers. Cost is associated with the number of students and teachers utilizing the software.

The building blocks of the Youth Conservatory program are:
- teachers who believe in and receive regular feedback and training opportunities,
- a curriculum that provides structure and flexibility,
- weekly group classes that promote peer interaction,
- frequent low-stakes performance opportunities, and
- yearly traditions like Monster Concert and PianoFest. (Ezola mentioned that the yearly tradition events are open to teachers in the community.)

The presenter described the weekly group classes in more detail. These classes are typically held in the keyboard lab, where students enjoy the benefits of practicing technique, sight reading, improvisation, and ensemble playing. Of special note is the AIM Program (Achievement in Music Program) run by the Utah Music Teachers Association. This program allows students to progress through ten levels and receive yearly testing in the areas of sight reading, technique, ear training, music theory, and performance. Ezola shared that switching these group classes to an online format due to the pandemic was "not as hard as you would imagine," and that it allowed teachers a sneak-peek into the learning environments of the students. Teachers focused on creating highly interactive game-based learning. A video clip was shared from one such class in which a teacher demonstrates how to build major five-finger patterns.

Next, Ezola described the performance opportunities that are held at the Youth Conservatory. To continue the standard monthly recital tradition, the Youth Conservatory moved to a pre-recorded format which was then broadcast via Zoom. All recitals were stored and later shared on the Youth Conservatory YouTube channel. Ezola mentioned that an added "perk" of the online format is that family members from far away could listen in and enjoy the performances. A video was also shared that featured six students playing a Halloween ensemble piece via Zoom. This was made possible with a click track (or backing track) so students could practice and then record their parts. These parts were then compiled into one video. Professionals were hired to do the video editing. Another popular performance opportunity is the yearly Christmas concert. For the 2020 year, students submitted videos of small sections of a piece that were then "cut and pasted" into one video. The presenter described this as a "musical chairs effect."

Ezola went on to describe the last major event of the year for the Youth Conservatory, which is the USC Piano Fest, which is also open to piano teachers from anywhere. Typically, students arrive at the USC campus and are invited to participate in as many categories as they wish, within their age categories. For 2020, students were invited to participate in an online, synchronous masterclass with members of the USC faculty. The presenter stated that the 2020 event had record enrollment, which is attributed to the accessibility of the online format. She then shared a video clip of this masterclass. Internet reliability is always an issue with this format, Ezola stated, but nevertheless it is a challenge that can be overcome.

The presenter opened the floor to questions, and also invited any attendee to reach out to her at a later point. She also noted that more information is available on the Youth Conservatory website, as well as on the Youth Conservatory YouTube channel. Future plans for the Youth Conservatory include a return to in-person events, depending on the COVID situation.

Reaching Digital Native Music Majors:
Pedagogy for Undergraduate Group Piano in the 21st Century
Presented by Rachel D. Hahn
Friday, July 30, 2021
Recorded by Angela Leising-Catalan

The presenter began by explaining that her research was a part of dissertation work completed at the University of Missouri in 2019. Members of her group piano classes inspired and contributed to this research over a three-year period. Dr. Hahn stated that group piano has been a core element of music major curriculum for decades. However, little empirical research exists regarding the specific practices that lead to student success.

The presenter stated that this study comprises three investigations, designed to investigate how instructors can best accommodate today's music majors. The first investigation was a review of the literature that summarizes what is currently known about group piano at the collegiate level. The second investigation was phenomenological, qualitative study involving first-semester group piano students experiencing the college adaptation process. The third investigation was an experimental study that was designed to explore the effects of various technology tools on student achievement in class practice sessions.

To understand our music majors, according to Dr. Hahn, it is important to find a few constructs that apply to this population. Today's music majors are digital natives and emerging adults, caught in the middle of a fundamental life transition. Research indicates that digital natives use different learning processes than their generational predecessors, and studies have identified a diverse array of twenty-first-century skills needed for modern life. These skills include the four Cs: creativity/innovation, critical thinking/problem solving, communication, and collaboration. It is also important to understand the value of group piano in today's collegiate coursework. Group piano is also one of the first classes that music makers encounter in college. Learning practice skills on a secondary instrument in a group environment sets this class apart from other core music classes and private lessons. In addition, Dr. Hahn stated that the fundamental skills learned in group piano provide a foundation for a variety of music careers.

Dr. Hahn spoke about the qualitative study; understanding how college students adapt to new coursework, specifically group piano, may help instructors to tailor their curriculum to the needs of individual students. Dr. Hahn interviewed six first-semester students who were enrolled in group piano level one. The interview questions included basic demographic information and literature-based questions describing the collegiate adaptation process. The presenter began analyzing the data with narrow units of analysis, and broadened to wider units as she analyzed interview transcripts, along with written student summaries. Each participant read the transcripts to check it for accuracy, and outside reviewers also analyzed the data coding to check it for accuracy.

Dr. Hahn went on to explain that coding resulted in the emergence of five themes. These themes were preparedness, motivation, priorities and expectations, support systems, and accomplishment/empowerment. These themes had been identified in previous literature; however, new traits within these themes were discovered that had not been researched previously.

- **Preparedness**
  The ability to prepare for college AND the specific demands of group piano class.
- **Motivation**
  Ability to motivate oneself for college and group piano tasks.
- **Priorities and expectations**
  Unique and individualized student priorities and expectations for college music study.
- **Support systems**
  The people (both on and off campus) who help students succeed.
- **Accomplishment/empowerment**
  Feelings associated with completing specific group piano assignments and mastering techniques and skills.

The presenter continued by explaining the "take-away" from the research. The complexity of relationships among these five themes highlights the importance of adaptation as a framework for planning group piano curriculum. Teachers and students may be better equipped to handle challenges and obstacles if they face those obstacles together, and work on related solutions in the context of everyone's adaptation experience.

Moving on, Dr. Hahn highlighted the findings of the third study, a quantitative experiment involving technology-assisted practice. Rapid changes in technology have encouraged many music majors' educators to use a variety of new tools in the classroom. The purpose of this study was to explore the use of three technology tools and compare them with a non-technology group, to ascertain how they assisted student achievement during class practice sessions. An added purpose was to explore how student background variables impacted technology use and achievement. The forty-three participants in this study were music majors enrolled in either Level 1 or Level 3 group piano. Students participated in two practice sessions at Week 5 and Week 10 of the semester. Students completed a pre-test survey, and were then given an unfamiliar piece of music, and recorded themselves. After the session, students were given thirteen-and-a-half minutes to practice that unfamiliar piece of music, using their assigned technology. (Or, in the case of the control group, no technology.) After these practice sessions, students completed another performance of the piece and recorded that final performance, and then completed a post-test survey and self-evaluation. Two expert judges rated the student recordings (both the original sight-reading recordings and the final recording) according to a multi-dimensional assessment rubric.

When comparing the performance achievement of students across all three technology groups and the control group, the findings of this research demonstrated that there were no significant differences in student achievement. This may be surprising, Dr. Hahn stated, and one might think that a student that had access to a YouTube video, for example, would do better than a student that had access to no technology. Or, a student that was practicing with Tempo SloMo, may do better than a student who had only a simple metronome. However, these results may be less surprising if we consider each student as a unique individual, with strong personal preferences. The presenter observed many students showed great emotional displays, either excitement or dismay, regarding the technology that they were randomly assigned. If students had been given the choice to practice with their favorite app, that may have had a greater impact on their achievement and success in practicing with that tool.

The second important finding of this study, according to Dr. Hahn, is that background experience variables did have a significant impact on student achievement. In particular, Dr. Hahn found that the Level 1 students scored significantly higher than their Level 3 peers during the Week 5 final performance. This may suggest that the more difficult nature of the Level 3 curriculum had outpaced the developmental skill levels of those Level 3 students. Instructors should consider the fast-paced nature of group piano curriculum, and how this routine and sequence may not fit the needs of all learners. Dr. Hahn stated that the results also indicate that students who had prior piano experience before coming to college scored significantly higher than their inexperienced peers, unsurprisingly. However, it is interesting to note that students that had prior piano experience did not score significantly higher on the final performance recordings, either in Week 5 or Week 10. This may suggest that the brief practice sessions in this study were enough to level the playing field and allow all students to reach a level of proficiency with these unknown pieces of music. This should be an encouraging development for group piano instructors and suggests that we all should continue implementing various technologies and exploring how brief, in-class practice sessions may help to level the playing field and assist all students, especially struggling or inexperienced students.

"So, what do we take away from this research?," Dr. Hahn asked. She stated that the experience of music majors in the group piano sequence seems to reveal common trends, as well as the importance of individual differences on student's success. Instructors should be well-versed in research regarding effective practice habits and classroom routines for undergraduate students, as well as literature that describes the characteristics of this age group. However, teachers can best reach their students by building relationships, learning about individual differences, and assessing each learner's unique needs in context, and adapting curriculum to meet those needs. Instructors also need to make explicit why students need piano skills. Pairing freshmen students with junior/senior mentors may help those students to understand how piano skills are applied in upper-level course work such as conducting or rehearsal techniques. In addition, connecting coursework with real, twenty-first-century jobs and gigging may help students see the big picture of how piano will affect their future careers. Students also value options and choice in their college coursework. Providing an array of pedagogically sound technology tools to choose from, as well as student projects, may help student motivation, as well as other challenges that come with college adaptation, such as procrastination and time management. Although teachers do not have to be experts in technology, they should have the knowledge and skills to help students with trouble shooting.

Dr. Hahn stated that technology is not a magical cure to solve all student problems. However, when combined with thoughtful planning, various technologies may assist students and teachers in developing successful practice routines. In addition, 93% of participants in the quantitative experiment indicated that technology helped them in their practice in some way. It is possible that technology can assist with student's perception and feelings of accomplishment. Research suggests that further research is needed to understand the complexities of teaching group piano. As we move forward with twenty-first-century teaching, it is important to consider the limitations of these studies and expand our knowledge with further investigations.

How to Approach Jazz and Pop for a Classical Teacher
Presented by Christopher Norton
Friday, July 30, 2021
Recorded by Kate Acone

This presentation covered ways to teach jazz, rock, and pop styles using three pieces from Norton's book *Connections 4 Piano*. Norton presented the pieces as notated in the book and then presented options for improvisation, preparation, and rearranging based on each piece. Some of these activities included harmonic progressions and chords, some involved playing with backing tracks, and some were based on scalar improvisation.

He first introduced "Deep in Thought," a lyrical 3/4 piece based on a harmonic progression of extended chords. After demonstrating the piece in its entirety, the presenter delivered a formal analysis of the sections to chart the harmonic patterns. These underlying harmonies were easily turned into blocked chords, a great start for an improvisation activity alongside the backing track. The next improvisational activity was to play an *ostinato* pattern in the left hand while improvising a melody based on an F-major scale with the right hand. This right-hand pattern could be decorated with grace notes or parallel fourths. Other ideas for the right hand include answering an "A" idea with a "B" idea, trying AABA or AABCAA forms, and playing very freely.

The second piece was "Open Window," an eight-beat piece with a Latin feel heard easily via the backing track rhythm. After a demonstration of the whole piece, he showed a two-hand rhythm pattern to prepare the piece. The harmonic progression was much simpler than "Deep in Thought," so his suggested preparation and improvisation centered around the rhythmic expression, in addition to playing and "savoring" the harmonic progression.

The third, "Positively Swinging," has a big-band style jazz swing backing track. The twelve-bar blues pattern is used throughout, and his suggested preparation included transposing the chords to other keys. The improvisation activity is to play the C blues scale on top of the backing track in various rhythms. Other ideas include making a two-bar idea and repeating it up the octave, making a two-bar question and answer, playing more than one note at a time, trying longer ideas, and to try continuous eighth notes, grace notes, and pedal notes. He also suggested rhythmic exercises for improvisation, like using a drum pattern to start ideas or making your own rhythm pattern and building on that.

Norton also suggested using modal improvisation to create more ideas for all three pieces. Finally, he presented options for reworking the left-hand voicing in all three pieces to highlight different scale options for improvisation in the right hand. One could choose to re-voice the left hand, use blocked chords, or use the left-hand patterns of the piece itself.

During the question and answer period, he discussed right- and left-hand coordination. He has students practice in two-bar stretches, even with improvisation, to practice patterns, chords, and coordination.

Should Folk Songs in Group Piano Be Scrapped?
Presented by Jeriel Jorguenson
Friday, July 30, 2021
Recorded by Jessie Welsh

Modern reflection of folk tunes and other "traditional" material used in group piano methods and materials has revealed that many of these songs have complicated—albeit, problematic—backgrounds and beginnings. The question lingers: what is the role of piano instructors in navigating this complicated issue? Should these folk songs be altogether removed from the group piano literature? This session addressed this issue in an honest, diplomatic, and strategic way, creating space for communication, reconciliation, and authentic classroom discussions. The three main points of the session included the benefits of folk tunes, the potential pitfalls of folk tunes, and practical solutions for including folk tunes in the group piano classroom.

Jorguenson began this session by defining folk literature. He described folk songs and tunes as dance songs, tunes shared through oral traditions, and cultural songs that often have unknown origins. He provided examples of American folk songs, including *Simple Gifts*, *Swing Low*, *Danny Boy*, and other spirituals.

Jorguenson framed the discussion of folk tunes in the group piano classroom by asking two related and important questions: how can these songs be used positively in the group/class piano setting? What is their teaching value? Among the benefits he noted were student familiarity; prior aural experience; the ability for the teacher to build on this familiarity and focus on technique, more complex patterns, arranging, *etc.*; and ensemble performance.

Immediately following this discussion of the benefits of folk music, Jorguenson examined the flipside, asking, "What are the negative implications for using these tunes?" Possible consequences he included were as follows:
- May amplify racial overtones and stereotypes
- May diminish a holistic and rich understanding of a culture by limiting it to a single viewpoint or representative tune
- May strip indigenous peoples and minorities of recognition by removing the music from its context

From this balanced perspective of the pros and cons of including problematic folk tunes in the class/group piano curriculum, Jorguenson examined specific folk tunes which are often included in piano texts. He openly discussed the roots of these problematic tunes and then provided practical strategies for teachers as they navigate this complex issue. These strategies include the following:

- Context matters and teachers ought to include this in any teaching use—provide students context rather than hiding it.
- Disregarding damaging stereotypes and overtones is extremely harmful—have the tough conversations in the classroom if you choose to include problematic folk tunes.
- These tunes could be replaced by original music by diverse composers—consider other music with comparable teaching value and less clouded history.
- Origins of the music must be acknowledged—for example, African American spirituals cannot be divorced from their original context, however difficult and tragic.
- Find comfort in discomfort—make the classroom a safe place to have these discussions, however uncomfortable.

Following Jorguenson's presentation, attendees engaged in a question-and-answer session via the chat feature. During this discussion, the presenter reiterated the importance of communication and discussion when choosing to include potentially problematic folk tunes. He emphasized that he personally does not feel these songs should be necessarily thrown out; instead, he views them as opportunities for conversation, reflection, and connection in the classroom. The presenter concluded by emphasizing that the musical goals of a lesson must always remain preeminent. His belief is that there must always be strong musical reasoning for including any tune, problematic or otherwise. He urged attendees to intentionally choose tunes with lasting musical value and purposefully provide a safe and honest space to discuss any clouded history surrounding problematic folk songs.

Score Study Experts: Using Conductors' Techniques to Enhance Audiation, Gesture, Understanding, and Conceptualization in the Private Piano Lesson
Presented by Anna Beth Rucker
Friday, July 30, 2021
Recorded by Jason Gallagher

Score study is the fundamental skill behind stories of great pianists learning entire works away from the piano. In this presentation, Rucker explored score study techniques used by conductors which can be useful in the private piano lesson. Using three different approaches, Rucker showed participants how students can gain an in-depth understanding of a piece before even approaching the piano.

Rucker began with Kahn's audiation exercise, leading the participants through the steps with Bach's *Minuet in A Minor*, BSV Anh. 120 as a model. In this exercise, students work in eight-measure sections, beginning with the upper voice, and audiate the example until memorized. Moving on to the bottom voice, students again audiate but without needing to memorize. Having audiated both lines and memorized the upper voice, students then work to audiate the entire two-voice texture. This process can be followed as a course of study continuing with Bach's *Two-Part Inventions*, then *Three-Part Inventions*, the fugues and string quartets. When approaching three voices, students should audiate and memorize the outer voices before adding the inner voice. Following this method of study helps students identify errors and solve problems, and it will also help the student gain a concept of the whole and retain the music.

The second approach follows Battisti and Garofalo's *Guide to Score Study*, adapted for the piano, which examines the score through four lenses: Melody, Harmony, Form, and Rhythm. Melody is examined through several fundamental attributes: form, scales/arpeggios, contour, musical sound (character), ornamentation, texture, dynamics, and articulation. Harmonic analysis begins with determining the pitch center and the approach to harmony (major, minor, chromatic, modal, whole tone, or other). Within that context, the student should then examine cadences, modulations, and progressions. Harmony is finished by examining chord structures—type (major, minor, seventh, etc.), inversions, and harmonic rhythm. Form is analyzed according to traditional structures, but also moves beyond these to look at symmetry and contrast, relative length of sections, and tonality within each section. Finally, rhythm is examined according to tempo, meter, and special rhythmic techniques (hemiola, syncopation, displaced accents, augmentation/diminution, thematic/motivic rhythms, and significant rests). Within these parameters, participants collaborated through Google Docs to adapt and narrow down the techniques for beginning and intermediate piano lessons.

After illustrating these two in-depth analysis techniques, Rucker concluded with the "Herford-Style Structural Graph." This is a visual technique that takes a broader approach to music analysis. A graph includes the tempo marking and time signature and large form headings (*e.g.* ABA) with measure numbers. Within these large form headings, phrases are indicated visually with curved lines between vertical dividers, also including measure numbers. The motivic structure within the phrases are indicated with numbers (*e.g.* 4+4), with the motives given identifiers and the cadences identified (*e.g.* Half Cadence – HC, Perfect Authentic Cadence – PAC). Finally, the overall tonal center with its functional label (*e.g.* dominant, tonic) is indicated underneath. Using this technique, students can construct a visual representation of the overall structure of the work they are studying. Participants then completed a Herford-Style Structural Graph for the Bach *Minuet in A Minor* used in Kahn's audiation exercise above.

Brooklyn's Post-Millennial Mozart: Missy Mazzoli
Presented by Christina Lai
Friday, July 30, 2021
Recorded by Allison Fog

The presenter began with a performance of *Orizzonte*, written by composer Missy Mazzoli. Mazzoli was born in 1980 and grew up in a small town, but later moved to New York, where she currently resides and teaches composition at the Mannes College of Music. She began composing at age ten, and her influences include Philip Glass, Meredith Monk, and Beethoven. She was particularly inspired by composers who used serialism, minimalism, and neo-romanticism. Her works feature strong elements of storytelling and drama.

Mazzoli is passionate about striving for gender equality, especially for women composers. She speaks publicly about gender disparities and expectations for women in the composition business. She founded Luna Composition Lab, a mentorship program for female composers from ages thirteen to nineteen. Her advocacy for social issues and gender equality is reflected in her musical works. She founded the all-female band *Victoire*, whose members perform Mazzoli's own compositions. Communication and human connection are valued greatly by her, and she shares this through her teaching and composition.

Orizzonte is Mazzoli's oldest published piece and features electronic sound waves that overlap with a melody played on the piano. This combination of piano and electronic sounds is eerie, with the tension rising and falling. The piece is written without bar lines, which gives the performer freedom to control the space and time between notes. The droning sound waves suggest horizons and their colors, lending a meditative and reflective quality.

Next the presenter introduced the audience to another piece by Mazzoli, *Isabelle Eberhardt Dreams of Pianos (*2007). The piece was based on the life of Swiss-Algerian writer and explorer Isabelle Eberhardt, who traveled extensively, and exemplified the unconventional life of a woman. Eberhardt wrote short stories under a male pseudonym, dressed as a male, and even changed her name to one more masculine. She was involved in Algerian politics, survived an assassination attempt by saber, and died in a flash flood. She believed that suffering was a positive thing, producing courage and devotion. The adventures of Eberhardt inspired Mazzoli, who "…imagines her riding on horseback through the desert, lost in thought, remembering sounds and sensations of her old life. Fragments of Schubert's *Sonata in A Major* pierce her consciousness and are quickly suppressed. In her fatigue she dreams of a piano half-buried in sand, a flash flood of sheet music swirling around her."

Musically, *Isabelle Eberhardt Dreams of Pianos* gives us a sense of searching for what is lost. The mood is pensive, and the music begins with pulsating electronic sounds and a sparse melodic line played on the piano. The piece also features a metronome backing track throughout, with *crescendos* that build gradually. When the Schubert sonata is quoted, the performer strives to make the melody sound new and fresh, unlike anything heard previously in the piece.

Dr. Lai's performance of the piece concluded the presentation.

가위 ("Scissors") Fantasia Toccata: An Unexpected Inspiration
Presented by April Kim
Friday, July 30, 2021
Recorded by Allison Fog

In this presentation, Dr. April Kim introduced the work of composer Jiyoun Chung, discussed the influences and inspiration for the piece 가위 *("Scissors") Fantasia Toccata*, and ended with a performance of the piece.

Jiyoun Chung was born in South Korea and started playing the piano at age four. Throughout her life, she was exposed to both traditional Western music as well as traditional Korean music. She came to the United States in 2008 as a graduate student at Illinois State University and is currently on the faculty at Illinois Wesleyan University. Her enjoyment of new music and of performing inspired her to pursue composition.

The *"Scissors" Fantasia Toccata* was inspired by many aspects from Korean culture, including the rhythm of the traditional Korean percussion instrument *changgo,* as well as the visual excitement and movements of the scissor hitting act. Korean percussionist Seok Jin Ko was inspired to include the scissors in his act after seeing them used in a theater festival. The scissors are also used to cut traditional taffy-like Korean candy, called *yeot*. Dr. Kim included a video that highlights one family who has been making *yeot* for many generations. The process of making the candy involves cooking rice and other spices, then fermenting to create a slight sweet flavor. The batter is pulled like taffy and becomes translucent. The *yeot* represents Korean culture and tradition, and the family who makes it takes pride in their work. *Yeot* dates back one thousand years, and for a time was only available to those in the privileged class. Now it is accessible to everyone, and sellers use the scissors in a very rhythmic and engaging way in order to attract those who pass by on the street.

Seok Jin Ko performs rhythms using the scissors called *Samulnori*. *Samul* means "four objects" and *Nori* means "folk entertainment." Although this is a modern tradition, it was inspired by performers from the eighteenth and nineteenth centuries. The four instruments used are *Ching* (a small gong), *K'kwaeng-gwari* (a small metallic, hand-held instrument), *Changgo* (an hourglass-shaped percussion instrument that uses two mallets), *and Buk* (a large drum that provides the bass). The mallets of the *changgo* have different uses: one is usually played on the downbeats, and the other is played on the off-beats. The *changgo* is used in the scissor hitting act, and a video clip highlighted both performers. Each shares the rhythm, trading it back and forth. The visual aspect is crucial as it strives to emulate the physicality and excitement of a street performer. At one point, the scissors are even thrown into the air!

Together the instruments perform a *Changdan*, which is a rhythm combination of long and short durational values. The *changdan* is the essential element of rhythm in Korean music.

In *Fantasia Toccata*, Chung wanted to bring out the combination of music and dance, without replicating the exact patterns used in Korean music. She uses the long-short pattern, duple and triple meter, and repetition. *Glissandi* are included to mimic the throwing of the scissors, and the hand crossings relate to the *chungoo* player. Chung felt it was imperative to preserve the visual element, to better connect with modern audiences.

The presentation continued with a performance of 가위 *("Scissors") Fantasia Toccata.*

Boomers on Eurhythmics
Presented by Jackie Edwards-Henry
Friday, July 30, 2021
Recorded by Autumn L. Zander

With the guiding tenet that the body is the instrument and that music acts as the motivator, stimulator, and regulator of movement, Dalcroze Eurhythmics is a valuable approach when exploring and experiencing musical concepts. All too often Eurhythmics is associated with pre-college students, but there are multiple ways in which the principles of Dalcroze Eurhythmics can be used with older students.

In order to fully grasp the elements of active listening, discovery-based experiential learning, and the relationships between time, space, and energy, the session began with Edwards-Henry asking attendees to participate in three preliminary activities. Because of the virtual setting, all movement was based on what could be easily done in a seated position. The first activity involved moving to a piano arrangement of the song *Sweet Dreams* by the pop group The Eurhythmics, as played by Edwards-Henry. Participants moved in any way they wished, such as snapping fingers, waving arms, "chair dancing," *etc.* This activity allowed for participants to experience a steady beat, gain a level of comfort with moving freely to the music, and provided a moment of fun. The second activity involved clapping or stepping to the music and freezing when the music stopped. This quick reaction activity explored active listening combined with the element of surprise due to the unpredictable nature of when the music stopped and started. The third activity addressed continuous rhythm. Participants began tapping the quarter-note pulse and then tapped different note values upon command, such as half notes or triplets. Throughout all of the subdivision changes, maintaining a steady pulse was the goal.

After the group participation activities Edwards-Henry stressed the importance of experiencing an activity before analyzing it by getting the body involved in the learning process. This concept was further emphasized via several pre-recorded teaching excerpts. In the first excerpt, an adult group piano class explored the concept of rhythm via walking to a musical excerpt and freezing when the music stopped. The unpredictable stops and starts of the music encouraged active listening, quick reactions, and fun! It proved to be an ideal activity for adults who might otherwise feel self conscious about participating in a movement-based activity. As the video progressed, the ease with which the adult students moved and reacted during the activity became apparent.

Another memorable segment involved an individual lesson with a senior citizen. Due to COVID precautions, this lesson took place in a large room without a piano and used a recording of Chopin's *Prelude in A Major,* Op. 28, No. 7. The student was studying this piece and had challenges with the dotted-eighth sixteenth-note rhythm and moments of slight *rubato*. Utilizing aspects of Dalcroze Eurhythmics, a specific stepping pattern was executed every time the dotted-eighth sixteenth-note pattern was heard. In the teaching video, Edwards-Henry is shown actively participating in the choreography with the student and coaching him throughout the movements. When incorporating this type of movement in lessons with senior citizens, Edwards-Henry reminded participants that due to the stamina of many older students, the amount of repetition teachers might normally expect in a lesson may not be physically possible for these students. However, many of these activities can be incorporated into an older student's daily practice routine, allowing for the individual to take as many breaks as he/she needs while still developing a sense of comfort and mastery of the skill.

The final pre-recorded teaching segment depicted how elements of Dalcroze Eurhythmics were utilized as a preparatory activity for sight reading with college music majors. Specific rhythms were experienced and explored via movements. These same rhythms were then included in various sight-reading excerpts that the students later practiced. Throughout all of the teaching segments, the session provided numerous moments of inspiration and tangible ways in which participants can incorporate movement and principles of Dalcroze Eurhythmics in their own teaching with adult students.

Designing an Effective Collegiate Sight-Reading Course
Presented by Brian Marks
Friday, July 30, 2021
Recorded by Curtis Pavey

In this presentation, Dr. Marks presented guiding principles and suggestions to help collegiate professors prepare a sight-reading course for undergraduate piano majors. With twelve years of experience developing his own sight-reading course at Baylor University, Marks presented a variety of information including a discussion of the different domains of sight reading, goal planning within the curriculum, assignments, tips for sight reading well, and in-class activities.

According to Dr. Marks, there are several challenges that occur while teaching a sight-reading course. Besides the variety of skill levels that each student will bring to the course, sight reading is difficult to teach because of the variety of skills needed to complete the task well. Marks refers to these components as the Four Domains: the visual, conceptual, tactile, and aural components. In his discussion, Marks combined the visual and conceptual components, describing them as how the students read and interpret what is on the page. From there, students must have developed good tactile senses to easily move around the keyboard, while also being able to hear or audiate different passages before playing them.

To help his students sight read, Dr. Marks suggests a number of instructions for practicing. He begins by having students scan the score and audiate the beginning passages. Students need to know in advance what passages may challenge them and how these passages will sound. Based on this information, students should determine a tempo they can maintain and then try to audiate the first phrase while tapping in tempo. Marks mentioned that some students may struggle to audiate pitch—this is okay especially in repertoire with challenging harmonies or pitch content, but students should be able to at least audiate the rhythm and the relevant pitch direction from the passage. From there the students should count off and play without stopping. A brief period of reflection occurs after, allowing students the opportunity to practice a few sections, replay, and then move on to the next page or score.

In designing a curriculum, Dr. Marks first suggested creating short-term and long-term goals for the students. While it is possible for students to make tremendous progress during a semester-long course, Marks cautioned participants in the session that students must be given clear short-term goals for the semester that help them develop independence to work towards long-term goals on their own. In his course, Marks focuses firstly on helping students to develop habits and a toolkit of exercises to improve their sight reading. After the course ends, he hopes the students will continue their study and learn to sight read increasingly difficult repertoire. In the course, students are required to sight read daily for five to ten minutes, to keep a log of these pieces, and then to learn a new intermediate-level piece each week and prepare it for a performance in the class. The course activities also include transposition, open score, figured bass, and singing. A few of the most interesting activities he mentioned included flashcard examples that depicted patterns that students would perform, playing their own repertoire *senza vista* (not looking at their hands), ensembles for eight hands, and realizing single-line canons. In his teaching, Marks emphasizes pattern-recognition development, tactile awareness, and aural skills development.

Dr. Marks' extensive experience in this topic showed in this thorough discussion of the challenges and possibilities of designing a sight-reading course for piano majors. With these tips in mind, participants left this session ready to design and implement these ideas in their own course.

Not Playing Around: Toy Pianos and Their Creative Potential in the Studio
Presented by Grace Huang
Friday, July 30, 2021
Recorded by Sarah Leonard

The presentation began with an overview of the history and use of the toy piano. It has been used as a child's toy since the mid-1800s, and in the 1940s, it made its way onto stage and into the recording studio. It has been used by a variety of musicians including classical artists, popular artists, and composers. Additionally, it has been used to champion new music. It also has pedagogical value and can be used as a creative outlet or practice tool. The presenter remarked that it is fun to play, but can still be used for serious practice.

In terms of toy piano history, Albert Shoenhut was born into a German toy-making family. When he was seventeen, he moved to the United States to continue making toys. Because toy pianos used glass rods for the sound, they were quite fragile and difficult to ship. Shoenhut replaced the glass with metal. This made the instrument more percussive, higher pitched, portable, and durable. The Shoenhut piano company was established in 1872 in St. Augustine, Florida, and still remains to this day. Michelsonne was a French toy piano company from 1939 until 1970, the year it burned down. Instead of reconstructing, the patents were sold to an Italian company. This makes these toy pianos more difficult to find, though they can still be heard in recordings from French musicians.

Dr. Huang noted some facts about more recent toy pianos. In 2001, the Library of Congress assigned a specific call number for toy piano music. The presenter showed images of vintage and newer models of the toy pianos. Earlier Shoenhut models did not have chromatic keys, but the black keys were painted on. To illustrate the difference in timbre, Dr. Huang demonstrated the tone of a newer Kawai model and Shoenhut using the tune from Seals and Croft's "Summer Breeze." Dr. Huang remarked on the Kawai's delicate tone and the Shoenhut's louder, more robust sound.

There are also events and festivals for toy pianos. YouTube highlights can be found of many of the following festivals:
- UC San Diego Toy Piano Festival
- UnCaged Toy Piano (NYC)
- Florida International Toy Piano Festival
- Non-Piano/Toy Piano Weekend (Hamburg, Germany)
- 100-Note Toy Piano Project

In popular music, the toy piano has been used in recordings from Neil Diamond to Radiohead, jazz pianist Angelica Sanchez, and French composer Yann Tiersen, who wrote the soundtrack to

Amélie. Dr. Huang encourages the audience to look up Richard Carpenter's live performance of "Dirty Fingers" on YouTube. In this video, Carpenter can be seen playing on five different pianos, including a vintage Shoenhut toy piano.

In classical music, John Cage wrote the first serious work for the toy piano in 1948, called *Suite for Toy Piano*, which is made up of five short movements. Each movement is less than two minutes in length. John Cage appreciated the small range of the toy piano, and its slightly percussive tone. American composer George Crumb liked to use the instrument for its unique timbral possibilities. Margaret Leng Tan, the first woman to earn a doctorate from Juilliard, began collaborating with John Cage using the toy piano, and is now a toy piano specialist.

Dr. Huang provided this abbreviated listening guide:
- John Cage *Suite for Toy Piano* (1948)
- Yann Tiersen *The Waltz of the Monsters* (1995)
- George Crumb *Ancient Voices of Children* (1970), *Todos Las Tardes*, and *Metamorphisis, Book 1* (2017) "Clowns at Night"
- Julian Grant *Etudes Transcendentales pour le toy piano* (2013)
- Karlheinz Essl *Whatever Shall Be* (2013)
- Margaret Leng Tan *The Art of the Toy Piano* (1997)

Toy pianos do not have a standardized range. Dr. Huang believes the largest range is forty-nine keys, though many are around two octaves. Additionally, the key width varies, which calls for different technical demands. The presenter also noted that a performer needs to keep positioning and seating in mind, meaning rehearsal is needed prior to a performance.

For use of the toy piano as a studio teaching tool, Dr. Huang stated an advantage of the toy piano is its portability and accessibility. It can be interactive and used by audience members as well as the performer. The toy piano can also be used as a practice tool, similar to practicing on different pianos as it requires a different technical and articulation approach. The presenter referenced Dr. Barbara Fast's presentation featuring "variable practice" in support of using the instrument as a tool during practice. When teaching, the presenter stated that it can be used for improvisation, and the smaller range of the keyboard is less intimidating to her students than a full piano. Dr. Huang pointed out that it can also be used collaboratively, then demonstrated an arrangement of *Carol of the Bells* for three-toy pianos.

Lastly, the presenter noted that it can also be used as a tool for composition. For her students, the different timbre from the piano can foster creativity while still allowing them to compose on a keyboard instrument. Dr. Huang referenced a chapter in Alan Shockley's *The Contemporary Piano*, to point out that the toy piano can be used in, as she called it, "prepared (toy) piano." The presenter also uses the toy piano as a composition tool in her class piano courses. To end the presentation, Dr. Huang performed five pieces written for the toy piano, four of which were written by students.

Mindful Movement:
Applying Yogic Principles to Preschool, Adolescent, and Senior Music Lessons

Presented by Lesley McAllister
Friday, July 30, 2021
Recorded by Elizabeth Smith

When thinking of yoga, people often imagine a good core workout or twisting into a pretzel. Dr. McAllister clarified that she would be talking about healthy practices that can engage attention, increase body awareness, and decrease anxiety. In preschool, students can have fun using their body, and in adolescence, yoga can help students decrease anxiety. The presenter then provided some research on yoga's benefits. Physical benefits include breath capacity/awareness, reduced fatigue, stronger immune system, and greater endurance. There are also cognitive benefits, which include better awareness, cognition, and retention. These strengths lead to a better planning ability and spatial memory. Finally, there are emotional benefits, which include decreasing performance anxiety and increasing what is called the "flow state."

In early childhood education, common challenges include short attention span, ADHD, special needs, and needing time to calm down. The "sushi roll" pose (rolling up in your mat) and *savasana* "resting pose" promote relaxation and give the child time to relax and reset after their lesson. For young children, movement is a vital part of the learning process, and skills like balance helps students self-regulate and process. Movement also helps students learn contrast through improved listening skills, by listening for commands like "up/down, major/minor."

Young students can also use cross-lateral poses to help gain body awareness. Cross-lateral movement links both sides of the body and requires "crossing the midline" for brain integration. There are several poses that achieve cross-lateral movement, including: revolved wide-legged forward fold, eagle pose (can be modified), "sprinkler" pose, and balancing table. There are songs that can be used to supplement this type of movement, including *Hot Cross Buns*, *Pat-a-Cake*, dancing with scarves, and *Simon Says*. Early childhood students also can benefit from brain breaks. Practicing different types of breath can help refocus the lesson or activity. Other activities include partner poses (like "see-saw") and eye exercises (like "eye rolling").

The presenter then switched to the demographic of seniors. Common issues in seniors are related to injuries and misalignments. Students of this age also might have impaired eyesight and a higher risk of falling, which means that teachers must exercise caution when practicing yoga with these types of students. Teachers must make appropriate modifications for their students and should spend the majority of their time on standing and restorative poses, like "stork" and "staff" pose. Forward flexion motion and seated positions should be properly limited for students with osteoporosis and osteoarthritis. Constructive rest can be beneficial for senior students to limit spine compression. If students are wary of combining yoga into piano lessons, there are several postures from chairs that can help release tension in the head and neck ("cat-cow," "prayer," "lotus," and "eye-palming"). Superposes are poses that are efficient in many ways for seniors and include "mountain" pose, "brainy-bridge" pose, and putting legs up the wall.

The last category of students presented was adolescents, a group which has been experiencing high levels of anxiety and stress during the pandemic. This is likely due to the fact that a large amount of a student's self-worth comes from social situations, which have been limited during the COVID-19 pandemic. Having quiet time for breath work or warm-up poses at the beginning of the lesson can help focus the rest of the lesson. Pre-lesson quiet time is highly encouraged for students of this age. Dynamic movements help open the body and prepare for the piano lesson; poses include "chest pulses" and "easy seated twist."

Breath work can help students calm themselves and reduce anxiety before a performance. The presenter then led the audience through an alternate-nostril breathing exercise. The biggest issues in advanced musicians are anxiety, depression, and performance anxiety. Advanced musicians may also have Performance-Related Musculoskeletal Disorder, which are also known as repetitive stress injuries. Ways to reduce these injuries can be to warm up with dynamic movements and take breaks to stretch with static movements during practice. Pre-performance routines can help calm the musician before a performance and include slow movements, forward holds, and long holds. If students want to be energized before a performance, exercises can include backbends and standing poses.

All the World's a Stage: Teaching Confident Performance Presentation through Acting
Presented by Andrea Johnson
Friday, July 30, 2021
Recorded by Omar Roy

Dr. Johnson began the presentation by sharing some meaningful benefits from her high-school experience with acting, including a reduction in stage fright, increased confidence, a sense of trust, using one's body to inhabit a character, remaining authentic, and having fun. She credited acting's total psychological involvement as a major factor in reducing fear simply because there is too much else to focus on, and volunteered that some of the practices common to acting could be beneficial to piano students.

Invoking Leschetizky, she quoted: "The whole art of piano playing is *most* akin to the art of acting."

This idea, Dr. Johnson noted, was a major driver of her research, which focused on how acting skills can help music students present themselves with more confidence on stage. The interactive nature of the workshop involved audience members in several physical exercises.

In the first exercise, participants were invited to stand up and take a bow as they would prior to performing. After the initial bow, Dr. Johnson reframed and repeated the exercise with the following Leschetizky quote, noting the different sensation that it may create: "I love you [the audience] so much that I will enjoy myself and be free."

Dr. Johnson then introduced warm-up activities she uses with her students. Typically, all of these warm-ups are conducted in a "drama circle" that fosters communication and eye contact between students, creating a sense of community. During this segment, she took the audience through physical movements and a series of exaggerated facial and body expressions to warm up the body. Another activity, called "Name, Gesture," invited audience members to introduce themselves to the group while making some sort of gesture, which was then repeated by the group. This series of warm-up activities concluded with an exercise Dr. Johnson dubbed "Emotional Spaghetti," in which participants repeated the word "spaghetti" with different emotional emphases to foster an embodied sense of emotion.

In the next segment, Dr. Johnson addressed the issue of communication, and emphasized that performers should have a specific idea in mind for each piece they perform and that they practice bonding with that idea over the weeks and months in preparation for a performance. She also suggested focusing on these objectives prior to walking on stage and accompanying them with a mantra to enhance focus and prevent the audience from breaking the performer's focus.

Dr. Johnson highlighted that one way in which a performer can begin communicating an idea is the way that they walk on stage. To emphasize this, she demonstrated an activity in which performers shift their movement center to different parts of their body to embody different moods and attitudes.

The presentation concluded with a quote by Stanislavski, encouraging performers to focus on presenting themselves authentically and to perform with confidence, and emphasized the positive benefits of these strategies for students.

Lightning Talks
Friday, July 30, 2021
Moderated by Todd van Kekerix; Presented by Esther Hayter, Jinkyung Kim,
Ricardo Pozenatto, Mengyu Song, Karen Yong
Recorded by Louie Hehman

Got Rhythm? Establishing Habits for Long-Term Wellness
Esther Hayter discussed rhythm as being more than the "time aspect" of music, defining it more scientifically as "a set of repeated processes." Reference was made to the definition of rhythm in Webster's dictionary. She referenced her own wellness training, and discussed how establishing a rhythm of daily life has been beneficial to her mental wellness. Scholarly articles discussing the importance of highly routine health behaviors were also referenced. Hayter suggests that teachers ask themselves how they could alter their own daily rhythms to improve their well-being. Starting small and consistency were also emphasized.

Teaching 20th-Century Intermediate Repertoire in Changing Meter
Jinkyung Kim discussed the idea that more straightforward time signatures are easiest to teach, but that as students reach the intermediate stage, more complex time signatures may present problems. Kim focused upon a piece titled "Counting" by Dianne Goolkasian Rahbee. This work is taken from a collection called *Modern Miniatures*, which shares certain similarities with earlier intermediate collections, such as those by Burgmüller. Kim provided excerpts that show the changing meter in the Rahbee piece, and emphasized that the simplicity of the left hand part allows students to focus on the changing metrical emphasis in the right hand. Kim mentioned that many teachers may avoid teaching such works, but strongly suggested that they consider doing so. She also mentioned several other works similar to "Counting" that teachers could use in their studios.

From the Known to the Unknown: The Lego-Blocks of the Sight-Reading Skill
Ricardo Pozenatto began with a definition of sight reading from Richard Chronister. Pozenatto used this definition to refute the idea that sight reading is only the playing of a piece for the first time. He provided certain "building blocks" that must exist in a student before attempting to sight read; technical proficiency with anything being sightread is a must. Knowledge of rhythmic patterns is also essential. In sum, familiar technique, familiar rhythm, and familiar pitch are all essential building blocks for successful sight reading. An analogy was made to reading English words—we don't stop and read every letter. According to Pozenatto, *practicing sight reading skills* actually happens separately from *doing sight reading*. The acts of reading both horizontally and vertically are essential. Pozenatto provided an example from Beethoven, in which the measures of a well-known piece are reordered for the student to read at sight. Pozenatto finished by encouraging teachers to practice sight reading with students.

Teaching Mixed Meter and Suggested Intermediate-Level Repertoire
Mengyu Song suggested that correctly executing mixed-meter pieces consists of three steps: 1) conducting a steady beat, 2) conducting a steady beat while counting the mixed meters, and 3) adding conducting patterns while counting the mixed meters. According to Song, conducting will help students to keep a steady beat. Several composers of mixed-meter pieces were suggested, including Robert Starer, whose "Evens and Odds" was shown as a good example. Song showed how she would apply her three-step conducting process to learning the Starer piece.

All the "Feels" About Open Sight Reading
Dr. Kathryn Sherman began humorously by simply saying the word "sight reading" and showing a frowning emoji. She stated that there are four components to sight reading: visual, cognitive, technical, and performance. Dr. Sherman focused on the "technical" aspect today, and asked the question, "what type of chops need to be developed for open-score sight reading?" She suggested that, in addition to the scalar and chordal patterns developed by many method books, open-score reading necessitates double-note technique, 2+2 textures, and contrapuntal playing. In this session, she focused upon the first of these—double notes. Specific exercises for double notes were highlighted, including an excerpt from Kohler. She showed the Kohler excerpt in an open-score format, and followed up with a Gurlitt example.

Introducing *Alicia's Piano Books* by Indonesian Composer Ananda Sukarlan
Dr. Karen Yong began by introducing Sukarlan and the *Piano Books*, initially named for his daughter, Alicia. These works combine elements of Western and non-Western cultures, and are appropriate for intermediate, early-advanced, and even advanced students. Yong explored some of Sukarlan's compositional approaches, including his canons, fugues, variations, and waltzes. Specific selections from the collection were highlighted. The Sukarlan books are available for purchase, but there is a specific Indonesian website through which they must be purchased. Yong concluded by encouraging teachers to consider using this collection in their own teaching.

Lost Gems: Piano Music of Bolivia
Presented by Walter Aparicio
Friday, July 30th, 2021
Recorded by Louie Hehman

This session began with the presenter, who is of Bolivian origins, introducing himself. Aparicio stated that there are three particular composers upon whom he planned to focus. The first of the composers presented was Eduardo Caba (1890-1953). Aparicio explained that Caba was quite cosmopolitan, starting his career in La Paz but later living in Buenos Aires, and then Madrid. A brief description of Caba's pieces was provided, followed by a performance. The works were two *Aires Indios (de Bolivia)*, No. 3 and No. 9, and then *Leyenda Keshua*. All of the works were highly expressive and contained elements of both dance and folk melody.

The next piece was by Simeon Roncall (1870-1953), who is most known for his 20 *cueca,* a type of folk dance which Roncall specifically adapted for piano. Aparicio gave a description of the type of the *cueca*, as well as the specific piece he would perform. This upbeat piece needed to be cut in half due to time constraints.

The last piece to be performed by Aparicio was by Marvin Sandi (1938-1968). According to Aparicio, little is known about this individual, but evidently it is known that he was a philosopher in addition to being a composer. Stravinsky and Schoenberg were influences, as was the nationalistic style of Eduardo Caba. The work for piano played by Aparicio was *Ritmos Panteisticos*, which contains several movements dedicated to various aspects of nature including "The Rock" and "The Moon." These were highly rhythmic and somewhat virtuosic in nature. The presentation then concluded with a reference to Aparicio's website, as well as his Instagram account.

Reach, Connect, and Heal: Online Piano Teaching of Adult Hobbyists
Presented by Carla Davis Cash, Laura Lennis Cortés, and Qin Ling
Friday, July 30, 2021
Recorded by Angela Leising-Catalan

Despite the many challenges of the last year, the presenters found that the same goals were attainable in the online format for adult piano students. The presenters stated that their presentation would focus on the adult amateur student, or hobbyist, and how this segment of the population can come to experience enriching and meaningful music making and learning. The presenters stated that piano study not only provides opportunities for students to learn or refine a skill, but also avenues by which adults can form meaningful personal relationships and find an important source of stress relief. Two projects studying adult online piano instruction were discussed in this presentation: case studies of two students returning to piano as adults, and the effects of online piano class on mood and sleep of university medical students.

For the case studies involving the students returning to piano as adults after quitting during their teenage years, Dr. Cash described weekly surveys that prompted students to self-reflect about instruction, practice, teacher effectiveness, and how childhood piano experiences compared to present experiences. An inductive approach was used to analyze raw data. Through multiple careful readings of participant text, the presenters ended up with categories from repeated word and phrase usage that captured the core message communicated by the participants. The categories that emerged were then grouped into broader themes that described the essence of participant experiences.

Dr. Cortés went on to describe her experience of teaching two returning adult piano students in the midst of the COVID-19 pandemic. Both of these students had quit piano lessons at a young age due to different reasons that resulted in the loss of motivation to continue their learning process. These students, named Alice and Ruby, filled out surveys every week during a twelve-week period. Four themes emerged as this data was analyzed:

1. The development of effective practice habits.
    Alice and Ruby both described increased satisfaction with their practice when they incorporated relaxation techniques and exercises to their routines.
2. The development of comfort and confidence in music expression.
    The guidance towards how to practice for expressivity was principally based on modeling, imitating, singing, playing, and audiation. Ruby and Alice described the effects of practicing with more expression.
3. The importance of well-being and enjoyment in music learning.
    Regarding music making as a source of stress relief, Ruby wrote that playing the piano helped her personally by allowing total concentration, and not having to

think about COVID, politics, racism, etc. Alice wrote that music making helped her calm her emotions on multiple occasions, and she was able to "get lost" in the music and not think about anything else.
4. The importance of the teacher-student relationship.
    The core of the teacher-student relationship that developed between the student and the researcher was based on communication rooted in empathy, respect, trust, and mutual support. Effective guidance meant choosing adequate lesson materials, modeling supported with precise verbal instructions, the effectiveness of the online learning setting, and precise and clear feedback.

Moving on, the presenters introduced their findings on the effects of online piano class on mood and sleep in university medical students, a typically high-stress group of individuals. Participants attended a weekly group class and then filled out surveys at the start, mid-point, and end of their twelve-week course of study. Stress and mood were examined. The Pittsburgh Sleep Index was used to measure quality of sleep. The Center for Epidemiologic Studies and Depression was used to measure mood. Preliminary results showed a modest-to-low lowering (or improvement) of numbers related to sleep and mood problems over the course of twelve weeks. This indicates that the group piano class had a protective effect on stress. The presenters discussed findings related to a free online piano class that was offered to Texas Tech medical students. Students had little-to-no prior piano experience. The teaching model used was Recreational Music Making (RMM).

The presenters then discussed a number of specific strategies for making online teaching effective and productive for adult hobbyists, especially in an online environment:

1. How to keep students engaged
    a. Provide opportunities for sharing and discussion in an open and relaxed learning environment.
    b. Show appreciation and interest in students' ideas and initiate inspiring discussions.
    c. Provide opportunities for student showcases in the class, if they wish. Even two to three measures is sufficient.
2. How to give students feedback
    a. Be honest, vulnerable and show the best version of oneself in teaching and interacting.
    b. Keep feedback mostly positive with several negative ones now and then in a detailed and encouraging way.
3. How to create activities for online recreational piano class
    a. Transfer (off-staff reading to intervallic reading).
    b. Ear training

       c. Transposition
4. Lead sheet music practice
    a. Happy Birthday
5. Music appreciation session
    a. Highlight a famous pianist or composer, and then watch a video featuring them.
6. Teamwork
    a. Pair strong and weak students.
7. Discussion for possible challenges
    a. Students discuss potential challenges and create practice plans.
8. Variability challenge session and class showcase
    a. As a practice technique, ask students to vary dynamics, articulation, and tempo.

In closing, quotes from class members were shared. The quotes expressed gratitude for having a dedicated time to enjoy the piano, and to temporarily disconnect from the stressors of everyday life.

Tonal or Spectral? An Alternative "Aural Skills" Workshop for Pianists
Presented by Yannis Rammos
Friday, July 30, 2021
Recorded by Kate Acone

This presentation introduced a philosophical and nuanced approach to aural skills. The presenter contrasted pitch-oriented (more traditional) aural skills with timbre-based aural skills. This was predicated on the notion that while the sound of a piano is assumed to be a universal neutral pitch delivery, it is actually made up of numerous complex partials. Pianists should be trained in listening to timbre and tone.

Dr. Rammos provided three contrasts between pitch-oriented and timbre-based aural skills. Pitch-oriented aural skills rely on working memory, prioritize the formal, and consider the notation to be the truth. Timbre-based aural skills rely on cross-modal metaphors, prioritize aesthetics, and consider notation to be an indication of intended effect.

The presenter then gave some background philosophies on piano tone and sound. It could be considered either as *Ton* (the music as experienced) or as *Klang* (the sound/noise as natural, not music). The piano is thought by some to be mimetic in that it flattens what it imitates. Others consider it as a black/white representation of tone, a position with which the presenter disagrees. He then discussed the difficulty of defining the start and end of a pitch. How loud does a sound have to be to be considered a pitch and not just sound? Similarly, he referenced a passage of a Granados piece, bringing up the question of whether or not pedal sonorities are pitches. He recommends a syllabus of 50% *Ton* and 50% *Klang*.

The next segment of the presentation discussed ways to think about the piano timbre. Dr. Rammos presented a three-stage way to hear the sound. The first part of the sound you hear is the transient, or the consonant, of the piano tone. The second is the decay, or the vowel, which is the sound most aural skills classes focus on. The last is the damper, or the end of the tone. This concept gives a more complex spectrum of the piano soundscape, including vowel changes in tone. A pianist could hear a transient in three ways: the hammer on the string, the key into the key-bed, or the fingertip on the key. The decay can be controlled with a default partial pedal. A "beating partial," an in-and-out soundwave, may be part of the soundscape. A pianist also has choices in shaping the cutoff with both the key release and the pedal release.

Dr. Rammos concluded by calling for more nuanced approaches to aural skills and for deeper listening.

Getting to It and Positive Actions: The Most Important, Most Forgotten Practice Tips
Presented by Barbara Fast
Friday, July 30, 2021
Recorded by Chloe Raber

During a Spring 2020 course, Dr. Fast asked students to experiment with two types of practice strategies: 1) tips for getting to the practice room, and 2) tips for positive actions. These remained popular with students for the entire semester, particularly with the challenges of the COVID-19 pandemic. Beyond the college setting, teachers can quickly see how both kinds of strategies are critical to teacher and student success and can be applied beyond studio and practice rooms.

In starting any new task (*e.g.*, working on a project or practicing an instrument), the initial "newness" of the task is the moment that is most effortful for the brain. Thus, "Getting to It" tips help people overcome that initial resistance to starting an activity. The effectiveness of these tips is highly individual, so the presenter encouraged listeners to go for the options they thought would be fun and helpful for themselves or for a certain student. One recommendation was Focusmate.com, a favorite of Dr. Fast for a variety of work, home, and life tasks (recommended for ages 14+). The site allows users to commit to a fifteen-minute co-working session with another user. It promotes accountability by having users report what they will be working on before the session and report how their work went after the session, with a rule of no conversation during the session. Another recommendation was the Pomodoro Technique, where a person has a set timer for working sessions alternating with breaks (*e.g.*, twenty minutes of work, followed by a five-minute break, then twenty minutes of work, then a longer break, etc.). It is especially useful for time management and for technology distraction management. There are many apps available, including: *Forest*, *Donut Dog* (recommended for young students), *Focus Cat*, *Study Bunny*, *STREAKS* (a checklist-style app), and even *Snapchat*.

In regards to positive actions, Dr. Fast prefaced her recommendations with an overview of negativity bias. Humans have a stronger memory for negative experiences than positive experiences due to ancient survival needs. The innate fight-flight-freeze response quickly identifies negative experiences and stores them in memory. On the other hand, it takes a full twelve seconds of holding a positive experience in the conscious mind to transfer it from short-term memory to long-term memory. For teachers, this is an important consideration during a lesson—they must be intentional about dedicating at least twelve seconds to a positive feedback statement for students to form a memory of it. Tips for incorporating positive actions into daily life include: keep a gratitude list; send a thank-you email or text; keep a "ta-da!" list of what you have accomplished (vs. the traditional "to-do" list); make the statement "already peaceful, already contented, already loved" at first waking (from Rick Hanson); name the support around you (from Rick Hanson); name three blessings or things that went well and explain why they went well (from Martin Seligman); try a breathing practice (*e.g.*, breathe in for four counts, hold for six counts, and breathe out for eight counts); name a stressor and follow it with the statement "…but at least…" (from *Commanding Performance* by Cody Commander); be outdoors and in nature; take a "Pic a Day"; "Pet the Lizard" (mentally imagine petting a lizard); try compassion practices (*e.g.*, Tara Brach has many videos on meditation and self-compassion). Dr. Fast also recommended the *STREAKS* app for consistently applying these tips. She concluded with the encouraging reminder that good in quantity outweighs the negative.

During the question-and-answer time following the presentation, attendees suggested additional apps related to the session topic: *Toggl*, *Flora*, and *Bear Focus Timer*. Multiple questions addressed how to convey and implement these tips with students, including those without access to technology. Dr. Fast's recommendation was to verbally discuss ideas with students because student buy-in is a must for effective adoption. Additionally, a teacher's excitement during presentations and ways of gamifying practice habits, even with paper and stickers, makes a big difference in student response.

Attendees interested in further reading can explore *Hardwiring Happiness* by Rick Hanson, *The Happiness Project* by Gretchen Rubin, *Mindset* by Carol Dweck, and *iPractice: Technology in the 21st Century Music Practice Room* by Dr. Fast.

A Year of Experimentation:
Piano Studio as a Place of Belonging, Engagement, and Ownership
Presented by Jihea Hong-Park
Friday, July 30, 2021
Recorded by Margie Nelson

Jihea Hong-Park began by stating that as educators we have gone through a time of uncertainty and pause, yet we have found creative ways to get through it all. This year has become a time of creativity, experimentation, and personal growth.

Attendees were asked to take out a pen and a piece of paper to take a walk down memory lane. They were directed to reflect on themselves as children, teenagers, and college students and to think about what the lesson studio was like.

Our first question was this: "What are some of the words, images, or associations that come to mind when you hear the word 'belonging'?" The second question was: "What does the word 'belonging' mean in the context of your applied studio? What are the ways that your piano teachers have fostered a sense of community in his or her studio?" The third question was: "To what extent did you know the other students in your studio? How did your peers affect your learning?" At this time, members of the audience shared their thoughts.

Hong-Park mentioned that she did not feel particularly close to her fellow students until she went to college, and she decided that when she was to have her own studio, she would make sure that her students felt safe, noticed, and empowered. Recently, she had an opportunity to build a new studio at BYU. In the midst of COVID, how was this going to be possible? Before meeting the students in her new studio, she sent out a Google Form with questions so she could get to know them. Some of the questions on the form were: "How are you practicing self-care?" "Where do you see yourself in ten years?" "What do you think about certain repertoire?"

In addition to the questionnaire, she made sure that each student felt important. She scheduled one-on-one Zoom calls, and then used the *Slack* app to continue the lines of communication. This app allows you to create channels where you can ask questions, upload videos and keep a dialogue going. This app helped to keep her studio connected. Once *Slack* was set up, Hong-Park asked her students to upload a short video about themselves, which enabled students to find others with similar interests and to visually see who was in their studio. Next, in her first class, instead of going through a syllabus, she had an icebreaker. The students put stickers on a board that allowed them to connect with common interests. Hong-Park then created "Learning Pods" where students were paired up with each other to form mentoring groups. This became a huge hit because they bonded. The upperclassmen mentored the younger students and often played for each other and met socially—particularly helpful for an introverted person. Using the app, she also created a "Student Leadership Council." In her studio, everyone has a job. For example, a student might make posters for upcoming events, manage the *Slack* app or be the emcee for a guest performer. Finally, during studio class, each class began with a reflective prompt and then after student performances, the students would give each other feedback. Because the students felt comfortable, this became a place where they could give constructive feedback, enabling them to be better listeners, teachers, and adjudicators in the future.

At the end of the year, Hong-Park sent out a short, anonymous survey asking students if they felt a sense of belonging in the studio this year and how the studio could be improved. The students responded with many positive comments about feeling close even though in the midst of a pandemic and enjoying the ability to contact each other. The next question was, "Did you feel engaged as a learner in the studio this year?" Many responded positively to this question. The third question; "Did you feel a sense of ownership this year in the studio?" Again, a positive experience was had by all. The fourth question was "How did your peers enhance or distract your learning experience?" Many suggested that hearing others motivated them.

The fifth question asked about career development which Hong-Park really encouraged her students to think about. The response was positive, mentioning that because of the class discussions, a student was made aware of a career choice that they may not have thought about.

In conclusion, Hong-Park summarized what she had learned from her year of experimentation and asked the attendees to reflect on how they might build a sense of belonging, community and ownership in their own studios.

Evaluation Insights
Presented by Sara Ernst, Asher Armstrong, Maria Case, Janet Lopinski, and Stephen Pierce
Friday, July 30, 2021
Recorded by Sarah Leonard

The presentation began with introductions by each of the panelists. All five presenters are members of the Royal Conservatory of Music College of Examiners.

Dr. Lopinski advocated for the audience to consider the concept of evaluation in a broad sense, and as an essential aspect of teaching and learning. The question she proposed was, "What do we listen for, and how do we engage our students in this process?" The presenters asked the audience to identify which of the following performance traits they found least and most difficult to coach:
- Rhythmic character and vitality
- Harmonic and structural awareness
- Melodic shape and direction
- Refined control of texture, balance and voicing
- Sound quality and tonal variety
- Communication of musical character and overall effect

Dr. Armstrong broke down "rhythmic character and vitality" into three main components: foundational, fundamental, rhythmic organization; stylistic understanding; and expressive space or personal inflection. He defined rhythmic organization as a sense of pulse and rhythm, comparing the two to a "heartbeat." A more advanced aspect discussed was inflecting metric undercurrents and cross rhythms. The presenter described "stylistic understanding" as "information that is beyond what is explicit on the page." He used hemiola in Baroque *courantes* and jazz rhythms as examples. He stated agogic stresses, up-bow and down-bow phrasing, and *rubato* are elements of expressive space and personal inflection.

Dr. Case proposed that it is possible to cultivate an awareness of harmonies and structures at the elementary and intermediate levels, though these topics are usually studied by advanced students. The presenter used Beethoven sonatas as an example, stating evaluators listen for clarity of thematic characters, dominant preparations, and unexpected modulations. She claimed these elements make the pieces' construction clear and students of this level should develop an understanding of theory that allows them to make these elements salient in performance. The presenter stated younger students can understand tension and release and direction of phrase within context of a piece, and students can be made aware of "same, similar, and different" at their fundamental level, which can be used to explore interpretive choices.

Dr. Pierce defined "melodic shape and direction" in the following way, "a hierarchy between horizontal consecutive notes in a line, and every phrase should have a destinational peak." He then explained three different kinds of phrases; one starts at a peak then hastens, one grows to a peak in the middle and then hastens, and then one grows to a peak at the end. As an evaluator, the presenter listens for a student's consideration of melodic contour, and whether they are portraying their choices to the listener, using dynamics and expressive markings to inform these decisions. He continued with a discussion about refined control of texture, balance, and voicing. These concepts refer to the vertical relationship of coinciding or simultaneous notes: in Classical repertoire, homophony; in Baroque repertoire, counterpoint; in Romantic repertoire, projecting multiple voices. The presenter believes this should be developed from the very first lesson.

Dr. Ernst used "color" to describe different levels of sound quality and tone. To build off of Dr. Pierce's point about eras, she explained each era has distinctive levels of sound. She emphasized the importance of pedal for opening the variety of tones available to the instrument. Dr. Ernst closed the discussion of the six criteria with her thoughts on musical character and overall effect. She highlighted the importance of tempos in musical flow and effect. The example she used was playing the first movement of a sonata *adagio* instead of *allegro*. She pointed out an *adagio* tempo cannot accurately portray the spirited character of *allegro*. The presenter explained that the student's ability to connect to the emotive quality of a piece is the most important aspect of a student's delivery of a personal performance.

The discussion of these criteria was further explored by evaluating student performances: Following the performance of *Etude in D Minor*, Op. 82, No. 65, by Gurlitt, Maria Case stated a student could use harmonies to emphasize the "drama" of the piece. After the performance of *Red Rose Rendezvous* by Martha Mier, Dr. Armstrong described how he thinks about what he would like to hear from professional performers, specifically, attention to detail and organicism, when evaluating a quality performance. Dr. Ernst continued by using the phrase "personal spark." In response to *Sonatina in G Major*, Op. 19/20, No. 1, Movement I by Dussek, Case pointed out the need for control in a more accomplished performance. Dr. Pierce spoke on clarifying the destination of phrases for a polished effect. Dr. Ernst spoke on the quality of balance and character in "Bright Orange" by Robert Starer. She suggested the performer could explore subtle shaping within the piece. Dr. Pierce and Dr. Armstrong stated they wished for a faster tempo. In *Etude in A-flat Major,* Op. 30, No. 19 by Concone, Dr. Pierce wanted more color and sound contrast. Dr. Lopinski wished the student to work on continuity. In *Etude-Tableau in E-flat Major*, Op. 33, No. 7 by Rachmaninoff, Dr. Lopinski wanted the student to explore balance and voicing, believing the student could bring out the layers in the texture.

Dr. Ernst discussed the audience's answers to the polls regarding easiest and most difficult performance traits to coach. "Melodic shape" was chosen for the easiest followed by communication of musical character. "Sound quality and tonal variety" was chosen as the most difficult to teach. Dr. Pierce highlighted the difficulties of teaching sound quality through an online platform. He recommended a color-coded map to spark imagination for timbre. Dr. Lopinski pointed out the naturalism of "melodic shape." Importance of quality instruments was emphasized by all of the presenters. Dr. Ernst stated that emphasizing this to parents early on can help. Dr. Pierce closed by explaining all six criteria should be instilled at the first lesson.

What If You Came First? Self-Care for Teachers in Turbulent Times
Presented by Laura Amoriello, Vanessa Cornett-Murtada, and Jessica Johnson
Friday, July 30, 2021
Recorded by Leonidas Lagrimas

How have teachers dealt with the mental and emotional difficulties brought on by the pandemic? What types of self-care have teachers utilized to maintain a sense of stability and sanity during these unprecedented times? While the concept of "self-care" might be a highly personal one, and no two teachers have experienced the pandemic in the same way, one thing is clear—self-care is no longer an occasional need, or an indulgent luxury, nor is it even optional. Rather, self-care is mandatory for each of us.

This session with panelists Laura Amoriello, Vanessa Cornett-Murtada, and Jessica Johnson explored the timely and relevant topic of self-care by presenting three unique, yet interconnected approaches to dealing with adverse and difficult moments and avoiding the burnout and exhaustion so prevalent among music teachers.

Amoriello framed the idea of "self-care" around the vital question: *What does my body need right now?* Constantly asking this question and staying attuned to your bodily needs (whether physical, mental, or emotional) forms the foundations of effective self-care. In order to be attuned to our needs, Amoriello offered eight dimensions of well-being, taken from Paola Savvidou's book *Teaching the Whole Musician: A Guide to Supporting Music Students' Wellness* (2021):

- Physical
- Emotional/mental
- Environmental
- Financial
- Occupational
- Social
- Intellectual
- Spiritual

By reflecting on these dimensions and placing them within the proper context of our daily lives, one can realize just how wide-ranging and extensive their needs truly are and take active steps to satisfy those needs. Another key component for effective self-care is modeling wellness for others, whether they are your family or your students.

To promote self-care and well-being, Cornett-Murtada used the idea of a revolution against cultural norms glorifying what she termed the "cult of ambition" and the "glorification of busyness." An apt metaphor for such thinking can be taken from the sports world, where several elite international athletes have made headlines for being vocal about prioritizing their mental health and well-being over the demands of competition and the need to win. One key question to consider, then, when considering our own self-care is: *Have we been brainwashed to value achievement over well-being?* For many teachers who work under a litany of internal and external pressures usually related to demands of excellence and proof of success, this question is both humbling and enlightening to consider.

One way that Cornett-Murtada encourages this "rebellion" against the cult of ambition is to widen the distinction between our identities and our jobs. One's value as an employee is not necessarily defined by how productive they appear to be, or by how intense their workload is, or how prolific their professional achievements are. Two key quotations that summed up this line of thought were "My value is irrefutable—I am enough," and "I'm a human *being*, not a human *doing*."

Johnson's segment of the session focused on the importance of physical activity as a way to respond to stress and burnout. While one often associates stress and burnout with the toll of mental and emotional exhaustion, dealing with stress and burnout requires a physiological shift in our bodies—the healing process is far more than just something we deal with "in our heads." This physiological shift can be achieved by taking a few simple measures. First, one must realize just how important the act of breathing truly is in grounding us and providing connection to our own inner selves. One way to experience this is through the practice of "finger breathing," where one lets the finger serve as a focal point of breath and a way to concentrate the inhalation and exhalation. Second, the concept of *rest* is critical for our well-being and needs to be normalized as a necessary element to our daily lives. While we may associate "rest" with sleep, it can also take the form of a beneficial leisure activity. Finally, the intentional practice of what Johnson called "cultivating joy" is an effective antidote to the "numbing" that many teachers do to block negative emotions. Rather than a mental/emotional approach, Johnson suggested that "moments of joy" can be a physical act, through sensory experiences like sights, smells, tastes, and sounds that are personally significant.

Although the three panelists had unique and highly personal takes on the concept of self-care, one common thread that linked the three presentations was the simple act of putting oneself first and thinking about your own needs. As teachers, this idea is one that needs to be reinforced daily if we are to practice self-care and be our best personal and professional selves in these turbulent and difficult times.

Links Between Music and Language
Presented by Sean Hutchins
Friday, July 30, 2021
Recorded by Luís Pipa

The presenter explained that, unlike many of the people in the audience, he was not an educator, but a scientist interested in the links between music and the mind. Music is often said to be a universal language, as it is found around the world in every culture. Every person feels its pull and it is one of the most important forms of communication that we have. However, people feel that formal training is required for music, and believe themselves to be lacking in this area. Contrasting that with speech, another major form of communication that, like music, is found everywhere, people are comfortable with it, feeling that it is natural, and that it requires no specialized training.

Speech and music, although seeming two worlds apart, actually overlap in many important ways, such as structure, usage, and even the neural signals that underlie speech and music.
There is ongoing research on music-language links at The Royal Conservatory of Music in Toronto, of which Dr. Hutchins is Director of Research, and his talk had the purpose of recognizing musical elements in language, communicating those links to students, parents and administrators, and helping educators to use language as a tool in their teaching practice more effectively.

Music and language overlap in many critical ways, mainly in having similar goals, having similar forms, and using similar elements:
- The shared goals include expressing emotions, strengthening interpersonal relationships, and demonstrating proficiency.
- The shared forms of expression include the emission of sound and the fact that it can be written. These forms of expression have vocal and non-vocal components and are both grounded in rule-based codes.
- The shared elements include speech, rhythm, timbre, and neural signals.

In rhythm, words like "object" acquire different meanings depending on stress: OB-ject and Ob-JECT. The poetry of limericks has a distinct rhythmic pattern in 6/8 meter. Different types of languages use rhythm in different ways. As an example, English is a stress-timed language and French is a syllable-timed one. The presenter gave examples of a study comparing rhythmic patterns in English and Japanese languages.

Fetuses can hear the outside world, but only the low aspects of the frequency. Thus, it is mostly the rhythmic information that passes through, and infants will distinguish their mother languages from others by rhythm alone. Dr. Hutchins mentioned another study referencing that French composers tend to write music with rhythms more like French, whilst English composers tend to write music with rhythms more like English, even for music with no words.

Pitch is also a distinctive feature. Mandarin, Thai, Yoruba and Navajo are languages where the same word, with the same vowels and the same consonants, changing only in pitch, can mean different things. This may explain the high rates of people possessing absolute pitch in Mandarin and Thai speakers. The presenter spoke then of the speech-to-song illusion, where hearing speech multiple times can make it sound like singing. It is often the context that defines whether it is speech or song.

Prosody is often referred to as the music of speech; it includes nuances not captured in writing such as statements versus questions, happy versus sad, and the emphasis of particular words in a sentence. Prosody also applies to infant-directed speech, which is more songlike and preferred by infants, also helping language comprehension and learning. In music, prosody is also used to create meaning and emotion by using elements such as articulation and dynamics.

The presenter identified three major routes to create emotion in music:
- Resemblance – music that resembles sounds in the world.
- Piggybacking – the way we use speech, movements, and body language, can have parallels in the music and create emotion.
- Self-reference – music's relationship to itself – setting up music expectations by means of structure allows for the unexpected to occur.

There is a strong connection in people's abilities to understand language and music. There is a common belief that there is a close connection between music and math, but the connection between music and language is much stronger. Musicians are better than the average citizen in picking out speech in noise and have the ability to isolate and manipulate the sounds of speech by removing or combining sounds. That is called "phonemic awareness." Musicians are also better at performing complex tasks, such as remembering lists, recognizing emotions, grammatical processing, and learning a second language.

Scientists believe that the reason why musicians outperform non-musicians is the so-called OPERA hypothesis, resulting from the initials of five words: **O**verlap, **P**recision, **E**motion, **R**epetition, **A**ttention. Evidence of this exists in monitoring the electrical signals made by neurons in response to music. Also, gray areas in the frontal lobe (executive function) and the temporal lobe (sound/language) of the brain tend to be bigger in musicians than in non-musicians. Similarly, there is a stronger connection between different parts of the brain in musicians compared to non-musicians. In the RCM research project on music and language, group music classes are given to children between ages 0-6, developed in-house, and based on neuroscience. This is called "Smart Start." The research center has an "in-house lab to measure cognitive, linguistic, and musical outcomes of children taking these classes."

On the opposite side, studies are carried out with students at the Glenn Gould School, the university-level program of the RCM, and musicians show also at this stage higher levels in all parameters than non-musicians.

In his concluding remarks, the presenter further stressed that speech and music are similar in many ways, briefly reviewing the main aspects of this strong connection.

Teaching Students to Fish: Developing Independent Learners from the First Lesson
Presented by Lynette Barney, Joy Morin, Christopher Oill, Tony Parlapiano, and Clinton Pratt
Saturday, July 31, 2021
Recorded by Michael Dean

Lynette Barney began with a description of the topic as "how to work ourselves out of a job," explaining that her long-term goal for students is to not need her as a teacher anymore. Following brief introductions, each panelist then answered a specific question regarding how one might foster independence in the various types of beginners one might encounter.

Barney answered the first question: "How do you foster independent learning in young beginners?" She stated that by the time students encounter a concept in printed music, they should already be intimately familiar with it through play, movement, improvisation, and exploration. In this way, the pieces in method books are exercises in sight reading, as students already have all the tools necessary to learn the music. In Barney's studio, students often encounter new concepts in group classes, such as learning about irregular meters through bouncing and catching a tennis ball or using a finger staff, art, and *solfège* before moving to a printed staff.

Tony Parlapiano discussed fostering independent learners in teenage beginners, noting that the primary differences between younger and teenage beginners involve pacing and the rate at which one can layer concepts together. Parlapiano mentioned that having quality materials, including a standard composition book and special pencil such as the Blackwing Pearl, can inspire students' creativity. This also gives students added responsibility for their own learning experience, using the notebook for recording interests, assignments, and creative ideas. He shared his method of using symbols to introduce the topography or geography of the piano, beginning with the white keys on the outside of the black key groups and moving to more complex concepts. By building on basic concepts and combining them into various shapes, students can create more complicated pieces and use graphic notation to write them in their composition books.

Christopher Oill presented ideas for working with non-traditional students, noting the wide variety of people to which "non-traditional" may refer. For example, a non-traditional student may be one not interested in traditional classical music or one who has specific learning or life challenges. Oill stressed focusing on the student's specific interests while making other things supplemental. He stated the importance of giving resources for discovery and process learning rather than providing quick answers, and the value of collaboration instead of control. He provided a case study to show how these processes might work in real life.

Joy Morin then gave three examples of independent learners from her studio, ranging in ages from 5 to 76 years old and in levels from beginner to advanced. She noted that independence looks different depending on age and level. In all examples, Morin stressed the involvement of the student in decision making regarding pacing and musical interests. She mentioned *Pianist*, a publication from the United Kingdom, as a wonderful resource for older students which offers beginning, intermediate, and advanced-level pieces with each issue.

Clinton Pratt considered the question, "How can we ensure students are effective and independent at home?" It is of primary importance that students learn how to practice at home, so that they can continue learning when the teacher is not present. When trying to play fluidly, it is easier to practice slowly in small sections and more difficult to play large sections quickly. Pratt reiterated that questions may be used to inform practice, both when asked by the teacher and when asked by the students themselves. He lauded William Westney's *The Perfect Wrong Note*, noting that students can be informed by their mistakes and should be taught to be non-judgmental observers of what is happening while practicing. Finally, students can demonstrate their practice during the lesson or through a video recording, and even switch roles with the teacher during the lesson.

Presenters concluded by answering questions submitted to them during the session. Parlapiano stated that he is not in a rush in moving from using graphic notation to note reading. Once the student comfortably recognizes certain patterns on the piano through creative work, the representation on the staff is much more easily understood. He starts by having students write what they can already play. When asked about teaching students with little or no motivation, Morin mentioned that building a relationship with the student takes time but is important in fostering motivation. The teacher needs to take time to discover the student's own interests and what might motivate him or her. Barney agreed, stressing that relationship building and community within the studio is a significant factor in motivating students in their learning. She mentioned that she does all group instruction for students under the age of seven, with other students receiving a private lesson, an ensemble class, and time in the piano lab each week. Other members of the panel have studio or group classes monthly or occasionally throughout the semester. Presenters offered additional resources and welcomed questions via their personal emails, available at pianosensei.com/nckp2021.

Piano Partnerships: Traits of Effective Teachers of Adults (as Reported by their Students)
Presented by Pamela D. Pike
Saturday, July 31, 2021
Recorded by Roger McVey

In her presentation, Dr. Pike examined aspects of being an effective teacher to adult students, based on her significant teaching experience, as well as case studies. This analysis of effective teaching is based on the overriding premise that the teacher and the adult student must view their work together as a partnership, creating a collaborative learning environment, rather than a hierarchical relationship. According to research, Pike states that some of the general characteristics of adult students can be summarized as follows: adults tend to be self-directed in their learning, motivated, and goal oriented. However, they can also be unrealistic in their expectations, resistant to change, and slower to learn compared to children. Despite this, they often can learn concepts "better" or more deeply than younger students.

Pike illustrated some common themes regarding adult piano study. First of all, adults may not always state their actual motivation for study. Dr. Pike addresses this by giving questions for the student to answer, prior to the first interview meeting, regarding their motivation for taking piano lessons. She stated that a constant reassessment of learning outcomes, and the parameters of what defines "success" for the student, is necessary, and only possible with open communication between teacher and student. She described how a student's motivation can change during the course of their study—for example, after a goal has been met. Another issue is that interest in one style (say, Chopin) may suddenly change to something else that the student was previously unaware of, such as jazz, or piano duets, or some unfamiliar repertoire. Dr. Pike sees this as an opportunity to "reframe" goals, and consequently renew the student's motivation for learning.

Next, Pike discussed the question of whether adults should be taught in a group lesson format or a private lesson setting, and the considerations of each. In her experience, she has found that some people like the group dynamic and are motivated by it, while others may feel intimidated by the group and as a result need to be taught individually. In addition, some students simply want a teacher's individual attention. Dr. Pike goes on to describe some of the extra-musical and psychological/social benefits that her students have reported, in general support of adult piano study. For example, adult students enjoy learning and staying active, and they benefit from the mental stimulation of lessons. Many students report improved focus and concentration from studying piano, as well as an improvement of listening skills (outside of listening to music). Some students report an improved sense of physical coordination, while others value the sense of fulfillment and the "spiritual benefits" that come from playing the piano. Finally, many adult students feel a sense of community or common purpose in their music study.

Finally, Dr. Pike described how the learning and processing of music changes during an adult's normal ageing process. This manifests in four areas: visual changes, auditory changes, physical changes, and cognition changes. Dr. Pike discussed the five stages of adulthood, and how this affects learning and lesson experience. She explained how thoughtful repertoire selection can make a huge difference to a student (considering aspects of level, style, genre, arrangements, etc.). She emphasized how teacher flexibility is crucial for student success and satisfaction—that we, as teachers, need to be patient, knowledgeable, respectful, and show that we love teaching. We also need to be adaptable, and to help our adult students find stimulating repertoire. There are many things which teachers of adult students can be aware of in order to make lessons more effective. For example, considering score size and the use of practice scores, with highlights, color, and bold markings; giving time between statements for a student to process or reframe the statement; reducing background noise while speaking or giving instructions; and, using slower tempi when necessary. Dr. Pike summarizes the characteristics of effective, motivating teachers as "four Es and one C": Expertise, Empathy, Enthusiasm, Expectancy, and Clarity. Her final point was that teacher flexibility also means understanding life's other demands, outside of music, that our adult students may be dealing with.

Uncovering Hidden Voices: Exploring Piano Works by Black Women Composers in the Helen Walker-Hill Collection

Presented by Bryan Chuan, Anastasiia Pavlenko, Angela Schmitt,
Elizabeth Smith, and Elizabeth Strickland
Saturday, July 31, 2021
Recorded by Michael Dean

Helen Walker-Hill, pianist and musicologist, collected numerous compositions by Black women composers to use in her own teaching and performing. This collection is hosted by the American Music Research Center at the University of Colorado at Boulder. Since 2019, the Hidden Voices project, supervised by Dr. Alejandro Cremaschi, has explored, documented, and annotated pieces from this collection. In this presentation, members of CU's MTNA Collegiate Chapter shared historical information and pedagogical relevance of several works from the collection.

First presented were three works from Zenobia Powell Perry's fourteen-piece collection entitled *Piano Potpourri*. Perry's work was influenced by Black American and Native American folklore, and includes pieces at a variety of levels. Two pieces, "Vignette No. 2" and "Orrin and Echo," are suitable for beginning students strengthening their understanding of melody and harmony. "Orrin and Echo" also includes a canonic call and response and requires rhythmic consistency. "A Jazz Trifle" contains sophisticated jazz and gospel harmonies and is suitable for an intermediate student focusing on voicing and pedaling.

Works by Montague Ring, though widely published in the early twentieth century, can be difficult to find now. The three dances of the *T'Chaka Suite* (1927) all contain strong rhythmic ideas, with the melodies occurring above harmonies using open fifths. The second movement, "Monarah," is a slower, lyrical piece suitable for a mid- to late-intermediate level student. *African Dances*, another set of three pieces, contains folk elements and themes with West African origins. This intermediate-level set concludes with "Dance of the Warriors," which uses material from the first two movements and requires rapid stride piano technique.

Avril Coleridge-Taylor's *Nocturne* was originally written for harpsichord, but is effectively performed on the modern piano. Although left-hand arpeggiation and position shifts make this an intermediate-level composition, the thin texture and easily memorized form make this a good early nocturne in a student's study, requiring a singing melodic tone and nuances of expression.

Valerie Capers' *Portraits in Jazz* is a set of twelve pieces inspired by the children's albums of composers such as Bach, Schumann, and Prokofiev. Drawing from both jazz and classical influences, it introduces intermediate students to the elements, styles, and important historical figures of jazz. "Billie's Song," a brief ballad dedicated to Billie Holiday, allows the performer many expressive possibilities, requiring flexible timing and rubato as well as an understanding of voicing and rich chromatic harmonies. "Cool-Trane" quotes and invokes John Coltrane's saxophone performances, and is the final and most difficult piece of the set. The movement is technically challenging and requires finger agility and speed.

Composer Anna Gardner Goodwin was known for her many marches and religious works. The *Educational Congress March*, a brief three-page work, utilizes tonal harmonies and an easily understood form. Its technical demands, including large rapid jumps in the left hand and right-hand melodies in octaves, make this piece appropriate for the early-advanced student.

Jacqueline Hairston's writing covers genres from spirituals to contemporary art songs. Her *"Great Day" Ode* is based on three African American spirituals. Utilizing a variety of sounds and tempi, the most difficult technical passages include rapid parallel octaves, *glissandi*, and arpeggios.

Presenters shared a portion of a video made when Mable Bailey discussed her compositional style as the balancing of tonal and atonal influences, arriving at a style uniquely her own. *Dance*, a good introduction to atonal composition, utilizes atonal trichords in a concise, clear form. Technical difficulties in this advanced piece include large left-hand leaps and overlapping rhythmic motives.

Jeraldine Saunders Herbison's *Sonata*, Op. 19, is a technically demanding work requiring knowledge of the music of the Baroque, Classic, and Romantic periods. Its outer movements ("Prelude" and "Air") are in a neoclassic style, while the inner movements ("Rondo" and "Scherzo") are denser, neoromantic, and brilliantly virtuosic.

Undine Smith Moore, often referred to as the dean of Black women composers, wrote over 100 compositions in a variety of genres. *Many Thousand Gone* is an advanced work requiring large hands, solid octave technique, and agility through arpeggios and chromatic runs.

Anastasiia Pavlenko described the development of the Hidden Voices project and the involvement of the MTNA collegiate chapter. Those interested in more information regarding the Hidden Voices project were invited to visit the website at colorado.edu/project/hidden-voices. Music from the Helen-Walker Hill Collection may be requested by emailing sca@colorado.edu, and some pieces (such as *Portraits in Jazz)* are still available from various publishers or on the IMSLP website. Mable Bailey also has a technical exercises collection, and the presenters continue to explore additional underrepresented composers and works.

Duels at a Distance: Adapting Games to a Remote Group Piano Environment
Presented by Erin K. Bennett
Saturday, July 31, 2021
Recorded by Leonidas Lagrimas

Every piano teacher forced into remote teaching by the pandemic has encountered the feeling of "teaching into the void." Even the most experienced and seasoned of pedagogues has endured the feeling of being disconnected, in the physical, emotional, and musical sense, from their remote-learning students. The problem is particularly noticeable for collegiate group piano teachers, where the in-person obstacles that these instructors may face—lack of motivation, lack of engagement, ambivalence towards the course content—are only amplified in virtual settings.

Presenter Erin K. Bennett's session highlighted the use of games in the remote group piano class as a means of "surviving" the remote-teaching void. Even before the pandemic, playing games was a valuable part of her group piano curriculum, in that they were an easy and fun way for students to work cooperatively, review for assessments, understand grading standards, and create a sense of engagement and intrinsic motivation towards class content. Since the pandemic, though, playing games has taken on an even more vital role in that they are a way to recapture the normalcy of teaching, restore a sense of community in a time of isolation, and bring joy into the virtual classroom—indeed, a way to "stop teaching into the void."

An interactive, hands-on session allowed attendees to experience each of the games firsthand and in real-time. While the structure and set-up of each of the games were quite specific, Bennett made it clear throughout the presentation that all games could be easily adapted to specific and varied teaching situations, student populations, class sizes, and experience levels.

Tic-Tac-Toe
- Traditional set up with either an online template Tic-Tac-Toe board or draw your own on Zoom whiteboard
- Class divided into two teams by last name initial
- Questions are asked to one team at a time; team members use the Zoom chat function to "buzz in" by entering a single letter in the chat
- Questions can take the form of demonstrating a skill correctly (*e.g.*, performing a scale or chord progression), or recalling facts (*e.g.*, identifying a key signature)
- Correct answers mean teams can place X or O on square of their choice
- Prizes can range from extra credit to first "dibs" on a quiz time slot to bragging rights, or chocolate treats for in-person classes

4 in a Line (Connect Four)
- www.mathsisfun.com/games/connect4.html
- This is a more advanced variant of Tic-Tac-Toe

Jeopardy
Online Jeopardy templates readily available online
- Can be used as a quiz review; Jeopardy categories reflect quiz content "categories"
- Can be played as teams or as individual "free-for-all" format
- Chat function on Zoom is a straightforward way to buzz in first
- Buzzin.live (www.buzzin.live) offers online buzzers that can also be used with a phone; premium version offers scorekeeping and flexible membership time periods
- Questions can be adapted for students who have access to a piano and those who do not (*e.g.* performing an arpeggio or spelling out the correct pitches of an arpeggio)

Wheel of Fortune
- Many Powerpoint templates for Wheel of Fortune are available
- The wheel component of the game makes for a fun and visually compelling way to "randomize" segments of a remote class (*e.g.* calling on students, selecting specific tasks to perform, *etc.*)
- If Wheel of Fortune word puzzles are used, answers can be drawn from all kinds of music theory/music history-based categories

Truth or Dare/Double Dare
- Based off the traditional "truth or dare" format of "daring" another person or team to answer
- Specific "Double Dare" format based off the 1980s Nickelodeon show
  - Questions are asked, teams can "dare" other teams to answer questions for increasing dollar amounts, or opt to take a physical challenge
  - Physical challenges can be skill-based, like sight-reading or performing a chord progression; can also incorporate fun/silly elements
- Student motivation to answer questions and/or perform skills was noticeably strong in this game format

Virtual Scavenger Hunt
- The virtual scavenger hunt worked well for remote, asynchronous classes
- Can be used as a tool to familiarize students with online learning sites and/or Learning Management Systems (LMS) like Canvas or Blackboard
  - Students navigate their LMS for "Easter Eggs" related to the course content

- Students upload photos and videos into LMS to familiarize themselves with the process and allow the teacher to establish expectations and guidelines for performance, correct posture, remote quizzes, *etc.*

While it was Bennett's hope that teachers might not have to rely on such games as part of a long-term remote curriculum for much longer, an important point to take away from this session is that these games (or specific components of each of these games) can still be a vital component of in-person learning. Teachers can turn to games/game elements at any time during the semester when students are in need of extra motivation or a change of pace in the piano lab. Perhaps the most powerful benefit of games, though, can be equally felt in both remote and in-person settings: Games are a quick and fun way to instantly create a sense of community and belonging in the group piano class.

Building the Dyslexic Brain with Music
Presented by Becki Laurent
Saturday, July 31, 2021
Recorded by Angela Leising-Catalan

Becki Laurent began the presentation by telling the audience about how her interest in dyslexia research was initially sparked by her daughter's close friendship with a child with dyslexia. Each year, Laurent chooses one topic for in-depth personal learning and research, so she decided to pursue a deeper understanding of dyslexia, and how this relates to learning music.

The presenter discussed the amount of overlap that is involved in learning to read with learning to read music. She mentioned her Orton-Gillingham training, which is an approach to teaching literacy when reading, writing, and spelling does not come easily to individuals. She has worked to convert this knowledge and apply it to her music teaching. According to the CDC, one in five people have dyslexia to varying degrees, so the probability is high that a teacher will have several students with dyslexia in the average-sized studio. The presenter mentioned her difficulties as a non-reader and non-speaker of Hebrew in a trip to Israel. She described it as mentally and physically exhausting. This was a good reminder of what it's like for dyslexic students on a daily basis. These difficulties are compounded by piano lessons typically being at the end of the student's day when students are fatigued.

The presenter stated that a common misconception about dyslexia is that it is the flipping around of letters or writing words backwards. This can be a component of dyslexia; however, it is much more complex than that. The International Dyslexia Association states, "Dyslexia is manifested by variable difficulty with different forms of language, often including, in addition to problems reading, a conspicuous problem with acquiring proficiency in writing and spelling." Notable characteristics of dyslexia include:
1. Difficulty in learning to read, write, spell, and do math
2. Difficulty in following oral and written instructions
3. Squished or illegible handwriting
4. Cannot stay on task
5. Easily distracted
6. Immature for their physical age
7. An inability to sequence, or has confusion in sequencing, ex: b and d
8. Delayed spoken language
9. Difficulty with spatial and/or time directions: up/down, left/right/, yesterday/tomorrow
10. Easily frustrated, escalated frustration
11. Difficulty retaining information
12. Extreme anxiety during tests
13. Extreme energy levels (super energetic or very lethargic)

The presenter then spoke about the behavior one might see in a piano lesson in relationship to each of the characteristics listed:
1. Look of panic when you ask student to do written theory pages, read instructions from the page or add counts in a measure.
2. Most commonly seen when you explain the method book page objectives and the student cannot follow.
3. You notice that all handwriting is "doctor scrawl" or the letters are not closed or finished.
4. Student has a hard time staying on the bench, finishing an exercise or piece.
5. The student stops mid measure to tell you a story or make a comment.
6. You'll see this in the preparation for class, in their conversation, and in their reactions to situations.
7. You might see this when you are asking the student to identify a note and *b* and *d*, or *a* and *e* gets flipped or confused.
8. It is very unlikely that you will come across this unless the student has been known to you from birth.
9. Difficulty identifying direction of intervals, or bass and treble clef.
10. "This is TOO HARD!" Often you'll see emotional outbursts for what you think are trivial issues or you might see escalated frustration when they are corrected.
11. The learning curve seems exceptionally long and you teach the same lesson many times, not due to practice habits.
12. You will see an utter freak out when you ask them to play last week's assignment.
13. Student either won't sit still or won't get out of the car. You have no way of predicting week to week which student you'll have.

Laurent explained how the Orton-Gillingham philosophies for literacy can apply to the teaching of music. Some of these philosophies are:
1. Teaching using a multi-sensory approach of visual, auditory, and tactile/kinesthetic methods
2. Super structured
3. A phonetically based program of reading and spelling that teaches the complete sound structure of the language
4. A tremendous amount of repetition and drill in both group and individual instruction

Teaching Techniques
1. Multi-sensory instruction—use more than sheet music to teach. Sheet music is visual, but you also need to incorporate kinesthetic and tactile techniques.
2. Musical phonetic/musical symbol—sounds to symbol.
3. OG synthetic/analytic—synthetic phonics is learning the smallest unit of sound and what it looks like. Analytic phonics is breaking down the whole word into parts. In music,

synthetic would be looking at each measure's individual pieces. Analytic would be looking at the whole piece and breaking it down into parts.
4. Structured lesson plan—materials are presented in an organized manner highlighting the relationship between new and previously taught information.
5. Sequential presentation—the approach moves from a simple concept to more complex concepts.
6. Repetition and mastery—the goal of repetition is automaticity. Mastery is not forgetting it.
7. Diagnostic/prescriptive—continuous monitoring of progress to assess areas of need and responsiveness to instruction, followed by your plan for progression.

The presenter went on to list suggested resources and activities:
1. *Sproutbeat* app worksheets and games—quick, great for eye tracking and fallboard exercises
2. "Fishing" with toy fish that have musical symbols for fast-paced recall activity
3. Paper plate sliding—this creates physical memories of *staccato* and *legato*.
4. Invisible ink rhythm cards—rhythm cards written in invisible ink. Students shine UV light and then must remember the pattern and clap it out loud.
5. Stomping rhythm patterns while wearing light-up shoes
6. Use of drawn imagery
7. The Most Amazing Sheep Game and Rhythm Cup Games
8. Chrome Music Lab

Giving students with dyslexia whatever tools they need to remember and learn musical information should never be looked down on or seen as a crutch. As a teacher, you are providing exactly the tools and support that they need.

Clarifying the Piano Teacher's Role in Playing-Related Injury
Presented by Barbara Lister-Sink
Saturday, July 31, 2021
Recorded by Todd Van Kekerix

Barbara Lister-Sink's presentation focused on how piano teachers can play a more supportive role in their student's journey through injury and rehabilitation after playing-related injuries. She framed her presentation by stating that musicians are artist athletes because playing piano is a highly complex and coordinating activity. Various statistics gave further proof of how important the teacher's role is. Among classical musicians, women are two times more likely to suffer an occupational injury. Additionally, eighty-seven percent of women have what's considered a small hand size, according to Lister-Sink.

So as a teacher, it is important to watch for warning signs and communicate what those may be to your student. The warning signs include muscle fatigue and soreness, burning sensations, pain, numbness, tingling, cramping, difficulty moving fingers. These warning signs could indicate an injury that requires attention.

Lister-Sink covered various types of injuries and provided possible treatments. Playing related disorders of the tendons include tendonitis, tenosynovitis, "tennis elbow," "golfer's elbow," ganglion cysts, and "texting thumb." Some of the treatments she suggested include RICE ("relative" rest, ice, compression, elevation initially) and retraining in efficient technique.

Common nerve entrapment disorders including carpal tunnel syndrome, cubital tunnel syndrome, thoracic outlet syndrome, and ulnar nerve entrapment are also problems that pianists encounter. Treatments that were suggested included splinting, physical therapy, modification of daily activities, and retraining overall body and muscle awareness.

Myofascial disorder, which simply refers to knots in the muscles, are common as well. Treatment options include acupuncture, massage therapy, and relaxation techniques.

Lastly, the presenter brought up Leon Fleisher's battle with focal dystonia. Symptoms for FD include involuntary muscle contractions due to the brain's impaired ability to control movement. Treatments include botox, relaxation techniques, and acupuncture. The research points to retraining overall body and muscle awareness as being the most effective.

Teachers must also be aware of playing-related risk factors including repetitive motion, accumulation of muscle tension, excessive practicing and overloading the body, over-challenging repertoire, insufficient time for preparation, sudden increase in practice time, poor practice habits, mismatch of instrument, practicing environment, and faulty technique or biomechanics.

In addition, there are lifestyle-related risk factors that include lack of awareness of the body, genetic conditions, body size, medical conditions, physical anomalies, sleep deprivation, poor nutrition, lack of exercise, and personal and professional stress.

The presenter mentioned joint hypermobility periodically as a condition that can sometimes lead to problems later in a student's musical studies. It is a genetic condition that is not brought on by poor technique or faulty biomechanics and affects musicians and females more. The presenter suggested using joint braces as they have been effective in her experience.

The presenter also emphasized the critical risk factor of having small hands, which is not recognized widely enough in our field. Research suggests a high rate of injury in female pianists with small hands. One study indicated that 87 percent of females have small hands based on the Steinbuler and Company hand gauge. The modern keyboard size poses a significant risk for these students.

The presenter clarified the role of teacher as a guide and wellness partner, supporter, advocate, protector, coach, and counselor. She suggested caring for the student through a commitment to their health and working with outside sources to navigate the injury. It's important to not diagnose nor tell the student what injury they have, such as saying "I think you might have tendonitis." Make sure that they don't continue practicing if there is pain and create an action plan. Keep a chronology indicating when pain started, how long it lasted, what type of pain there was, and what other activities bring on the pain. She also suggested looking into the Performing Arts Medicine Association (PAMA) online courses and webinars.

The difficulty in finding healthcare providers with enough experience in complex disorders of pianists can result in diagnoses that are incomplete or inaccurate. Because of this, the presenter suggests networking with other teachers, pianists, and performers with similar injuries who have had successful diagnoses and treatments. When there's an injury, it's important to be a mediator on behalf of the student and deal with potential pressure from parents and peers to keep practicing and performing through the pain. It is also important to help the student maintain an identity as a musician.

If long-term healing becomes necessary, it's important for the teacher to play the role of a coach by urging the student to think of the piano as a partner in the rehabilitation process, create an action plan with healthcare providers, and continue with regular lessons that follow the appropriate action plan. For accountability, the presenter requests daily video clips of rehabilitation exercises.

In the role of counselor, it's important to remember that injuries are psychologically devastating. Work to create a respectful, supportive, and positive environment for rehabilitation and retraining and to help the student maintain hope throughout the process. As a means of coping, students should be encouraged to journal about the process or do an audio reflection if they need to let their hands rest. Students may have to work through emotional and psychological issues because of potential financial loss and academic consequences, such as losing their scholarship.

Bringing the Pop to Popular Music—Teaching Performance Practice in Pop, Rock, and R&B
Presented by Nicolas Lira and Bridget O'Leary
Saturday, July 31, 2021
Recorded by Fiona Christano

The presenters opened by highlighting the fact that for many students, popular music may be the most important style they learn in piano lessons, and one that they will return to again later in life. As educators and performers, it should be our goal to teach and perform popular music with the same authentic performance practice as repertoire from previous eras. Just like classical music, popular music has its own various distinguishing stylistic elements and musical idioms. These elements and idioms are seldom notated; they are mostly learned through listening to the music, using the guidance of a teacher. The presenters used four examples: *Love Song* by Sara Bareilles, *If I Ain't Got You* by Alicia Keys, *Your Song* by Elton John, and *Hello* by Adele. Finding the groove of the particular music is essential. One needs to be able to feel it and later on, produce it. *Groove* is described as establishing a background pattern of rhythm and meter with multiple levels from the subdivision of the beat to groupings of multiple beats. For the purpose of the discussion, there are several terms that are used. The presenters set a specific definition to each of those terms: *pulse*, defined as tempo as heard from the metronome; *beat*, defined as the heard/felt rhythmic impulse; *meter*, defined as the pattern of strong and weak beats.

Pulse and beat may line up with each other but that may not necessarily be the case. Knowing whether the beat falls before or after the pulse is crucial to finding the groove. Not all musical accents in the phrase will align with the meter. For example, in blues, R&B, and jazz there will sometimes be emphasis on two and four. Meter can exist with pulse groupings in multiple levels—shorter than, equal to, or longer than the measure. Consistent subdivision of the beat is also important to maintaining the groove. In pop music, the subdivision needs machine-like consistency to maintain the groove whether it occurs in even or swung time. Singing is essential to more easily internalize the groove of a piece of popular music. Elton John's *Your Song* uses a very even subdivision of the beat into four parts. Alicia Keys' *If I Ain't Got You* is propelled by its triplet subdivision. Sara Bareilles' *Love Song* uses the swung subdivision.

As with any musical style, the piano utilizes common idioms in popular music—some are percussive and driving, others more melodic and textural. *Idiom* is used to refer to musical patterns and techniques characteristic of pop music. The presenter then gave several examples of the popular music idioms with various elements such as a metronomic, evenly separated, and emphasized pattern; a syncopated pattern that utilizes rests to provide space for the melody sung by the artist; a pattern that is sustained, syncopated, and leaning towards melodic in the upper line; and one using a bass line with sixteenth notes in the right hand which most likely flows underneath a vocal melody sung by the artist. Listening to the recording of the actual song is crucial to convincing understanding and, later, production of the music.

In trying to help students break down and understand the pop piano idioms of popular music, there are some questions that are important to ask:
- What is the meter of the song?
- What beats/subdivisions does the piano play on?
- Swing or straight?
- Does the piano rest anywhere, and why?
- Is the piano part melodic, rhythmic, or both?
- What kind of textures are in the piano part?
- How does the articulation of the piano part impact that texture?

More questions to consider specific to each song:

Sara Bareilles: *Love Song*
- If a rock band was playing the piano part, which instruments would be playing what?
- Why is the left hand syncopated and not playing on the same parts of the beat as the right hand and what is the effect of the left-hand syncopation?

Alicia Keys: *If I Ain't Got You*
- Meter of chorus vs. verse? How does rhythm in the piano part affect the feel of the tempo?
- How does the album version sound different from live recordings? (Hint: the piano is more dominant in live recordings!)
- Where are dynamic swells heard and felt?

Elton John: *Your Song*
- Why does the song flow better in 2/2?
- Rhythm challenge: try to play with the metronome at one click per measure!

The final song the presenters used was *Hello* by Adele. It has a relatively simple piano part. However, it does warrant a short discussion of harmony, especially with a more advanced student. Being a modal composition (revolving around the F Aeolian mode and the diatonic triads a third away—Ab Major and Db Major), it does not provide resolutions from the major-dominant chord to a tonic. This gives the song a feeling of suspension and unsettled emotions. The beat falls slightly behind the pulse, contributing to the song's ruminating sound.

Some questions to consider when working on Adele's *Hello*
- Have students experiment with different voicings/inversions of the chords. What differences do they notice?
- In each section, which chord receives the most emphasis?

In closing, listening to the artist's performance of the popular song is an integral part of learning for our students. It is also crucial to the production of a convincing and energetic performance. As teachers we can ask some of the questions listed above to help our students understand the groove, articulations, and rhythm of the music. With an extensive understanding of those elements and the pop piano idioms we can help our students learn pop, rock, R&B, and electronic music with the same authentic performance practice as repertoire from other eras.

Electronic Chamber Music: Collaborating with Computers
Presented by Brendan Jacklin
Saturday, July 31, 2021
Recorded by Fiona Christano

The presenter opened the session by highlighting the benefits of working with computers as chamber music partners. The use of a computer enables musicians to access collaboration whenever it is desired, with a high degree of control over tempo and pitch consistency, and at the frequency and duration that is needed, in the comfort of the user's home.

Many people are uncomfortable with the use of technology and computers to help with practicing, editing music and teaching. This past year, musicians and educators had to learn to do it due to the pandemic. What is overlooked is the computer's compatibility to be a chamber musician/partner that can play its own music and at the same time, respond to what it hears. The lecture recital explored the three different ways to interact with computer-generated music, including the necessary technology and where to find this genre of music through three different pieces: *Disturbed Earth* by J. Andrew Smith, *David Lynch Etudes* by Nicole Lizee, and *Prayala* by Evan Williams.

Though the technology involved can be quite intimidating and complex, the basics are quite simple and use much of the same equipment as the ones we have become acquainted with this past year. There are only a few pieces of equipment (hardware) that are actually required:
- A pair of microphones with stands. These microphones are needed to amplify/modify the live sound of the instrument(s) connected to the usual microphone or using the XLR cables.
- Audio Interface (at least two inputs). The interface allows microphones to talk to the computer which then allows it to react to the live sound—much like performing with a regular chamber musician. There are many kinds of audio interfaces but a two-input interface is enough to get started.
- A pair of speakers. These speakers need to be connected to the interface. If possible, run the sound from the interface through a mixer before connecting it to the speakers. This will result in a better control for balance as well as other musical details.

In addition to the hardware listed above, there are two types of software that are needed:
- DAW (Digital Audio Workstation). DAW allows users to record, edit, and playback the audio. It works better than music players such as iTunes because it gives users more control of balance and playing time, and enables the use of an equalizer to adjust the sound to fit the space. Some examples are: Audacity, Pro Tools, Studio One, Reaper, Logic, and Ableton Live.

- MaxMSP. In order to perform interactive music with electronics, one needs a program that can modify live sounds. MaxMSP is a visual programming language that allows for interactive electronics with both audio and video. It is available to users for free.

Disturbed Earth for piano and live electronics is inspired by a poem by Margaret Atwood (with the same title) that dwells on the human tendency to reject things that "thwart" our wishes and desires. Near the end, the speaker undergoes a "transmutation" and becomes the very thing rejected. The poem encourages the readers to seek out the speaker in "the Disturbed Earth." The piece is a perfect example of how interactive chamber music is performed with a computer that samples and modifies the sounds of the live performance in real time.

David Lynch Etudes takes sounds and visuals from Lynch's film and TV catalogue and merges them with the piano to form an immersive and psychedelic journey. It is a perfect example of a performance with interactive electronics with the use of a complex pre-recorded track. Different from the previous performance, this piece requires the pianist to react to the electronics and has an end goal of immersing and becoming one instrument with it.

Prayala is a Hindu term defined as dissolution in the cycles of life and death. The fourth movement is a chaconne based on the opening bars of Mahler's *Urlicht*. It is accompanied by beautiful images of nature and the Aurora Borealis. It combines all the elements of live sampling in modulations, pre-recorded sound, and pre-recorded video, and requires the use of MaxMSP, audio interface, speakers and microphones, as well as a projector.

These types of music can be difficult to find in a more traditional repertoire resource. Listed below are good sources to find them:
- **Specialized Publishers:** Wise Music Classical, Hildegard Publishing
- **Composer Collectives:** Frog Peak Press, Adjective New Music
- **Competitions and Festivals:** SEAMUS, The Pulitzer
- **Specialized Databases:** Canadian Music Centre, Pytheas Center for Contemporary Music, Institute of Composer Diversity, musicbyblackcomposers.org, and A Seat At the Piano

Six Hands on Deck: "Six Hands is the New Four Hands"
Presented by Martin David Jones, Rosalyn Floyd, and Clara Park
Saturday, July 31, 2021
Recorded by Fiona Christano

The presenters began by highlighting the importance of ensemble playing to provide a social element to the often-solitary nature of piano playing/studying. The presenters have worked together in preparing the presentation and have decided that due to the joy they have had together, they wanted to share that "Six Hands is the New Four Hands!"

The lecture recital program started with Martin David Jones' arrangements of four American folk tunes ("I've Been Working on the Railroad," "The Arkansas Traveler," "Home on the Range," and "When the Saints Go Marching In") from his *American Folk Music Suite for Six Hands.* Each piece is about three minutes long with the two middle movements in moderate tempo and lyrical style and the last one set in a ragtime-like, swing-rhythm style. Attendees interested in obtaining any or all of the *American Folk Music Suite for Six Hands* by Martin David Jones, were advised to contact Dr. Jones at mdjones@augusta.edu. These pieces are distributed through JW Pepper.

Following the first presentation, a commentary was given prior to each performance to give the audience a historical background on the piece.

The Rachmaninoff *Valse and Romance for Six Hands* were composed around 1891 and was dedicated to Rachmaninoff's cousins: Natalya, Lyudmila, and Vera Skalon. The *Valse* was based on a theme that was written by Natalya. Dr. Floyd mentioned that it was a "light and frothy salon type of music." The *Romance* was a more serious composition with a theme that opens the second movement of Rachmaninoff's second Piano Concerto. The whole piece lasted about two minutes. They are both set in the key of A major and are appropriate for late-intermediate students. Rachmaninoff gave a specific direction on how to work on the piece: "Study each part separately; then, as necessary, play them together."

The *"Hallelujah Chorus" from Messiah* (excerpt) was an arrangement by Carl Czerny. Dr. Park highlighted that the arrangement was published by Alfred Publishing Company in the *Essential Keyboard Trios – Ten Intermediate to Early Advanced Selections,* selected and edited by Lucy Mauro and Scott Beard. The book also includes other six-hands arrangements such as Mozart's *Marriage of Figaro*, Rachmaninoff's *Valse and Romance*, W. F. E. Bach's *Das Dreyblatt*, Carolus Fodor's *Sonata for Six Hands*, Gurlitt's *Capriccietta, Gavotte,* and *Impromptu*, as well as J. L. Streabbog's *Bolero.*

The last presentation was W. F. E. Bach's *Das Dreyblatt,* lasting about four minutes. The composer was J. S. Bach's grandson. Dr. Jones highlighted the fact that this is a humorous piece—one that students will really take to and one that will generate a lot of laughter. The performance was not only a musical offering but also a theatrical one, involving a couple of fun props as well as choreography to accommodate the outstretched, bookending hand positions of the secondo part.

**Distantly Social: Creating Meaningful Virtual Recital Experiences
for Students, Families, and Communities**
Presented by Mario Ajero
Saturday, July 31, 2021
Recorded by Omar Roy

Dr. Ajero introduced his session by highlighting the difficulty of transitioning to virtual recitals due to the pandemic and emphasized that, despite improving conditions for in-person events, teachers should have the technological capabilities to successfully create meaningful, virtual performance opportunities. The session addressed a large range of skills and experience, providing solutions for teachers with limited technological experience as well as those with significant experience. The presenter provided step-by-step, detailed walkthroughs in real-time for the following virtual performance options:

Creating a YouTube Playlist

Dr. Ajero provided instruction for uploading and combining videos into a YouTube playlist to avoid creating extremely large video files and/or exceeding the time limits of various video hosting services. He also delineated the difference between Public, Private, and Unlisted videos so that teachers can manage the public visibility of their videos and playlists.

Making a "YouTube Premier"

For teachers that prefer one long video, Dr. Ajero suggested a YouTube Premier. This allows teachers to upload a video and have it available for viewing at a scheduled day and time, and can be supplemented by Live Chat features.

Live Broadcasting on YouTube or Facebook

Dr. Ajero suggested live broadcasts as an alternative to pre-recorded performances. He also provided suggestions to enhance the professionalism and quality of live broadcasts through the use of external cameras and microphones, and demonstrated the use of dedicated streaming programs such as Open Broadcaster Software (OBS). Programs like OBS can be used in conjunction with the live broadcast options available on YouTube.

Some of the equipment that Dr. Ajero recommended included the following:
- Camera: Nikon D750 DSLR Camera
- Camera-to-Laptop adapter: UltraStudio Mini Recorder
- Microphone: Zoom H4N Handheld Recorder

Dr. Ajero included a recorded example of a previous live broadcast and highlighted that virtual recitals he had organized at Stephen F. Austin State University reached a much larger audience than in-person attendance alone could allow for. Additionally, whereas in live concerts audience members must limit their applause to between movements, live broadcasts on services like Facebook can allow for a constant outpouring of support through the text chat and other functions available through the streaming platform. Dr. Ajero concluded by stating he will continue implementing these virtual performances to continue reaching larger audiences.

Teach Them to Believe: Strategies for Cultivating Self-Efficacy Beliefs in Piano Students
Presented by Lynn Worcester Jones
Saturday, July 31, 2021
Recorded by Allison Fog

This presentation served to introduce the concept of self-efficacy, discuss why it's important in piano study, explore sources of information used to increase self-efficacy beliefs, and offer strategies in research and experience to help cultivate self-efficacy beliefs in students. "Whether you think you can or think you can't, you are right."~ Henry Ford. Research suggests that Ford's comment was accurate, in that a student's perceived ability to perform tasks is just as important as actual ability.

Albert Bandura created the concept of self-efficacy in 1986, and states that "self-efficacy is the belief we have in our ability to perform tasks successfully, which helps us reach our goals." Furthermore, self-efficacy is "concerned not with the number of skills you have, but what you believe you can do with what you have under a variety of circumstances."

Piano study offers many situations for assessment, including technique, sight playing, ear training, and performance. These assessments can challenge our students' beliefs in their own abilities, so it is imperative that self-efficacy beliefs are as strong as our students' pianistic skills. Students must gain the ability to manage fears and to cope, especially when their skills are tested under stressful circumstances.

Constructs of the "self" include self-esteem, self-efficacy, confidence, and motivation. Self-efficacy is a belief in a set of abilities needed to achieve a goal; self-esteem is related to one's worth and value in themselves. According to Bandura, "confidence is a nondescript term that refers to strength of belief but does not necessarily specify what the certainty is about." Motivation to achieve is driven by desire but self-efficacy is driven by belief. A student may not want to practice, but they know that once they try, they can achieve success. Examples of high self-efficacy beliefs in piano students include a student who is worried about an upcoming performance, but believes she has the skills to succeed. Another is a student who perceives musical challenges as tasks to be mastered. Examples of low self-efficacy beliefs include a student who avoids tasks even though they are age and level-appropriate, or a student who loses belief in their skill sets because of one poor performance.

There are three sources of information that can help students to increase self-efficacy beliefs: Mastery Experiences, Social Modeling, and Verbal Persuasion.

Mastery Experiences are previous performances that are perceived to be successful, and students use these successful experiences to increase self-efficacy beliefs. The four strategies below can increase mastery experiences:
1. Create more high-stakes performances
2. Create low-stakes performances
3. Master one piece before moving on
4. Assign independently learned parallel repertoire

High-stakes performances are those which contain meaningful consequences, and include musical examinations, as well as studio classes and formal recitals. An ordinary lesson can become an opportunity to create a high-stakes performance by asking another family member or a friend to attend. Low-stakes performances are those with little to no consequences. For example, a teacher could sit far away from the student to hear a new scale, treating this as a mini-performance. One study suggests that achievement is greater when incorporating more low-stakes experiences into teaching.

Self-efficacy beliefs can be strengthened by encouraging a student to fully master one piece before moving on to new repertoire, as well as assigning a parallel piece that is easier. (The new piece must be significantly easier than the student's original piece).

Social Modeling involves observing others perform similar tasks successfully. Self-efficacy beliefs increase while watching others play without mistakes, but those beliefs are further strengthened by watching peers struggle and then overcome obstacles. Teachers can provide opportunities for students to interact, observe, and share by overlapping lessons, holding studio classes every two to four weeks, and pairing up less experienced students with more experienced ones. Competitions and festivals also provide chances for observation and sharing of music and experience.

Verbal Persuasion involves using positive language to convince students they can perform a task. A focused pep talk before a performance can be an excellent opportunity to discuss the path of the music versus the outcome. Students can be reminded of successful past performances, because too often the brain holds onto negative experiences, and students can have a type of "false memory" when it comes to a performance that they remember to be unsuccessful when in fact it wasn't.

Self-efficacy beliefs are in a state of flux throughout one's life. One bad experience can corrupt even the most seasoned professional. Students who genuinely believe in their ability to achieve their goals experience the most success.

Nurturing Interest and Cultivating Motivation: Investigating the Intersection of Educational Psychology and Piano Pedagogy
Presented by Jared Rixstine
Saturday, July 31, 2021
Recorded by Allison Fog

The presenter began by giving attendees a quiz focused on learning styles, goals, and modalities. The questions were as follows:

Question 1: What are learning styles?
   A. ways teachers teach
   B. a problematic myth
   C. an individualized approach to teaching based on how one learns

Question 2: Information should be presented in multiple modalities simultaneously. True or False?

Question 3: Should students have *performance* goals or *mastery* goals?

The answer to the first question included a brief explanation of learning styles and learning modality. Research from forty years has shown that learning styles are a myth, and educational psychology has tried to dispel the myth. Learning styles seem to work because they are intuitive, however studies have found that human beings have preferences for learning, but not styles.

Learning modalities are more helpful in understanding the process of learning. In the brain, the "Central Executive" takes incoming stimulus, and moves it into the Phonological Loop (auditory information) and the Visual Spatial Sketchpad (visual information). A bimodal modality involves two ways to process and decode incoming content simultaneously. The role of the central executive in the brain as described above is compared to the editor of a newspaper. The editor assigns reporters to specific stories, choosing the best reporter for each story. The central executive in the brain also chooses the best path: auditory or visual.

How can educators maximize teaching and learning, using modalities? A driver education class was given three ways to learn how to negotiate a roundabout. The first involved showing a video, followed by commentary. The second way involved watching the video, followed by a lecture of the same content from the video. In the third example, students watched the video while the teacher led them through a discussion of the implications of the actions taken by each driver. It was found that the third option outperformed the other two groups, because it used a bimodal modality. Thus, the answer to the second quiz question is "True."

A grid illustrating Goal Orientation, or motivation, was presented. The four categories of goals on the grid were Mastery, Performance, Approach, and Avoidance. Mastery goals are those done for their own sake, while Performance goals are centered on the outcome and for one to look competent. An Approach goal is about correctness and moves toward success, while an Avoidance goal focuses on the negative, and moves away from success. The intersection of the categories on the grid showed that goals can be Mastery-Approach, Mastery-Avoidance, Performance-Approach, and Performance-Avoidance. It has been found that mastery goals produce the most success and motivation, while performance goals can lead to anxiety and frustration, with negative motivation often attached. The goals of our students can fall anywhere on this grid and in many combinations, but teachers need to encourage mastery goals over performance ones.

Teachers can encourage students to focus on mastery goals in three ways. First, explain issues of execution through the music, not performance. For example, ask "what did you hear in the music?" or "what is the music communicating?" The material in the music should be the primary focus. Second, the word "good" should not be used by a teacher. Group class students also can be encouraged to offer comments to one another that don't involve the word "good." For example, "I liked the way your steady pulse made me feel like dancing!" Students can be encouraged to "share their gift," moving the emphasis away from a strictly performance goal.

A Million Little Etudes: Enhancing Artistic Expression and Technical Ease
Presented by Catharine Lysinger
Saturday, July 31, 2021
Recorded by Angela Leising-Catalan

Dr. Lysinger began by describing the scope of her teaching experience at Southern Methodist University in the precollege program and in the pedagogy program. She has taught applied piano to students of all ages and levels. She stated that this presentation is based on what she has learned over the years. What to teach, and when to teach it, are concepts that typically are easy for teachers, Dr. Lysinger said, but the more difficult concept for teachers is typically how to teach students how to spend their practice time and effort. She stated that her idea of "a million little etudes," or practice boxes, reflects this idea of how to guide students in focused practice from day one and beyond, in specific ways.

The presenter shared a slide setting out the "Fundamentals First" of what needs to be secure initially, or the "little etudes" may not be helpful:
- rhythm
- notes
- fingering
- articulation
- dynamics
- and, in advanced levels, balance, pedaling, and phrase shaping.

Goals of created etudes are projection and communication of musical detail. This involves enhancement of character and physical comfort and ease. To find "little etudes," Dr. Lysinger suggested reading through pieces to find the basic pitfalls and trouble spots of a piece, while thinking about gestures and technique that would be needed. She reminded attendees that we are our student's most important sound model.

As an example, the presenter shared a video of a beginning student playing the piece *The Juggler*. Lysinger and the student indicated practice boxes for focused practice that included eighth-note phrases going over a bar line, and isolated *staccato* notes.

Another video showing a student, age nine, was shared. The student played James Hook's *Lesson One*. Lysinger created boxes for focused practice where the student may have been tempted to run musical ideas together, and perhaps would need extra attention to alignment between the hands.

The next video example was a student playing *Petite Prelude* by Schytte. Boxes were created to help the student achieve proper pedaling and to create more flow. Dr. Lysinger described how short etudes keep the teaching dialogue moving without long explanations.

Another video was shared of a Dr. Lysinger playing *Through Forest and Field* by Gurlitt. Here, practice boxes were created to help isolate practice spots, with the goal of layering the sound entrances with fine nuance.

An attendee asked if these boxes were assigned in advance. The presenter answered that generally she assigns pieces in sections, or subsections, but this can vary based on the student, literature, or circumstances. She also stated that small "etudes" can also be used to play very small segments up to tempo, with less danger of building in mistakes.

Next, a video was shared of a student playing Grieg's *Notturno,* Op. 54. Here, practice boxes were created to help focus practice on voicing and smooth movement of the hands.

The next segment of the presentation was a video of a student playing *Butterfly,* Op. 43, by Grieg. The student was able to self-identify where in the music a gesture between two hands was required. Multiple other musical ideas were quickly discussed and demonstrated. At the end of the video, the presenter discussed how this etude strategy helps busy students focus and make their practice time efficient.

Dr. Lysinger went on to share examples of more advanced works of music. The presenter shared a video of herself playing the first movement of Haydn's *Sonata in E-flat Major,* Hob. XVI/49, with etude boxes indicated.

Another video was shared of a student playing Chopin's *Grande Polonaise,* Op. 22, showing multiple elements of movement and events, and connecting physical gestures.

The presider indicated some comments from the attendees regarding the helpfulness of boxes, and how the boxes can add a sense of purpose to each individual practice session. The presider asked if colors were specific to any particular concern; the presenter indicated that it depended on each individual student. Dr. Lysinger indicated that digital or paper versions of markings are helpful. She then discussed how advancing students gain skill in self-identifying where etude spots should occur in their own music.

The last video of the presentation was a student playing "Aufschwung," Op. 12, No. 2, by Schumann. Here, practice boxes were used to highlight spots to practice with balance and voicing within the hand in mind.

How to Play by Ear (Really!)
Presented by Bradley Sowash
Saturday, July 31, 2021
Recorded by Jessie Welsh

This session discussed principles of playing by ear and gave practical, hands-on opportunities for attendees to apply these strategies in the session. Bradley Sowash discussed his admiration for classically trained pianists and his desire to assist them in developing the skill of playing by ear. He also asked attendees to position themselves near an instrument in order to best participate in this interactive session.

The four intended sections of the presentation included the following, with the caveat that each would be addressed in order, time permitting:
- *Intro*
- *Melody*
- *Chords*
- *Melody and chords*

In the *Introduction*, Sowash discussed that "playing by ear" can mean many different skills and skill sets, including (but not limited to) performing from memory, mixture of muscle memory and audiation, improvisation, learning by rote, "faking" an arrangement, embellishing a melody, sitting in with a band, *etc.* For the purpose of this session, however, Sowash described playing by ear as "working out tunes without written music." He discussed how this skill is in fact a "bundle of related skills" and ultimately *learned* (not merely inborn) skills. These "bundled" skills include the following:
- Predictive listening
- Filling in unknowns between knowns
- Hearing lines and shapes around "target" notes
- Testing educated guesses
- Leaps of faith

While there may be a wide range of inborn abilities, all individuals can develop the necessary skill set. According to Sowash, these skills are not typically taught to classically trained pianists, and so development of these skills is often most challenging for musicians who have been taught to read *only*. The presenter discussed his own experience with playing by ear, his strengths and weaknesses, and his ultimate belief that "regardless of aptitude, playing by ear improves with experience."

Under the *Melody* heading, Sowash examined possible beginning strategies for playing by ear. He suggested attendees begin with the melody if the chords are already known or if the melody is tuneful and memorable. Alternatively, they might begin with the chords if the melody is already known, or if the melody is "nondescript" or secondary to the chords. Furthermore, attendees may work out both together if they are related or intertwined; for example, if the melody features broken chords that suggest the harmony. For the purpose of this interactive session, Sowash noted that the group would begin with melodic exercises and then move to chordal and simultaneous decoding, time permitting.

When building one's skill of playing by ear, begin by choosing repetitive diatonic tunes appropriate to the learner's level and experience. The following strategies provided by the presenter may also assist:
- Listen first—allow the melody and structure to sink in.
- Identify the meter, key, and tonality to narrow note choices.
- Hum, then play the *last* note to confirm the key (often tonic).
- Hum or play the scale in the key of the tune at hand to hear the character of each scale degree.
- Identify the first note (often a note in the triad).

Sowash also equated melodic decoding with components of the human body, using the metaphor of *bones, tendons, flesh* to represent *target notes, connecting notes*, and *filling in the blanks*, respectively. This process of decoding also allows musicians to play *something* from the very beginning as they listen.

Following this discussion of melody, Sowash invited attendees to participate in the trial-and-error, interactive part of the session. He featured three public-domain tunes in turn, asking attendees to capture as much as possible during the repetitions by playing along. He also engaged the attendees by giving them different goals for each repetition and asking them to rate themselves on their ability to play each particular song by ear.

The presentation concluded with specific tips for decoding melodies, including the following:
- Think in scale degrees/letter names, not intervals.
- Remember the "pull" of notes within the tonality.
- Learn songs for hearing scale degrees.
- Think of the logic of the line (*e.g.*, pickup notes, repeated strains, sequences, cadences, direction changes, *etc.*).
- Visualize or "air play" the notes on your instrument as you listen.
- Play your best guess—avoid hunting and just go for it! Fix it next time!
- Don't fix as you go!
- Hum mystery notes as the tune progresses. Compare on the next repeat.
- Read written music only if you must!
- Notice any non-diatonic chords suggesting secondary dominants, modes, or quirks.

- Recognize "cells" and any stylistic "clichés" (*e.g.*, cadences, melodic fragments that we hear often).
- Notice melodic embellishments that are decorations of "main note" chord tones.

New to the Job! (Collegiate Faculty)
Presented by Todd Van Kekerix, Andrea Johnson, Ivan Hurd, and Margarita Denenburg
Saturday, July 31, 2021
Recorded by Jessie Welsh

The session opened with introductions by the four presenters. They shared brief biographical information, communicated pertinent information about their faculty positions, and explained their professional relationships and connections to one another. The goals for the session included sharing recent experience of applying to and interviewing for jobs, providing the audience with practical ways to prepare for jobs within academia while still in graduate school, and helping the audience to know what to expect within the first several years of an academic position.

The presenters discussed how they discovered shared themes within their individual experiences. They explored each of these in light of their former perspectives as students and their current perspectives as young faculty members:
1. *Resources*
2. *Versatility*
3. *Academia*
4. *Materials/Other*

Within the *Resources* category, the panelists discussed the importance of students utilizing what their universities have to offer. This included building relationships with faculty mentors, collaborating with colleagues within the same program, seeking assistance from university career centers and writing centers, utilizing library and health center facilities, and seeking opportunities to represent the university at outside conferences. For example, a student could take advantage of the university career center to work on a *curriculum vitae*, participate in mock interviews, and take advantage of free headshots.

The faculty perspective on *Resources* included becoming familiar with a university's Division of Research, understanding research requirements for a tenure-track position, applying for grants and awards (both inside and outside the university), and seeking university and departmental support through colleagues, funding, and continued development of writing skills.

The *Versatility* category for students centered on the importance of continued development of an increasingly diverse experience in both performing and teaching. All the presenters spoke of the necessity of strong performance and pedagogical skills in securing a faculty position. They stressed the importance of performing music by living and underrepresented composers, participating in collaborative performance, viewing course projects and papers as stepping stones for future publications and presentations, and carefully crafting lesson plans. Additionally, they emphasized the importance of continued academic skill development (particularly writing skills), participation in a collegiate chapter of the Music Teachers National Association, and seizing a variety of teaching opportunities for one's graduate assistantship or fellowship.

The faculty perspective on *Versatility* included insights about interdisciplinary collaborations, finding one's own niche in the field, and building a diverse professional resume to fulfill tenure requirements. For example, one presenter mentioned the possibility of mixed-media recitals by collaborating with dance or art departments. Other possible interdisciplinary collaborations discussed included working with medical or psychology students and faculty. The group of presenters recommended that faculty members pursue two to three niche areas of interest and pursue a variety of publications, presentations, and collaborations to support their research.

The student perspective on *Academia* emphasized the importance of learning about the job application process as a student, building a professional resume while in graduate school, looking at job postings often, and applying to as many jobs as possible. The presenters emphasized the importance of knowing one's audience in the application process. This included understanding the type of school (*e.g.*, state university vs. liberal arts college), the university culture, and national trends in job postings. They emphasized the importance of reflecting this knowledge in a cover letter, music philosophy, and any teaching and/or performance videos. Furthermore, current graduate students should take advantage of performance and teaching spaces at their universities, recording performances, classes, and lessons often. Lastly, graduate students should begin asking themselves, "What am I passionate about? How do I want to contribute to the larger field?" The answers to these questions can guide research projects, course selection, and recital design—all elements which the presenters assert will contribute to a strong job application.

The faculty perspective on *Academia* explored requirements for promotion and tenure, university service, and professional activities files. The presenters underscored the importance of knowing the requirements specific to a university and getting to know both the music faculty and the university faculty at large.

The final category, *Materials/Other*, explored additional elements which did not fall within the previously discussed categories. It also served as a final wrap-up and way to emphasize the most important takeaways, especially for current graduate students. From a student perspective, the presenters shared the importance of regularly recording teaching and performing (in both high- and low-stakes environments), frequently conducting teacher self-assessments, writing (and re-writing) one's philosophy, updating one's *curriculum vitae*, and maintaining a current professional web presence with promotional materials.

From a faculty perspective, the presenters offered their own biggest takeaways as young professionals. The *Materials/Other* included prioritizing organization, time management, strategies for email organization, working in short bursts of energy, utilizing breaks, delegating, mentoring, and finding work-life balance.

The presenters concluded the session with a final reminder that the work—whether completed by a student or faculty member—is all about relationships.

Choral Music Educators and "Real World" Piano Applications:
A Collective Case Study—Professional Musicians
Give Their Perspectives on Piano Training
Presented by Leonidas Lagrimas
Saturday, July 31, 2021
Recorded by Amy Glennon

Dr. Lagrimas began with a concept first presented by Pamela Pike: The college class piano lab is a "place with the potential for musical synthesis (Pike, 2018) of skills/concepts across multiple disciplines." For choral musical education majors, musical synthesis of applied piano skills within a choral conducting context is essential. This raises the question: Does the class piano format/curriculum prepare choral music educators for "the real world?"

Purpose

The purpose of this session was to highlight selected preliminary results of an ongoing collective case study of a select group of choral educators. This study involved two categories of questions: 1) Perception of the effectiveness of their class piano curriculum in preparing them for choral music careers and 2) Utilization of applied piano skills in their current jobs (how do they use the piano?).

Procedure/Methodology
- Potential case study subjects from a university alumni list were asked to complete a qualitative survey questionnaire (open-ended questions).
- Responses were analyzed and classified according to Saldana's (2013) model of holistic coding for qualitative research methodology.
- All case study subjects are in the first two to three years of a full-time choral position and received a bachelor's degree in choral education.

*Codes and Coding (*Saldana, 2013)
- A code is a researcher-generated construct.
- Holistic Coding: An exploratory method of coding that attempts to capture an overall sense of the data and suggests possible themes for investigation.

Survey Questions
- Describe your current teaching position and course load.
- What specific applied piano skills do you use in your teaching?
- Describe the piano preparation you received as a choral music education major. Were you prepared adequately for your current job? Are there any areas of piano you wish you had received more training in?

- Do you experience performance anxiety/stage fright whenever you must utilize piano skills in your teaching? If so, what are some ways you deal with it?

Holistic Coding: Analyzing Larger Units of Data
- "Real world" piano
- Utilizing piano daily
- Variety of courses
- "I wish that…"/Regrets about class piano
- Time/Not enough time
- Stage fright/Nervous
- Repertoire selection: The repertoire they teach in the choir in relation to piano skills.

Emergent Themes for Further Study
- Class piano vs. "real world" piano (for example, exploring stage fright/performance anxiety)
- Wide range of teaching load/duties, besides choir (AP Theory, General Music, extracurricular activities)
- Wide range of applied skills utilized (accompanying, improvisation, vocal warm-ups, open score reading)
- Needing MORE from class piano (higher standards, more structure)
- Effects of piano ability on choral repertoire selection

Potential Research Questions
- How do choral music educators utilize piano in their teaching?
- What effect does a choral conductor's piano ability have on repertoire selection?
- How do in-service choral music educators perceive the effectiveness of the piano training they received as undergraduate music majors?
- What effect does class piano study have on choral music educators' performance anxiety/stage fright?

Discussion/Implications for Further Research
- Does our class piano curriculum accurately reflect piano in the "real world?"
- Does success in class piano equal success in the "real world?" (In other words, does the mark of an "A" in Class Piano equal success in the "real world?")
- Need for research investigating utilization of piano skills *after* graduation.
- Musical Synthesis: Are we teaching individual skills or finding ways to synthesize concepts?
- Training/experience of class piano educators: What should they know?
- Course model: Class piano for in-service educators/graduate students?

Question and Answer Session

- "How many participants do you hope to have?" There is not a set number at this stage. This could end up being a case study on one person, or a study of a large group of participants. "This is the beauty of an open-case study."
- "Why did you choose two to three years post-graduation?" This was a way to "narrow down" results. The first- and second-year teacher is not necessarily a good indicator of anything we would label in a larger context.

What Did They Say?
Professional Musicians Give Their Perspectives on Piano Training
Presented by Margaret Young
Saturday, July 31, 2021
Recorded by Amy Glennon

Dr. Young has been interested in the topic of best practices for undergraduate non-piano group classes ever since her Class Piano students asked: "Why do I need to take this class?" An outline of this session:
- *Background*
- *Methodology*
- *Results*
- *Implications*

Background

The National Association of Schools of Music (NASM) requires students to take Class Piano in large part because professional musicians report their use of piano in their professions.

What we know:
- Students need *keyboard competency*. Functional skills include sight reading, improvisation, harmonization, open-score reading, and transposing.
- Professional musicians value the ability to play the piano.
- Group piano curricula need to reflect the needs of the twenty-first-century musicians.

In short, we need to find out what professional musicians want from their piano training, and this is what Dr. Young set out to find.

Methodology

Dr. Young conducted semi-structured interviews with twenty-six musicians with a variety of backgrounds who engage in a variety of music traditions.

- Musical Background
  The highest number of participants had performance degrees. This was followed by Music Education. Other participants included those in the fields of Music Theory, Music Technology, Business, and "No Degree Earned." Dr. Young interviewed vocalists, pianists, violinists, guitarists, a bass player, a trumpeter, a flutist, and a percussionist. In terms of educational background, sixty percent had master's degrees, and fifty percent had doctoral degrees. Fifty-eight percent of participants did not study a secondary instrument at the undergraduate level. For those who had studied a secondary instrument, the piano was the most studied instrument, followed by the organ.

- Piano Training
Eighty-one percent had piano study before starting college, and nineteen percent were self-taught prior to college. All participants had some piano training in college. This training included learning repertoire, building healthy technique, and to a lesser-extent, functional skill training.

- Current Position
Most participants held positions in higher education or engaged in a "portfolio career" (they did a "little of everything to make ends meet").

- Piano Use
College piano use: Twenty percent did not use piano at all during college, and those who did used it to learn their repertoire, accompany others, earn money, or for "other reasons" (creativity, composition, enjoyment, *etc.*). Those who earned money accompanying were exclusively piano majors.

Results
- Skill perception: Seventy-two percent felt positively about their skills upon completing undergraduate degrees.

- Current Use, Work: Teaching was the most common use of piano skills. Other skills included accompanying, learning repertoire, and performing. Five participants reported never using their piano skills in their current work.

- Current Use, Pleasure: Twenty-five percent said "no," twenty-five percent said piano was used for creative pursuits like improvising and composing, and fifty percent played repertoire for pleasure in a variety of styles.

- "What do you wish you had more training on during your piano studies?" Participants wanted more of training in technique, score study, hymns, improvisation, and pedagogy (pianists-only).

- "If you could design a piano curriculum for the next 'you,' what would you include?"
    1. Playing from chord charts
    2. Building technique
    3. Accompanying
    4. Improvisation
    5. Learning a variety of styles (not just Western Art Music)
    6. Reading open scores and transposing them

Thematic Analysis and Emerging Themes
Using Braun and Clark's thematic analysis, and using NVivo Qualitative Data Analysis Software, Dr. Young analyzed the results and some themes emerged:

- Confidence and Use: A lack of efficacy also meant lack of use.
- Creativity and Communication: Many participants indicated that the piano is used for communication with other musicians and creating something new, a "therapeutic presence." Implication: Allowing students to work together on group projects will enable them to gain confidence in sharing what they know about the piano with others.
- Building Skills: Students wanted to know how they were progressing, and how what they were doing related to the music making experiences they were familiar with. A vocalist said: "I wanted a class that had you work on a piano tune, then read it as a lead sheet, then transpose it, then perform it with another person. I never felt like my assignments in piano class meant anything. I just played it for the teacher and that wasn't motivating. I needed an audience. I needed it to feel like I was playing music."

Implications
- Make it musical.
- Connect and create.
- Practice success: Provide opportunities for independent learning.
- Use our colleagues: Ask your colleagues how they use the piano in their own work and share this with the students. Ask your students to interview other faculty.

My Piano Arrangement is Better Than Yours (and Here are the Secrets!)
Presented by Jeremy Siskind
Saturday, July 31, 2021
Recorded by Autumn L. Zander

Crafting a piano arrangement that goes beyond just playing the melody in the right hand and blocked chords in the left hand can feel daunting. A great arrangement that goes beyond these basic melodic and accompaniment roles, regardless of genre, is a satisfying experience for both the performer and audience member. Utilizing the lead sheet for the jazz standard, *God Bless the Child*, the process of crafting a memorable arrangement was demystified by focusing on three broad categories; melody, harmony, and pianism. Attendees, regardless of whether they were a novice or experienced arranger, were presented with a sequential series of ideas to consider and explore when crafting their own arrangements or guiding their students through the process.

Rather than playing the melody in a straightforward manner, Siskind suggested attendees "think like a singer." He demonstrated this by speaking the lyrics in a conversational manner while a metronome maintained a large steady pulse. This process allowed for the natural rhythm of the lyrics to flow within the parameters of a large pulse. The conversational rhythm was then transferred to his playing of the melody. This casual, yet purposeful, approach to melodic pacing invites further rhythmic exploration, such as changing duple rhythms into triple rhythms and back phrasing. Added melodic embellishments, such as grace notes, ornaments, and non-chord tones, were demonstrated with the kindly reminder that in order to achieve a "pitch bend," grace notes are not to be played cleanly, but overlapped in order to create a slightly blurred effect. For the classical pianist, the demonstration of "ghost notes," notes that are not part of the melody but act as a timekeeper in contrast to the relaxed melody, served as an important learning moment in the creation of an arrangement in a jazz idiom. The ghost notes created a melody full of depth of character and style all within a sparse texture. Inclusion of added intervals, such as 3rds and 6ths to the melody, were demonstrated as well.

Equally important in crafting an interesting piano arrangement is listening to multiple recordings of a tune performed by varying artists and instruments. Listening to the various ways singers approach phrasing, tone color, and rhythm offers a plethora of ideas to explore in one's playing. Likewise, instrumentalists present new perspectives to phrasing, articulation, and dynamics.

When approaching elements of harmony, Siskind discussed the use of emotion words within the lyrics to help influence chord choices that highlight a desired effect for specific passages and the overall delivery of the piece. In the effort to expand one's harmonic world, Siskind demonstrated the various personalities a tune could take on via stylistic changes such as using triads in the style of a four-part hymn, 7th chords that channel a jazz style, the exploration of modes, and the use of clusters and atonality to explore a twenty-first-century vibe. Throughout these various accompaniment styles, easy reharmonization via chord inversions reinforced the rule that a good bass-line melody helps to create a more satisfying arrangement. Aspects of harmonic rhythm, the use of non-chord tones, and altered dominants to create moments of tension were also demonstrated.

As with many pieces, the roles of melody and harmony are not always separated between the hands. The final area of the session addressed the broad aspect of pianism and how to approach melody and harmony in a stylistic manner. Sharing the chords between the hands, shuffling (alternating back and forth between roles akin to ragtime bass lines) and draping (allowing a single hand to play both the melody and harmony) added to the final layer of piano arrangement craftsmanship.

The Aural Underground:
Laying the Ear-Brain-Body Foundation for a Lifetime of Piano Success
Presented by Amy Rucker
Saturday, July 31, 2021
Recorded by Linda M. Fields

Rucker started with a question for attendees: "If I had more time in the piano lesson, I'd include…" Answers included: rote teaching, sight reading, singing, movement, listening to orchestral works, etc. These things are all important, but often students need help with more basic things like note or rhythm accuracy. Using examples of teaching pieces in triple meter often distorted to duple meter, Rucker admitted that short-term solutions such as using words that reflect the proper rhythm can help, but what the student really needs is movement. However, many are not comfortable using their voice, much less leaving the bench. In addition, finding time for these kinds of activities is an ongoing challenge.

So, Rucker had participants take a step back to consider the student's "aural pathway," and what may be missing there. Displaying a matrix, Rucker showed two progressions that start from birth. In the Child Development list, Listening is the beginning. Motor Response follows, leading to Language, then Social and Emotional milestones, culminating in Cognitive skills. Next, she traced Musical Development, again starting with Listening—"the cornerstone of all learning." Movement in response to music comes next, followed by Vocalizing (language), then Ensemble (social music making) and Creativity (expressing feelings). Reading and Writing music are a natural final step.

Yet, she pointed out, we typically start lessons with Reading and Writing—having missed many, if not all, of the earlier steps. Using the example of struggling to open a tightly shrink-wrapped bottle, ignoring the perforations, Rucker made the point that we don't have to open the child's musical mind the hard way. Instead, we can seize upon "open windows" (sometimes called "critical periods") along the developing aural pathway.

Neural science shows that the window for developing an internalized and controlled steady beat is three to six years of age, when the frontal lobes are developing toward their future role as executor of the brain. Experience with steady beat enables neural connections, priming the frontal lobes' awakening, possibly avoiding symptoms of weak executor function (similar to ADHD) that may surface later.

Referencing Dr. Dee Joy Coulter, a neuro-science educator, Rucker shared that, in infancy, a steady beat is basically a subconscious reflex. Around age three to four, as the child is realizing they can control their own beat, they may play around, often with syncopation and other "messy" rhythmic expressions. Around the fourth year, many will regain control, evident in the ability to stop and start, to move at different speeds, to fit their steady beat with an external rhythm, etc. This can be an ideal time to introduce short rhythmic echoes, with the goal of helping them move from beat awareness to owning an independent steady beat. At any age, a steady beat is best heard and absorbed into the body, using the aural pathway from ear to brain to body to instrument. Rather than making pianists into musicians, she stressed, we want to help musicians become pianists.

Rucker agrees with many that age six to eight is a good time to start lessons, but *music* learning can occur earlier. The challenge for us today is to find ways to bridge the cultural gap in social musical experience that would normally build the aural pathway. Rucker listed some options for helping to fill that gap right now. She suggested experiences beyond the method such as:
- Sing, especially the resting tone.
- Chant rhythm patterns.
- Start early with movement and even drumming.
- Look at the music, focusing on what should be heard. Express an element with the body before playing it on the piano.

Sample activities followed. Attendees were invited to use a scarf to move with Beethoven's "Ode to Joy," keeping a half-note beat until the phrase ending, when the gesture became a loop.

Rucker then modeled, and had participants try, a variety of physical movements to help a student feel triple beat in the body, using a dance called "Cathrineta" from Musikgarten's *Music Makers Around the World*. She recommended clapping, drumming, or dancing, using both macro and micro beats, noting that it's important to keep moving through the large, slow beats, so students feel the space in their body. Additionally, when students change their movement with sections, it leads to awareness of form.

The presenter wrapped things up with some suggestions for additional steps to take as educators, to foster an "underground" aural pathway in our students. These included:
- Add an early childhood department to your studio.
- Take early childhood music training.
- Grow your own musicians and educate parents at the same time.
- Teach in groups.

Finally, Rucker made the point that it all starts with the ear. If we don't help them focus their listening, how many will be able to develop it on their own? From steady beat on, she admonished, give your students the gift of deeply ingrained musical awareness and they will thank you!

A question and answer period concluded the session:
- *Is it possible to compensate for lack of these experiences from 3-6 years?*
  Yes! The learning will take longer, but it's worth it.
- *What size is best for a group?*
  6-8 is ideal; 4-10 at the outside.
- *Please talk about the ear-body activities that encourage parent involvement.*
  A curriculum-provided CD with suggested home activities for parents is ideal.
  Include parents for the last 10-15 minutes of class.
- *How to encourage families to buy CD players?*
  Many publishers are moving to links to be downloaded to various devices.
  Rucker still likes a child-dedicated listening area with a CD player, scarves, sticks, etc.
- *Do you use any childhood education methods, such as Orff?*
  Rucker has found success with a curriculum that pulls the best from Orff, Dalcroze, Kodaly, Montessori, Tomatis, etc., in development-appropriate pacing.

RECOMMENDED REFERENCES:
Dr. Dee Coulter - *Mind and Music: Insights from Brain Science* (4 CDs, c/o Worldcat libraries)
Dr. Edwin Gordon - *Music Learning Theory for Newborns and Infants*
Eric Bluestein – *The Way Children Learn Music, an Introduction and Practical Guide to Music Learning Theory* (an easier-to-read, partner book to Gordon's)
Paul Maudale – *When Listening Comes Alive* (about children and their possible aural needs)

Technique Through the Repertoire
Presented by Jani Parsons and Christopher Madden
Saturday, July 31, 2021
Recorded by Megan Blood

While many instrument families use excerpt books in their core curriculum, Dr. Parsons and Dr. Madden noticed a lack of excerpt books for piano. A few such books do exist, such as Maurice Aronson's *The Pianist's Digest* (1942), which uses excerpts from advanced literature within the public domain, but these do not include intermediate repertoire. Drs. Parsons and Madden sought to fill this void by collecting a list of excerpts for piano categorized by skill and level.

Studying excerpts can provide many benefits for intermediate students given the variety of styles and connection to standard repertoire. When choosing excerpts, Drs. Parsons and Madden selected repertoire which cultivates the technical skills necessary to play advanced repertoire such as articulation, scales, bass patterns, finger independence, ornamentation, etc.
The excerpt used to demonstrate varied articulation was Bartók's *Song "Come Home, Lidi."* Dr. Madden demonstrated several different ways to teach and practice this excerpt in order to achieve the desired lengths of slurs. Other pieces that may be used to teach articulation to late-intermediate and early-advanced students include Zipoli's *Fughetta in E Minor* and Weber's *Scherzo*.

Türk's *The Scale Ladder* was used as an example of a scale-focused excerpt. Dr. Parsons recommended purposeful pauses and repetition to help students master these scales, as well as flexibility and support in the hand. Advanced pieces in this category include Streabbog's *The Cadets,* Op. 64, No. 11 and Bach's "Gavotte" from *French Suite No. 5 in G Major*.
Excerpts such as Schumann's *Little Etude,* Op. 68 and Beethoven's *Minuet in D Major* cultivate skills involving broken chords and chord inversions, while Le Couppey's *Sonatina in G Major* and Gedike's *Sonatina in C Major* are ideal for teaching the Alberti bass pattern. Waltz bass excerpts include Amy Beach's *Waltz,* Op. 36, No. 3 and Schubert's *Waltz in B Minor,* Op. 18, No. 6. Bartók's "Ballad" from *For Children* and Albéniz's *Capricho Catalan* are excellent excerpts for teaching left-hand melodies.

For the skill of alternating hands, in which the performer is required to pass a melody or accompaniment pattern from one hand to the other, Dr. Madden recommended using Heller's *Avalanche,* Op. 45, No. 2, and Dr. Parsons performed Heller's *Fluttering Leaves,* Op. 46, No. 11, providing an advanced excerpt option. Excerpts that are ideal for double notes, or thirds, include Rebikov's *The Bear* and Kuhlau's *Sonatina in C Major,* Op. 55, No. 3. The early-intermediate selection provided for teaching ornaments was Beethoven's *German Dance in B-flat Major,* WoO 13, No.6, and the advanced option was Czerny's *Etude* Op. 823, No. 62. The final skill presented was *legato* pedaling, and the excerpts included were Heller's *Tolling Bell* Op. 125, No. 8 and Maykapar's *Pedal Prelude No. 5*.

The presenters included a handout in their presentation, which included even more excerpts, categorized by skill and level, and encouraged the audience to find and use more excerpts in piano lessons. During the question and answer session, they discussed playing excerpts in studio classes and how useful excerpts can be as sight reading, "quick-learn" pieces, or in the development of transfer students' skills.

Action Research in the Piano Lab:
An Auto-Ethnographic Exploration of Developing Ear Playing in Beginner Pianists
Presented by Gemma O'Herlihy
Saturday, July 31, 2021
Recorded by Amy Glennon

This session explored the problem, method, analysis, and findings of Dr. O'Herlihy's research.

The problem: "Many beginner pianists are not taught to play by ear, impeding balanced musicianship." Research question: "How has the recursive action research process, balancing an aural-reading equilibrium, changed me to be a different teacher?" Answer: "Dialogic relationships with the pupils and parents lead to a different model of practice. Pupils teach me to teach better."

In 1999, the Cork School of Music Piano Lab was set up to improve sight reading and worked alongside private lessons. This piano lab provided an opportunity to explore an aural approach. Phase 1: Group interviews with piano teachers. Phase 2: Action Research using *Jump Right In: The Instrumental Series.* Dr. O'Herlihy taught four groups of beginning pianists (age 6–10) with a focus on ear-playing and music reading. On an ongoing basis, she engaged in group interviews with pupils and parents, observed videos of her teaching, and maintained a teacher reflective diary. Both parents and children were made aware of the research project through informational leaflets. Open communication with parents and students was maintained throughout the three-year research study.

Through dialogue with parents and students, Dr. O'Herlihy learned that students were reluctant to read the score after a long time spent with aural skills. As a result, she shortened the interval between the aural introduction and the introduction to the score. Students read the song immediately after being able to play hands together by ear, usually in two to three weeks' time, which worked well. Engaging parents can have a profound impact on the self-identity of the instructor; the instructor is vulnerable and open to feedback, and this dialogue creates an entirely different model of instruction. In addition, the students in the group became active participants, vs. passive listeners. "They teach me to teach better."

Improvisation in Collegiate Private and Group Piano Settings
Presented by Grace Choi
Saturday, July 31, 2021
Recorded by Amy Glennon

Dr. Choi's interest in improvisation began when she started teaching as a graduate student. As she learned more about the benefits of improvisation and creativity, she became more and more convinced that there is a great value in incorporating creativity in piano pedagogy. Notably, Dr. Choi experienced great fulfillment and success in applying her own study of eighteenth-century performance practice to collegiate class piano.

"Mozart's performances were designed to display his talents as improviser, pianist, and composer (that is the order his contemporaries assigned to his gifts)." (Robert Levin, *Improvising Mozart,* p. 144). This quote was meaningful to Dr. Choi, as a performer and teacher. For most keyboardists of the sixteenth to eighteenth century, improvisation was an integral part of musicianship. Particularly for organists, improvisation was a regular part of auditions, and was as much a part of daily practice as repertoire study. In the eighteenth century, virtually all composers were performers, and all performers were composers. In contrast, today's "Urtext mentality" or "museum mentality" has shifted our thinking to the extent that the only important thing is what the composer put in the score. This is contrary to what eighteenth-century performers were doing. These performers considered the score as a starting point, open for interpretation. "In Mozart's letters we find a pervasive stress on musicianship, expression, and taste—*"gusto"*as he calls it—as final arbiter in matters of execution (Frederick Neumann, *Ornamentation and Improvisation in Mozart,* p. 5). This included not only ornamentation, but dynamic shadings and *rubato*. Mozart left many passages in sketched form, relying on the performer to fill in the empty spaces. When preparing for publication or student performances, Mozart included dynamics and wrote out embellishments.

Today's students can develop musicianship through improvisation. Dr. Choi incorporated "Seven Skills in Pedagogy" (*Developing Musicianship through Improvisation,* Azzara & Grunow*)* into her work with class piano students and private students.

Seven Skills in Pedagogy
Skill 1 – improvise rhythm patterns to the bass line
Skill 2 – sing harmonic functions
Skill 3 – learn harmonic rhythm
Skill 4 – improvise rhythm patterns to the harmonic progression
Skill 5 – improvise tonal patterns to the harmonic progression
Skill 6 – improvise tonal and rhythm patterns
Skill 7 – improvise

The *Sonata in B-Flat Major,* K. 570 was used with class piano students to explore the seven skills listed above. (The question-and-answer session revealed that this activity would certainly not be used with beginning class piano students). It is important to note that each skill begins aurally, without the notation. Students begin by singing the bass line on a neutral syllable. The bass line was written out by Choi for her reference and included the root of each harmonic shift. After singing on a neutral syllable, students then added *solfège*. Students then add harmonic functions by switching parts of the harmonies. Next, rhythmic improvisation, then tonal, then a combination of rhythm and tonal, Choi performed what might be considered a "finished product."

After three years of exploring an aural approach to improvisation in collegiate class piano, Choi wrote her dissertation, with the intent of improving pedagogy in collegiate class piano.

Research Questions
- What is the improvisation achievement of beginning collegiate class piano students?
- What is the relationship between beginning piano students' music aptitude and music achievement?
- What are students' perceptions of improvisation in class piano pedagogy?

This research was descriptive in nature and involved students their first year.

Rating Scale (Azzara and Grunow, and Choi)
- Tonal Rating Scale
- Rhythm Rating Scale
- Expressive Rating Scale
- Improvisation Rating Scale

Quantitative Data
Collected after fourteen weeks of instruction. Each student sang the melody of "Happy Birthday," improvised the melody of "Happy Birthday" vocally, played the melody of "Happy Birthday" in the right hand, with appropriate left-hand accompaniment, improvised the melody of "Happy Birthday" in the right hand with appropriate left-hand accompaniment, and then repeated these steps with a melody composed by Dr. Choi, experienced for the first time on the day of the assessment. These assessments were conducted by three independent judges, using the rating scales shown above. Dr. Choi projected the statistics for the pilot study, including the dissertation data. Qualitative data was collected by pre-study surveys, mid-study group interviews, and post-study individual interviews. Students expressed that they loved improvising and overall, the improvisation created a meaningful experience.

Learning from Limitations: The Indianist Piano Pieces of Amy Beach and Arthur Farwell
Presented by Natalie Khatibzadeh
Saturday, July 31, 2021
Recorded by Charl Louw

In the 1880s, American men were worried about the effects of Industrialism and supported efforts to connect spiritually with the natural surroundings. With artists creating works like "The Song of Hiawatha" by Henry Wadsworth Longfellow, the American Indians were romanticized.

Jill Carolyn Meehan explains that The Second New England School felt they rarely attempted to arrange Native American songs because they needed direct contact and knowledge of that culture, so they stayed with their own musical ethnicities. Boston composers depicted nature scenes upon prior European traditions. This group included Amy Beach (1867-1944) who said, "We are all Europeans by descent, and therefore these Indian airs can never really become a part of us." Beach was interested in universal connections and emotions in transcriptions of Native American songs.

Eskimos, Op. 64 (1907), a work for teaching children containing four movements, is based on Franz Boaz's *The Central Eskimo* (1888) where all harmonies, modulations, interludes are from the original composer. It was followed by the longer seven-page children's piece *From Blackbird Hills* (1922).

Arthur Farwell (1872-1952) advocated for American composers and for piano melodies derived from native North America. As a child, he and his family visited two Minnesota Sioux villages where he listened to Sioux singers and was intrigued by the variety of emotion he heard. He established The Wa-Wan Press in 1901 to feature American compositions expanding on prior traditions, incorporating native North American music. The term Wa-Wan means to sing for someone in a ceremonial way, like passing a Pipe of Fellowship. The ceremony promotes peace among the tribes, and the blessing of children.

American Indian Melodies, Op.11 (1901), is a set of ten movements, each with a different song transcription. Farwell described it as each melody having "a problem, to be worked out by itself…to study the spirit and temper of American Indians."

The presenter provided three reasons why non-native people cannot compose indigenous music.
1) Indigenous people's music is produced from their own experience.
2) Indigenous composers write music to empower their own tribes
3) More indigenous role models are needed to support young indigenous people who are trying to find their own identity.

Brent Michael Davids explains how approaches in Western music have assisted in the elimination of Native American musical curricula and public performances. "Erasing peoples also erases their music, so the resultant naivete about Native Americans may sit somewhere along the ignorance-is-bliss scale as a byproduct of ethnic cleansing."

David Treuer (b. 1970) is an Ojibwe author and professor of English at USC. He is the recipient of the Pushcat Prize, two Minnesota Book Awards, fellowships from the NEH, Guggenheim Foundation, and Bush Foundation. His work exposes realities of Native American life that are not covered in history courses and media. He sees the Native languages he had as a child as being better at describing the ideas that attend Native peoples than English.

The presenter recommended Treuer's book: *The Heartbeat of Wounded Knee: Native America from 1890 to the Present*. Police were assigned to reservations but had no laws or policies that they had to follow. Soon they had the authority to punish Native Americans for performing traditional dances because they were a hindrance to civilization.

Jerod Tate (b. 1968) a composer-pianist, and citizen of the Chickasaw Nation, taught composition to high school students through the Joyce Foundation and American Composers Forum. He blends Chickasaw traditions with classical music and features the music and language of other tribes. He was recently named Cultural Ambassador for the U.S. Department of State for 2021-22.

Dr. Lisa Cheryl Thomas' research, lecture recitals, and recordings are focused on American Classical Native Piano Repertoire and Indianist Piano Repertoire. A citizen of Sovereign Cherokee Nation Tejax, Dr. Thomas was featured on Dallas classical radio station WRR 101.1 FM through the series, "North Texas Women Who Have Made a Difference in the Arts." Comparing print transcriptions to wax cylinder recordings of original indigenous music, she said, "The wax cylinder recordings are the most accurate renditions of the original tribal melodies, but these were not as available to the public as the printed transcriptions."

"Go Big ~~Or~~ AND Go Home!": Adult Group Teaching Pedagogical Takeaways
Presented by Yeeseon Kwon
Saturday, July 31, 2021
Recorded by Louie Hehman

Dr. Kwon began her presentation by talking about the idiomatic phrase, "go big or go home," which evidently began as a sales slogan for Harley-Davidson, although some insist that it is derived from skiing or surfing. Dr. Kwon suggested that this mentality perfectly captures the current moment, with the caveat that the conjunction "or" be replaced with an "and." The presenter discussed her experiences teaching group piano for adults, and then shared a poll with the attendees: "How would you evaluate your overall teaching experience this past year teaching remotely?" The attendees voted, and then Dr. Kwon shared the results: 80% said that they were "satisfied." She noted that this actually does not surprise her. Studies showed that online teachers were generally satisfied, and the satisfaction is more likely if there is appropriate training, and if online teaching allows for flexibility in their schedules.

For Dr. Kwon, this showed that the embracing ("going big") of online teaching helped teachers feel more satisfied. This was true for her in her own teaching. According to her, there are opportunities available for adult teaching that may be opened up by online teaching. She then shared a video of her group class playing "St. Louis Blues." Following this, she stated that choices of repertoire are important for adult learners, as are their options for how they receive their instruction. Dr. Kwon also insisted that: "Ultimately, adults learn best by doing and by watching." She then went to a slide that showed the technological items she utilized in her lessons, including *Classroom Maestro* and internet MIDI. This was followed by an excerpt from one of the presenter's collegiate class piano courses.

These technological tools were clearly helpful, but Dr. Kwon also showed a video of a couple playing simply on an acoustic piano, showcasing that even simple setups can be very effective. This video also showed how important assessment of students is in an online setting. Watching a video can be a very passive experience, so a good assessment tool that Dr. Kwon utilized was a program called *GoReact*. A recording of *GoReact* in action was then played, followed by a video of a student upload. This student recorded himself playing an accompaniment, and then playing the melody on his primary instrument (saxophone). The presenter stated that this exemplifies how teachers can reimagine their ensemble activities. She then concluded her presentation by sharing another poll. This time, she asked if teachers were planning to utilize online platforms of any kind in the coming year. The response was similar: roughly 83% answered in the affirmative. Dr. Kwon thanked everyone for participating and challenged all attendees to "go big" in their group teaching.

Dr. Kwon was asked to share about her experiences teaching adults in both private and group settings. She answered this by saying that many adult students make the choice for themselves whether to stay in group settings, or move to private lessons. Another question was about software, specifically *Classroom Maestro*. She gave a quick demonstration of the program. She was then asked if she had any new materials that she was planning to add. Dr. Kwon responded that background accompaniments may be something that she adds to help raise the level of motivation.

Dr. Kwon summarized her thoughts by stating that the idea is "engagement, in all the different ways that we can." She followed up by saying that she always asks herself, "How do I make this more economical?"

Bringing Your Online Teaching to the Next Level:
Using OBS Studio and Creative/Fun Activities
Presented by Joao Paolo Casarotti and Daiane Raatz
Saturday, July 31, 2021
Recorded by Louie Hehman

Having started teaching online in 2009, Dr. Casarotti noted that this was long before the pandemic began. He also began presenting about online teaching in 2014, at a time when he noted that many teachers believed he was "out of [his] mind." Several pictures were shown from this pre-pandemic era; Dr. Casarotti emphasized that, even at this time, he and other forward-thinking teachers utilized multiple camera angles in their online teaching.

Dr. Casarotti offered several advantages to online teaching: better visual communication, different forms of delivery, and comfort of students, among others. He mentioned that he believes that the world has changed permanently because of the pandemic, and that online teaching (of some type) is likely to stay. The visual elements were addressed: the ability to simultaneously show the score, the piano itself, and the relationship with the body and the piano is a distinct advantage. He suggested the possibility of *virtual cameras* as a strong option. To showcase all of this, he showed an example where he utilized his cell phone in coordination with multiple camera angles to toggle back and forth between views. Dr. Casarotti then discussed his Top 10 Scenes for OBS, addressing each of their usefulness in turn. Then, he mentioned several of the important apps that he uses: *ForScore*, *Classroom Maestro*, *Reflector*, and *Stream Deck*. Casarotti then concluded by showing a tutorial in which he uses all his technology to teach Rebikov's "The Bear." Dr. Casarotti then shared a playlist containing his technology and teaching tutorials.

After this, Daiane Raatz took over the presentation. Her focus was on "Creative Resources for Piano Teachers: Zoom Tools in Online Lessons." She stated that she herself had the experience of both learning and teaching online, but she was particularly concerned, when the pandemic began, that she could not keep her young students engaged. She mentioned that she had two "big surprises" that she encountered: first, that the kids were naturally engaged with their online classes, and second, she was amazed when she discovered that she could adapt all her in-person activities into a virtual format using Zoom. The specific tools which he utilized were: whiteboard with annotation ability, screen sharing with annotation ability, iPad screen sharing, remote control, and virtual background. She then discussed each one of these tools, offering a brief introduction to how they work, and then showing an example of one of her students utilizing these tools in the context of a lesson. She then finished up by sharing a fun, light-hearted video that showcased her video editing skills (and sense of humor).

During the question and answer period, the presenters were asked, "If you have students with limited means, how can they best set up their home studio with decent equipment?" Dr. Casarotti mentioned that there are ways to use just a normal phone through a TV; a cheap connecting cable will negate the need for an iPad or a laptop.

MAIN CONFERENCE PRESENTATIONS IN SPANISH

Danzas y ritmos ecuatorianos: estrategias para la enseñanza pianística.

Presentación de Angélica Sánchez
30 de julio de 2021
Resumen de Alejandro Cremaschi

Los maestros de piano nos vemos frecuentemente en la necesidad de encontrar repertorio con el cual los alumnos se identifiquen y que los motive. El objetivo de la presentación de Angélica Sánchez fue, justamente, ofrecernos música de Ecuador que motiva, inspira y enseña. La presentación se enfocó en tres danzas tradicionales de Ecuador: el Sanjuanito, el Pasacalle y el Pasillo. Mostró videos de músicos populares tocando estos ritmos. Luego de los videos de cada género, la maestra Sánchez mostró arreglos propios de estas danzas y ritmos, clasificados a nivel intermedio de dificultad, y de excelente calidad didáctica. Al final de la presentación, la conferencista introdujo algunas estrategias pedagógicas para enseñar esta música.

El Sanjuanito es una danza que se hace presente en festividades relacionadas al sol, por ejemplo, del solsticio de verano, que coincide con la fiesta de San Juan. Actualmente se baila también en otras festividades tradicionales en Ecuador. Contiene ritmos alegres y rápidos, y se escribe en modo menor y compás de 2/4. El Pasacalle es una danza que puede verse en las calles de Ecuador, y fue influida directamente por la Passacaille europea. Contiene el mismo tipo de ostinatos en el bajo que la danza europea relacionada. Como el Sanjuanito, también se escribe en 2/4 y en modo menor. Se lo danza durante las celebraciones de la Independencia en distintas ciudades. Finalmente, el Pasillo es una mezcla de música autóctona con el Vals europeo. Se lo encuentra en muchos países de América Latina, incluidos Perú, Colombia y en América Central. Está escrito en ¾ y contiene el lirismo y romanticismo típico de la música de Ecuador. La maestra Sánchez compartió un arreglo propio del Pasillo "Cuanto te quiero" de Salvador Bustamante Ceni.

Para cerrar, la conferencista presentó consejos pedagógicos para enseñar estas piezas y arreglos, así como algunos beneficios musicales de estas piezas. Uno de los aspectos atractivos de estas piezas es que la melodía utiliza un rango limitado con pocos cambios de posición de mano, lo que las hace ideales para alumnos de los niveles iniciales.

Ecuadorian Dances and Rhythms: Strategies for Piano Teaching
Presented by Angélica Sánchez
July 30, 2021
Recorded by Alejandro Cremaschi

Teachers are often faced with the need to motivate students by selecting or arranging meaningful repertoire they can connect with. This was exactly the goal of the music presented by Angélica Sánchez. According to this presenter, Latin American and Ecuadorian music present a rich variety of rhythms that may inspire and motivate students. The presentation focused on three traditional dances from Ecuador: the *sanjuanito*, the *pasacalle* and the *pasillo*. It featured authentic examples through videos of popular musicians performing these rhythms. After playing videos of each genre, Sanchez showed and played full arrangements of those pieces and rhythms. These arrangements, which can be classified at the intermediate level in terms of difficulty, feature many pedagogical benefits. At the end of the presentation, the presenter addressed some strategies to teach these pieces.

The *sanjuanito* is a dance present in festivities related to the sun (*e.g.* summer solstice, which coincides with the San Juan festivities), though now it tends to be danced in all traditional festivities in Ecuador. It features a happy and upbeat rhythm, and is written in minor keys and in 2/4. The *pasacalle* is a dance present in the streets of Ecuador directly influenced by the European *passacaille*. It features the same type of bass *ostinatos* found in its European cousins. Like the *sanjuanito*, it is also written in 2/4 and minor keys, and *allegro* tempo. It is danced during the independence celebrations in different cities. Finally, the *pasillo* is a mix of autochthonous music and the European waltz. It is present throughout Latin America, in countries like Perú, Colombia, and countries in Central America. It is written in minor keys and in 3/4 is characterized by a lyricism and romanticism typical of Ecuadorian music. Sanchez showed an arrangement of the *pasillo* "Cuanto te quiero" ("How much I love you"), a traditional *pasillo* written by the musician Salvador Bustamante Ceni.

To close the presentation, Sanchez shared general pedagogical tips to teach these pieces and arrangements, as well as some of the benefits of incorporating this music. For example, one of the attractive aspects of this music is that the melody uses a limited range and has few changes in hand position, which makes it ideal for students at the early intermediate level.

Obras latinoamericanas para piano a cuatro manos: etapas.
Presentado por Mariana Garrotti, Ana Paula Oyola, Beatriz Yacante, y Andrea Zanni
30 de julio de 2021
Resumen: Alejandro Cremaschi

Las cuatro conferencistas presentaron esta conferencia desde la provincia de San Juan, Argentina. Esta presentación es parte de un proyecto de investigación en la Universidad Nacional de San Juan sobre la música para cuatro manos y dos pianos de compositores latinoamericanos. El contenido de esta presentación se enfocó en obras apropiadas para el primer y segundo nivel de estudios en dicha Universidad, para las edades de 7 a 11 años.

Se concentraron en cuatro obras específicas: "Emilia", del compositor venezolano José Ángel Montero, "Amarelinha", del brasileño Ricardo Tacuchian, "En la Guagua", del compositor español Jorge Gómez Labraña, y "Arrorró" de la argentina Celia Torrá. Incluyeron información biográfica sobre cada compositor, ejemplos musicales, y la partitura anotada y animada, que se mostró mientras se tocaba la música. Luego de cada interpretación, las conferencistas se refirieron a varias características musicales y pedagógicas de las piezas, y sus dificultades.

"Emilia," de Montero, fue compuesta en fecha desconocida. La pieza se asemeja a un vals, y presenta la parte del primo en unísono, con un acompañamiento acórdico en manos alternadas en el secondo. La mayor dificultad para el secondo es el frecuente cambio de posición y acordes. El primo es adecuado para alumnos de primer nivel, mientras que el secondo puede ser tocado por el maestro o un alumno más avanzado.

"Amarelinha" de Tacuchian, fue clasificada por el mismo compositor como de nivel básico. La Amarelinha es el nombre en portugués del juego popular conocido en español como rayuela o tejo. De acuerdo con el compositor, esta pieza sugiere el ritmo del juego infantil. Así como en otras piezas, las conferencistas se refirieron a las características de la pieza y su potenciales problemas. Esta pieza es apropiada para alumnos del mismo nivel.

Gomez Labraña fue un compositor español que vivió en Cuba por varios años, donde compuso "Un Paseo por el Zoo," un conjunto de piezas educativas que usan títulos y motivos populares cubanos, e incluye piezas para piano solo y a 4 manos. "En la Guagua" contiene sonoridades que recuerdan los sonidos producidos por el autobús, conocido como "guagua" en la isla de Cuba. La pieza es ideal para la práctica del portato en el piano. El secondo utiliza una escala en tonos enteros, mientras que el primo está escrito en do mayor. A diferencia de otras piezas a 4 manos, el primo utiliza las claves de sol y fa.

"Arroró" fue escrito por la compositora argentina Celia Torrá, quien también fue una importante violinista y directora coral y orquestal. La pieza se basa en la canción de cuna tradicional de

Argentina, y contiene una parte para triángulo. Uno de sus desafíos es el balance entre las partes, y mantener un pulso constante en un tiempo lento. El primo es apropiado para alumnos de primer nivel, y el secondo para alumnos de segundo.

La presentación ofreció opciones frescas y atractivas de América Latina que enriquecen y expanden el repertorio a cuatro manos para alumnos principiantes.

Latin American Works for Piano Four Hands: Initial Stages
Presented by Mariana Garrotti, Ana Paula Oyola, Beatriz Yacante, and Andrea Zanni
July 30, 2021
Reported by Alejandro Cremaschi

The four presenters spoke from the province of San Juan, Argentina. They have been working on this presentation as part of a research project that seeks to survey, analyze, level, and disseminate information about the music for piano four hands and two pianos by Latin American composers. The project is being conducted at the Universidad Nacional de San Juan, with the goal of enriching and expanding the piano canon. This particular presentation focused on works appropriate for the first and second levels of study at the preparatory program at the Universidad de San Juan, which includes ages 7 through 11 years old. The presentation put an emphasis on describing and analyzing the challenges and benefits of this music.

The presenters focused on four pieces for four hands: *Emilia* by the Venezuelan composer José Ángel Montero, *Amarelinha* by the Brazilian Ricardo Tacuchian, *En la Guagua* by the Spanish composer Jorge Gómez Labraña, and *Arrorró* by the Argentine Celia Torrá. The presentation included biographical and contextual information about each composer, musical examples, and scrolling scores that showed the piece while it was being performed. After each performance, the presenters showed detailed information about their formal and textural characteristics and their challenges.

Emilia by Montero was composed at an unknown date. The piece sounds like a waltz, and presents a *primo* mostly in unison and a chordal accompaniment with alternating hands in the *secondo*. The main difficulty for the *secondo* is the frequent position shifts and chords. The *primo* is appropriate for students in the first level, while the *secondo* could be performed by the teacher or a more advanced student.

Amarelinha by Tacuchian was classified by the composer himself as elementary. "Amarelinha" is the Portuguese name of the popular children's game known as "hopscotch" in English. According to the composer, the piece suggests the rhythm and movement of the game. Like in the other pieces, the presenters discussed its characteristics and potential challenges, such as the intertwining of the parts, which pass along melodic lines. This piece may be appropriate for two students of the same level.

Gomez Labraña was a Spanish composer who lived in Cuba for many years, where he composed *Un Paseo por El Zoo* (*A Promenade at the Zoo*), a pedagogical set that uses titles and motives familiar to people in Cuba, and includes pieces for solo piano and piano four hands. "En la Guagua" ("In the bus") features sonorities that imitate the horn and the sounds produced by the city bus. This piece was intended to develop the *portato* touch at the piano. The *secondo* uses a whole-tone scale, while the *primo* is written in C major. Unlike other four-hand pieces, the *primo* is written in treble and bass clefs.

Arrorró (*Lullaby*) was written by the Argentine composer Celia Torrá, who also was an important violinist and choral and orchestral conductor. The piece is based on a traditional lullaby from Argentina, and interestingly, features a triangle part in addition to the *primo* and *secondo*. Among its challenges is balance of the parts (which are very contrapuntal) and maintaining the pulse at a slow tempo. The *primo* is appropriate for students in level 1, while the *secondo* is appropriate for level 2.

This presentation offered fresh options from Latin America that will definitely enrich and diversify the repertoire for beginning students.

Partita mestiza
Baroque Meets Latin America
Presentado por Manuel Matarrita
31 de julio de 2021
Resumen: Florencia Zuloaga

La suite "Partitura Mestiza" fue concebida por el compositor Manuel Matarrita como una combinación de los esquemas formales y danzas típicos de la suite barroca y los ritmos tradicionales de danzas latinoamericanas. El primer movimiento, "Preludio-Son", incorpora al típico movimiento inicial los ritmos del "son montuno" cubano. En segundo lugar, "Allebossa" reúne la típica alemanda con una bossa nova brasileña. El tercer número, titulado "Coruantillo", es una courante inspirada en el "pasillo", una danza típica de Colombia, Panamá, Costa Rica y Ecuador. "Courantillo" es seguido por la "Sarabandala", la cual combina la típica danza lenta del siglo XVII con la vidala argentina. En quinto lugar está "Mirania", la cual se caracteriza por la incorporación de la "Guarania" (danza típica de Paraguay) con el minuet. "Bohuayno", en el sexto lugar, demuestra una combinación de boureé y "huayno", un género musical tradicional de Bolivia y Perú. El número final de esta suite es una giga, en este caso incorporando ritmos del "tambito", una danza típica de Costa Rica. El uso de una cadencia frigia en "Partita Mestiza" actúa como núcleo unificador a lo largo de todos los movimientos. Si bien "Partitura Mestiza" fue compuesta con fines pedagógicos, puede utilizarse también como parte de repertorio para la sala de concierto. Esta pieza es ideal para pianistas de nivel intermedio y avanzado. Puede utilizarse tanto como obra introductoria a las danzas barrocas; asimismo es una pieza útil para introducir al estudiante en los ritmos modernos de Latinoamérica.

Partita mestiza
Baroque Meets Latin America
Presented by Manuel Matarrita
Saturday, July 31, 2021
Recorded by Florencia Zuloaga

The suite *Partitura mestiza* by composer Manuel Matarrita was conceived as a combination of the traditional dances seen in the Baroque keyboard suite and rhythms typical of Latin American dances. The first movement, "Preludio-Son," incorporates the *son montuno* from Cuba to the traditional opening movement. This is followed by "Allebossa," an *allemande* featuring rhythms of Brazil's *bossa nova*. The third movement, titled "Coruantillo," is a *courante* inspired by the *pasillo* (a dance from Colombia, Panama, Costa Rica and Ecuador). The "Courantillo" is followed by the "Sarabandala," a combination of the seventeenth-century *sarabande* with Argentina's own *vidala*. The suite's fifth movement, "Mirania," demonstrates a combination of minuet with *guarania*, a dance typical from Paraguay. "Bohuayno," the sixth piece, features a combination of *bourreé* with *huayno*, a traditional dance from Bolivia and Perú. The suite closes with a *gigue*, in this case combining the original French dance with Costa Rica's own *tambito*. A Phrygian cadence reappears throughout the entire suite, acting as a unifying theme between all movements.

While the suite "Partitura Mestiza" was created with a pedagogical end in mind, it can also be used in the concert hall. This suite is geared towards the intermediate and advanced level. "Partitura Mestiza" can be used as an introductory piece towards both the dances of the Baroque era and Latin American modern dances.

Las Sonatas para teclado de Padre Antonio Soler
Presentado por Marina Bengoa Roldán
31 de julio de 2021
Resumen: Florencia Zuloaga

Padre Antonio Soler (1729-1783) nació en Girona, España en 1829. A lo largo de su carrera ocupó distintos puestos en la corte, trabajando como Maestro de Capilla en Lleida y más tarde en El Escorial (Madrid). Escribió "Llave de la modulación y antigüedades de la música" en 1752. Este libro fue el primer tratado que discutía reglas e instrucciones para el abordaje de la modulación, incluyendo el concepto de "modulación agitada". Como Maestro de Capilla en El Escorial (lugar que fue, además, sede de la Familia Real durante ciertas temporadas del año) Padre Antonio Soler desarrolló una fructífera carrera como pedagogo, enseñando a figuras como el Infante Don Gabriel (hijo de Rey Carlos III) y Pedro de Santamant, entre otros. Mientras vivió en Montserrat, Soler estudió piezas para clave de compositores italianos, cuyas influencias son evidentes en su obra. Su música también recibió influencias de sus profesores, José de Nebra y José Elías, como también de C.P.E. Bach, J. Haydn y D. Scarlatti. Es importante mencionar que Scarlatti visitó El Escorial en numerosas ocasiones. Soler continuó con la tendencia española de añadir nuevos giros estilísticos a la sonata, en particular con el uso de modulaciones enarmónicas. El género sonata no conllevaba la implicación de una cierta estructura formal; en su lugar, las sonatas eran piezas escritas con fines pedagógicos. Muchas piezas escritas durante este período tales como los "essercizi" (Scarlatti), "toccatas" (Nebra y Soler), y "obras" (Soler) fueron publicadas más tarde bajo el nombre de sonatas, una denominación que persiste hasta hoy. Gran parte de las sonatas del Padre Antonio Soler son consideradas de nivel intermedio y avanzado. Muchas de las sonatas de Soler no siguen el esquema típico de forma bipartita ni las prácticas comunes del estilo Galant o Barroco. Uno de los catálogos más completos fue hecho por el musicólogo Samuel Rubio. La primer pieza de esta presentación es la Sonata en La mayor, R 53, titulada "Sonata de Clarines". El título surgió como referencia al clarín, un tipo de trompeta sin pistones típico en la música de la corte española. El órgano ibérico contiene registros similares a los del clarín, por lo que se infiere que esta sonata fue escrita para órgano. Algunos de los elementos compositivos de la Sonata R 53 son el uso de terceras, octavas rotas, bajos Alberti y escalas. Es importante enfatizar la sólida digitación de las terceras, cuyo sonido imita el llamado de los clarines. Dado que esta sonata asigna especial énfasis a la repetición, se puede animar al alumno a experimentar con distintas dinámicas, de forma similar a la alternancia de registros en el órgano. La segunda sonata en esta presentación es R 24 en Re menor. Es considerada de nivel intermedio-avanzado dado a la sensibilidad y atención necesaria en cuanto a su armonía, melodía, e individualización de voces, en el contexto de una tonalidad menor. Está escrita en tiempo ternario y demuestra el uso de forma bipartita con repeticiones. Debido al amplio uso de ornamentación, se sugiere que el estudiante experimente alternando distintas ornamentaciones en la repetición. La segunda mitad de esta sonata demuestra el uso de ornamentación imitando giros del folklore español. Para enfatizar los rápidos cambios de color harmónico, se sugiere el uso de "una corda" y la individualización de las voces dentro de la misma mano. Durante la segunda mitad de la sonata, es importante evitar estiramientos innecesarios de la mano derecha; la alternación de pulgar en la negra con puntillo y dedos 3 y 4 en la voz superior hasta llegar a la octava final con 1 y 5 es recomendada. La presentación concluye con la Sonata en Re major (R 84). Esta sonata fue ponderada por Jane Magrath debido a su carácter de danza, su especial abordaje de la armonía, y el uso de octavas paralelas en la mano derecha. Es una pieza para estudiantes en la etapa inicial del nivel avanzado. Está escrita en forma bipartita con repeticiones. El compás de 3/8 de esta Sonata recuerda a otros géneros españoles como la jota o el flamenco. Posee ciertos gestos que recuerdan a la escritura para guitarra, por lo que se infiere que esta Sonata fue escrita para el clave. Esto se hace particularmente evidente en el uso de arpegios y notas repetidas. Para una interpretación óptima de las notas repetidas, se recomienda la alternancia de dedos "3-2-1".

The Keyboard Sonatas of Padre Antonio Soler
Presented by Marina Bengoa Roldán
Saturday, July 31, 2021
Recorded by Florencia Zuloaga

Padre Antonio Soler (1729-1783) was born in Girona, Spain, in 1729. Throughout his career, he was appointed to several positions and worked as Chapel Master in Lleida and El Escorial (Madrid). He wrote *Llave de la modulación y antigüedades de la música* in 1752, which was the first written treatise addressing rules and instructions for modulation procedures, including rapid modulations or *modulación agitada*. During his appointment at El Escorial (which was the place of residence for the Royal Family during certain seasons of the year) Padre Antonio Soler developed a fruitful career as a pedagogue, teaching the Infante Don Gabriel (the son of King Charles III) and Pedro de Santamant among others. During his time in Montserrat, Soler studied keyboard pieces of Italian composers, whose influences can be traced throughout his works. Other major influences include those of his teachers José de Nebra and José Elias, as well as C. P. E. Bach, Haydn and Scarlatti, who visited El Escorial on several occasions. Soler followed a trend in Spain that consisted of adding new features to the sonata, in particular with the use of enharmonic modulations. The term "sonata" did not imply a specific formal structure; instead, sonatas were written as pedagogical pieces. Many pieces during this time, such as Scarlatti's *essercizi*, Nebra and Soler's *toccatas*, and Soler's *obras* were later published as sonatas—a practice that persists today.

Most of Soler's sonatas are considered intermediate to advanced pieces; a possible reason for this lies in the fact that Soler never taught beginner-level students. These works do not follow the typical binary form seen in this period, nor the style of *galant* or Baroque pieces seen at the time. Samuel Rubio has one of the most complete catalogs of Soler's works. The first piece in this presentation was Soler's Sonata R 53 in A Major, titled *Sonata de Clarines*. The title was given as a reference to the *clarín* (bugle), an instrument similar to a trumpet typically seen in royal courts during this time. The Iberian organ featured organ stops *en chamade*, including some sounding like the trumpet. Hence, it is inferred that this sonata was written for the Iberian organ. Some of the keyboard devices used on the Sonata R 53 are thirds, broken octaves, Alberti bass, and scales; in regard to these thirds, the student should aim for solid fingering, imitating the ringing call of the *clarines*. Since the piece is very repetitive, the student should be encouraged to experiment with different dynamics, much like the organist using different stops each time.
The second sonata in this presentation was R 24 in D minor. This sonata is considered as late-intermediate to advanced level due to the sensibility and attention needed towards harmony, melody, and voicings, all within the context of a minor key. It is written in triple meter, featuring a two-part form with repetitions. There is a heavy use of ornamentation, and the student is encouraged to improvise different ornamentations on the repeats. The second half of this Sonata features the use of ornamentation in the style of Spanish folklore. The sudden changes in key as seen in Soler's Sonata in D minor are perfect examples of the composer's approach to fast

modulations. The attention to voicings and use of the *una corda* pedal are necessary to highlight these changes in the harmonic color. Equally important in the second half is the attention to appropriate fingering to avoid unnecessary stretching of the right hand for the broken octaves; an alternation of thumb on the dotted-quarter note and fingers 3 and 4 on the top voice until reaching final octave with thumb and finger 5 are recommended.

Soler's Sonata in D major (R 84), has been highlighted by Jane Magrath because of its dance character, unique harmonic colors, and the use of parallel octaves in the left hand. This piece is suitable for students in the early-advanced level. It is written in a two-part form with repeats. The 3/8 rhythm seen in this sonata is typical of other Spanish dances such as the *jota* or *flamenco*. Certain gestures of this Sonata in D major resemble those of a guitar; therefore, it is implied that this sonata was written for the harpsichord. This is particularly evident in the use of arpeggiation and repeated notes. For an optimal performance of the repeated notes, an alternation of fingers 3-2-1 is recommended.

MAIN CONFERENCE PRESENTATIONS IN PORTUGUESE

Persona: a utilização de fantoches como recurso lúdico-afetivo nas aulas de piano
Palestrante: Vanessa Bormann
Quinta-feira, 29 de julho, 2021
Escrito por Ana Paula Machado Simões

Nessa palestra, a professora Vanessa Bormann compartilhou de uma maneira bem-humorada e cativante sua experiência com o uso de fantoches (no seu caso, bonecos de Bach, Mozart e Beethoven) nas aulas de piano e como essa prática refletiu positivamente no aprendizado das crianças. Os fantoches têm sido utilizados desde a Antiguidade por diversas civilizações ao redor do mundo. Seu uso foi verificado, por exemplo, na China, no Egito, na Grécia e na América pré-colombiana. Grandes artistas, como Molière, Goethe, Picasso, Haydn e Manuel de Falla também eram muito interessados em marionetes e as incorporaram em suas criações.

Os fatos de os fantoches não terem consciência de sua natureza material, estarem desvinculados de uma expectativa de seriedade e serem a própria personificação das vontades e emoções imbuídas por seu manipulador, tornam-os um instrumento de cativação e comunicação poderoso, atraindo a atenção do público e sendo capazes de inspirar reflexões sérias. No ramo educacional, seu poder e carisma podem se tornar aliados do professor. Além de deixarem a atmosfera de aprendizado mais criativa, eles facilitam a comunicação e a transferência de ensinamentos aos alunos.

A interação e o diálogo com os fantoches contribuem para que as crianças absorvam e lembrem-se com mais facilidade do que foi ensinado, uma vez que elas tendem a prestar mais atenção aos ensinamentos transmitidos pelos bonecos do que pela própria professora. Além disso, eles estimulam a conversa, o pensamento independente, e afetam positivamente o relacionamento entre o professor e o aluno e entre o aluno e a matéria. Eles também auxiliam o professor a compreender a personalidade e as características de cada criança, ajudando-o a compreender suas necessidades e a planejar novas abordagens. Para que o poder dos fantoches seja potencializado, é importante que eles sejam figuras frequentes na aula e não apenas utilizados esporadicamente em datas especiais.

Vanessa Bormann compartilhou diversas atividades que podem ser realizadas com os fantoches, por exemplo:
- Hora da conversa: durante os últimos cinco minutos da aula, os alunos podem interagir e conversar com os fantoches.
- Apreciação musical: os bonecos podem acompanhar as crianças em concertos.
- Levar para casa: na semana do seu aniversário, as crianças podem escolher um dos compositores para levar para casa.

- Hora da tarefa: os compositores gravam vídeos introdutórios e em resposta às tarefas dos alunos. Esta atividade estimulou os alunos a praticarem mais regularmente e com mais qualidade.
- Ajude o compositor: jogos e atividades de revisão e reforço onde os alunos precisam ajudar os compositores, já velhinhos, a se lembrarem de conceitos musicais.
- Salve o compositor: os alunos precisam resolver enigmas musicais para salvar o compositor sequestrado. As atividades são feitas no Google Forms e o aluno só avança para a questão seguinte ao acertar a pergunta. A cada resposta certa, ele fica mais perto de libertar o compositor.
- Corrida de obstáculos: atividades realizadas de forma presencial e envolvendo movimentação física, como por exemplo, atravessar um campo minado de notas, acordes invertidos, ou escalas. Os alunos precisam vencer os desafios para chegar até o compositor.
- Compositor da "vida real": os fantoches participam de eventos e atividades da vida da professora e dos alunos. Dessa forma, além de os compositores ensinarem às crianças sobre quem foram, eles vivem uma nova vida ao lado delas.

O uso de fantoches como recurso didático mostrou-se um meio efetivo para promover o engajamento dos alunos nas aulas e contribuiu para o relacionamento entre professora e aluno. Seu caráter lúdico-afetivo é um instrumento poderoso para atrair a atenção das crianças e envolvê-las ativamente no aprendizado. As diversas sugestões de utilização dos bonecos apresentada por Vanessa Bormann podem deixar as aulas mais divertidas e estimulantes, ajudando na absorção e retenção de conhecimentos pelos alunos.

Persona: The Use of Puppets as a Ludic-Affective Resource in Piano Lessons
Presented by Vanessa Bormann
Thursday, July 29, 2021
Recorded by Ana Paula Machado Simões

In this lecture, Vanessa Bormann shared, in a humorous and captivating way, her experience in the use of puppets (in her case, Bach, Mozart, and Beethoven) in piano lessons and how it reflected positively in the children's learning experiences. Puppets have been used since ancient times in several civilizations around the world, such as Chinese, Egyptian, Greek, and in pre-Columbian America. Well-known artists, such as Molière, Goethe, Picasso, Haydn, and Manuel de Falla were also very interested in puppetry and incorporated them in their works.

The facts that puppets are not conscious of their material nature, that they are unrelated to an expectation of seriousness, and that they are the personification of the desires and emotions of whom is controlling them, make them a powerful instrument of communication and captivation that captures the attention of the audience and can inspire profound reflections. In the educational field, their power and charisma can become teacher allies. They set up a creative learning atmosphere and facilitate the communication and the transfer of knowledge to the students.

The interaction and dialog between puppets and students help children absorb and recall information, since they tend to pay more attention to what is taught by the marionette rather than the teacher. Furthermore, they stimulate conversation, independent thinking, and positively affect the relationship between teacher and student, and student and subject. They also assist teachers in comprehending the personality and the characteristics of each child, which helps them diagnose their needs and plan future approaches. To maximize the power of the puppets, it is important that they are used frequently and not only sporadically in special occasions.

Bormann shared various activities that can be done with puppets, for example:
- *Talk time*: during the last five minutes of the lesson, students can interact and chat with the puppets.
- *Music appreciation*: students can take the puppets to concerts.
- *Take home*: students can choose one puppet to take home during their birthday week.
- *Homework time*: the composers record introductory and response videos to the students assignments. This activity stimulates regular and better practice habits.
- *Help the composer*: review and reinforcement games and activities where students need to help the old composers remember music concepts.
- *Save the composer*: students solve musical challenges to rescue the composer. The activities are created on Google Forms and the student can only move to the next question and get closer to saving the composer after getting the correct answer.

- *Composer obstacle course*: in-person activities involving physical movement, such as crossing a minefield of notes, inverted chords, or scales. Students need to solve challenges to get to the composer.
- *Composer "real" life*: the puppets take part in events and activities in the teacher's and students' lives. This way, in addition to teaching about who they were, they live a new life with the children.

The use of puppets as a pedagogical resource has shown to be an effective way to engage students during lessons and contribute to the relationship between teacher and student. Its ludic-affective character is a powerful tool to attract children's attention and involve them in the learning process. The various suggestions on how to include puppets in piano lessons presented by Bormann can make lessons more fun and engaging, contributing to students' knowledge assimilation and retention.

O primeiro repertório para o piano: As Sonatas de Giustini
Palestrante: Bernardo Scarambone
Quinta-feira, 29 de julho, 2021
Escrito por Diego Caetano

O professor de piano da Eastern Kentucky University, Bernardo Scarambone, apresentou sobre as Sonatas de Giustini, uma das primeiras obras compostas para o piano na História da Música Ocidental. Ele dividiu a palestra em três partes: a história da peça, o processo de transcrição da obra para uma notação moderna e gravação, e aspectos pedagógicos das peças. O projeto começou quando Bernardo Scarambone queria achar peças barrocas antes de Bach e Scarlatti, e Giustini chamou sua atenção. Como só havia o manuscrito da obra, Scarambone teve que transcrever cada nota e se familiarizar com a notação antiga. Ele, então, explicou quais os aspectos problemáticos da notação no manuscrito e possíveis soluções para estes problemas. Ele continua a palestra explicando o processo de edição e publicação das obras, o que não foi fácil. Felizmente, a obra está publicada em uma edição crítica em três volumes.

O professor Scarambone recentemente lançou, em 2021, a gravação das sonatas em um CD triplo usando o piano moderno. Esta palestra teve o objetivo de mostrar que a música de Giustini é de extrema valia para estar nos palcos e nos estúdios pelo mundo, pois pode ser uma substituição ou uma adição às obras standard no repertório Barroco. A meu ver, o apresentador fez um excelente trabalho apresentando, tocando e convencendo a plateia sobre este repertório.

The First Repertoire for the Piano: Giustini *Sonatas*
Presented by Bernardo Scarambone
Thursday, July 29, 2021
Recorded by Diego Caetano

Bernardo Scarambone presented on Giustini's *Sonatas*, one of the first compositions for the piano in the Western music history (1732). He divided the presentation in three parts:
1. history of the pieces,
2. the process of transcription of the pieces for a modern notation and recording, and
3. pedagogical aspects of some of the pieces and performance of the pieces.

This project started because the presenter wanted to find underrepresented pieces before Bach and Scarlatti, and Giustini caught his attention. Since there was only a manuscript, Scarambone had to transcribe every note, and get familiar with the ancient notation. He explained what the problems of the notation were and possible solutions for the notation. He proceeded to explain the process of getting them published, which was not easy. Fortunately, the music is now published in a three-volume critical edition.

Scarambone has recently released the recordings of the pieces in a three-volume album in 2021 using the modern piano. This presentation had the goal to show that Giustini's music is worthy to be on the concert stage and in the piano studios around the world, as it can be a substitution or an addition to the standard Baroque repertoire.

Danzas Fantásticas, op. 22 de Joaquín Turina:
construindo a performance para piano solo a partir de sua orquestração
Palestrante: Diego Caetano
Quinta-feira, 29 de julho, 2021
Escrito por Ana Paula Machado Simões

O recital-palestra se iniciou com uma breve introdução sobre o compositor Joaquín Turina e seu estilo composicional. Turina (1882–1949) nasceu em Sevilla, na Espanha, e faz parte da segunda geração de compositores espanhóis, juntamente com Manuel de Falla. Ele estudou em Paris, tendo sido aluno de piano de M. Moszcowski e de composição de Vincent d. Indi. Apesar de ter absorvido elementos da música francesa, ele foi inspirado por I. Albéniz a escrever música de caráter espanhol. Uma de suas inspirações foi sua cidade natal, que figura em algumas de suas obras mais pitorescas, entre elas *Rincones Sevillanos* e *La Leyenda de la Giralda*, para piano. Turina trabalhou também como crítico musical e escreveu uma enciclopédia de música.

Suas *Danzas Fantásticas* estão entre suas obras mais conhecidas. Elas foram compostas primeiramente para piano em 1919 e foram orquestradas pelo próprio compositor no mesmo ano. A versão orquestral foi a primeira a ser estreada e se tornou também a mais famosa. As *Danzas Fantásticas* foram baseadas no romance *La Orgía* do escritor sevilhano José Mas e cada um de seus três movimentos ("Exaltación," "Ensueño," e "Orgía") possui uma citação da livro. Conhecer a versão orquestral da obra ajuda na interpretação pianística, pois sabendo-se qual instrumento toca determinado trecho, pode-se buscar diferentes cores, timbres e ataques ao piano. Por exemplo, pode-se imitar a articulação das cordas (como *legatos, pizzicatos*), o fraseado e a respiração dos sopros e os ataques da percussão. Além disso, o uso do pedal pode ser pensado de modo a capturar a atmosfera e o timbre orquestrais.

Cada movimento foi inspirado em uma dança diferente de várias partes da Espanha. Elas são bem contrastantes entre si, formando um conjunto musical muito rico e interessante. O primeiro movimento, "Exaltación," foi inspirado na dança Jota, da região de Aragão. Essa dança utiliza compasso 3/4 ou 6/8 e é acompanhada por castanholas, violões e percussão. O segundo, "Ensueño," foi baseada em um canto folclórico e inspirada na dança Zortziko, do País Basco. Essa dança é em 5/8 e é marcada por ritmos pontuados. Ela foi também utilizada por Albéniz e Ravel em suas composições. O último movimento, "Orgía," foi inspirado na Farruca, um tipo de flamenco originado na Andalusia. Ela é marcada pelo virtuosismo, pelo sapateado e pelas mudanças dramáticas de tempo.

Após a explanação, a obra foi executada de maneira primorosa pelo pianista. Ele soube explorar o caráter e as particularidades de cada parte e utilizou diferentes timbres pianísiticos para enriquecer a performance. Os três movimentos formam um belo conjunto e evidenciam a riqueza de ritmos e cores presentes na música espanhola.

Danzas Fantásticas, Op. 22 by Joaquín Turina:
The Performance for Solo Piano Based on His Orchestration
Presented by Diego Caetano
Thursday, July 29, 2021
Recorded by Ana Paula Machado Simões

The lecture recital began with a brief introduction about the composer Joaquín Turina and his compositional style. Turina (1882–1949) was born in Sevilla, Spain, and is part of the second generation of Spanish composers along with Manuel de Falla. He studied in Paris and was a piano student of Moszkowski and a composition student of d'Indy. Despite having absorbed elements from French music, he was inspired by Albéniz to write music with Spanish character. One of his inspirations was his hometown, which is featured in some of his most picturesque works, such as *Rincones Sevillanos* and *La Leyenda de la Giralda*. Turina also worked as a music critic and wrote a music encyclopedia.

His *Danzas Fantásticas* are among his most well-known works. They were composed for piano in 1919 and were orchestrated by the composer in the same year. The orchestral version was the first to be premiered and became the most famous. *Danzas Fantásticas* were based on the novel *La Orgía* by José Mas and each one of its movements ("Exaltación," "Ensueño," and "Orgía") feature a quote from the book. Listening and studying the orchestral version helps the pianist in their interpretation, because by knowing which instrument plays a passage, one can choose different tone colors, timbres, and attacks in the piano. For example, it is possible to imitate the articulation of the strings (such as *legatos* and *pizzicatos*), the phrasing and breathing of the woodwinds and the attacks of the percussion. Furthermore, the pedal can be used to create orchestral atmospheres.

Each movement was inspired by a different dance from various parts of Spain. They are very contrasting between each other and form a rich and interesting set. The first movement, "Exaltación," was inspired by the dance *jota* from Aragon. This dance is in 3/4 or 6/8 meter and is accompanied by castanets, guitars, and percussion. The second, "Ensueño," was based on a folk song and inspired by the dance *zortziko* from the Basque Country. This dance is in 5/8 and is marked by dotted rhythms. It was also used by Albéniz and Ravel in their compositions. The last movement, "Orgía," was inspired by the *farruca*, a type of *flamenco* originated in Andalusia. It is characterized by virtuosity, tap dance, and dramatic tempo changes.

After the lecture, the work was performed exquisitely by the pianist. He explored the different elements and characters of each movement and utilized various tone colors that enriched the performance. The three movements make a beautiful set and highlight the richness of rhythms and timbres present in Spanish music.

Música contemporânea brasileira para iniciação ao piano: enriquecendo o repertório de estudantes de níveis elementares e intermediários
Palestrantes: Claudia Deltregia & Luís Cláudio Barrios
Sábado, 31 de julho, 2021
Escrito por Ricardo Pozenatto

Na palestra intitulada "Música contemporânea brasileira para iniciação ao piano", a professora Claudia Deltregia, da Universidade Federal de Santa Maria (Brasil), e o professor Luís Barrios, da Universidade Estadual de Santa Catarina (Brasil), compartilharam de forma detalhada sua pesquisa sobre o rico repertório contemporâneo brasileiro de piano para alunos elementares e intermediários.

No início da sessão, a professora Claudia salienta a definição "repertório didático para piano." Este tipo de repertório pode ser dividido em dois grupos gerais. O primeiro grupo considera compositores que criaram uma literatura pianística das mais diversas formas e níveis (ex. peças camerísticas, concertos, peças solo, peças de nível avançado, etc.) mas que também reservaram parte de suas criações a composições de níveis elementares e para iniciantes ao estudo do instrumento. O segundo grupo contém uma literatura escrita por compositores e professores com objetivos didáticos claros. A pesquisa dos professores Claudia e Luís abordaram obras do segundo grupo da literatura pianística brasileira.

Claudia explica que a atual pesquisa é resultado de sua investigação iniciada há alguns anos durante seus estudos no curso de mestrado. Algumas observações da época da pesquisa inicial são relatadas: a falta de diálogo entre professores de piano, alunos e compositores da atualidade; práticas bastante conservadoras/inadequadas em relação ao ensino do piano; ausência de leis para proteger direitos autorais; e tendências da música contemporânea brasileira, presentes em congressos e festivais de música mas que não estavam presentes em peças didáticas. Assim, os objetivos de tal pesquisa incluíram a promoção da conexão entre professores, alunos e novos compositores para tornarem acessível peças didáticas da chamada geração pós-nacionalista.

Houve então um levantamento de partituras para a iniciação ao piano a partir de bibliotecas (universitárias e públicas) e das principais editoras do país, resultando num catálogo com 155 obras de compositores da geração pós-nacionalista. Este catálogo temático inclui nome dos compositores, das obras e das editoras, data da composição, fonte de onde a obra foi encontrada, e também uma pequena análise da obra. A pesquisa prosseguiu com encomendas de obras a diversos compositores, resultando em 20 peças inéditas (hoje disponíveis gratuitamente pela internet), as quais revelaram diferentes tendências composicionais.

A fase atual da pesquisa apresenta dois objetivos principais: (1) dar continuidade ao projeto original, e (2) ampliar o acervo de repertório pianístico para os níveis iniciais e intermediários.

O professor Luís menciona uma lacuna temporal de mais de 20 anos entre a primeira pesquisa e a pesquisa atual. Ele expõe que os novos contextos sociais (como avanços tecnológicos) nortearam a metodologia da pesquisa de forma que a democratização ao acesso do acervo de partituras tornou-se uma das prioridades do atual projeto. Da mesma forma, a construção de uma interlocução e um diálogo entre compositores e professores de piano tornaram-se importantes na pesquisa, de modo que o trabalho em conjunto pudesse trazer contribuições ao pensamento pedagógico das obras, visando introduzir o pianista iniciante a uma linguagem musical contemporânea.

Luís apresenta os delineamentos pedagógicos da atual pesquisa, ressaltando que não são rígidos e nem sequenciais. São eles:
- Contactar compositores que escreveram composições de cunho pedagógicos (para revisarem obras e escreverem obras novas);
- Digitalização de obras a serem gravadas;
- Gravação das obras pelos pesquisadores;
- Feedback das gravações pelos compositores;
- Transformação das gravações em videopartitura (buscando a democratização do acervo);
- Transcrição das partituras em Braile; e
- Organização de um e-book de partituras

A apresentação foi concluída com os professores Luís Barrios e Claudia Deltregia tocando algumas obras que serão gravadas para a atual pesquisa. São elas: Peça no. 2, das Cinco Pequenas Peças para Piano, de Marcus Ferrer; Estudo no. 3, dos 3 Pequenos Estudos, de Rafael dos Santos; e Chôro, de Cyro Pereira.

Contemporary Brazilian Music for Piano Beginners:
Enriching the Repertoire of Elementary and Intermediate Students
Presented by Claudia Deltregia and Luís Cláudio Barrios
Saturday, July 31, 2021
Recorded by Ricardo Pozenatto

In this presentation, Claudia Deltregia of the Federal University of Santa Maria (Brazil), and Luís Barrios of the State University of Santa Catarina (Brazil) shared in detail their research on the rich contemporary Brazilian piano repertoire for elementary and intermediate students.

At the beginning of the session, Deltregia highlighted the definition of "didactic repertoire for piano." This type of repertoire can be divided into two general groups. The first group considers composers who created pianistic literature of the most diverse forms and levels (*e.g.*, chamber pieces, concertos, solo pieces, advanced level pieces, *etc.*) but who also reserved part of their creations for elementary-level compositions and beginning students at the instrument. The second group contains literature written by composers and teachers with clear didactic objectives. The research by Deltregia and Barrios addressed works from the second group of Brazilian literature for piano.

Deltregia explained that the current research is the result of her investigation that started a few years ago during her studies in the master's course. Some observations from the time of the initial research were reported: the lack of dialogue between piano teachers, students, and composers from that present time; very conservative/inadequate practices concerning piano teaching; absence of copyright laws; and trends in Brazilian contemporary music, present in conferences and music festivals but not present in educational pieces. Thus, the objectives of such research included the promotion of the connection between teachers, students, and new composers to make didactic pieces of the so-called post-nationalist generation accessible.

There was then a survey of piano scores for beginning study through libraries (university and public) and main publishers of the country, resulting in a catalog with 155 works by composers of the post-nationalist generation. This thematic catalog included the names of the composers, works, and publishers; date of composition; source from which the work was found; and also a small analysis of the work. The research continued with commissions of works from several composers, resulting in twenty unpublished pieces (now available for free on the internet), which revealed different compositional tendencies.

The current phase of the research has two main objectives: (1) to continue the original project, and (2) to expand the piano repertoire collection for elementary/beginners and intermediate levels.

Barrios mentioned a time gap of more than twenty years between the first and the current research. He explained that the new social contexts (such as technological advancements) guided the research methodology so that the democratization of access to the sheet music collection became one of the priorities of the current project. Likewise, the construction of an interlocution and dialogue between composers and piano teachers became important in the research, so that working together could bring contributions to the pedagogical thinking of the works, aiming to introduce the beginning pianist to a contemporary musical language.

Barrios presented the pedagogical outlines of the current research, noting that they are neither rigid nor sequential. They are:
- Contact composers who have written compositions of a pedagogical nature (to review works and write new works);
- Digitization of works to be recorded;
- Recording of works by researchers;
- Feedback of recordings by composers;
- Transformation of recordings into video scores (seeking the democratization of the collection);
- Transcription of scores in Braille; and
- Organization of an e-book of sheet music.

The presentation ended with Barrios and Deltregia playing some works that will be recorded for the current research. They are "Piece No. 2" from *Five Small Pieces for Piano* by Marcus Ferrer; "Study No. 3," of the *3 Small Studies* by Rafael dos Santos; and *Chôro* by Cyro Pereira.

O Guia Prático Para A Juventude: A Obra Pedagógica De Heitor Villa-Lobos
Palestrante: Verena Abufaiad
Sábado, 31 de julho, 2021
Escrito por Ricardo Pozenatto

Em sua palestra *O Guia Prático Para A Juventude* a doutora Verena Abufaiad abordou o repertório pianístico didático da obra *O Guia Prático* do compositor brasiliero Heitor Villa-Lobos. Sua pesquisa, fruto de estudos durante seu doutorado, incluiu análises formais e estilísticas das obras para piano que compõem essa coleção. Além disso, Verena propôs níveis de dificuldade das peças, apontando adversidades técnicas, e também sugerindo estratégias de ensino.

O contexto histórico do surgimento da obra *O Guia Prático* encontra-se em âmbitos de música vocal. Villa-Lobos compôs diversas obras canto-coral para crianças e jovens, estudantes de escolas públicas brasileiras durante a primeira metade do século 20 com o intuito de criar um programa musical sólido e de acesso a todos onde valores como patriotismo, comunidade e disciplina seriam integrados. O projeto inicialmente idealizado consistiria de uma coleção estruturada de materiais de ensino, dividida em seis volumes, chamada *Guia Prático*. Apenas um volume foi concluído, contendo 137 peças vocais. Alguns anos depois, durante as décadas de 1940 e 1950, o compositor redistribuiu várias dessas obras em diversas coleções para piano. Uma dessas coleções resultou em *O Guia Prático, Álbum Para Piano*, incluindo 59 peças para piano, catalogadas em 11 álbuns, cada um contendo de cinco a sete peças.

Após uma breve contextualização histórica, a professora Abufaiad apontou algumas características da coleção. São elas:
- Linguagem simplificada através de materiais musicais acessíveis baseados em canções infantis;
- Peças curtas, com forma e estrutura harmônica claras;
- Texturas compactas e atraentes ao público alvo (jovens estudantes);
- Associações extra musicais como canções folclóricas, cantigas de roda, lendas e narrativas populares;
- Incorporação de gêneros musicais e danças (como o samba)

A apresentação prosseguiu com a professora Abufaiad explorando e performando peças de diversos formatos de *O Guia Prático, Álbum Para Piano*. As duas primeiras foram as cirandas *O Ciranda, O Cirandinha* e *Vestidinho Branco*, onde buscou representar composições dos níveis mais acessíveis de toda a coleção, classificando essas duas obras como nível pré-intermediário. Ela explicou que Villa-Lobos era fã de cirandas, incorporando seus temas folclóricos em diversas composições.

Após a performance das cirandas, Verena abordou duas obras de nível intermediário, *Samba-Lelê* e *Manquinha*, as quais são elaboradas ritmicamente e possuem texturas musicais densas. Ela explicou que o caráter do *samba*, em *Samba-Lelê*, está presente no ritmo, acrescentando que a melodia sincopada viaja entre as mãos do intérprete. Em *Manquinha*, Verena ressaltou o aspecto programático da obra. A mesma célula rítmica sincopada de *Samba-Lelê* encontra-se nesta obra de maneira ambígua, representando tanto a felicidade da personagem em questão (uma menina manca – "manquinha") quanto o seu andar. Esse aspecto é reforçado pela tonalidade da obra, incluindo modos maiores e menores.

Em *Rosa Amarela* e *A Maré-Encheu*, obras de nível intermediário tardio, a apresentadora ressalta que os ritmos sincopados presentes em ambas, capturam a cultura e os estilos musicais típicos brasileiros. Verena realçou que *Rosa Amarela* apresenta dificuldades técnico-musicais maiores se comparada as peças anteriormente apresentadas. *Rosa Amarela* exige um uso mais refinado de pedal, justamente por apresentar frequente passagens cromáticas e sonoridades densas (acordes). As letras iniciais de *A Maré Encheu* representam rituais da natureza: "*A maré encheu / A maré vazou / Os cabelos da morena / O riacho carregou.*" Estes são ditos e crenças populares, presentes no cancioneiro infantil brasielito, nas cantigas de roda. Verena ainda ressaltou que o aspecto programático da obra são representados pelos acordes iniciais (a maré enchendo) seguido por semicolcheias descendentes (a maré vazando). Essa mesma ideia retorna na *coda* para concluir a peça. A apresentadora mencionou alguns aspectos de dificuldade durante a parte central da obra, como a precisão rítmica e o cruzamento das mãos.

Ao finalizar sua apresentação, Verena compartilhou seu desejo de que este tipo de repertório fosse mais conhecido e mais performado, principalmente entre jovens músicos. Afinal, essa foi a verdadeira intenção de Villa-Lobos.

The *Guia Prático* for the Youth: The Pedagogical Work of Heitor Villa-Lobos
Presented by Verena Abufaiad
Saturday, July 31, 2021
Recorded by Ricardo Pozenatto

In her presentation "The *Guia Prático* for the Youth," Dr. Verena Abufaiad addressed the didactic pianistic repertoire of the work *The Practical Guide* by Brazilian composer Heitor Villa-Lobos. The research, the result of her doctorate studies, included formal and stylistic analysis of the works for piano that make up this collection. In addition, Abufaiad proposed levels of difficulty for the pieces, pointing out technical adversities, and also suggesting teaching strategies.

The historical context of the emergence of the work *The Practical Guide* is found in areas of vocal music. Villa-Lobos composed several choral and vocal works for children and teenagers, students from Brazilian public schools during the first half of the twentieth century, to create a solid musical program, accessible to all, where values such as patriotism, community, and discipline would be integrated. The project was initially conceived as a structured collection of teaching materials, divided into six volumes, called *The Practical Guide*. Only one volume was completed, containing 137 vocal pieces. A few years later, during the 1940s and 1950s, the composer redistributed several of these works in various piano collections. One of these collections resulted in *The Practical Guide, Album for Piano*, including fifty-nine piano pieces, cataloged in eleven *álbum*, each containing from five to seven pieces.

After a brief historical contextualization, Abufaiad pointed out some characteristics of the collection. They are:
- Simplified language through accessible music materials based on children's songs;
- Short pieces, with clear shape and harmonic structure;
- Compact and attractive textures to the target audience (young students);
- Extra-musical associations such as folk songs, round songs, legends, and popular narratives;
- Incorporation of musical genres and dances (such as *samba*).

The presentation continued with Abufaiad exploring and performing pieces of different formats from *O Guia Prático, Álbum Para Piano*. The first two were the rounds "O Ciranda," "O Cirandinha" (Circle Dance, Little Circle Dance) and "Vestidinho Branco" (Little White Dress), where she sought to represent, with these, compositions from the most accessible levels of the entire collection, classifying these two works at the early-intermediate level. She explained that Villa-Lobos was a fan of round songs, incorporating their folkloric themes in several compositions.

After the performance of the two rounds, the presenter shared two intermediate-level works, "Samba-Lelê" and "Manquinha" (Little Lame Girl), which are rhythmically elaborate and have dense musical textures. She explained that the *samba* character in "Samba-Lelê" is present in the rhythm, adding that the syncopated melody travels between the performer's hands. In *Little Lame Girl*, Abufaiad highlighted the programmatic aspect of the work. The same syncopated rhythmic cell of "Samba-Lelê" is ambiguously found in this work, representing both the happiness of the character in question (the lame girl) and her walk. This aspect is reinforced by the tonality of the work, including major and minor modes.

In "Rosa Amarela" (Yellow Rose) and "A Maré-Encheu" (Full Tide), late-intermediate works, the presenter emphasized that the syncopated rhythms present in both capture the culture and musical styles that are typical in Brazil. She emphasized that "Yellow Rose" presents greater technical and musical difficulties when compared to the previously presented pieces. "Yellow Rose" requires a more refined use of the pedal since it frequently presents chromatic passages and dense sounds (chords). The initial lyrics of "Full Tide" represent nature's rituals: "The tide has risen / The tide has run out / The hair of *morena* / The stream carried." These are popular sayings and beliefs, present in the Brazilian children's songbooks, in the round songs. Abufaiad also emphasized that the programmatic aspect of the work is represented by the initial chords (the rising tide) followed by descending sixteenth notes (the ebbing tide). This same idea returns in the *coda* to end the piece. The presenter mentioned some aspects of difficulty during the central part of the work, such as demanding rhythmic precision and crossing of the hands.

At the end of the presentation, Abufaiad shared her desire for this type of repertoire to be better known and more performed, especially among young musicians. After all, that was Villa-Lobos's real intention.

National Program Committee
David Cartledge
Diana Dumlavwalla
Yeeseon Kwon
Christopher Madden
Artina McCain
Nicholas Phillips

Jennifer Snow, CEO and Executive Director
Sara Ernst, Director of Teacher Engagement
Esther Hayter, Associate Director
Anna Beth Rucker, Associate Director
Executive Committee: Sara Ernst, Andrea McAlister, Pamela Pike, and Jennifer Snow

Made in the USA
Middletown, DE
22 October 2022